THE CAMBRIDGE COMPANION TO
CHRISTIAN ETHICS

Following the same formula as other *Cambridge Companions*, this book is written by leading international experts in Christian ethics and is aimed at students on upper-level undergraduate courses, at teachers and at graduate students. It will be useful as well to ministers and other professionals within the church. Its eighteen chapters provide a thorough introduction to Christian ethics which is both authoritative and up to date. All contributors have been chosen because they are significant scholars with a proven track record of balanced, comprehensive and comprehensible writing.

The *Companion* examines the scriptural bases of ethics, introduces a variety of approaches to ethics including those informed by considerations such as gender and by other faiths such as Judaism, and then discusses Christian ethics in the context of contemporary issues including war and the arms trade, social justice, ecology, economics, and medicine and genetics. The book offers a superb overview of its subject.

CAMBRIDGE COMPANIONS TO RELIGION
A series of companions to major topics and key figures in
theology and religious studies. Each volume contains specially
commissioned essays by international scholars which provide
an accessible and stimulating introduction to the subject for new
readers and non-specialists.

Other titles published
THE CAMBRIDGE COMPANION TO CHRISTIAN DOCTRINE
edited by Colin Gunton

THE CAMBRIDGE COMPANION TO BIBLICAL INTERPRETATION
edited by John Barton

THE CAMBRIDGE COMPANION TO LIBERATION THEOLOGY
edited by Christopher Rowland

THE CAMBRIDGE COMPANION TO KARL BARTH
edited by John Webster

THE CAMBRIDGE COMPANION TO DIETRICH BONHOEFFER
edited by John W. de Gruchy

THE CAMBRIDGE COMPANION TO JESUS
edited by Markus Bockmuehl

THE CAMBRIDGE COMPANION TO FEMINIST THEOLOGY
edited by Susan Frank Parsons

Forthcoming
THE CAMBRIDGE COMPANION TO THE GOSPELS
edited by Stephen C. Barton

THE CAMBRIDGE COMPANION TO ST PAUL
edited by James D. G. Dunn

THE CAMBRIDGE COMPANION TO ISLAMIC THEOLOGY
edited by Tim Winter

THE CAMBRIDGE COMPANION TO REFORMATION THEOLOGY
edited by David Bagchi and David Steinmetz

THE CAMBRIDGE COMPANION TO MARTIN LUTHER
edited by Donald K. McKim

THE CAMBRIDGE COMPANION TO JOHN CALVIN
edited by Donald K. McKim

THE CAMBRIDGE COMPANION TO FRIEDRICH SCHLEIERMACHER
edited by Jacqueline Mariña

THE CAMBRIDGE COMPANION TO HANS URS VON BALTHASAR
edited by Edward Oakes and David Moss

THE CAMBRIDGE COMPANION TO KARL RAHNER
edited by Declan Marmion and Mary E. Hines

THE CAMBRIDGE COMPANION TO POSTMODERN THEOLOGY
edited by Kevin Vanhoozer

THE CAMBRIDGE COMPANION TO

CHRISTIAN ETHICS

Edited by Robin Gill
University of Kent at Canterbury

CAMBRIDGE
UNIVERSITY PRESS

PUBLISHED BY THE PRESS SYNDICATE OF THE UNIVERSITY OF CAMBRIDGE
The Pitt Building, Trumpington Street, Cambridge, United Kingdom

CAMBRIDGE UNIVERSITY PRESS
The Edinburgh Building, Cambridge CB2 2RU, UK
40 West 20th Street, New York, NY 10011–4211, USA
477 Williamstown Road, Port Melbourne, VIC 3207, Australia
Ruiz de Alarcón 13, 28014 Madrid, Spain
Dock House, The Waterfront, Cape Town 8001, South Africa

http://www.cambridge.org

First published 2001
Reprinted 2002, 2003

Printed in the United Kingdom at the University Press, Cambridge

Typeface Severin 10/13 pt   *System* QuarkXPress™   [SE]

A catalogue record for this book is available from the British Library

ISBN 0 521 77070 x hardback
ISBN 0 521 77918 9 paperback

Contents

Notes on contributors

Stephen C. Barton is Senior Lecturer in New Testament in the Department of Theology, University of Durham, and a non-stipendiary minister at St John's Church, Neville's Cross. His books include *Discipleship and Family Ties in Mark and Matthew* (Cambridge: CUP, 1994) and *Invitation to the Bible* (London: SPCK, 1997).

Don Browning is Alexander Campbell Professor of Religious Ethics and the Social Sciences at the Divinity School of the University of Chicago. Among his recent books are *A Fundamental Practical Theology* (Minneapolis: Fortress Press, 1991) and, as co-author, *From Culture Wars to Common Ground: Religion and the American Family Debate* (Louisville: Westminster John Knox, 1997). He is director of the Religion, Culture, and Family Project, sponsored by a grant from the Lilly Endowment.

Lisa Sowle Cahill is J. Donald Monan, S. J., Professor of Theology at Boston College. Two of her recent works are *Sex, Gender and Christian Ethics* (Cambridge: CUP, 1996) and *Family: A Christian Social Perspective* (Minneapolis: Fortress Press, 2000).

James F. Childress is Edwin B. Kyle Professor of Religious Studies and Professor of Medical Education at the University of Virginia. He is co-author of *Principles of Biomedical Ethics*, 4th edn (New York: OUP, 1994) and co-editor of *Christian Ethics: Problems and Prospects* (Cleveland: Pilgrim Press, 1996).

Gavin D'Costa is Senior Lecturer in Theology at the University of Bristol. He has recently published *The Trinity and the Meeting of Religions* (Maryknoll/Edinburgh: Orbis Books/T. & T. Clark, 2000) and *The Trinity and Gender* (London: SCM Press, 2000). He is consultant to the Roman Catholic Church and the Church of England on other religions.

R. John Elford is Pro-Rector Emeritus of Liverpool Hope University College and Provost of Hope at Everton. Among his recent publications are *The Pastoral Nature of Theology* (London: Cassell, 1999) and *The Ethics of Uncertainty* (Oxford: Oneworld, 2000).

Duncan B. Forrester was Professor of Christian Ethics and Practical Theology at the University of Edinburgh 1978–2000. He at present holds a personal chair in Theology and Public Issues. Among his recent publications are *The True Church and Morality* (Geneva: World Council of Churches, 1997) and *Christian Justice and Public Policy* (Cambridge: CUP, 1997).

Robin Gill is Michael Ramsey Professor of Modern Theology at the University of Kent at Canterbury. Amongst his recent books are *Churchgoing and Christian Ethics* (Cambridge: CUP, 1999) and *A Textbook of Christian Ethics*, 2nd edn (Edinburgh: T. & T. Clark, 1995). He is also the series editor for CUP's New Studies in Christian Ethics.

Tim Gorringe is Professor of Theological Studies at the University of Exeter. He has just finished *Till We Have Built Jerusalem: A Theology of the Built Environment*. Among his recent publications are *Karl Barth: Against Hegemony* (Oxford: OUP, 1999) and *God's Just Vengeance: Crime, Violence and the Rhetoric of Salvation* (Cambridge: CUP, 1996).

Ronald M. Green is the Eunice and Julian Cohen Professor for the Study of Ethics and Human Values at Dartmouth College in Hanover, New Hampshire. He is also Director of Dartmouth's Ethics Institute. His books on philosophy of religion include *Religion and Moral Reason* (Oxford: OUP, 1988) and *Kierkegaard and Kant: The Hidden Debt* (Albany: State University of New York Press, 1992).

Timothy P. Jackson is Associate Professor of Christian Ethics in the Candler School of Theology at Emory University. He is the author of *Love Disconsoled: Meditations on Christian Charity* (Cambridge: CUP, 1999) and a member of the Board of Directors of the Society of Christian Ethics.

Gareth Jones is Professor of Christian Theology at Canterbury Christ Church University College. Amongst his recent books are *Christian Theology: A Brief Introduction* (Cambridge: Polity Press, 1999) and *Critical Theology: Questions of Truth and Method* (Cambridge: Polity Press, 1995).

He is also co-editor of the Blackwell Publishers series Challenges in Contemporary Theology.

Michael S. Northcott is Senior Lecturer in Christian Ethics at the University of Edinburgh. Recent publications include *The Environment and Christian Ethics* (Cambridge: CUP, 1996), *Urban Theology: A Reader* (London: Cassell, 1998) and *Life after Debt: Christianity and Global Justice* (London: SPCK, 1999).

Stephen J. Pope is an associate professor in the theology department of Boston College, Chestnut Hill, Massachusetts. He has written *The Evolution of Altruism and the Ordering of Love* (Washington, DC: Georgetown University Press, 1994) and edited *Essays on the Ethics of St Thomas Aquinas* (Georgetown, forthcoming), and is currently working on a project entitled *Human Evolution and Christian Ethics.*

Jean Porter is Professor of Moral Theology and Christian Ethics at the University of Notre Dame, Indiana. Her most recent books are *Natural and Divine Law: Reclaiming the Tradition for Christian Ethics* (Ottawa: Novalis Press and Grand Rapids: Eerdmans Press, 1999) and *Moral Action and Christian Ethics* (Cambridge: CUP, 1995).

John Rogerson is Emeritus Professor of Biblical Studies at the University of Sheffield. His most recent books are *An Introduction to the Bible* (London: Penguin Books, 1999) and *Chronicle of the Old Testament Kings* (London: Thames & Hudson, 1999). He is currently working on a theology of the Old Testament.

Max L. Stackhouse is Professor of Christian Ethics at Princeton Theological Seminary. He is the primary editor of *On Moral Business: Classical and Contemporary Resources for Ethics and Economic Life* (Grand Rapids: Eerdmans, 1995) and author, amongst other books, of *Covenant and Commitment: Faith, Family and Economic Life* (Louisville: Westminster John Knox, 1997).

Rowan Williams is Archbishop of Wales and a former Lady Margaret Professor of Divinity at the University of Oxford. His recent publications include *Sergii Bulgakov: Towards a Russian Political Theology* (Oxford: Blackwell, 1999), *On Christian Theology* (Oxford: Blackwell, 1999) and *Lost Icons: Reflections on Cultural Bereavement* (Edinburgh: T. & T. Clark, 2000).

Preface

Over the last twenty-five years the study of Christian ethics has seen a considerable revival in both Britain and the United States. After a period of relative neglect in the 1950s and 60s, most theology departments, seminaries and theological colleges now teach the subject and have a Christian ethicist on the staff. In a number of secular universities Christian ethics also acts as a bridge with other disciplines. The success of the Cambridge University Press series New Studies in Christian Ethics over the last decade also provides evidence of the strength of the subject today. The *Cambridge Companions* would not be complete without a volume on Christian ethics.

Following the same formula as other *Cambridge Companions*, this collection of eighteen chapters has been written by leading British and American experts in the subject and is aimed at students in upper-level undergraduate courses, graduate students, teachers and other interested parties within the church or in adjacent academic disciplines. It should provide a fairly comprehensive introduction to Christian ethics that is both authoritative and up to date. All of the contributors have also been chosen because they have a proven track record of balanced, comprehensive and comprehensible writing.

The *Companion* is in three parts. The first of these considers the crucial relationship of Christian ethics both to the Bible itself and to modern biblical studies. Rowan Williams' opening chapter sets the broad theological and ecclesiastical contexts for this relationship. An earlier version of this chapter was given at a key plenary session of the Anglican Lambeth Conference of Bishops in the summer of 1998 at Canterbury, England. Underlying many of the debates at this vexed international conference was the question of the authority of scripture. The second chapter, by Gareth Jones, a colleague of mine at Canterbury, turns to this very question. John Rogerson then examines the challenges facing Christian ethics in its use of the Old Testament. Timothy Jackson next offers a strikingly original chapter comparing the four canonical gospels with Gnostic gospels, arguing that there are moral grounds for preferring the former. Finally in this part Stephen Barton looks critically at the epistles and Christian ethics.

The second part of the *Companion* examines different, and sometimes competing, approaches to Christian ethics. Stephen Pope provides a wide-ranging survey of natural-law approaches to the discipline. This is followed by a similar critical survey by Jean Porter of different forms of virtue ethics. Lisa Sowle Cahill then examines the contentious questions of gender and Christian ethics and, in the process, makes extensive use of Susan Parsons' well-received threefold typology of feminist ethics. Tim Gorringe next examines the concept of liberation in Christian ethics, a concept which has been highly influential within both political and gender issues. Ronald Green and Gavin D'Costa then provide contrasting chapters on the relationship of Christian ethics to other forms of religious ethics. Ronald Green writes as a Jew who also has extensive knowledge on Christian ethics. Indeed, an earlier version of this essay was first given as his Presidential Address to the Society of Christian Ethics meeting at San Francisco in January 1998. Gavin D'Costa writes as a Roman Catholic who has a high reputation as a mediator between Christians and Jews.

The third part of the *Companion* examines a number of crucial issues in modern Christian ethics. It would be impossible to cover adequately all of the issues that currently concern Christian ethicists, so inevitably I have been selective. As the cover of this book hints, Christian ethics has been influential in a number of political and social contexts around the world over the last few decades. The statue of the African Madonna in Cape Town Cathedral, South Africa, continues to make a powerful theological statement against apartheid. The crowd scene from the window of the Crucifixion in Birmingham Cathedral, England, represents the Christian story set amidst the challenges of modern urban industrial society. Despite evidence of growing pluralism and secularity in many countries, a number of theologians and church leaders have been instrumental in effecting crucial changes. Pope John Paul II, Mother Teresa, Archbishop Desmond Tutu, Archbishop Robin Eames and Dr Martin Luther King, Jr, all proved to be surprisingly influential in deeply troubled political and social contexts in the second, supposedly godless, half of the twentieth century.

The first two chapters in this third part, by John Elford and myself, analyse an area of Christian influence in social ethics which has been more abiding than almost any other, namely just war discussion. John Elford's chapter sets the broad frame of this discussion, whereas my own locates it specifically in the debate about the arms trade in a context of recent wars and conflicts in the Gulf, Iraq and the Balkans. Duncan Forrester's chapter then examines rival accounts of social justice and locates them specifically in the context of welfare provision. Michael Northcott next provides a forceful theological case for deeper ecological involvement by Christian ethicists. Max Stackhouse's chapter presents a broad critical survey of different Christian ethical approaches to business and economics. Don Browning's chapter offers a powerful Christian critique of family trends around the world. And finally James Childress provides a wide-ranging chapter in the area which he has made so effectively his own, namely medicine and genetics as they relate to Christian ethics.

Of course, this *Companion* is only a taster. However, I hope that these chapters and the notes attached to them will inspire readers to delve more deeply into Christian ethics in the future. For thoughtful Christians who are concerned about the modern world there surely cannot be a more important discipline.

Robin Gill
University of Kent at Canterbury

Part one

The grounds of Christian ethics

1 Making moral decisions

ROWAN WILLIAMS

What is it like to make a choice? The temptation we easily give way to is to
think that it's always the same kind of thing; or that there's one kind of
decision-making that's serious and authentic, and all other kinds ought to be
like this. In our modern climate, the tendency is to imagine that choices are
made by something called the individual will, faced with a series of clear
alternatives, as if we were standing in front of the supermarket shelf. There
may still be disagreement about what the 'right' choice would be, but we'd
know what making the choice was all about. Perhaps for some people the
right choice would be the one that best expressed my own individual and
independent preference: I would be saying no to all attempts from outside
to influence me or determine what I should do, so that my choice would
really be mine. Or perhaps I would be wondering which alternative was the
one that best corresponded to a code of rules: somewhere there would be
one thing I could do that would be in accord with the system, and the challenge would be to spot which it was – though it might sometimes feel a bit
like guessing which egg-cup had the coin under it in a game. But in any case
the basic model would be much the same: the will looks hard at the range of
options and settles for one.

But of course we don't spend all our lives in supermarkets. There are
plenty of environments in which this kind of consumer choice is at best a
remote dream, where it can sound like a cruel mockery to talk of such
choices. And for those who do have the power to exercise such choices, is
this model a sensible account of what it's like to make decisions in general?

Whom shall I marry? Shall I marry at all? Which charity shall I support
this Christmas? Shall I resign from this political party, which is now committed to things I don't believe in – but is still better than the other parties in
some ways? Should I become a vegetarian? Should I break the law and join
an anti-government protest? Should I refuse to pay my taxes when I know
they are partly used to buy weapons of mass destruction? How should I
finish this poem or this novel? How should I finish my life if I know I'm

3

dying? Think about these and choices like them. Each of them – even 'Which charity shall I support?' – is a decision that is coloured by the sort of person I am; the choice is not made by a will operating in the abstract, but by someone who is used to thinking and imagining in a certain way: someone who is the sort of person who finds an issue like this an issue of concern. (Another person might not be worried in the same way by the same question.) And this means that an answer only in terms of the 'system', the catalogue of right answers, would help us not at all; what kind of code, we may well ask, would give us impersonally valid solutions to the dilemmas just listed? We believe that, in some contexts, we can say, 'You ought never to do that'; but there is no straightforward equivalent formula allowing us to say. 'You ought to do that.' As the Welsh philosopher Rush Rhees argues in an unpublished paper, telling someone else what they ought to do is as problematic as telling someone else what they want. There is a significant sense in which only I can answer the question 'What ought I to do?' just as only I can answer 'What do I want?' But for me to answer either question is harder than at first it sounds. Rhees is careful to say that 'What ought I to do?' is drastically different from a question about my preferences, what I just happen to want (or think I want) at some specific moments.

Herbert McCabe, a prominent British Catholic theologian and moralist, wrote many years ago – not without a touch of mischief – that 'ethics is entirely concerned with doing what you want',[1] going on to explain that our problem is that we live in a society, and indeed as part of a fallen humanity, that deceives us constantly about what we most deeply want. The point that both Rhees and McCabe are trying to make is emphatically not that ethics is a matter of the individual's likes or dislikes but, on the contrary, that it is a difficult discovering of something about yourself, a discovering of what has already shaped the person you are and is moulding you in this or that direction. You might put it a bit differently by saying that you are trying to discover what is most 'natural' to you, though this begs too many questions for comfort. Rhees notes, very pertinently, that if I say I must discover something about myself in order to make certain kinds of decisions with honesty, this is not purely 'subjective': I am in pursuit of a truth that is not at my mercy, even if it is a truth about myself. And when the decision is made, I shall not at once know for certain that it is 'right' – in the sense that I might know if it were a matter of performing an action in accordance with certain rules: it may be that only as years pass shall I be able to assess something I have done as the 'natural' or truthful decision.

That too tells us something significant about our decision-making: we may in retrospect come to believe that – however difficult a decision seemed at the time – it was the only thing we could have done. We were less free to choose than we thought: or, we might say, we were more free (in a different sense) to do what was deepest in us. Some of our problems certainly arise from a very shallow idea of what freedom means, as if it were first and foremost a matter of consumer choice, being faced with a range of possibilities with no pressure to choose one rather than another. But we have to reckon with the freedom that comes in not being distracted from what we determine to do. Saints are often recognised by this freedom from distraction. They may not be – subjectively – eager to do what they are going to do, but they have a mature and direct discernment of what 'must' be done if they are to be faithful to the truth they acknowledge. And their confidence comes not from knowing a catalogue of recommended or prescribed actions, but from that knowledge of who or what they are that enables them to know what action will be an appropriate response to the truth of themselves and the world.

SELF-KNOWLEDGE

But it is time now to look harder at this matter of self-knowledge. We can easily misunderstand it if we think first and foremost of the self as a finished and self-contained reality, with its own fixed needs and dispositions. That, alas, is how the culture of the post-Enlightenment world has more and more tended to see it. We romanticise the lonely self, we are fascinated by its pathos and its drama; we explore it in literature and psychological analysis, and treat its apparent requirements with reverence. None of this is wrong – though it may be risky and a courting of fantasy; but we have to think harder, in the 'Western', or North Atlantic, world about the way the self is already shaped by the relations in which it stands. Long before we can have any intelligent account of our 'selfhood' in absolutely distinct terms, we already have identities we did not choose; others have entered into what we are – parents and neighbours, the inheritance of class and nation or tribe, all those around us who are speaking the language we are going to learn. To become a conscious self is not to say no to all this: that would be flatly impossible. It is to learn a way of making sense and communicating within an environment in which our options are already limited by what we have come into.

If this is so, self-knowledge is far more than lonely introspection. We discover who we are, in significant part, by meditating on the relations in which we already stand. We occupy a unique place in the whole network of human and other relations that makes up the world of language and culture; but that is not at all the same as saying that we possess an identity that is fundamentally quite unlike that of others and uninvolved in the life of others – with its own given agenda. Thus the self-discovery we have been thinking about in the process of making certain kinds of decision is also a discovery of the world that shapes us. I wrote earlier of finding out what has shaped the person I am, and this is always going to be more than the history of my own previous decisions.

And this is where we may begin to talk theologically (at last). How do Christians make moral decisions? In the same way as other people. That is to say, they do not automatically have more information about moral truth in the abstract than anyone else. What is different is the relations in which they are involved, relations that shape a particular kind of reaction to their environment and each other. If you want to say that they know more than other people, this can only be true in the sense that they are involved with more than others, with a larger reality, not they have been given an extra set of instructions. The people of Israel in the Old Testament received the Law when God had already established relation with them, when they were already beginning to be a community bound by faithfulness to God and each other. The Law did not come into a vacuum, but crystallised what had begun to exist through the action of God. When the Old Testament prophets announce God's judgement on the people, they do not primarily complain about the breaking of specific rules (though they can do this in some contexts) or about failure to live up to a moral ideal; they denounce those actions that signify a breaking of the covenant with God and so the breaking of the bonds of faithfulness that preserve Israel as a people to whom God has given a unique vocation – above all, actions such as idolatry and economic oppression. They denounce Israel for replacing the supremely active and transcendent God who brought them out of Egypt by local myths that will allow them to manage and contain the divine; and for creating or tolerating a social order that allows some among God's chosen nation to be enslaved by others because of poverty; and that is unworried by massive luxury and consumption; or sees its deepest safety in treaties with blood thirsty superpowers. If you had asked one of the prophets about moral decision-making, he might have responded (once you had explained what you meant to someone who would not be starting with such categories) by saying, 'What we seek as we choose our path in life is what reflects the demands of the covenant, what is an appropriate response to the complete commitment of God to us.' The Law tells me what kinds of action in themselves represent betrayal of God; but in deciding what, positively, I must do, I seek to show the character of the God who has called me through my people and its history.

The truth sought by such a person would be a truth shared with the community of which they were part, the community that gave them their identity in a number of basic respects. When we turn to the New Testament, it is striking that the earliest attempts at Christian ethical thinking echo this so closely. We can watch St Paul in Romans 14 and 15 or 1 Corinthians 10 discussing what was in fact a profoundly serious dilemma for his converts. To abstain from meat sacrificed to pagan gods was regarded as one of the minimum requirements for fidelity to the true God by Jews of that age (as an aspect of the covenant with Noah, which was earlier and more comprehensive than the covenant made through Moses); and it had been reaffirmed by the most authoritative council we know of in the church's first decades, the apostolic synod described in Acts 15. But the growing recognition that the sacrifice of Christ had put all the laws of ritual purity in question, combined with the practical complications of urban life in the Mediterranean cities, was obviously placing urban converts under strain.

Paul is, it seems, fighting on two fronts at once. He warns, in Romans 14, of the risks of the 'pure', the ultra-conscientious, passing judgement on the less careful, at the same time as warning the less careful against causing pain to the scrupulous by flaunting their freedom in ways that provoke conflict or, worse, doubt. In the Corinthian text, he offers an even clearer theological rationale for his advice in arguing that any decision in this area should be guided by the priority of the other person's advantage and thus by the imperative of building the Body of Christ more securely. What will guide me is the need to show in my choices the character of the God who called me and the character of the community I belong to; my God is a God whose concern for all is equal; my community is one in which all individual actions are measured by how securely they build up a pattern of selfless engagement with the interest of the other – which in itself (if we link it up to what else Paul has to say) is a manifestation of the completely costly directedness to the other that is shown in God's act in Christ.

So for the early Christian, as for the Jew, the self that must be discovered is a self already involved very specifically in this kind of community, in relation to this kind of God (the God of self-emptying). The goal of our decision-making is to show what God's selfless attention might mean in prosaic matters of everyday life – but also to show God's glory (look, for example, at Romans 15:7 or 1 Corinthians 10:31). What am I to do? I am to act in such a way that my action becomes something given into the life of the community and in such a way that what results is glory – the radiating, the visibility, of God's beauty in the world. The self that I am, the self that I have been made to be, is the self engaged by God in love and now in process of recreation through the community of Christ and the work of the Holy Spirit.

MORAL DEPTH

What might this mean in more depth? The model of action which actively promotes the good of the other in the unqualified way depicted by Paul, and which reflects the self-emptying of God in Christ, presupposes that every action of the believer is in some sense designed as a gift to the Body. Gifts are, by definition, not what has been demanded or the payment of a debt or the discharging of a definite duty. To borrow the terms of one of our most distinguished Anglican thinkers, John Milbank, a gift cannot just be a 'repetition' of what is already there.[2] At the same time, a gift has its place within a network of activities; it is prompted by a relationship and it affects that relationship and others; it may in its turn prompt further giving. But in this context it is important that a gift be the sort of thing that can be received, the sort of thing it makes sense to receive, something recognisable within the symbolic economy of the community, that speaks the language of the community. In the Christian context, what this means is that an action offered as gift to the life of the Body must be recognisable as an action that in some way or other manifests the character of the God who has called the community.

And this is where the pain and tension arises of Christian disagreement over moral questions. Decisions are made after some struggle and reflection, after some serious effort to discover what it means to be in Christ; they are made by people who are happy to make themselves accountable, in prayer and discussion and spiritual direction. Yet their decisions may be regarded by others as impossible to receive as a gift that speaks of Christ – by others who seek no less rigorously to become aware of who they are in Christ and who are equally concerned to be accountable for their Christian options. It would be simpler to resolve these matters if we were more abstract in our Christian learning and growing. But the truth is that Christians learn their faith in incarnate ways; Christ makes sense to us because of the specific Christian relationships in which we are involved – this community, this inspirational pastor or teacher, this experience of reading scripture with others. Of course (it ought not need saying) such particularities are always challenged and summoned to move into the universal sphere, the catholic mind of the whole body. But this is what can be a struggle. If we learn our discipleship in specific contexts and relations, as we are bound to, our Christian identity will never be an abstract matter. We are slowly coming to acknowledge the role of cultural specificities in the Christian practice. But it is more than that, more than a matter of vague cultural relativity, let alone allowing the surrounding culture to dictate our priorities. It is that local

Christian communities gradually and subtly come to take for granted slightly different things, to speak of God with a marked local accent. At a fairly simple level, we might think of different attitudes to the Christian use of alcohol in many African contexts as opposed to prevailing assumptions in the North Atlantic world, or differences as to whom you might most immediately ask for help over matters of moral or even spiritual concern – a cleric or an elder in a community or a family council. At first sight, when you encounter a different 'accent', it can sound as though the whole of your Christian world is under attack or at least under question, precisely because no one learns their Christianity without a local accent.

And it would be easy to resolve if Christians had no concern for consistency, no belief that the church ought to speak coherently to its environment about discerning the difference between ways that lead to life and ways that lead to death. We want our faith to be more than just what we learn from those who are familiar and whom we instinctively trust, because we remember – or we should remember – how the faith moved out from the familiar territory of the eastern Mediterranean to become 'naturalised' in other cultures. Tribalism is never enough. Yet when we begin to put our insights together, deep and sometimes agonising conflict appears. What are we to do?

MORAL DISCERNMENT

So much is being said in all the churches about issues of sexuality as the paradigm tests of moral coherence or faithfulness that I believe it is important to look seriously at some other matters also when we reflect on moral decision-making and the character of our moral discernment. So let me take a different set of questions, one in which I have long been involved. I believe it is impossible for a Christian to tolerate, let alone bless or even defend, the manufacture and retention of weapons of mass destruction by any political authority (see below, pp. 187f). And having said that I believe it is impossible, I at once have to recognise that Christians do it; not thoughtless, shallow, uninstructed Christians, but precisely those who make themselves accountable to the central truths of our faith in the ways I have described. I cannot at times believe that we are reading the same Bible; I cannot understand what it is that could conceivably speak of the nature of the Body of Christ in any defence of such strategy. But these are the people I meet at the Lord's table; I know they hear the scriptures I hear, and I am aware that they offer their discernment as a gift to the Body. At its most impressive, the kind of argument developed in defence of their stance reminds me that in a violent world the question of how we take responsibility for each other, how we avoid a bland and uncostly withdrawal from the realities of our environment, is not easily or quickly settled. In this argument, I hear something that I need to hear which, left to myself, I might not grasp. So I am left in perplexity. I cannot grasp how this reading of the Bible is possible; I want to go on arguing against it with all my powers, and I believe that Christian witness in the world is weakened by our failure to speak with one voice in this matter. Yet it seems I am forced to ask what there is in this position that I might recognise as a gift, as a showing of Christ.

It comes – for me – so near the edge of what I can make any sense of. I have to ask whether there is any point at which my inability to recognise anything of gift in another's policy, another's discernment, might make it a nonsense to pretend to stay in the same communion. It is finely balanced: I am not a Mennonite or a Quaker. I can dimly see that the intention of my colleagues who see differently is also a kind of obedience, by their lights, to what we are all trying to look at. I see in them the signs of struggling with God's Word and with the nature of Christ's Body. Sixty years ago, Bonhoeffer and others broke the fragile communion of the German Protestant churches over the issue of the anti-Jewish legislation of the Third Reich, convinced that this so cut at the heart of any imaginable notion of what Christ's Body might mean that it could only be empty to pretend that the same faith was still shared. How we get to such a recognition is perhaps harder than some enthusiasts imagine, and Bonhoeffer has some wise words about the dangers of deciding well in advance where the non-negotiable boundaries lie. Our task is rather to work at becoming a discerning community, ready to recognise a limit when it appears, a limit that will have a perfectly concrete and immediate character. For him, the limits are going to be set 'from outside': 'the boundaries are drawn arbitrarily by the world, which shuts itself off from the church by not hearing and believing'.[3] But of course the discerning of such boundaries has quite properly involved the church in drawing boundaries 'from within', in the form of baptism and credal confession. To paraphrase Bonhoeffer: if we did not have these markers of Christian identity, there would be no ground on which the church as a community, a body with a common language, could discuss and discern a possible boundary being set by the world's refusal of the gospel.

The question is when and where the 'world' so invades the church that the fundamental nature of the church is destroyed, and to this question there is – by definition, Bonhoeffer would say – no general and abstract answer. Up to a certain point we struggle to keep the conversation alive, as long as we can recognise that our partners in this conversation are speaking the same language and wrestling with the same given data of faith. If I might put in a formula that may sound too much like jargon, I suggest that what we are looking for in each other is the grammar of obedience: we watch to see if our partners take the same kind of time, sense that they are under the same sort of judgement or scrutiny, approach the issue with the same attempt to be dispossessed by the truth they are engaging with. This will not guarantee agreement; but it might explain why we should always first be hesitant and attentive to each other. Why might anyone think this might count as a gift of Christ to the church? Well, to answer that I have a great deal of listening to do, even if my incomprehension remains.

And there is a further turn to this. When I reluctantly continue to share the church's communion with someone whose moral judgement I deeply disagree with, I do so in the knowledge that for both of us part of the cost is that we have to sacrifice a straightforward confidence in our 'purity'. Being in the Body means that we are touched by one another's commitments and thus by one another's failures. If another Christian comes to a different conclusion and decides in different ways from myself, and if I can still recognise their discipline and practice as sufficiently like mine to sustain a conversation, this leaves my own decisions to some extent under question. I cannot have absolute subjective certainty that this is the only imaginable reading of the tradition; I need to keep my reflections under critical review. This, I must emphasise again, is not a form of relativism; it is a recognition of the element of putting oneself at risk that is involved in any serious decision-making or any serious exercise of discernment (as any pastor or confessor will know). But this is only part of the implication of recognising the differences and risks of decision-making in the Body of Christ. If I conclude that my Christian brother or sister is deeply and damagingly mistaken in their decision, I accept for myself the brokenness in the Body that this entails. These are my wounds; just as the one who disagrees with me is wounded by what they consider my failure or even betrayal. So long as we still have a language in common and the 'grammar of obedience' in common, we have, I believe, to turn away from the temptation to seek the purity and assurance of a community speaking with only one voice and embrace the reality of living in a communion that is fallible and divided. The church's need for health and mercy is inseparable from my own need for health and mercy. To remain in communion is to remain in solidarity with those who I believe are wounded as well as wounding the church, in the trust that in the Body of Christ the confronting of wounds is part of opening ourselves to healing.

This is hard to express. It may be clearer if we think for a moment of the past of our church. In the Body of Christ, I am in communion with past

Christians whom I regard as profoundly and damagingly in error – with those who justified slavery, torture or the execution of heretics on the basis of the same Bible as the one I read, who prayed probably more intensely than I ever shall. How do I relate to them? How much easier if I did not have to acknowledge that this is my community, the life I share; that these are consequences that may be drawn from the faith I hold along with them. I do not seek simply to condemn them but to stand alongside them in my own prayer, not knowing how, in the strange economy of the Body, their life and mine may work together for our common salvation. I do not think for a moment that they might be right on matters such as those I have mentioned. But I acknowledge that they 'knew' what their own concrete Christian communities taught them to know, just as I 'know' what I have learned in the same concrete and particular way. And when I stand in God's presence or at the Lord's table, they are part of the company I belong to.

Living in the Body of Christ is, in fact, profoundly hard work. Modern liberals are embarrassed by belonging to a community whose history is infected by prejudice and cruelty (and so often try to sanitise this history or silence it or distance themselves from it). Modern traditionalists are embarrassed by belonging to a community whose present is so muddled, secularised and fragmented (and long for a renewed and purified church where there are apparently clear rules for the making of moral decisions). If we cared less about the truth and objectivity of our moral commitments, this would matter infinitely less. But if I say that our moral decisions involve a risk, I do not mean by that to suggest that they have nothing to do with truth; they are risky precisely because we are trying to hear the truth – and to show the truth, the truth of God's character as uniquely revealed in Jesus Christ. And there are times when the risky decision called for is to recognise that we are no longer speaking the same language at all, no longer seeking to mean the same things, to symbolise or communicate the same vision of who God is. But that moment itself only emerges from the constantly self-critical struggle to find out who I am and who we are in and as the Body of Christ.

Can we then begin thinking about our ethical conflicts in terms of our understanding of the Body of Christ? The first implication, as I have suggested, is to do with how we actually decide what we are to do, what standard we appeal to. An ethic of the Body of Christ asks that we first examine how any proposed action or any proposed style or policy of action measures up to two concerns: how does it manifest the selfless holiness of God in Christ? And how can it serve as a gift that builds up the community called to show that holiness in its corporate life? What I have to discover as I try to form my mind and will is the nature of my pre-existing relation with God and with those others whom God has touched, with whom I share a life of listening for God and praising God. Self-discovery, yes; but the discovery of a self already shaped by these relations and these consequent responsibilities. And then, if I am serious about making a gift of what I do to the Body as a whole, I have to struggle to make sense of my decision in terms of the common language of the faith, to demonstrate why this might be a way of speaking the language of the historic schema of Christian belief. This involves the processes of self-criticism and self-questioning in the presence of scripture and tradition, as well as engagement with the wider community of believers. Equally, if I want to argue that something hitherto not problematic in Christian practice or discourse can no longer be regarded in this light, I have a comparable theological job in demonstrating why it cannot be a possible move on the basis of the shared commitments of the church. I may understand at least in part why earlier generations considered slavery to be compatible with the gospel or why they regarded any order of government other than monarchy to be incompatible with the gospel. I may thus see something of what Christ meant to them, and receive something of Christ from them, even as I conclude that they were dangerously deluded in their belief about what was involved in serving Christ.

I cannot escape the obligation of looking and listening for Christ in the acts of another Christian who is manifestly engaged, self-critically engaged, with the data of common belief and worship. But, as I have hinted, there are points when recognition fails. If someone no longer expressly brings their acts and projects before the criterion we look to together; if someone's conception of the Body of Christ is ultimately deficient, a conception only of a human society (that is, if they have no discernible commitment to the risen Christ and the Spirit as active in the church); if their actions systematically undermine the unconditionality of the gospel's offer (this was why justification by faith became the point of division for the Reformation churches, and why anti-Jewish laws in the Third Reich became the point of division for the Confessing Church in 1935) – then the question arises of whether there is any reality left in maintaining communion. This is a serious matter, on which generalisations are useless. All we can do is to be wary of self-dramatising, and of a broad-brush rhetoric about the abandonment of 'standards'. As the Confessing Church knew well, such a case requires detailed argument – and the sense also of a decision being forced, a limit being encountered, rather than a principle being enunciated in advance of legitimate divisions.

Unity at all costs is indeed not a Christian goal; Christian unity is 'Christ-shaped' or it is empty. Yet the first call, so long as Christians can think of themselves as still speaking the same language, is to stay in engagement with those who decide differently. This, I have suggested, means living with the awareness that the church, and I as part of it, share not only in grace but in failure; and thus staying alongside those on the other side, in the hope that we may still be exchanging gifts – the gift of Christ – in some ways, for one another's healing.

One of the major problems, especially in our media-conscious age, is that we talk past each other and in each other's absence; and even when we speak face to face, it is often in a 'lock' of mutual suspicion and deep anxiety. But the Body of Christ requires more than this. It requires, I have suggested, staying alongside: which implies that the most profound service we can do for each other is to point to Christ; to turn from our confrontation in silence to the Christ we all try to look at; to say to one another, from time to time, hopefully and gently, 'Do you see that? This is how I see him: can you see too?' For many Christians, the experience of ecumenical encounter is like this when it is doing its work. I wonder whether we are capable of a similar methodology when churches divide over moral questions. It does not preclude our saying – in the ecumenical context – 'I can't see that; that sounds like error to me'; and in the ethical context, 'I can't see that; that sounds like sin to me.' It's what I want to say to those who defend certain kinds of defence policies, as I've noted. But what if I still have to reckon with my opponent's manifest commitment to the methods of attention to Christ in Word and worship? I risk an unresolvedness, which is not easy and may not be edifying, and trust that there may be light we can both acknowledge at some point.

And I am brought back to the fundamental question of where and who I am: a person moulded by a specific Christian community and its history and culture, for whom Christ has become real here with these people; but a person also committed, by my baptism, to belonging with Christian strangers (past, present and future – do we think often enough of our communion with Christians of the future? we are 'their' tradition). I am not sure what or how I can learn from them. They may frighten me by the difference of their priorities and their discernment. But because of where we all stand at the Lord's table, in the Body, I have to listen to them and struggle to make recognisable sense to them. If I have any grasp at all of what the life of the Body is about, I shall see to it that I spend time with them, doing nothing but sharing the contemplation of Christ. At the very least, it will refresh the only thing that can be of a real and effective motive for the making of Christian moral decision: the vision of a living Lord whose glory I must strive to make visible.

Notes

1 Herbert McCabe, *Law, Love and Language*, Sheed & Ward, London 1969, p. 61.
2 John Milbank, *The Word Made Strange: Theology, Language, Culture*, Blackwell, Oxford 1997.
3 D. Bonhoeffer, *The Way to Freedom: Letters, Lectures and Notes, 1935–1939*, ed. E. H. Robertson, SCM Press, London 1966, p. 79

2 The authority of scripture and Christian ethics

GARETH JONES

In their daily lives, human beings make decisions about what and how and why they want to do things. Sometimes such decisions are practical; for example, whether one walks to work or takes the train. On occasion such decisions are simply emotional ones; for example, whether one feels like wearing the red or the green dress to tonight's party. And sometimes they are ethical decisions; for example, deciding not to drink and drive. With each of these examples most people will agree that there are certain straightforward motives that explain why people make the decisions they do: it makes more sense; it feels better; it is 'the right thing to do', respectively.

On closer examination, however, one can see that such decisions are not as straightforward as they might at first appear. Walking to work can be a decision made for environmental as much as practical reasons. One might wear the red dress to avoid clashing with the hostess. And not drinking and driving is a very practical thing to do if one already has ten points on one's driving licence. The reasons why we make certain decisions, therefore – even, perhaps especially, ethical ones – are complex. We might appeal to such concepts as justice, equality, freedom and civic consideration, but the ways in which such concepts justify or authorise our decisions always raise significant epistemological questions.[1] That we normally answer these questions without too much thought does not mean that the questions disappear. It means, rather, that we are too often unreflective at just that point where we need to do most of our thinking.

When one speaks of Christian ethics, then questions of justification and authorisation become ones of epistemology; that is, they require answers that are derived from explicitly religious sources. Such sources might be the church, understood both as an institution and as a community of fellow believers. They might be the history and traditions of one's denomination. They might be religious experience, however that is defined. Very often, however, the source of people's justification and authorisation of their Christian ethical decisions is the Bible.[2] One sees this constantly; for example, in the difficult area of human sexuality (see below). While it is necessary to understand the complexity of this decision-making process, one may also legitimately speak of 'the authority of scripture and Christian ethics' as one of the central theological-epistemological questions in this process. In short, the Bible often looms large as the principal authority to which most Christians appeal when they seek to justify their ethical decisions. The key question is how they do this, which is the subject of this discussion.

INITIAL DEFINITIONS

Later in this chapter it will be necessary to illustrate this argument with some specific examples drawn from contemporary life. At this stage, however, one can make a more general point as a way into some initial definitions. When one writes of the Bible in relation to questions of justification and authorisation, one is arguing that the Bible has authority. More specifically, the argument is that the Bible has the authority of ethical decisions because it is the Word of God. For example, if I say that committing adultery is wrong, and when challenged argue that I am right because it says adultery is wrong in the Bible, then a biblical passage, in this case Exodus 20:14, determines the truth of my statement.[3] The Bible is the Word of God, on this reading, and is therefore true.

This example is quite simplistic, and it would not be difficult to think of more difficult decisions and more complex interpretations of biblical texts.[4] Even a simple example such as this one, however, illustrates the decision-making process, a process whereby, starting with an ethical question, authority for a position is sought from the Bible in order to return to the question with some kind of resolution. In his recent book *Scripture and Ethics: Twentieth-Century Portraits*,[5] Jeffrey S. Siker identifies five distinct questions that must be asked when addressing the relationship between scripture and Christian ethics:

- What biblical texts are used?
- How does the author use scripture?
- How is the authority of scripture envisioned?
- What kind of hermeneutic is employed in approaching the Bible?
- What is the relationship between the Bible and Christian ethics?

The thing one immediately notices about Siker's scheme is that the explicit relationship between scripture and Christian ethics is the final stage of the process, there being previous questions. This illustrates one of the most difficult things about our initial definitions, namely, what is scripture?

If one argues that scripture is one text, or a canon of sixty-six distinct texts, or a much larger collection of separate texts that have been formalised into the present books of the Old and New Testaments, then one is making a judgement prior to the matter of 'appealing to scripture'. The answer to the question 'What is scripture?' therefore itself involves a matter of judgement (see below, pp. 42f).

There are aspects of this question that can be informed by textual analysis and historical criticism, a development that has greatly influenced the modern discussion of our central question.[6] However one decides, the really significant question is to what extent one understands the authority of the Bible to be, where by 'normativity' one means the quality of determining truth. The key emphasis here is rightly placed on the word 'always': 'normative' means 'always', not 'sometimes'. Thus, if I argue that adultery is wrong, and I support this statement by appealing to Exodus 20:14, then I am recognising the normative authority of that text to determine truth. Adultery is wrong, therefore, if it says so in the Bible. (This, in fact, is the obvious corollary of believing that the Bible is the Word of God in an objective, straightforwardly literal sense.)

This is a stark position, and the reader should not assume that it goes unquestioned. Rather, I cite it here as a way of fixing our initial definitions with clarity and precision, so that in what follows one might recognise the complexity of making Christian ethical decisions in relation to the Bible. In his important study *The Uses of Scripture in Recent Theology*, David H. Kelsey writes: 'Our suggestion is that scripture may properly be said to be "authority" for a theological proposal when appeal is made to it in the course of making a case for the proposal.'[7] Kelsey is making a general methodological point; but in the terms of our discussion, 'making a case for the proposal' means appealing to the normative authority of the Bible in order to determine the truth of an ethical statement or decision. This is the same process we are involved in whenever we seek to use the Bible in this way. Kelsey writes: 'The sole point of importance here is that in making an appeal to scripture in order to justify a theological claim, a theologian is in fact framing an informal argument.'[8] Making a case for a proposal, and framing an informal argument, is what Christians do when they appeal to the Bible to support ethical decisions.

Kelsey's points provide a general or formal way of interpreting the construction of theological and (for us) ethical arguments. There is not too much about this process that is difficult to understand – the difficulty arises in appreciating how it works in specific instances – but the one exception to this simplicity is the question of normativity. In his seminal essay 'The

Moral Authority of Scripture: The Politics and Ethics of Remembering',[9] Stanley Hauerwas argues that although the Bible is profoundly important in the process of ethical decision-making, it is not normative. Normativity, reasons Hauerwas, is something that arises within a community rather than from a biblical proof text or – worse – a set of abstract principles like 'justice' and 'freedom': 'It is a process of judgement of a community determining what the community is all about. It is always a question of authority and power.'[10] And, as Siker rightly observes, such questions of communal polity, for Hauerwas, are matters of contextualised discrimination: they are judgements made for a given situation, in that same given situation.[11] For Hauerwas, therefore, matters of authority, still less those of normativity, are far more complex than they appear to be for Kelsey.[12]

What do we learn from this discussion of Hauerwas and Kelsey? The important thing to recognise here is that when we make ethical decisions in a thoughtful and responsible way, then we look for some authority to support them. This is Kelsey's point. When we do this, however, we must recall that we always do so in a specific time and place, a given situation. This is Hauerwas' point. Together, these two points help us to understand how an appeal to biblical authority works. Remember, it is not a matter of thinking that certain biblical texts are 'right' and others 'wrong'. Nor is it necessarily a matter of reading the Bible ethically, something that is subtly different.[13] Rather, it is a matter of defining a process of interpretation: what happens when someone makes a decision and appeals to the Bible to justify it? What happens is that questions of authority and normativity arise at just that point where they are most problematic. To appreciate this point one needs to think a little about how 'the truth' is understood in the modern world.

BIBLICAL AUTHORITY AND THE CHALLENGE OF MODERNITY

An example here will illustrate the point being made, as well as leading into the next stage of the argument. In Matthew's gospel one finds the story of Jesus' encounter with the rich young ruler who comes to Jesus and asks, 'Teacher, what good deed must I do, to have eternal life?' (Matt. 19:16). After some debate Jesus says to him, 'If you would be perfect, go, sell what you possess and give to the poor, and you will have treasure in heaven; and come, follow me' (v. 21). This turns out to be a bad answer, however, because the young man is very rich and Jesus' words make him sorrowful. This in turn gives rise to Jesus' famous statement: 'Truly, I say to you, it will be hard for a rich man to enter the kingdom of heaven. Again I tell you, it is easier for a camel to go through the eye of a needle than for a rich man to enter the kingdom of God' (vv. 23–4). The beauty of this story is that someone approaches Jesus with an ethical question and receives a seemingly definitive answer.

But is it true?

Let us answer this question in a series of stages. First, let us say, 'Yes, it is true': it is indeed difficult to be rich and to enter God's kingdom. Second, let us pose Kelsey's question: 'Is this always the case?' Again, I think we need to answer, 'Yes': Jesus does not say it is sometimes true, sometimes not true. Third, however, let us address the normativity of Jesus' statement from Hauerwas' perspective: if it is true in my community that the rich always find it very difficult to enter God's kingdom, what can they do about it? The answer for Hauerwas – give money away and follow Jesus – is not normative 'because it's in the Bible'. It is normative because it is what Christians do in their own lives, in the midst of their communities.[14]

The question of the ethical difficulties surrounding wealth is important because it illustrates many of the challenges of modernity to a straightforward understanding of biblical authority. Christianity's historic appeal to the poor has always had much to do with its message of hope to the disenfranchised; something that is as true today in Latin America as it was in first-century Palestine.[15] In the medieval church the Franciscan Order made 'holy poverty' its guiding principle, reasoning that Christ's injunctions on this matter could become a lived and shared life of prayer and service. This remained a powerful message even into the time of the Reformation and Counter-Reformation in the sixteenth century (and was authoritative because it was biblical and therefore taken to be true).

Thereafter, however, the steady rise in influence of trade and commerce led to a distinction between so-called spiritual questions and material ones; that is, those to do with economic and commercial matters. In the eighteenth century, Adam Smith made this distinction between value and fact central to his book *The Wealth of Nations*.[16] Today Smith's understanding of the value-free working of markets and the equations of supply and demand of goods and services is the principal tenet of capitalism, as even a cursory reading of *The Economist* demonstrates.

The question 'Was Smith right?' is impossible to answer, even if we can say with confidence that he certainly seems to have been right, given the great success of capitalism over the last two hundred years. For our inquiry, however, this question is actually misleading; for the reality we need to address is the modern acceptance of the separation of fact and value, not its truth. More pertinently, what do we have to say about a world in which re-

ligious and ethical questions are increasingly divorced in popular perception from the material circumstances in which people live? And what, then,
does this say about the way in which people appeal to biblical authority to
support their ethical decisions?

The most important thing to say is that the effective split between fact
and value is very damaging to the question of the relationship between biblical authority and Christian ethics, for two reasons. First, when such a split
is accepted, biblical authority is deemed to be relevant solely to questions of
a so-called spiritual order. Thus, such questions of 'value' become reduced to
what one might call individual ethics, in which personal decisions and
judgements are made but are divorced from the actual circumstances of our
daily lives. A good example of this is the modern response to questions of
human sexuality, and the previously cited appeal to the authority of the Ten
Commandments (Exod. 20). One of the constant refrains of contemporary
life – often muttered by politicians – is that 'His sex life is nobody's business
but his own'. This privatisation of what originally was a very public morality
now typifies the modern approach to such questions (see below).

The second point is subtler, but potentially every bit as damaging.
When biblical authority is relegated to questions of value, new principles –
freedom, justice, law, order and equality – are identified in abstract and then
used to regulate matters of fact. One sees this constantly, for example, in
courts of law in the United Kingdom, where the principle that one is innocent until proven guilty is used to govern inquiries that are required to demonstrate guilt 'beyond a reasonable doubt' – not about values, but about
facts. Of course much of this is very significant, and modern civil society
could not function democratically without such guiding principles.
Nevertheless, their development has significant implications for the status
of religious and in particular biblical authority: if one can appeal to justice
normatively to authorise behaviour, where does that leave authority? Or
stated another way: if it is true that one is innocent until proven guilty, what
is the relationship between this truth and the biblical truth?

One might argue here that modern conceptions of justice and equality
before the law are in fact biblical themes, and that civil society is founded
upon biblical understandings of just and godly community.[17] But the fact is
that this is not how many people understand things today. And the fact is
that a document like the Constitution of the United States of America, and
indeed its Bill of Rights, enshrines the individual's right to religious freedom
within a greater understanding of freedom itself. When freedom is taken to
be something greater than biblical authority, then this relativises the authority of the Bible when it comes to making ethical decisions. In short, biblical

truth is part of a greater truth, one that human reason understands as much as it understands the Word of God. This, in general, is the situation facing Christians in the modern, developed world.

CONTEMPORARY ISSUES

It would be wrong of me to suggest now that this is a good or a bad situation, when in fact it is simply a situation, by which I mean it just happens to be the contingent circumstances in which many modern Christians find themselves. Nor would it be right to suggest that 'modernity' has been a period in which biblical authority has been entirely questioned, either in the name of a variety of different religious communities, or in the name of such enlightened principles as liberty, equality and fraternity. There have always been communities and churches that have understood biblical authority to be normative. Indeed, one of the most important developments, comparatively recently, has been the growth of particularly energetic forms of evangelical fundamentalism, for example in Latin America, which have a very strong reliance upon a straightforwardly normative understanding of biblical authority.

If we return to the question of scripture as the Word of God, then we will be able to find a way through this situation towards certain contemporary issues. As we have seen, a traditional view of the Bible was that it was straightforwardly the Word of God, and as such normative for all church teaching, including ethical teaching. When the Bible began to be seen as primarily a text written in community, however, with the implication that its relationship to God was more indirect, then other authorities began to be important, too. Today many Christians think that the sacraments, the life of the church, people's experiences and respect for personal integrity and privacy are as authoritative as the Bible. Under such circumstances ethical decisions can be made with a variety of different justifications, each of which will have significance for certain individuals or groups.

A simple illustration of this can be found in the area of sexual ethics, particularly the distinct though related questions of birth control and abortion. In the unhappy circumstances of an unwanted pregnancy, a woman has a variety of different possibilities when it comes to making a Christian ethical decision, each of which has advocates. If she believed the Bible to have normative authority, she might cite Exodus 20:13, 'Thou shall not kill', and have the baby. Alternatively, she might regard her decision as private and personal, a matter relating to the integrity of her relationship with God. She might think of the specific circumstances in which she could bring a child into the world, and be influenced by her experiences and her social and economic conditions. And she might be influenced by a conviction that giving birth itself is an expression of the sacramental, and therefore an encounter with God. As one can see, the normativity of the Bible is solely one of these potential responses; and there can be others.

A similar situation can be seen with the related question of contraception. In order to prevent unwanted pregnancies, women and men can take a variety of measures to prevent conception. To someone for whom biblical authority is normative, this can seem a direct contradiction of the Ten Commandments (Exod. 20:13 again). But it can equally seem an affirmation of private and personal responsibility, with a considerable awareness of the potential damage to community of unwanted pregnancies and births. In India, for example, birth control has recently been seen as imperative if the terrible economic distresses associated with overcrowding and poverty are to be alleviated. Of course, this is not to suggest that all (or any) of India's problems will be solved by contraception. But such a method of birth control is at least addressing the situation, and can be justified by reference to a variety of authorities other than the Bible.

It is at this point that the reader is justified in wondering whether the Bible can ever be integrated into the modern world, rather than simply imposed upon it 'from above': whether, that is, biblical authority is simply normative, or simply relative to any other. As Jeffrey S. Siker demonstrates, however, Stanley Hauerwas offers a very clear understanding of a responsible Christian alternative to this very monochromatic choice.[18] Hauerwas writes of a 'scripture-shaped community' in which the Bible has no authority apart from the community of believers. Hauerwas speaks of narrative as the correct hermeneutic of the Bible, by which he means that the Bible has to be read and interpreted from within the community of believers, rather than from without ('from above'). When people in community read the Bible in community, they recognise its authority as being part of their own authority, and vice versa. In fact, one of their responsibilities as Christians is to understand their own story as being wrapped up with the Bible's story, and again vice versa. And, most important, they must understand that the same God who speaks to them from the Bible is the same God who speaks to them in the midst of their own community. In this way God draws people towards reconciliation, a process the Bible reflects with profound beauty and revelation, but without coercive authority.

If one returns to Siker's own five-point scheme for understanding the relationship between biblical authority and Christian ethics, one sees that the important stages are the third and fourth: how is the authority of scripture envisioned; what kind of hermeneutic is employed in approaching the Bible? If one thinks about these questions for a moment, then one can see that they boil down to a simple proposition: when one looks at the Bible as a text, how does one see it in relation to one's own context? If one sees it as something complete and separate, monumental and eternal (Word of God), then its authority is absolute: outside of time, it applies equally to all time. If, however, one sees it as something to be read and understood and embraced within one's own world, and that one's own world must always be a part of that reading, then one sees the Bible, and its authority, in a different light. It is no longer something complete and separate, but is rather part of the same process of reconciliation and mission that all Christians are part of. Christians then become a genuinely biblical community, and their ethical decisions, if made responsibly and spiritually, reflect this same complex, interpretative story.

A WAY FORWARD

This approach will not be satisfactory to someone who wants to see the Bible as a repository of correct answers to ethical questions. Nor can it be; for it does not regard the Bible as a repository of anything. On the contrary, it regards the Bible as the revelation of God's story of redemption for the world; but that story continues, and Christians today are as much a part of it as Christians were in the time of the gospels. If this realisation does not make the business of making ethical decisions any easier, it does at least have the virtue of revealing what ethical decisions actually are, at least for Christians: reflections of the love of God. By this one simply means that a Christian ethical decision is one that reflects God's loving embrace of the world; it reflects what Jesus Christ died for.

If one now asks, 'What is love?' expecting to receive a longer answer than that given in 1 John 4:16 ('God is love'), then one can respond by returning to Matthew 19 and the story of the rich young ruler. Jesus' reply to the young man is a word of judgement: 'If you would be perfect, go, sell what you possess and give to the poor, and you will have treasure in heaven . . .' But it is not expressed with intolerance and harshness. Jesus looks upon the man's predicament with compassion, embracing his circumstances and condition: '. . . and come, follow me'. That the man is subsequently incapable of doing so is in itself a reflection of Christ's love and compassion. For the essence of the matter is that the rich young ruler is free to decide: he cannot be coerced into selling his possessions and following Jesus. A decision made under such circumstances would not be a decision. It would be a sentence.[19]

This matter of freedom from coercion goes to the heart of the relationship between the Bible and Christian ethics. On any scale, a genuine decision must be one that is freely made; without freedom, there can be no genuine decision. Coercion is arbitrary and abusive, using power and authority to constrain people to events and actions that they might not wish to choose. Biblical authority cannot be coercive if it is to be a reflection of God's authority. Nor can one understand the Bible as somehow constraining people to act in a certain way rather than in others, if such constraint removes from them their ability to respond freely and wholeheartedly. People must be free to respond as themselves part of the same story that the Bible is part of, namely, God's story. Without this fundamental identification, one loses the spirit, retaining solely the letter. As St Paul has shown, this is not the gospel, but rather a peculiar and inadequate version of canon law (see Rom. 8).

The positive side of this approach is that it allows people to concentrate upon the genuinely important aspect of a Christian ethical decision. Rather than having to worry about whether or not one's decision precisely correlates to a given biblical text, people are free to think about their part within a worshipping community, their relationship with God within that same community, and the effects their decision will have on others. And, just as they themselves must be free from coercion and the abuse of power, so must their decisions not coerce and abuse others. This understanding of freedom from coercion and abuse as a commutative relationship among God, the individual and the community is the cornerstone of Christian decision-making. Any understanding of biblical authority that undermines this freedom is not, finally, Christian.

The negative side of this definition is relative, but is important enough to be identified. As has already been indicated, an understanding of freedom in the modern world will be influenced by the secular definitions of liberty and equality that have been discussed, particularly in political and economic circles, since the mid eighteenth century. This is unavoidable in the western world, and with the increasingly global character of modern capitalism it is soon likely to be the case everywhere else, too. It need not be problematic in and of itself, however. There is no reason why the concept of freedom as one finds it in modern democratic theory should not inform a Christian understanding of freedom, and indeed vice versa (this being, after all, the foundation of liberal theology). The important thing is to understand the derivation of each definition. For the democratic theorist, freedom is an inalienable right, worthy of publication in a bill and subsequently of defence (by force, if necessary). For the Christian, freedom is a gift from God. Just as Jesus gave the rich young ruler the freedom to make his decision, so God gives us that same freedom. Moreover, whereas the democratic theorist will speak of the rights of the individual, Christianity always speaks of God's gifts to the church as a whole. Taken together, these emphases on gift and community defend the faith from misunderstanding and misappropriation.

Once again, therefore, one can turn to the words of Stanley Hauerwas to summarise the definition of the relationship between biblical authority and Christian ethics: 'non-coercive reconciliation'.[20] For Christians, the Bible is indeed the Word of God. It is not, however, a catalogue of correct decisions and information; it is not law in this reductive sense. The Bible is spirit, just as the Word of God is Spirit. And just as Christians believe that the Bible is one of God's gifts to the church, so they believe also that the Spirit, at Pentecost, is given to the church. Christians live today in continuity with that biblical event, and in so doing become part of God's story of redemption. In making ethical decisions, Christians affirm this membership, thereby affirming, too, the Bible's authority in their lives. It is the authority of non-coercive reconciliation, an authority that, as God's, is the eschatological reality for which, and in which, Christians are called to decision.

CONCLUSION

From this last comment it will be clear that I consider all discussion of Christian ethics to be discussion, and consequently itself part of the ongoing story of God's Word. To speak of this event as eschatologically real is to acknowledge that it has a specific origin in God's historic act of self-revelation in Jesus Christ, an act to which the New Testament as scripture witnesses. From this understanding arises any meaningful interpretation of the relationship between biblical authority and Christian ethics.

At the same time, however, I have argued throughout this chapter that such a relationship is not a simple thing, and cannot be reduced to a straightforward correlation between the events recorded in the Bible and the decisions Christians have to make today. On the contrary, since Christians remain part of the old creation even as they pray for their new creation (2 Cor. 5:17), so our decisions and actions today remain conditioned, in part at least, by the world in which we live. To understand this is to understand the life of faith, hope and love to which all Christians have been called.

Notes

1 By 'epistemology' here I mean the science or analysis of the good reasons why people do or believe certain things. Theological epistemology is, consequently, the science or analysis of the theological good reasons why people do or believe certain things. It follows that Christian ethics is subject to analysis by theological epistemology.

2 In this chapter I use 'Bible' and 'scripture' as synonyms, depending on context; sometimes usage is determined by source. On the general question of the relationship between the Bible and Christian ethics, see the following: J. I. H. McDonald, *Biblical Interpretation and Christian Ethics*, Cambridge University Press, Cambridge 1993; C. F. Sleeper, *The Bible and the Moral Life*, Louisville 1992; S. E. Fowl & L. G. Jones, *Reading in Communion: Scripture and Ethics in Christian Life*, Grand Rapids 1991.

3 Exodus 20:14 is part of the Ten Commandments. I will not enter the debate as to the cultural and historical origins of this text: my point here is a straightforward one and concerns interpretation, not textual criticism.

4 Simple or complex, one of the biggest difficulties with attempting to find biblical 'solutions' to ethical questions is their sheer arbitrariness, something that always undermines notions of genuine ethical inquiry.

5 Oxford 1997, pp. 3–4

6 By 'textual analysis' and 'historical criticism' I mean the practice of subjecting biblical texts to objective or scientific analysis, on which question cf. McDonald, *Biblical Interpretation*.

7 London 1975, p. 125.

8 *Ibid.*

9 In Stanley Hauerwas, *A Community of Character: Toward a Constructive Christian Social Ethic*, University of Notre Dame Press, Notre Dame 1981, pp. 53–71.

10 Hauerwas, quoted in Siker, *Scripture and Ethics*, p. 111. In a more general sense, Hauerwas distinguishes between what he calls 'Constantinianism' and 'the Enlightenment', and their detrimental impact upon religious belief. Constantinianism is the conviction that Christianity is about being religious in a general and diffuse sense. The Enlightenment makes Christians into apologists to and for the modern world. On these definitions in Hauerwas' work cf. Siker, pp. 109–11.

11 'Contextualised discrimination' is my own expression, not Siker's.

12 I should reiterate that Kelsey is specifically offering a formal case for the construction of theological arguments, though by inference this case must also apply to Christian ethical decisions if it is genuinely an exercise in theological epistemology.

13 'Reading the Bible ethically' is about the ethics of interpretation, and therefore involves considerable reflection upon such things as perspective and context. Of course, one would hope that people read the Bible ethically in using the Bible for ethical decision-making, but the two inquiries are distinct.

14 For the sake of clarity here, I should explain that neither Hauerwas nor Kelsey

writes explicitly about Matthew 19. The application of their general arguments to this particular text is my own, not theirs.

15 One of liberation theology's central tenets is the material correlation between the situation in first-century Palestine and that pertaining today in Latin America.

16 Adam Smith, *An Inquiry into the Nature and Causes of the Wealth of Nations*, London 1991.

17 On another occasion I would go further and say that civil society is founded upon biblical understandings of just and godly society. For the antithetical argument, cf. John Milbank, *Theology and Social Theory: Beyond Secular Reason*, Blackwell, Oxford 1990.

18 Siker, *Scripture and Ethics*, p. 120.

19 NB here the proximity to civil and criminal law.

20 Siker, *Scripture and Ethics*, p. 122.

3 The Old Testament and Christian ethics

JOHN ROGERSON

In the past twenty years there has been a move in British and North American scholarship to use the term 'Hebrew Bible' (less often, 'Jewish Bible' or 'Jewish scriptures') in place of 'Old Testament'. The question affects ethics, as will be shown shortly. The reason for the move has been a wish to be sensitive to Judaism, and to avoid the impression, undoubtedly created in many people's minds by the term 'Old Testament', that the books designated by this name are inferior to or superseded by those known as the New Testament. In addition, there has been the feeling in some quarters that the Christian term 'Old Testament' is inappropriate in academia.

It is easier to be sympathetic to the reasons for the move than to feel that the underlying problem has been satisfactorily dealt with. The terms 'Jewish Bible' and 'Jewish scriptures' most naturally refer to texts held sacred by and used distinctively within Judaism. They are legitimate designations in that context. 'Hebrew Bible' is more problematic, because, on analogy with 'English Bible', it most naturally refers to the Bible in Hebrew, although few students who take courses in 'Hebrew Bible' in universities and colleges actually read it in that language. There is the further problem that 'Hebrew Bible' and 'Old Testament' are not synonymous. For the majority of Christians for most of the history of the church, 'Old Testament' has designated not only the twenty-four books of the Bible in Hebrew, but has also included the thirteen to sixteen books that Protestants call the Apocrypha but which are scripture for the Roman Catholic and Orthodox churches.[1] A partial compromise would be for 'Jewish Bible/scriptures' to be used in the context of Judaism and 'Old Testament' in the context of Christianity.

The matter is particularly relevant for ethics, because the two faiths have developed markedly different approaches to using the texts that they have in common in their scriptures. In Judaism the scriptures reveal God's explicit guidance for the regulation of every facet of the daily life of the faithful believer. This belief has two implications. First, because the laws actually contained in the scriptures deal with only very limited areas of life, Jews believe that God revealed two laws to Moses on Mt Sinai – a written law and an oral law. The former is found in the Jewish scriptures, and pre-eminently in the first five books (the Torah). The second was passed down by word of mouth from Moses to Joshua to the prophets, and eventually to the rabbis of the era after the fall of Jerusalem in 70 CE, who began to write it down in the Mishnah (early 3rd century CE) the Tosephta (4th century CE) and the Babylonian and Jerusalem Talmuds (4th to 9th centuries CE).[2] This leads to the second implication, which is that there has been, and continues to be, a process of legal and scriptural interpretation within Judaism designed to discover God's will for every detail of daily life. Further, although there have been, and continue to be, great authorities on how to interpret the laws, the field is not occupied merely by experts. In orthodox Judaism, all devout believers are students of the laws, and have devoted many hours of their lives to studying not only the scriptures but the dozens of volumes which contain the oral law.

Within Christianity a quite different path was taken; and it is clear that the question of the extent to which Christians, and in particular Christians who were not Jews, should obey the laws of the Old Testament deeply divided the early church and left its mark on the New Testament. The matter was made more difficult by the fact that church and synagogue congregations were often rivals in areas such as Syria and Asia Minor. The letters of Paul indicate that there were conflicts between those who believed that Christ's death and resurrection had 'fulfilled' the law and removed from Christians the obligation of strict observance of it, and 'Judaisers' in the church, who took strict observance to be part of Christian discipleship. The Pauline party came out on top, and in the Acts of the Apostles, a book representing the Pauline viewpoint, a 'Council of Jerusalem' is described, which decided that non-Jewish Christians should observe only the following Old Testament laws: to abstain from eating meat that had been sacrificed to idols (not an explicitly Old Testament law but an interpretation of the prohibition of idolatry in the Ten Commandments), to avoid blood (i.e. to eat only 'kosher' meat) and to avoid unchastity (Acts 15:1–29, especially vv. 28–9). Whether or not there was a Council of Jerusalem, the point is that Acts 15 expresses a view about Christian obligation that was held in at least some Pauline churches.[3] As this chapter will indicate later, this 'minimalist' view of Christian obliga-tion to the Old Testament laws contrasts sharply with some Reformation and modern reformed views that as much of the Old Testament as possible should be legislated upon contemporary societies.

PROBLEMS OF THE MORAL CONTENT OF THE OLD TESTAMENT

Popular misconceptions about the Old Testament, such as that its God is a God of wrath, spill over into its moral tone, with passages being cited such as those about dashing the heads of babies against rocks (Ps. 137:9) or the demand of 'an eye for an eye' (Exod. 21:24). There is no denying that the Old Testament contains material that is offensive to modern readers, and that some of its leading characters behave in ways that are illegal as well as offensive in a modern society. For example, Jacob (Gen. 29:21–30) and Elkanah (the father of Samuel, 1 Sam. 1:2) have two wives, a reminder that ancient Israelite society was polygamous. Joshua, at God's command, kills the entire population of conquered towns (Josh. 6:21), something that would be regarded as a war crime today. David commits adultery with the wife of one of his soldiers who is away fighting, and then arranges for the man to be killed in battle when it is discovered that he has made the woman pregnant (2 Sam. 11). David does not go uncensored (see 2 Sam. 12:1–15), yet he is described elsewhere as a man after God's own heart (1 Sam. 13:14) and as one whose heart was wholly true to God (1 Kings 15:3).

For much of Christian history, these and other difficulties were explained and justified in various ways. The inhabitants of cities destroyed by Joshua were said to be wicked people who deserved to be punished; and in any case, if God commanded something it must be right – not, incidentally, the view of the author of Genesis 18:22–33, who argued that God must act in accordance with what is just.[4] The actions of David were justified on the basis of the distinction between what he did in his official capacity as a king, where he was blameless, and what he did as a private individual, where he was morally culpable. Although this is not an arbitrary distinction – an army officer acting in accordance with proper 'rules of engagement' will not be held guilty of murder if he orders his men to shoot at an enemy, whereas a civilian who tells an accomplice to shoot a member of the public will be accused of murder – it is unlikely to convince modern readers that David can be held up as a moral example in the ways that the Old Testament does. Indeed, one of the factors that led to the rise of modern critical study of the Bible was the refusal of scholars to go on justifying the questionable moral behaviour of Old Testament characters.

This is not the only problem, however. Some of the actual laws contained in the Old Testament are illegal in modern society. For example, the death penalty is prescribed not only for homicide (Exod. 21:12) but also for striking one's father or mother, stealing a man (i.e. depriving him of his freedom), cursing one's parents, sacrificing to any god other than the God of Israel and apostasy (Exod. 21:15–17, 22:20; Deut. 13:6–11). Also to be put to death are a stubborn and rebellious son, a woman found not to be a virgin on her first night of marriage, a man and woman caught in the act of adultery, a man and woman who commit incest and a man who has intercourse with a male as with a woman (Deut. 21:18–21, 22:13–21, 22–4, Lev. 20:11–13).

There is evidence that the death penalty was not being enforced in Judaism for at least some of these offences by the end of the first century CE;[5] but one of the implications of the presence of laws such as those listed immediately above is that any use of the Old Testament in ethics which simply quotes a passage and seeks to apply it directly to modern society must confine itself to those laws which are not yet illegal in modern society, and must explain why these laws continue to be applicable today when others are so much at odds with modern ethical sensitivity.

HOW THE OLD TESTAMENT HAS BEEN USED IN CHRISTIAN ETHICS

One striking feature of the New Testament is how little reference it makes to the Old Testament in regard to conduct and morality.[6] Jesus is presented as someone who rejects the common interpretation of the law about not working on the sabbath (Mark 2:23–8, 3:1–6) and who radicalises the law in such a way that it can hardly be observed (e.g. Matt. 5:27 'every one who looks at a woman lustfully has already committed adultery with her in his heart'). Paul summarises some of the Ten Commandments and 'any other commandment' under the heading of loving one's neighbour (Rom. 13:8–10). It is also arguable that in sending back the slave Onesimus to his master Philemon (if this is what the letter to Philemon is about), Paul is ignoring the stipulation in Deuteronomy 23:15–16 that 'you shall not give up to his master a slave who has escaped from his master to you'.

The absence of reference to the Old Testament law continues with the texts known as the Apostolic Fathers. The *Didache*, which aims to guide its readers in the way of righteousness, has hardly any reference to the Old Testament, while *The Shepherd of Hermes*, which sets out twelve commandments for Christian living, has only one commandment which could be derived from the Old Testament, that on divorce. However, the author of *The Shepherd* is probably dependent on Matthew's gospel in this instance. *The Epistle of Barnabas* explicitly rejects the Old Testament sacrificial system, quoting Isaiah 1:11–14 and Jeremiah 7:22 (famous prophetic critiques of sacrifice) in support (Barnabas 2:5–6). It spiritualises ordinances such as those about clean and unclean foods (these laws actually refer to different types of person whose company should be avoided), and it declares that Old Testament laws about the sabbath are not be taken literally by Christians (Barnabas 10:1–9, 15:1–9).

When the Old Testament begins to be taken more seriously, it is on the basis of a kind of dispensationalism. The *Apostolical Constitutions* (probably dating from the fourth century and compiled in Syria) distinguishes between laws given before the incident of the Golden Calf and those given after it (Exod. 32; see *Apostolical Constitutions* vi, chs. 19–30). The laws and sacrifices prescribed after the Golden Calf incident are designed to correct Israel's apostasy and are not binding on Christians. The laws given prior to this incident include the Ten Commandments (which become increasingly important for the church) and laws of which many begin with the word 'if'. These laws must be taken seriously by Christians; but they are not necessarily prescriptions. For example, Exodus 20:24 does not say 'make an altar of earth'; it says 'if you make an altar, make it of earth'.

Sophistication in handling the Old Testament is increasingly evident as it wins back the ground that it appears to have lost, at any rate in moral issues, in the early church. Aquinas was influenced by the Jewish scholar Maimonides' masterpiece *The Guide of the Perplexed* (c. 1190) and by its argument that the Old Testament laws could be defended rationally as instruments designed to keep the Israelites from paganism and to promote their physical health. Like others before him, Aquinas distinguished Old Testament laws that were moral from those that were ceremonial and judicial. The moral laws contained the obligations of natural law, and were therefore binding upon all humans. The ceremonial and judicial laws were applications of natural law directed to the specific circumstances of ancient Israel. In the form that they took in the Old Testament they were not, therefore, universally binding. Indeed, even the supreme expressions of the moral law in the Ten Commandments, immutable as they were, needed to be interpreted in order to be applied; and it was permissible for the sabbath law to be broken if one was acting in the interests of human welfare.[7]

The distinction between moral laws and ceremonial and judicial (or civil) laws was taken up with the Reformation, and stated, for example, in the seventh of the Thirty-Nine Articles of Religion of the Church of England. The article states that, of the 'Law given from God by Moses', those 'touching Ceremonies and Rites, do not bind Christian men, nor the Civil precepts thereof ought of necessity to be received in any commonwealth'. Only the moral commandments were necessarily binding. However, it was not always easy to decide which commandments were moral and which were ceremonial and civil. The main reformers, Luther, Calvin and Tyndale, apparently took the view that the sabbath commandment was ceremonial and therefore not binding upon Christians. In the view of Calvin and Tyndale it was up to a local congregation or community to decide which day should be the Lord's Day (it did not have to be Sunday), while Luther objected to any ecclesiastical authority that declared a day such as Sunday to be holy, and he regarded such a declaration as an affront to Christian liberty.[8]

If it is a surprise that such radical attitudes to the Old Testament law should have been followed, in certain areas of Protestantism, by the development of strict sabbatarianism, the reason is that some strands of the Reformation believed that as much of the Old Testament as possible should be legislated upon Christian nations. Representative of this view is Martin Bucer's *De regno Christi* (On the kingdom of Christ), written shortly before Bucer's death in 1551 and dedicated to Edward VI of England.

Bucer accepted that Christians were not bound by the civil and ceremonial laws of Moses; but he also argued that

> since there can be no laws more honorable, righteous, and wholesome than those which God, himself, who is eternal wisdom and goodness, enacted, if only they are applied under God's judgement to our own affairs and activities, I do not see why Christians, in matters which pertain to their own doings should not follow the laws of God more than those of any men.[9]

In practice this meant that the king, like David, Solomon, Asa, Hezekiah, Josiah and Nehemiah, should regulate the life and attitudes of the people through education, decrees and the administration of justice. Bucer advocated the death penalty for blasphemy, violation of the sabbath, adultery, rape and certain types of false testimony.

Examples of the differing ways in which the Old Testament has been used in ethics could be multiplied. Although they do not necessarily inform us about how the Old Testament can or should be used today, they indicate that there has been a good deal of variation and of hermeneutical sophistication in such use. Anyone who gives the impression that to use the Old

Testament simply involves taking a passage and applying it straightfor-wardly to today's world, and that this procedure upholds biblical principles, is flying in the face of history.

CONTEMPORARY USES OF THE OLD TESTAMENT IN CHRISTIAN ETHICS

Contemporary uses can broadly be divided into 'conservative' and 'liberal' approaches, with considerable diversity within each division. Walter C. Kaiser's *Toward Old Testament Ethics* is a learned attempt to defend the moral integrity of the Old Testament and to advocate the view that its commandments are the revealed will of God.[10] Thus he tackles head-on the moral deficiencies of some Old Testament characters and laws that were pointed out in 'Problems of the Moral Content' above, and seeks to blunt the criticism that these deficiencies provokes. He uses, for example, the distinction between people acting in their capacity as holding an office, and people acting as private individuals. His particular view of the Bible and of God leads him to conclude that, in some cases, our conviction that some of God's commands are immoral rests upon 'a deficiency in our view of things and our ability to properly [sic] define terms or grasp the whole of the subject'.[11] Kaiser recognises that Old Testament laws cannot necessarily be plucked from their context and applied directly to today's world, and he sets out some 'Principles for Moral Interpretation of the Old Testament', which are ways of getting at universal moral statements behind Old Testament laws that are situated in Hebrew language and culture. At the same time, he argues that God's will as revealed in the Old Testament for all sexual rela-tionships is monogamous heterosexual marriage (Gen. 2:24) in spite of the evidence that Old Testament society was polygamous. Kaiser's book is a scholarly attempt to defend 'biblical principles' against modern secular atti-tudes, yet it acknowledges the force of modern secular attitudes by conced-ing that Old Testament morality has to be defended against the charge of immorality.

A quite different 'conservative' approach is that of Christopher Wright, whose work is characterised and to some extent shaped by awareness of the history of how the Old Testament has been used in ethics.[12] Wright argues that Israel is God's paradigm of what a nation ought to be. This enables him to take full account of the historical and cultural conditions in which ancient Israel existed and to contrast Israel with its neighbours so as to point out striking differences which ultimately indicate the moral charac-ter of God.

The application of Old Testament laws is seen as a sophisticated process in which laws must be understood in their Old Testament context so that their primary objective can be discerned. Once this has been found, it needs to be reformulated in terms of modern circumstances, also taking into account the fact that, in ancient Israel as well as in modern society, moral decisions were not and are not made in neutral circumstances, but in circumstances where the choice will be between two evils. Wright asks, when interpreting and applying an Old Testament law, 'What is the balance of creation ideals and fallen realities, of justice and compassion, in this law?'[13]

Two aspects of Wright's work are problematical. First, as a 'conservative' scholar he accords a much higher literal historical value to the Old Testament than most critical scholars would. Secondly, in his reconstructions of Israel as a paradigm in contrast to Canaanite society, he is too dependent on Norman Gottwald's pioneering work in *The Tribes of Yahweh*.[14] Few scholars would now accept that it is possible to know anything about ancient Israel in the period 1250 to 1050 BCE. On the other hand, Wright's general position is similar to that of scholars who approach Old Testament ethics and their application to today's world from 'liberal' historical-critical standpoints.

This position sees the value of the Old Testament in terms of example rather than precept. It holds that within the Old Testament there are attempts to define and legislate compassion towards the poor and the oppressed, as well as towards the environment and the non-human inhabitants of the earth. These attempts cannot be directly applied to today's industrialised world, since they deal with the problems of a society based upon subsistence agriculture; but they stress the importance of justice and solidarity, including solidarity with the natural environment, and are a challenge to today's world to work out these values under modern conditions.

A notable example of an historical-critical presentation of this position is in Eckart Otto's *Theologische Ethik des Alten Testaments*, which concentrates on major collections of laws in the Old Testament, such as the Book of the Covenant (Exod. 21:1 – 23:19) and Deuteronomy 12–26.[15] Otto sees these collections as attempts to bring originally secular moral precepts into the realm of Israel's religion, so that they express, and are used to put into practice, God's solidarity with humankind and especially with the poor and oppressed.

Working along similar lines, I have drawn attention to the presence in the Old Testament of 'imperatives of redemption' and 'structures of grace'.[16] Imperatives of redemption are motive clauses, that is, statements which give the reason why God commands certain things. A frequently found motive clause is 'you shall remember that you were slaves in the land of Egypt, and the Lord your God redeemed you; therefore I command you this today' (Deut. 15:15). It is an imperative of redemption because it refers to God's freeing of Israel from slavery in Egypt. In turn, this action has certain implications for Old Testament morality. God did not liberate a people so that they could enslave or oppress each other. This leads to the enjoining of the 'structures of grace', which are administrative and practical arrangements designed to introduce graciousness and compassion into the details of everyday life. In Deuteronomy 15:13–14 there is a 'structure of grace' in the form of a command that a released slave should receive from his master generous gifts of animals, grain and wine. The implication is that these will enable him to start life as a free man with better prospects of avoiding future slavery than if he were merely released penniless. Another 'structure of grace', in Exodus 23:12, makes the main beneficiaries of the command that no work should be done on the sabbath, the domesticated ox and ass and the slaves of a household.

If it is accepted that the Old Testament can best contribute to Christian ethics by example rather than precept, that is, by challenging modern society to imitate its principles in ways appropriate to today's world, three factors can be dealt with satisfactorily. First is the fact that the laws of the Old Testament cover only very limited areas of everyday life even in the context of ancient Israel. It was pointed out at the beginning of this chapter that orthodox Jews believe in an oral law which supplements the written law; and Roman Catholic moral theology has traditionally appealed to 'natural law' in order to supplement what is contained in the Bible. Any use of the Old Testament in terms of precepts, that is, applying Old Testament laws directly to modern society, is going to find itself restricted by the limited coverage of the Old Testament itself. Secondly, this restriction will be further limited by the fact that many Old Testament laws are either illegal or unacceptable in a modern society. The 'precept' approach limits itself in practice to the area of human sexuality and the family. The 'example' approach, fully recognising the particularity and situatedness of many Old Testament laws, can address far wider areas of modern life, including matters of justice, the economy and the environment. Thirdly, the 'example' approach recognises fully that morality and ethics are of concern to secular as well as religious interests. To the extent that some Old Testament laws have close parallels with, for example, the much older laws of Hammurabi, it can be said that the Old Testament acknowledges and draws upon a 'natural morality'.[17] If contemporary Christian ethicists are to devise 'structures of grace', they will need the help and expertise of modern 'secular' experts in the fields of law and sociology. Yet the 'example' approach maintains that religion has a part to play in the shared religious and non-religious enterprise of morality and ethics by providing prophetic insights that can shape morality and deepen sensitivity.

FURTHER CONSIDERATIONS

The Old Testament contains a good deal of evidence of moral debate that went on in ancient Israel. If this is noticed, the view that the Old Testament is primarily a source of commandments in the form 'thou shalt not' will be considerably modified. Secondly, recent developments in ethics and in particular the discourse or communicative ethics of Jürgen Habermas and his followers can shed new light on moral discourse in the Old Testament.[18]

Three stories about an ancestor (Abra(ha)m twice and Isaac once) saying that the man's wife is in fact his sister (Gen. 12:10–20, 20:1–18, 26:6–11) raise the question whether it is legitimate to deceive people in order to secure a more important end. In these stories, the purpose of the deceit is to save the life of a male ancestor, who believes that he will be killed by the foreign ruler in whose territory he finds himself so that the ruler can take the wife into his harem. These stories can also be seen in a new light in terms of discourse ethics, as will be argued shortly. The same dilemma is explored in 1 Samuel 20:1–34, where both Jonathan and David lie about the reason for David's non-appearance at Saul's new-moon festival. They know that Saul is likely to try to kill David if he is present. Thus a lesser evil – lying – is agreed upon in order to avoid a greater evil – attempted murder. That the lie will be wrong, even if necessary, is indicated by the fact that Jonathan will not volunteer the lie but tell it only if challenged by Saul about David's absence.

A different dilemma is explored in Exodus 1:15–20 where the two(!) midwives charged with killing the burgeoning number of Hebrew boys at birth on the orders of the pharaoh, refuse to carry out the orders. In order to justify themselves, they tell the lie that robust Hebrew women (unlike Egyptian women) give birth before the midwives get to them. The question of whether or not one should obey the unjust orders of those in authority is one that has become particularly acute in the modern world.

In Genesis 18:22–33, a long discussion (again illuminated by discourse ethics) is recorded between God and Abraham concerning whether God should destroy Sodom if even ten righteous people are found in the city. Two questions are raised. 'Shall not the Judge of all the earth do right?' asks

Abraham (Gen. 18:25). In other words, is there a notion of justice derived from 'natural morality' to which God should be subject? Secondly, is the just punishment of a wicked majority more important than the unjust punishment of a righteous minority, or vice versa? The passage implies the answer that it is more desirable to avoid wrongly punishing the innocent (which means that the wicked would go unpunished), if any can be found. It is also important to note that parts of the Old Testament attack the view that the universe is a moral universe, one in which virtue is rewarded and vice is punished. This attack is most explicitly mounted in Ecclesiastes and is based upon the author's observations of life. There are the oppressed for whom there is no help against their oppressors (Eccles. 4:1), there is wickedness in the place where justice should be administered (3:16), there are people who accumulate wealth and honour but who do not live to enjoy them (6:2), there is a poor wise man whose wisdom delivered a city but whose deed is forgotten (9:14–16). There are wicked people who succeed in life and righteous ones who do not (7:15). At the very least, such observations indicate that there are realism, compassion and even despair at the heart of the Old Testament's wrestling with moral issues. In this regard, Ecclesiastes becomes one of the most appealing texts for modern readers.

Discourse, or communicative, ethics as worked out by Habermas is an attempt to define the conditions under which ethical norms could be agreed by all those who had a legitimate interest in a matter, without coercion. The approach is directed especially against ethical relativism, and Habermas lays particular stress upon willingness to be persuaded by the force of the better argument. The twin ideas of discourse and of willingness to be persuaded by the force of the better argument are clearly evident in Genesis 18:22–33. They are also apparent in Genesis 20:1–17, the second of the three stories in which an ancestor deceives his foreign host by saying that his wife is his sister. The foreign host is Abimelech, king of Gerar, and the narrative contains an interesting dialogue between Abimelech and God, who comes to the king in a dream. God warns Abimelech that he is a dead man because he has taken a married woman into his harem. Abimelech, in his reply, appeals to the force of the better argument:

> Lord, wilt thou slay an innocent people? Did he [Abraham] not himself say to me 'She is my sister'? And she herself said, 'He is my brother'. In the integrity of my heart and the innocence of my hands I have done this.

The narrator justifies God's warning by making God say that it is he who has prevented Abimelech from having intercourse with Sarah; but the boldness with which the narrator describes Abimelech's dialogue with God is evidence for moral agonising in ancient Israel, and recognition of the importance of appeal to the force of the better argument.

CONCLUSION

According to popular perceptions, the Old Testament contains crude morality and operates mainly at the level of 'thou shalt not'. This chapter has not tried to evade any difficulties. It has tried to show, however, that throughout Christian history the Old Testament has been used in sophisticated ways in ethics and that modern research has revealed its moral sensitivities, the important of dialogue, the appeal to the force of the better argument and its attempts to make the practical arrangements of society reflect and express God's compassion for and solidarity with the world and all its inhabitants. A full appreciation of the range of its ethical concerns guards against simplistic application and enlarges the challenges that it presents to modern readers, including ethicists.

Notes

1 For more details see J. W. Rogerson, *An Introduction to the Bible* (London: Penguin Books 1999), chapter 1.
2 See E. E. Urbach, *The Sages – Their Concepts and Beliefs* (Jerusalem: Magnes Press 1975, translated by I. Abrahams from *Hazal: Pirqe Emunot veDe'ot*, Jerusalem: Magnes Press 1971), chapter xii ('The Written Law and the Oral Law').
3 For a recent discussion see C. K. Barrett, *A Critical and Exegetical Commentary on the Acts of the Apostles*, vol. II, xv–xxviii (Edinburgh: T. & T. Clark 1998), pp. 706–745.
4 See the use of these arguments and the general defence of the Bible against the charge of 'contradictions to morality' in T. H. Horne, *An Introduction to the Critical Study and Knowledge of the Holy Scriptures* 10th edn (London 1856), pp. 597–612.
5 See Urbach, *The Sages*, pp. 430–436 (Hebrew, pp. 380–384).
6 For what follows see J. W. Rogerson, 'The Old Testament' in J. W. Rogerson, C. Rowland, B. Lindars, *The Study and Use of the Bible* (Basingstoke: Marshall Pickering 1988), pp. 1–150.
7 See *ibid.*, p. 71.
8 D. S. Katz, *Sabbath and Sectarianism in Seventeenth-Century England* (Brill's Studies in Intellectual History 10, Leiden: E. J. Brill 1988), p. 4.
9 M. Bucer, *De regno Christi* (in Library of Christian Classics, 19, London: SCM Press 1959), p. 319.
10 Walter C. Kaiser, Jr, *Toward Old Testament Ethics* (Grand Rapids: Academie Books 1983).

11 *Ibid.*, p. 269.

12 Christopher J. H. Wright, *Walking in the Ways of the Lord: The Ethical Authority of the Old Testament* (Leicester: Apollos 1995).

13 *Ibid.*, p. 145.

14 N. K. Gottwald, *The Tribes of Yahweh: A Sociology of the Religion of Liberated Israel, 1250 to 1050 B.C.E.* (London: SCM Press 1980).

15 E. Otto, *Theologische Ethik des Alten Testaments* (Stuttgart: Kohlhammer 1994).

16 J. W. Rogerson, 'Christian Morality and the Old Testament', *Heythrop Journal* (36) 1995, pp. 422–430; 'The Family and Structures of Grace in the Old Testament' in S. C. Barton (ed.), *The Family in Theological Perspective* (Edinburgh: T. & T. Clark 1996), pp. 25–42.

17 See N. H. G. Robinson, *The Groundwork of Christian Ethics* (London: Collins 1971), pp. 31–32.

18 For the remainder of this section see my articles 'Discourse Ethics and Biblical Ethics' in J. W. Rogerson et al. (eds.), *The Bible in Ethics: The Second Sheffield Colloquium* (Journal for the Study of the Old Testament, Supplement Series 207, Sheffield: Sheffield Academic Press 1995), pp. 17–26; 'Old Testament Ethics' in A. D. H. Mayes (ed.), *Text in Context* (Oxford: Oxford University Press, forthcoming).

4 The gospels and Christian ethics

TIMOTHY P. JACKSON

> Then Jesus went about all the cities and villages, teaching in their
> synagogues, and proclaiming the good news [gospel] of the kingdom,
> and curing every disease and every sickness. (Matt. 9:35)[1]

> The world came about through a mistake. (Gospel of Philip 75,3)[2]

Every gospel implies an ethic, and every positive ethic (unlike nihilism)
implies some sort of good news (if only that life can be made bearable). But
whose gospel and which ethic should engage us? 'The gospels' once referred
more or less uncontroversially to Matthew, Mark, Luke and John of the
canonical New Testament, with 'Christian ethics' being the more ambiguous
or problematic phrase. Significant differences between the synoptics and
John, and among the synoptics themselves, were admitted, as were tensions
between their literal and allegorical readings. Yet the traditional gospels were
assumed to be four perspectives on one and the same Christ, such that the
gospels could be singularised and capitalised to 'the Gospel'. The central
questions for ethics concerned how to interpret and apply scripture to concrete issues (war, sexuality, medicine, political authority, economic justice
etc.), and the answers differed across denominational lines. As revealed
truth, nonetheless, the canon was the essentially fixed variable. Alternative
scriptures were known about, but these existed largely as fragmentary manuscripts or partial quotations from their critics (e.g. Irenaeus and Tertullian).

With the historical-critical scholarship of the last century and a half,
however, this situation has progressively changed. The pseudepigraphy and
evident redaction of various canonical texts and the diversity of extracanon-
ical accounts of Jesus' life and teachings, together with the variability of
community appropriations of those teachings, have contributed to a more
pluralistic picture of Christian origins and a more pragmatic attitude
towards Christian ethics. The discovery in 1945 of the ancient Coptic library
at Nag Hammadi, together with its subsequent translation/publication, was

a watershed. Several Gnostic documents never before known or not known in so complete a form became widely available, including *The Gospel of Truth, The Gospel of Thomas, The Gospel of Philip, The Gospel of the Egyptians, The Gospel of Mary, The Apocryphon* (i.e. secret book) *of James* and *The Apocryphon of John*. Before the important discovery at Nag Hammadi, 'gnostic' writings were largely known through the polemical works of anti-gnostic theologians. The latter were highly suspicious of the Gnostics' claim to special, secret 'knowledge' (the literal meaning of the Greek word *gnosis*) of the origin and destiny of humankind, by means of which the spiritual element in people could receive redemption. Gnostics first came to prominence within the church in the second century. By the end of that century, however, they had already begun to form sectarian movements separated from 'orthodox' Christians.

In 1999, perusal of the biblical reference section of my university's bookstore found the following titles: *The Five Gospels: The Search for the Authentic Words of Jesus; The Complete Gospels; The Gospel According to Jesus; The Other Bible: Ancient Alternative Scriptures; The Lost Gospel of Q: The Original Sayings of Jesus; Unearthing the Lost Words of Jesus: The Discovery and Text of the Gospel of Thomas; Behold the Man: Re-reading Gospels, Re-humanizing Jesus; Gospel Fictions*. These volumes are just across the aisle from the 'Catholic Studies' and 'Ave Maria Press' sections at the University of Notre Dame Eck Center, no less, making unmistakable the contemporary ferment among 'Gospel' translators and exegetes.

I write primarily as a Protestant ethicist. Rather than treating Matthew, Mark, Luke and John as the fixed points and ethics as the dependent variable, I use ethical reflection in this essay to probe both canonical and non-canonical gospels. More specifically, I compare orthodox and Gnostic conceptions of three fundamental moral notions: love, sin and salvation. Is one set of conceptions preferable to the other, and if so why? Broadly Gnostic modes of thought – the denigration of the body and of the material world generally, coupled with the elevation of esoteric forms of 'knowledge' as the means of escape to a purely spiritual realm – are arguably perennial aspects of western culture. Intellectualist or imaginative dualism takes robust form in Mani and Valentinus, but hints of it are evident in figures as diverse as Socrates and Plato, Kant and Blake. Nevertheless, with the qualified exceptions of Manicheanism and Mandeanism, early Gnostic literature failed to sustain a distinctive organised movement. Again, why? Some find the explanation in purely political factors: this literature was suppressed as 'heretical' by an increasingly powerful institutionalised church, with the

church Fathers leading the polemical way. Still others insist on the acciden-
tal character of both Gnosticism's historical defeat and Christianity's historical triumph: the real 'good news' for the latter, they suggest, was the Milvian
Bridge and the Edict of Milan, not the life, death and resurrection of Jesus.

My argument, in contrast, is a theological and ethical one: in spite of its
ongoing appeal, Gnosticism failed as a church and creed for good internal
reasons. Its bad news outweighed its good, and it could not articulate a
livable social ethic. The four canonical gospels deserve their pride of place
not because they were preferred by the historical 'victors', but because they
enable the kind of embodied yet spirited fidelity to God and neighbour that
is Christianity's lasting legacy. Christianity is a revelation of 'hard sayings',
and these sayings will always invite faith rather than claim proof, yet they
remain credible news about God and ourselves. This is not to say that
Matthew, Mark, Luke and John are scientific historians in the modern sense;
they, like their Gnostic competitors, mix factual recollections of Jesus' words
and deeds, handed down in oral tradition, with moral exhortation, religious
proclamation and mythological panegyric. Even so, in a time when there is
an abundance of media gossip and technical data but very little genuine
good news, the four biblical evangelists still present a 'living Jesus'[3] who
ministers to human beings in all their psychic complexity but also in all
their corporeal vulnerability. The canonical Jesus forgives sins and preaches
mercy and peace, but he also heals the sick, feeds the hungry, makes the lame
to walk and the blind to see. This gospel endures precisely because it makes
it possible to be in the world but not of it.

LOVE AND THE GOSPELS

A. Christian

The biblical good news is that 'the kingdom of heaven has come near'
(Matt. 10:7). It has come near, most fundamentally, in the person of Jesus
Christ and through his incarnation 'among you' (Luke 17:21) of a love[4] that
is beyond calculation and payment (Matt. 10:8).[5] The heart of the canonical
gospels, more specifically, is a spontaneous love that forgives sins and serves
others. As insouciant as Jesus encourages his followers to be, he nevertheless
commands three forms of love (*agape*): unconditional love of God, love of
neighbour as oneself and love of 'one another . . . as I [Christ] have loved you'
(Matt. 22:37–9 and John 13:34; see also John 15:12). The first two commandments are Jesus' echoing of the Shema (Deut. 6:4–5) and of Leviticus 19:18,
respectively, and, though a powerful distillation of 'the law and the
prophets', they are not new. The third commandment, however, provides a

concrete, and finally cruciform, model of moral excellence that is novel; it does not gainsay the natural self-love that is presupposed by the second love command, but it does distance it as a standard. In going to the cross, Jesus sets a pattern that is radically self-sacrificial, a stumbling block to common-sense ideas of prudence. Any strict reciprocity, in which one treats others as one has been treated, is left behind, but so is the Golden Rule that Jesus himself affirms at times. The positive principle of '[i]n everything do to others as you would have them do to you' (Matt. 7:12) is demanding enough, but under the right circumstances Jesus requires more. One does not nor-mally ask or even hope that innocent others be willing to die for one's good, but Jesus insists that the disciples 'take up their cross' and follow him (Matt. 16–24; Mark 8:34; Luke 9:23), and he implies that their willingness to lay down their lives for one another, in imitation of him, makes them his 'friends' (John 15:13–14).

Even if one accepts that the 'new commandment' of John 13:34 is not a contradiction of self-love but rather a specification, many worry that the command is at odds with the other half of Matthew 22:39: love of neigh-bour. That is, some see Jesus' instruction to the disciples to 'love one another ... as I have loved you' as a circling of the sectarian wagons, a pulling back by the early church from a universal charity that elsewhere encompasses even enemies (cf. Matt. 5:44).[6] Some find a growing anti-Semitism in John in which 'one another' refers to fellow Christian believers in self-conscious contrast to the stereotyped and increasingly vilified Jews. Perhaps the first thing to be said in response to this concern is that, taken out of context, John's belligerent remarks about 'the Jews' (e.g., 5:9–18 and 10:19–39) can be, and have been, used to support a programme of scapegoating. The second thing to say, however, is that this use is a falsification. It must always be remembered that '[e]arly Christianity arose as an eschatological sect within Judaism',[7] and that the author of the Gospel of John was almost cer-tainly a Jew writing to a community struggling to understand its identity as simultaneously Jewish and Christian. Because they had affirmed Jesus as the Messiah, these sincere believers had been put out of their synagogues by the religious authorities. But 'Jesus himself and all the disciples, men and women, mentioned in the gospel [of John] are Jews', and the gospel writer's 'polemic is not directed against the Jews as a nation but against the leaders who were the most strongly opposed to Jesus and eventually brought about his condemnation and death'.[8] In fact, crucifixion was a Roman form of exe-cution (for sedition), and even if some Pharisees acquiesced in it for Jesus, it remains the case for Johannine Christians that 'salvation is from the Jews' (John 4:22).

Because we often do not know how to love ourselves rightly, and because we need a concrete model of loving relations in any case, Jesus offers the new and christocentric commandment of John 13:34, reiterated at 15:12. His own death on the cross, freely accepted, becomes the standard of perfect love. Yet we need have little doubt that the intracommunal accent on loving 'one another' is but a starting point. A new disciple, troubled by her alienation from and possible persecution by her own Jewish people, must learn to walk before she can run. The faithful are called first to lead a rigorously service-oriented existence within the church: they are to establish and sustain their identity in contrast to 'the world' precisely by displaying how selflessly they support each other (13:35). But even as Christ the Logos creates the world and Jesus the Incarnate Son redeems it, so those who are made one with Jesus Christ are to witness to the world. Charity begins at home, but it does not end there. There is no denying that John's Jesus emphasises that both he and his followers 'do not belong to the world' (17:16). If simple escape or a small mutual aid society were what John was encouraging, however, then there would be no commissioning and no sending of the disciples into the world to preach and to forgive sins (17:18 and 20:21–3; cf. 20:31). As Richard Hays writes,

> We should . . . note that John unmistakably understands the death of Jesus as being for the sake of the whole world (1:29, 3:16): God loved the world so much that he gave his only Son up to death. Consequently, even though their primary mandate is to manifest love and service within the commuity, the disciples who share in Jesus' mission in the world can hardly remain indifferent to those outside the community of faith. The call to lay down one's life may have broader implications than those explicitly articulated in the 'new commandment'.[9]

Indeed, Hays finds in the fourth gospel not mere exclusionary self-righteousness or complacent self-sufficiency, but rather 'prophetic resistance' to the hatred and prideful materialism abroad in the land.[10]

In the other canonical gospels as well, Christlike love is more than compatible with love of self and of neighbour: it is the key to each, to appreciating both the fractious ego and opaque others. The key is timeless, however, and so must be turned counter-clockwise. We do not discover how to love our whole selves until we follow the model of compassion and self-forgetfulness found in Jesus: 'For those who want to save their life will lose it, and those who lose their life for my sake, and for the sake of the gospel, will save it' (Mark 8:35). Similarly, we cannot live well as either Jews or Gentiles until we see that we are all the Samaritans of Jesus' parables, traditional enemies called to be neighbours (see John 4:9–10; Luke 9:51–6; and, of course, Luke 10:29–37). At John 8:48–9, Jesus himself is called a Samaritan demoniac, and though he denies he has a demon, he does not deny that he is a Samaritan.

As the New Testament Greek word used in all three love commands (Matt. 22:37–9 and John 13:34), *agape* is the only form of love that is explicitly commanded in Christian scripture. (*Philia* is praised but not directly commanded, and *eros* is seldom if ever even praised.) I want to conclude this section by addressing the question, How can good news take the form of rigorous commands? Before doing so, however, I must head off a possible misunderstanding. I spoke above of outstripping reciprocity 'under the right circumstances', because it is tempting to see the love ethic of Jesus as one of 'complete selflessness' or 'pure non-resistance' in which the interests and claims of the self are entirely ignored or denied.[11] Jesus does say, after all, 'Do not resist an evildoer. But if anyone strikes you on the right cheek, turn the other also . . .' (Matt. 5:39). Literal quietism cannot be Jesus' ideal, nevertheless, since he himself opts for self-preservation at various points (e.g. Matt. 12:15; John 7:1–9 and 8:58) and clearly resists the moral evils and physical afflictions facing him in others. He cleanses the temple (John 2:13–16), heals the leper (Matt. 8:2–3; Mark 1:40–2; Luke 5:12–13) and when struck on the face by 'one of the police' does not just take it but responds: 'If I have spoken wrongly testify to the wrong. But if I have spoken rightly, why do you strike me?' (John 19:23).[12] To enjoin an uncritical self-denial or passivity, utterly insensitive to context, would be a prescription for injustice, as many feminists have pointed out. But Jesus is mainly communicating a way of being in the world, one that refuses to hate and thus to be conformed to evil, not generating exceptionless moral rules. He is wise enough to know that motives and consequences matter, even as we should recognise that to embrace a masochistic or profligate form of self-sacrifice is no Christian virtue. Coercion too is incompatible with genuine *agape* – '[i]f any want to become my followers', Jesus says (Luke 9:23) – so self-surrender must be both constructive and consensual. Yet self-surrender, rightly construed, does lead to true self-realisation, according to the New Testament, however painful and thankless this process may be.

B. Gnostic

Gnostic materials are so diverse, in both theological content and literary style, that they elude ready characterisation. Even more than Matthew, Mark, Luke and John, the Gnostic gospels resist systematic, or even consistent, exposition. Still, Hans Jonas' classic description remains serviceable:

Gnostic 'currents' of thought, he observed some forty years ago, 'maintain a radical *dualism* of realms of being – God and the world, spirit and matter, soul and body, light and darkness, good and evil, life and death – and consequently an extreme polarization of existence affecting not only man but reality as a whole'.[13] Visible reality, from physical objects to human bodies to social institutions, is generally considered corrupt and corrupting, the result of error and ignorance – usually on the part of a 'Sophia' or 'Demiurge' subordinate to the truly transcendental God. Created in ignorance, the world continues in darkness for the most part. Careless powers 'threw mankind into great distraction and into a life of toil' ('Hypostasis of the Archons' 91,8–9), or error itself 'fell into a fog' and thereby produced for human beings 'oblivions and terrors' (Gospel of Truth 17,30–3). As a result, the tangible world is not stably an object of love, God's or humanity's, either as first created or as currently constituted.

Because embodied human existence is akin to a prison, Gnosticism is fundamentally a gospel of personal escape rather than of social amelioration. Love, in the form of pity for other trapped spirits, has a place, but it is always on the verge of losing any real object. It is dauntingly hard to keep the self and others who are pitied in focus as actual persons of flesh and blood, as opposed to idealised forms translated intellectually out of a too-painful environment. There are no love commands per se in the Gospel of Truth, the Gospel of the Egyptians or the quite fragmentary Gospel of Mary, for instance. The Gospel of Truth speaks of faith's dissolving 'division' and bringing 'the warm pleroma of love' (34,29–31), but Truth's first mention of 'love' refers to the wish of 'the Father' to *be* loved rather than to love (see 19,14). Nevertheless, one must not overstate the case.

In the end, the Gospel of Truth at least prescribes a generous attention to others:

> Speak of the truth with those who search for it and (of) knowledge to those who have committed sin in their error. Make firm the foot of those who have stumbled and stretch out your hands to those who are ill. Feed those who are hungry and give repose to those who are weary, and raise up those who wish to rise, and awaken those who sleep. For you are the understanding that is drawn forth. If strength acts thus, it becomes even stronger. (33,1–11)

This is my favourite passage in all of the Gnostic literature I know, and it stands out as uniquely solicitous of both bodily and psychic need. The ongoing tension between self-absorption and other-regard is highlighted even here, however, by the fact that these words are followed immediately by the admonition: 'Be concerned with yourselves; do not be concerned with other things which you have rejected from yourselves. Do not return to what you have vomited to eat it' (33:11–16). As psychological advice about the importance of catharsis and of not dwelling on past follies or phobias, this is wise counsel. But when it is translated into interpersonal ethics – as in 'the lawless person is someone to treat ill rather than the just one' (33:24–5) – it falls below even the most petulant saying attributed to Jesus in the New Testament (e.g. Mark 6:11).

In the Gospel of Thomas, we read: 'Jesus said, "Love your brother like your soul, guard him like the pupil of your eye"' (saying 25). This is a lovely imperative, but one feels the subtle loss of moral force in the difference between Matthew's 'neighbour' and Thomas' 'brother' and between Matthew's 'yourself' and Thomas' 'your soul'. For the Gnostic, it is the soul that is dear, not the whole human being. In Thomas, as in Truth, it is unclear how compassion can lead one to feed the hungry or to stand in solidarity with the politically oppressed, because body (*soma*) and city (*polis*) are both finally impediments to, rather than contexts of, genuine liberation. Gnostic 'good news' focuses on recognition of the truth about oneself (*gnosis* concerning the *psyche* or the *pneuma*), which is equated with an ascent to God, instead of on enactment of practical love for others (*agape* for the neighbour), which orthodoxy equates with the descent of God. Thomas' Jesus is 'amazed at how this great wealth [spirit] has made its home in this poverty [the body]' (saying 29). And reminiscent of William Butler Yeats, his most poignant injunction is: 'Become passers-by' (saying 42).[14]

Though written as much as two centuries later, the Gospel of Philip contains a cosmology and anthropology as dualistic as that of Thomas' gospel. Thomas' Jesus says, 'Whoever has come to understand the world has found (only) a corpse, and whoever has found a corpse is superior to the world' (saying 56). For Philip, '[t]his world is a corpse-eater' (73,19), and the soul 'is a precious thing and it came to be in a contemptible body' (56,25–6). Such metaphysical beliefs have consequences, and, again, it is hard to imagine a sustainable social conscience flowing out of these opinions. 'If the world is a corpse and, by the fact of our recognizing it for what it is, unworthy of our attention, then we are not going to waste much time laboring for, say, a more just economic order or better housing for the poor'.[15] It does not follow that there is no place for moderation towards 'the world' or no room for love in 'the world.' But, to repeat, the love and moderation are equivocal. Thomas' Jesus says, 'Whoever does not hate his [father] and his mother as I do cannot become a [disciple] to me. And whoever does [not] love his [father and] his mother as I do cannot become a [disciple to] me' (saying 101). On the face of it, this appears to be a moderating of the parallel saying in Luke (14:26). But the next line makes clear the dualistic meaning: 'For my mother [. . .], but [my] true [mother] gave me life' (saying 101). It is usually thought that what the (earthly) mother gave is death or falsehood, while the true mother gave life.[16] The Gnostic Jesus is even more vehement than the Christian Christ in thinking of his true father as God and his true mother as the Holy Spirit – vehement to the point of insulting his mother in the flesh.

In the Gospel of Philip, however, we find this instructive, even touching, passage on love, partially echoing St Paul:

> Faith receives, love gives. [No one will be able to receive] without faith. No one will be able to give without love. Because of this, in order that we may indeed receive, we believe, and in order that we may love, we give, since if one gives without love, he has no profit from what he has given. (61,36 – 62,5)

If Marcion and Carpocrates are the lunatic fringe of Gnosticism, Philip is the staid reasonable man. Marcion's muscular flesh hatred rejected procreative sexuality, while Carpocrates' natural licentiousness accepted sexual promiscuity; and it is possible to see in these two figures the playing out, in separate keys, of the basic Gnostic refusal of the body and 'revolt against the cosmos'.[17] But the Gospel of Philip suggests that Gnostic ethics need not *always* take the form of either extreme asceticism or extreme libertinism, and that there is not *necessarily* a Gnostic drive among the 'elect' to 'solitary' navel-gazing (cf. Gos. Thom., saying 49). It is clear, even so, that the only form of 'building up' that can make sense for Philip is pedagogical: minds and their knowledge are to be expanded, but bodies and their needs are at best to be tolerated. And even in the midst of the comparatively balanced sentiments quoted above, a bitter dualism reasserts itself:

> Frequently, if a woman sleeps with her husband out of necessity, while her heart is with the adulterer with whom she usually has intercourse, the child she will bear is born resembling the adulterer. Now you who live together with the son of God, love not the world, but love the lord, in order that those you will bring forth may not resemble the world, but may resemble the lord. (78,15–24)

Of course, canonical scriptures are not free of ambivalence towards their surroundings. The Gospel of Philip's comments on 'the world' are verbally similar to passages in the canonical Gospel of John, arguably the most Gnostic of the four traditional evangelists. I noted previously a significant tension in John concerning love of 'the world', and the debate continues over just how dualist he is.[18] Whatever the precise outcome of this debate, it seems clear that, on the spectrum of canonical gospels, Luke is the furthest removed from Gnostic ideas and John the closest to them. There is still a recognisable divide between the canonicals and the non-canonicals, however. In the Christian scriptures, it is one and the same Love who makes the world and redeems it, and it is one and the same love that we are to extend to others and ourselves. Christ is the pivot in both cases, in the sense that his kenotic *agape* is the beginning and the end of the world: both its causal origin and its final purpose. This commitment to moral monotheism is what permits orthodox biblical faith to avoid the alienation and elitism lurking in the background of many Gnostic scriptures.

SIN AND THE GOSPELS

A. Christian

Few matters are more telling in discerning the core of a gospel than what it considers sin and what sin's remedy. In accepting the Hebrew Bible and the Genesis account of the fall of Adam and Eve, the Christian evangelists inherited a view of sin as at bottom pride, the overrunning of divinely given limits. Over the centuries, this central perception has been elaborated in a number of ways. When primary concern is for the character of agents, accent falls on who one loves: am I motivated by or in pursuit of realities other than God's Spirit? When primary concern is with the form of actions, accent falls on how one is lawed: am I performing God's mandated will or my own? When primary concern is for the consequences of action, accent falls on what is being achieved: am I helping to build the kingdom of God or the kingdom of the earth? The most adequate picture of sin will take into account all three of these dimensions, noting that it is unholy intentions and unjust acts as well as abominable effects. Jesus displays this kind of attention to both inner orientation and outer behaviour or consequence when he says that 'everyone who looks at a woman with lust has already committed adultery with her in his heart' (Matt. 5:28) and that both the 'right eye' and the 'right hand' can cause one to sin (Matt. 5:29–30).

It is common to aver (1) that classical Greek conceptions of morality focus on the intellect, with virtue being identified with knowledge and vice with ignorance, and (2) that Christian ethics, in contrast, highlights the will, with righteousness being intentional obedience to God's commands and sin being stubborn disobedience. The holism of the New Testament Jesus illustrates that this is only a partial truth. Socrates, Plato and Aristotle all defend a highly intellectualist version of human flourishing, and Christian theologians (e.g. St Augustine) do often allow for a perversity of will that would have been a puzzlement to Hellenes who think that to recognise the good is to do it. But the four gospel writers are aware that sin is a function of the whole person (a disordering of her reason, volition, emotion and/or bodily sensation) that leads to misrelation to the wider community (estrangement from neighbours and God). Sin and its opposite are neither entirely mental nor merely private. What else does Jesus mean when he warns the man recently made well and able to walk, 'Do not sin any more, so that nothing worse happens to you' (John 5:14). And what else does Jesus imply when he affirms that one is to love God 'with all your heart, and with all your soul, and with all your mind', and to love 'your neighbour as yourself' (Matt. 22:37–9)?

What, then, is the Christian remedy for sin? The usual, and altogether accurate, answer is: from the side of God, Christ, and from the side of humanity, faith. Jesus Christ is 'the Lamb of God who takes away the sin of the world' (John 1:29), and a trusting confidence in his love re-establishes right relations with God, other human beings and oneself. This is the case, perhaps most centrally, because Jesus makes it possible both to be forgiven and to forgive. This is at the heart of the good news preached in the canonical gospels: Christ is the forgiveness of sins incarnate. By his obedience to God, even unto death on the cross, he empowered the willing surrender of condemnation and animosity, however justified, both by God and by human beings. Christ's Passion vicariously satisfied God's righteous judgement of the world, that is, and it also delivered creatures from the need to condemn themselves and one another for past wrongs.

As 'son of Adam, son of God' (Luke 3:38), Jesus corrects the original disobedient act of eating by the first parents in the Garden. By turning away from God and consuming the fruit of the tree of the knowledge of good and evil, Adam and Eve perverted their characters, problematised their actions and polluted their environment. One need not believe with Augustine that original sin is transmitted biologically to all subsequent generations to hold that sin builds on sin and that human history represents, in many respects, a corporate bondage to hatred and futility. The cumulative effects of hostility to God and disregard for one another are inscribed in cultural attitudes, political institutions, even church practices such that individual innocence is hard to imagine. Again, one need not believe with Augustine that all meaningful human freedom is lost after the fall to recognise the staggering power of collective hostility and guilt: one need look only at slavery in the United States and what it took to abolish it, or at the Holocaust in Nazified

Europe and what it took to resist it. We are often carried along by a tide of fear, resentment and obliviousness (racial, ethnic, gender etc.) that makes refusal of social injustice and reform of personal vice seem fruitless endeavours. Yet Jesus offers the means to such heroism in his life of love and forgiveness.

Jesus shows his followers how to break the cycle of sin. Via an apparently abominable ritual, making a meal of his flesh and blood, he teaches others to internalise his spirit of charity and thus to reverse the truly abominable effects of that other eating in Eden (Matt. 26:26–9). In realising himself by serving others, Jesus demonstrates the essential mystery of grace: how to fall up. Other than his ascent of the cross, where power is perfected in weakness, there is no more edifying Christian symbol of patient self-giving than this. In Holy Communion, Christians who know themselves to be sinners partake of table fellowship with one another and make use of a God who has objectified himself for their sakes. 'God is a man-eater', according to the Gospel of Philip (62,35 – 63,1), but man is a God-eater, according to the New Testament.[19]

Again, at Matthew 5:31, Jesus states that 'blasphemy against the Spirit will not be forgiven'. Some find this assertion of an unforgivable sin to be out of character for the Christ and not a little unenlightened.[20] It does indeed seem at odds with the exhortation to forgive 'seventy-seven times' (i.e. unconditionally) found in Matthew 18:22. What are we to make of this? The key to reconciling the two verses is to see that realised forgiveness has two sides or moments: the offering and the accepting. The example of Christ points unmistakably to an unflagging willingness to extend forgiveness to everyone who sins against us (see Luke 11:4). But the offer of forgiveness alone does not insure a cessation of againstness; in addition to the generous giving, without precondition, there must be an active receiving. For forgiveness to 'take', so to speak, both parties must acknowledge the wrongdoing, then refuse hatred and let go of the past – if not re-establish relations. (Forswearing hatred and vengeance does not dictate staying in an unjust situation; it may even necessitate leaving it.) Without confession, contrition and restitution on the part of the sinner, however, this process cannot be completed. When Jesus maintains that blasphemy against the Spirit is unforgivable, he is gesturing, I believe, towards this truth. To mock the Paraclete is to deny that God is just and that one is in need of divine forgiveness; it is to refuse, in turn, all mercy that might placate that justice and communicate that forgiveness. Blasphemy makes it impossible, not for God to give forgiveness, but for the sinner to receive it.

Lest my previous comments on structural sin be misunderstood, it remains to add only this. To the extent that each of us turns away from God, the neighbour and ourselves, the New Testament suggests that every man is his own Adam and every woman her own Eve. Similarly, to the degree that each allows past sin to govern us and thus says no to forgiveness, whether for others or for ourselves, every person is Christ's Pilate – crucifying the Lord anew.

B. Gnostic

'Ignorance is the mother of [all evil]', the Gospel of Philip assures us (83,30–1). Because Gnosticism commonly associates sin with cognitive deficiency (error and ignorance) rather than wilful perversity (pride and disobedience), it often savours more of Hellenism than of Judaism. In fact, several of the Gnostic manuscripts construe the God of the Hebrew Bible not as the truly good and unchanging deity but rather as a fraud who mistakenly created human beings and arrogantly claims dominion over them. It is the foolish Yahweh (*Yaltabaoth* or *Yaldabaoth*) and his jailer minions (*archons*) who would keep humans trapped in the body and benighted about their spiritual condition, and it is the transcendent Son ('Christ' and/or 'Seth') who comes down to earth to enlighten creatures and enable them to ascend to the Truth, who is both Mother and Father.[21]

It is sometimes suggested, even by Christians, that the original sin of Adam and Eve was a 'fortunate fall' orchestrated by God herself to usher human beings into moral self-awareness. After all, a deity who would actually forbid to creatures, on pain of death, a full knowledge of good and evil, is manifestly tyrannical; even as a God who would stunt creatures for fear that they should become godlike, is transparently petty and jealous (see Gen. 3:1–5, but cf. Gen. 2:16–17). The real tragedy, so the argument goes, would have been if the first parents had been cowed by a blustering 'divine' authority and remained ignorant and innocent. The human drama is pre-eminently one of self-discovery, and unconsciousness is to be overcome precisely by eating the forbidden fruit. Whatever its plausibility as Old Testament exegesis, however, this is a Gnostic rather than an orthodox conception of sin and human history.

For traditional Judaism and Christianity, the first sin was a genuine disaster, violence done to humanity's best interests by its refusal of all limits. Rather than a transition to a higher intelligence, the fall was a decline into lust and death. In contrast, 'On the Origin of the World', a Gnostic cosmogony, casts God in the role of martinet and the snake (a.k.a. 'Beast') in the role of liberator. Referring to God's prohibition against eating (or touching) the 'tree of acquaintance (*gnosis*)', the serpent says to Eve:

> Do not be afraid. In death you shall not die. For he [God] knows that
> when you eat from it, your intellect will become sober and you will
> come to be like gods, recognizing the difference that obtains between
> evil men and good ones. Indeed, it was in jealousy that he said this to
> you, so that you would not eat from it. (118,33 – 119,6)

The serpent invites human beings to see lack of self-restraint as a matter of
'pride' in a positive sense: autonomy becomes heroic enlightenment in
which mental shackles are cast off. In basic ways, Gnosticism is defined by
acceptance of this gambit.

> Now Eve had confidence in the words of the instructor. She gazed at
> the tree and saw that it was beautiful and appetizing, and liked it; she
> took some of its fruit and ate it; and she gave some also to her husband,
> and he too ate it. Then their intellect became open. For when they had
> eaten, the light of acquaintance had shone upon them. (119,6–13)

It must never be forgotten, however, that the biblical God does not forbid
Adam and Eve to look at the tree of knowledge, only to consume it. The
canonical prohibition in the Garden is not designed to keep the first parents
ignorant of moral distinctions, but rather to prevent them from thinking
that they invented good and evil and thus can manipulate them (and one
another) for their own pleasure. The orthodox lesson of Genesis 2 and 3 is
that when creatures try to eat, rather than appreciatively attend to, the tree
of knowledge, they forget their finitude. Thereafter lust for possession
replaces respect – husbands claim to control wives, parents to own their children, human beings to dominate nature etc. – even as murder soon follows.
As Simone Weil observes:

> It may be that vice, depravity, and crime are nearly always, or even
> perhaps always, in their essence, attempts to eat beauty, to eat what we
> should only look at. Eve began it. If she caused humanity to be lost by
> eating the fruit, the opposite attitude, looking at the fruit without
> eating it, should be what is required to save it.[22]

The teachings of Carpocrates, a second-century Gnostic, highlight the
essential distinction between the two types of gospels on sin. Carpocrates
and his followers accepted sexual promiscuity as natural and maintained
that one ought to experience every sin so as realise oneself as spirit and
escape the cycle of reincarnation. They were not sensualists, revelling in the
flesh for its own sake, nor were they intentionally malevolent or hateful.
Rather, they sought to live out an utter indifference to the body, believing

that what it did was inconsequential but also holding that experiencing all that embodied life had to offer (pleasure and pain) was necessary to getting beyond it.

> ... souls are always made reincarnate until they have completed all sins; when nothing is lacking, then the freed soul departs to ... the God above the world-creating angels, and thus all souls will be saved. The souls which in a single life on earth manage to participate in all sins will no longer become reincarnate but, having paid all their 'debts', will be freed so that they no longer come to be in a body.[23]

There is a crazy logic to this once one accepts the basic premises that the physical world is a mistake and that transgressive self-consciousness is the way of deliverance. One escapes sin by flamboyantly embracing it, rather like dieting by bingeing on so much candy that one vomits. The sybarite wants to lose consciousness via fleshly indulgence, while the true Gnostic aims to heighten it. One is seldom so self-aware as when one is sinning, and what better way to express contempt for the world than to break all its rules. If one rejects the Gnostic premises, on the other hand, then one will detect here the moral equivalent of bulimia. (Marcion represents but the other side of the same coin: a kind of metaphysical anorexia.)

What, in summary, is the Gnostic remedy for sin? The Gospel of Philip (84,10–11) suggests the shortest answer: 'Ignorance is a slave. Knowledge is freedom'. Yet, even more than an overly intellectual account of sin as ignorance, as opposed to perversity of will, what is questionable about most forms of Gnosticism is their refusal to take responsibility for human vulnerability: both for evil and its correction and for dependency and its address. Because the world and the flesh are primarily phantoms to be fled, rather than realities to be redeemed, there is little place for patience as an aid to curbing hubris or for self-sacrifice as a means to overcoming others' want. To affirm the constructive uses of adversity, in contrast, is not theological masochism but rather, when suitably framed, the wisdom of God's presence in the world.

SALVATION AND THE GOSPELS

A. Christian

Any attempt to depict the richness of biblical salvation must remain a gesture by the inarticulate towards the ineffable. The kingdom of God can be adumbrated in parables, but human language ultimately fails: salvation has to be experienced and enacted. That said, an understanding of God's

kingdom can be hinted at by describing sin and then reversing the proposi-
tions: instead of obsessive hatred, spontaneous charity; instead of revenge
for the past and fear of the future, a peaceful attentiveness in the present;
instead of focus on self, a focus on God and the neighbour. Right relation to
God in Christ means that a 'new creation' appears in the person of the
believer, to use a phrase from Second Corinthians (5:17), but this is a recognisable redemption or resurrection of the old, rather than its utter destruction. Moreover, the good news is proclaimed '*to* the whole creation' (Mark
16:15), not against it. Creation is restored or justified by the coming of the
Messiah.

An enduring question is the extent to which justification (restoration
of right relation with God) and sanctification (growth in holiness in imitation of God) can be or have been realised by believers. 'Salvation' may be
associated with both, though justification is often understood as an immediate event and sanctification as a gradual process. Especially urgent is the
issue of how the faithful experience the coming of the kingdom: in this
world only? in the next only? in both? The Gospel of John, in particular,
seems to express a 'realised eschatology' in which 'eternal life' with God in
Christ is possible here and now: 'Very truly, I tell you, anyone who hears my
word and believes him who sent me has eternal life, and does not come
under judgement, but has passed from death to life' (5:24). A more pronounced eschatological reservation prevails in Matthew, however, such that
salvation (and judgement) can only be fully identified with a 'future' consummation. Even if this consummation represents the end of time, it also
promises the resurrection of the dead in a decidedly more 'delayed' fashion
than in John.[24]

I have written at some length elsewhere about the relation between personal immortality and Christian ethics,[25] and I will not repeat that entire
performance here. With both friends and foes of Christianity, I worry that
allowing a place for a post-mortem existence within the motivational structure of *agape*, either as reward or punishment, enmeshes believers in economies of exchange that are alien to Christlike love at its best. A too-dogmatic
certainty about immortality may also tempt us to denigrate this life.[26] An
afterlife remains a blessed hope, but for ethical purposes I would direct our
attention to the call to repentance and servanthood that is at the centre of
the Gospel of Mark (e.g. 1:15 and 9:35). An eschatological vindication 'in the
age to come' is promised in Mark (10:29–30), but the Marcan Jesus takes
great care to caution his followers against seeing discipleship as instrumental to future glory or reward (e.g. 10:35–45).[27] Discipleship is costly, and
'[w]hoever wants to be first must be last' (9:35). Jesus makes the essential

point paradoxically: 'For those who want to save their life will lose it, and those who lose their life for my sake, and for the sake of the gospel, will save it' (8:35).

The New Testament good news is that salvation takes the form not of autonomy or heteronomy but of theonomy: 'Your kingdom come. Your will be done, on earth as it is in heaven' (Matt. 6:10). Jesus is the mediator of God's will for the world, but that will is suffering love rather than coercion (John 3:16). The rule of God would mean radical reversals of existing conditions, most notably for the weak and marginalised who pine for God's kingdom against the odds – as in the beatitudes' proclamations concerning the 'poor in spirit', 'those who mourn', 'the meek' et al. (Matt. 5:3–12). Blessedness carries with it practical implications, such as being 'peacemakers', but the first thing needful is to be unself-consciously open to the gift of God's holiness: 'whoever does not receive the kingdom of God as a little child will never enter it' (Mark 10:15).

B. Gnostic

Gnostic salvation is highly cognitive, a matter proximally of knowledge, and this knowledge is usually highly self-referential. The Gospel of Truth refers to the initiated as 'the sons of interior knowledge' (32,23 *sic*), for instance, even as the Gospel of Mary has 'the blessed one' proclaim that 'the Son of Man is within you' (8,19). But it is a mistake to judge Gnosticism to be merely self-absorbed or narcissistic. 'The Exegesis of the Soul' (135,21–6) holds that 'the beginning of salvation is repentance ... And repentance takes place in distress and grief.' Moreover, although Gnosticism is introspective, most of its gospels treat other objects of saving knowledge than the self and allow other agents of saving knowledge than the self. The Gospel of Truth affirms:

> Since oblivion came into existence because the Father was not known, then if the Father comes to be known, oblivion will not exist from that moment on.
>
> Through this, the gospel of the one who is searched for, which <was> revealed to those who are perfect through the mercies of the Father, the hidden mystery, Jesus, the Christ, enlightened those who were in darkness through oblivion. (18,7–17)

Here God the Father is an (even the) object of knowledge, and Christ the Son is a (even the) causal agent who brings about knowledge.

In certain contexts, to be sure, 'Father' and 'Son' seem but alternate names for the ideal self. In the Gospel of Philip, Christ is called 'the perfect man' (55,12), and the restored person is 'no longer a Christian but a Christ' (67,26). Moreover, it is easy to find numerous Gnostic passages in which the self 'becomes light', rather than merely receives illumination (see Gospel of the Egyptians, 67,4), and in which saving *gnosis* is identified with uncovering some buried aspect of one's own psyche. Perhaps the most famous of these is saying 70 of the Gospel of Thomas:

> Jesus said, 'That which you have will save you if you bring it forth from yourselves. That which you do not have within you [will] kill you if you do not have it within you'.

And in 'The Book of Thomas the Contender', a Nag Hammadi manuscript following in the tradition of the Gospel of Thomas, we read:

> he who has not known himself has known nothing, but he who has known himself has at the same time already achieved knowledge about the depth of the all. (1,1–17)

Commenting on these and related lines, Elaine Pagels writes:

> Convinced that the only answers [to suffering] were to be found within, the gnostics engaged in an intensely private interior journey.
> Whoever comes to experience his own nature – human nature – as itself the 'source of all things', the primary reality, will receive enlightenment.[28]

Interpreting the Gnostic 'Hymn of the Pearl', Hans Jonas goes so far as to contend that 'the interchangeability of the subject and the object of the mission, of savior and soul . . . is the key to the true meaning of the poem, and to gnostic eschatology in general'.[29] There is indisputable insight in these remarks, but both Pagels and Jonas risk leading us astray. Even the Gospel of Thomas has Jesus declare that

> the kingdom is inside of you, and it is outside of you. When you come to know yourselves, then you will become known, and you will realize that it is you who are the sons of the living father. (Saying 3)

Note that subject/object and son/father distinctions are preserved in this passage. Although a virtual identity obtains between knowledge and salvation, the connection is not so intimate between self-knowledge and self-salvation. It is not clear, at any rate, that we can equate Gnosticism with a theological subjectivism in which the divine is 'nothing but' a dimension of the human. A creeping solipsism is a perpetual Gnostic danger, as I have pointed out, but it is not always in evidence. In some places, an accent on the soul and *anamnesis* goes hand in hand with an accent on God and contemplation, without the suggestion that these can or should be entirely conflated. As the Gospel of Truth puts it:

> Now, the end is receiving knowledge about the one who is hidden, and this is the Father, from whom the beginning came forth, to whom all will return who have come forth from him. And they have appeared for the glory and the joy of his name.
>
> Now the name of the Father is the Son . . . the Father's name is not spoken, but it is apparent through a Son. (37,37 – 38,1–7 and 38,22–4)

> . . . (it is fitting) to be concerned at all times with the Father of the all and the true brothers, those upon whom the love of the Father is poured out and in whose midst there is no lack of him . . . his children are perfect and worthy of his name, for he is the Father: it is children of this kind that he loves. (43,3–8 and 43,20–2)

It is always possible to give such verses a psychologised reading – as some exegetes do of 'the kingdom of God is among [or within] you' (Luke 17:21) – but the Valentinian sentiments certainly sound theistic.[30]

For all the polysemance of the literature, Gnosticism is essentially retrospective, while Christianity is essentially future-oriented, which in turn leads each faith to view the present quite differently. Gnostic 'salvation' is usually a repristination, in which the self returns to a timeless and pre-existent perfection,[31] whereas Christian 'salvation' is a process of redemption, in which the self journeys within or evolves across time to reach eternity, however defined. Whether or not one thinks of this as the difference between Plato and Moses, the salient point is clear: the Gnostic *eschaton* is severed from the visible world of creation. There is no inherent end (*telos*) of the tangible universe that is realised in an afterlife, no damaged promise that is healed even in this life. The Gnostic initiate is not concerned to save the world but to be saved from it. Therefore, neither the physiological nor the sociological – e.g. neither 'medicinal' practice nor 'political' reform – can have much if any current import. As is often pointed out, the bodily raising of Lazarus from the dead (John 11:43–4) must appear a cruel biblical hoax to a Gnostic mind. Although heightened awareness is made possible by the Gnostic Jesus, this does not normally imply his ethical imitation *in time* – asceticism and libertinism being flights *from time*.[32] There is perhaps also no personal communion with Christ in an eternity to come.

CONCLUSION

The biblical gospel is not that humans can save themselves inwardly or that whatever happens outwardly is meant to be, but rather that a personal God loves them and that, with divine help, they can freely love others. Human beings are not God, and human sin and suffering are real; to think otherwise is false consolation. That forgiveness and charity can be equally real, however, is the good news that does not grow old. Humans can participate in the grace manifest in Christ, and, being forgiven by God, both give and receive joy. Embodiment of that joy is all that Christian ethics has ever been or will be.[33]

Notes

1   All biblical quotations are from *The New Oxford Annotated Bible, with the Apocrypha*, New Revised Standard Version, ed. by Bruce M. Metzger and Roland E. Murphy (New York: Oxford University Press, 1991).
2   All Gnostic quotations are from *The Nag Hammadi Library*, third edition, ed. by James M. Robinson (New York: HarperSanFrancisco, 1990), unless otherwise noted.
3   See Luke Timothy Johnson, *Living Jesus: Learning the Heart of the Gospel* (New York: HarperSanFrancisco, 1999).
4   For more on love in the canonical gospels, see my *Love Disconsoled* (Cambridge: Cambridge University Press, 1999), from which I draw in this section.
5   According to Philip L. Shuler, 'the term "gospel" originally referred to the "reward" given to a messenger who brought [good] news, and it soon became identified with the news itself'. See Shuler, 'The Meaning of the Term "Gospel"', in *The International Bible Commentary*, ed. by William R. Farmer (Collegeville, MN: Liturgical Press, 1998), p. 1229.
6   See Wayne Meeks, *The Origins of Christian Morality* (New Haven: Yale University Press, 1993), p. 61.
7   George W. E. Nickelsburg, 'The Jewish Context of the New Testament', in *The New Interpreter's Bible*, vol. 8, ed. by Leander Keck (Nashville: Abingdon Press, 1995), p. 39.
8   Teresa Okure, 'Commentary on John', in *The International Bible Commentary*, ed. by William R. Farmer (Collegeville, MN: Liturgical Press, 1998), p. 1446.
9   Richard B. Hays, *The Moral Vision of the New Testament* (New York: HarperSanFrancisco, 1996), p. 145.
10 *Ibid.*, p. 147.
11 See Reinhold Niebuhr, *Love and Justice*, ed. by D. B. Robertson (Gloucester, MA: Peter Smith, 1976), pp. 27–40.
12 Some interpret the 'turn the other cheek' directive to be exclusively relevant to a personal insult delivered with the back of the hand. Whether such a reading can be sustained is not crucial to my analysis, since I do not think we should look for seamless generalisations here.

13 Hans Jonas, *The Gnostic Religion*, second edition (Boston: Beacon Press, 1963), pp. 31–32.

14 Yeats' famous epitaph, taken from his poem 'Under Ben Bulben', reads in part: 'Cast a cold eye on life, on death. Horseman, pass by!' See *The Yeats Reader*, ed. by Richard J. Finneran (New York: Scribner Poetry, 1997), p. 127.

15 Meeks, *Origins*, p. 52.

16 See the 1977 edition of *The Nag Hammadi Library*, ed. by James M. Robinson (San Francisco: Harper and Row).

17 Jonas, *Gnostic*, p. 145.

18 Some scholars deny that there is any ontological dualism in the fourth gospel; see Teresa Okure, 'Commentary on John', pp. 1447 and 1489, and Hays, *Moral*, pp. 142 and 148. Yet other writers find elements of both ontological and moral dualism in John; see Meeks, *Origins*, pp. 58–61. The extent to which the Gospel of Thomas is dualistic is also debated, but most scholars agree that it is less so than the other Gnostic gospels.

19 See my *The Priority of Love: Christian Charity and Social Justice*, forthcoming from Princeton University Press, Chapter 5.

20 See Stephen Mitchell, *The Gospel According to Jesus* (New York: HarperCollins, 1991), pp. 193–194.

21 See, for example, 'The Apocryphon of John' (11,15 to 15,13).

22 S. Weil, *Waiting for God*, tr. by Emma Craufurd (New York: Harper and Row, 1951), p. 166. Weil herself was fascinated by Gnosticism, especially by the Cathars, but she understood the issues at stake.

23 'Carpocrates', in *The Other Bible: Ancient Alternative Scriptures*, ed. by Willis Barnstone (New York: HarperSanFrancisco, 1984), p. 649.

24 See Hays, *Moral*, esp. pp. 149–150.

25 See my *Love Disconsoled*, Chapter 5, esp. pp. 151–169.

26 See Friedrich Nietzsche, 'The AntiChrist', in *The Portable Nietzsche*, ed. by Walter Kaufmann (New York: Viking Press, 1968), sects. 33 and 34, pp. 606 and 608.

27 Hays, *Moral*, p. 84.

28 E. Pagels, *The Gnostic Gospels* (New York: Random House, 1989), p. 144.

29 Jonas, *Gnostic*, p. 127; Jonas' line is quoted in *The Other Bible*, p. 308.

30 In Blake's 'Everlasting Gospel', the equation of man and God is more transparent, the antinomianism more complete: 'Thou art a Man God is no more / Thy own humanity learn to adore . . . Good & Evil are no more / Sinais trumpets cease to roar'. See *The Complete Poetry and Prose of William Blake*, ed. by David V. Eerdman (New York: Doubleday, 1988), pp. 520–521.

31 As John Dominic Crossan perceives; see his *The Birth of Christianity* (New York: HarperSan Francisco, 1998), p. 267.

32 Crossan argues that 'the theology of the *Gospel of Thomas* had public social consequences', that it was even a kind of 'social radicalism' implying a critique of accepted family relations and political powers (*ibid.*, pp. 269–270). I am disinclined, nevertheless, to call it a (sustainable) *social* ethic, precisely because it seems so vehement in its refusal of the world of real people.

33 Compare the opening line of the Gospel of Truth: 'The gospel of truth is joy for those who have received from the Father of truth the grace of knowing him . . .'

5 The epistles and Christian ethics

STEPHEN C. BARTON

IS THERE SUCH A THING AS 'NEW TESTAMENT ETHICS'?

The moral teaching of the New Testament epistles may be summed up as a radical reinterpretation of the scriptures and the story of Israel in the light of the life, death and resurrection of Jesus of Nazareth. This teaching took shape to serve the needs of groups of believers in the first century seeking to live out their Christian discipleship in the towns and cities of the Roman empire, from Palestine and Syria in the east to Rome in the west. Taken together, it is a body of practical wisdom on how to live in holiness as the people of God in the time between the resurrection and parousia of Christ. This practical wisdom covers matters like Jew–Gentile relations, how to avoid idolatry, food and sex rules, household order, work and obligations to those in authority. It is indebted to the moral traditions of Israel on the one hand and Greece and Rome on the other,[1] all refracted through the lens of the story of Jesus and the experience of the Holy Spirit in daily life and in gatherings for worship.

Against this background, it is not possible to talk about 'ethics' in the normal sense of the word. The New Testament does not present abstract reflection of a philosophical kind on the nature and grounds of moral action. It is not a compendium of systematic reflection on the good. Rather, it represents a variety of attempts to articulate the implications of conversion and baptism.[2] It invites its readers to a new way of life under the one true God revealed in Jesus Christ. This way of life is presented variously as an invitation to 'take up the cross', to become followers of 'the Way', to 'die with Christ' in order one day to 'rise with him', to show forth the 'fruits of the Spirit', and so on. What is important is not individual ethical decision-making by appeal (along Kantian lines) to the deductions of universal reason but faithful obedience in the light of tradition and revelation. The exemplary figure here is not so much the philosopher as the martyr. The exemplary society is not so much the philosophical school or academy as the communion of saints on earth and in heaven.

Seeing the 'ethics' of the New Testament in this way – that is, as reflecting the lives of a particular people seeking to display in their attitudes and actions the glory of God – should not come as a surprise, for it is basically the same with the 'ethics' of the Old Testament, that collection of sacred texts so influential in the shaping of the moral world of early Christianity. Thus, what John Barton says about the particularity of Old Testament moral teaching is equally true of the New:

> Our first impression, that the Old Testament presents its morality unsystematically and through a variety of vehicles, none of them much like the way we write about ethics, is misleading if it encourages us to think that it is just a muddle. But it is perfectly accurate in so far as it reminds us that the biblical way of conveying moral truth is always through the particular and the specific. Old Testament writers are maddeningly unsystematic. Asked for a general statement of moral principle, they reply with a little rule about local legal procedures, a story about obscure people of dubious moral character, or a hymn extolling some virtue in God with which human beings are supposed somehow to conform. Knowledge of the good for humankind lies through the observation of particulars, if Old Testament writers are to be believed.[3]

In the case of the New Testament, this 'observation of particulars' focuses above all on Christ. The gospels display the good in the form of narratives of the life of Christ seen in the light of his resurrection; the epistles display the good in the form of strenuous argument about the fulfilment of the scriptures in Christ and exhortation about what life 'in Christ' might mean for Christian identity and practice.

THE CONTOURS OF THE ETHICAL TEACHING OF THE EPISTLES

Before we say something about the 'use' of the epistles in Christian ethics, however, it is important to sketch briefly the contours of the ethical teaching they contain. A good focal point is 1 Corinthians.[4] What we find in this epistle is true of the epistles as a whole: that early Christian ethics is communal or ecclesial ethics set within the broader horizon of God's covenant love for the world. We may sum up the moral–theological thrust of the epistle under four headings:

1. *The word of the cross and the transformation of humanity.* At the heart of Paul's appeal for unity in the faction-ridden church in Corinth is a vision of the transformation of humanity. This transformation is under-stood as an act of God's mysterious power bringing a new creation into being through the 'foolishness' and 'weakness' of the cross of Christ: 'but to those who are the called, both Jews and Greeks, Christ the power of God and the wisdom of God' (1 Cor. 1:24). That short phrase 'both Jews and Greeks' speaks volumes. It expresses the claim that salvation in Christ is a matter not just of individuals but of peoples, not just of the personal but of the political as well. Today it is like saying 'both Serb and Croat', 'both Arab and Israeli', 'both Hutu and Tutsi', 'both Protestant and Catholic'. For the cross of Christ is the revelation of a power greater than the power of human pride and self-assertion. Such 'boasting' blinds humanity to the hidden wisdom of God and sows the seeds of a social and political order oriented on fear, violence, dom-ination and intolerance of the other. The cross is the revelation *as gift and grace* of God's power-in-powerlessness available to all without distinction, imparting new life and new peoplehood (see 1 Cor. 1:26–31).

2. *The resurrection and the economy of hope.* Like the teaching about the cross, the importance of the resurrection is that it is a message of hope in God's creative power through which every manifestation of death-dealing pessimism or party spirit in church and society may be overcome. The resur-rection of Christ is the great eschatological reality which offers new life to all alike. It brings the hope of transformed bodies to human beings weighed down with a sense of the body's relentless vulnerability to decay, dishonour and weakness (1 Cor. 15:42–3). It offers assurance of victory in the battle with mortal humanity's final enemy: death (verse 54). And because the ulti-mate victory is the gift of God, it is no person's boast. That is why the resur-rection is the basis for a whole new economy: 'Therefore, my beloved, be steadfast, immovable, always excelling in the *work* of the Lord, because you know that in the Lord your *labour* is not in vain' (verse 58). This is not pious platitude, for Paul goes on to say what this means: the Corinthians are to demonstrate their hope in the resurrection of the dead by contributing to the collection for the poor in Jerusalem (16:1–4).[5] The reordering of their energies away from self-preservation and competitive display releases them to work sacrificially with and for those in other churches. This represents the coming into being of a new, translocal and multi-ethnic polity unprece-dented in antiquity and still today able to transcend the ofttimes tribal loyal-ties of the modern nation-state.

3. *God's call to holiness in the Spirit and the church as a community of character.* In response to a church afflicted by lack of social discernment and

the exaltation of individual liberty over communal responsibility, Paul offers the resources for building (what Hauerwas calls)[6] a 'community of character'. Fundamental here is the idea of God's call to holiness (1 Cor. 1:2). This draws upon the biblical moral tradition (cf. Exod. 19:4–6) according to which holiness is a divine vocation to separate from evil in order to worship God and, by witnessing to the character of God, become a blessing to 'the nations'. Integral to this idea is the holiness of the temple, where 'temple' is extended metaphorically to stand for the community of God's people indwelt by God's Spirit: 'Do you not know that you [plural] are God's temple and that God's Spirit dwells in you?' (1 Cor. 3:16). Drawing upon his moral and sacerdotal tradition in this way is central to Paul's attempt to *resocialise* the Corinthians and to nurture a conversion of their corporate imagination by helping them to see themselves as heirs of the story of Israel.[7] His aim in so doing is not to take them out of 'the world' (5:10), but to consolidate their life together as a new people of the Spirit under the lordship of Christ.

4. *The primacy of love.* 'Knowledge puffs up, but love builds up' (1 Cor. 8:1b). This is the radical, counter-cultural dictum which Paul introduces as a corrective to the Corinthians' self-centredness. Nor is the meaning of 'love' (*agape*) left contentless, captive to ideological manipulation. On the contrary, it is given a specific, christological point of reference and is set within the overarching narrative of the life-giving cross of Christ: 'So [says Paul to the 'strong'] by your knowledge those weak believers *for whom Christ died* are destroyed' (8:11). Famously also, it is the focus of the long digression on 'the more excellent way', in 1 Corinthians 12:31b – 14:1. This has become a favourite text at weddings and funerals. But the danger is that the real force of what Paul has to say is seriously weakened: at a wedding, 'love' becomes romantic love; at a funeral, nostalgia. In context, however, Paul is talking about that virtue of regard for 'the other' at the heart of the life of God, the practice of which inaugurates and sustains a new, eschatological sociality. According to this conception, love is not primarily a matter of feeling: it is *action for the common good* in both the church and society at large, grounded in the scriptures of Israel and the story of the crucified Christ.

RELATING THE EPISTLES TO CHRISTIAN ETHICS

If there is no such thing as 'New Testament ethics', and '*the* ethics of the epistles' is an abstraction, the question arises: How may the epistles and Christian ethics be related?[8]

The most common answer in New Testament scholarship is to separate the descriptive and the normative tasks and order them sequentially. First

let the historian ask what the texts meant in their original historical contexts, then hand over the results to the ethicist to draw whatever conclusions
are possible.[9] The value of this approach is that it helps us to appreciate the
particularity and even peculiarity of early Christian moral teaching and
practice. We see that they were shaped by the traditions, social patterns and
events of the world in which the epistles were written, a world which in
many respects was quite *different* from our own. In consequence, we are less
likely to read the epistles in a simplistic way as speaking in oracular fashion
directly to our situation or as all saying the same thing or as all applying
equally in every respect in every time and place. Otherwise we might find
ourselves having to justify an insistence that women wear hats in church
(see 1 Cor. 11:2–16) or, much more seriously, having to justify the moral
probity of an hierarchical, class-based society which permitted the subordination of women and children and the owning of slaves (see Col. 3:18 – 4:1;
also the Epistle to Philemon). So the strengths of the historical approach are
considerable.

On the other hand, there are weaknesses also.[10] One is the danger that
because the task of historical reconstruction is ongoing and never complete,
the 'assured results' of the historian are never finally available for the ethicist! In consequence, the epistles become almost unusable for Christian
ethics. At most, they provide only choice quotations for ethical norms or
principles reached on other grounds. Another danger is that such heavy
emphasis is placed on the 'gulf' between the past and the present that significant points of continuity between past and present are overlooked. To put it
another way, it sometimes happens that the historian's energies are so nar-
rowly focused on the period of *origins* that the history of subsequent developments in Christian ethical tradition and practice are neglected.[11] A third
weakness has to do with epistemology. It is often made to appear that historical criticism is 'objective' and 'scientific' (*wissenschaftlich*) and produces
'hard' data about early Christian morality, whereas the appropriation of this
data for Christian ethics involves the 'soft' (i.e. unstable and constantly negotiable) business of personal judgement and interpretation. But this is both to
obscure the thoroughly interpretative nature of the act of historical description and to collude with a liberal view of ethics as essentially an expression
of individual preference or group interests.[12]

Is there, then, a way of reading the epistles which takes seriously the
need to situate them historically but which is less prone to tying them irre-
trievably to the past? The answer lies in reconceiving what is meant by
reading *contextually* such that our reading of the epistles is even more con-
textual than traditional historical criticism allows.[13] Arguably, the historical

critic's understanding of the context of the epistles is too narrow: ancient texts firmly tied to a context in Jewish and Greco-Roman antiquity. But from the viewpoint of Christian faith the epistles are not just ancient texts. They are also constituent parts of the canon of scripture, the appropriate context for the interpretation of which is *the ongoing life of the Church in its partici- pation in the life of God in the world*.[14] In other words, the context for inter- preting the epistles is *the present*: a present informed by the past – by an understanding of how the life of God has been understood and shared from the very beginning – and open to a future, an *eschaton*, which is in God's hands.

This means that the truth about God's ways with the world to which the epistles bear witness is a truth which is discerned as the epistles are read and reread in communities of faith generation after generation seeking, by God's Spirit, to live in creative fidelity to God's Word, Jesus Christ. The *trini- tarian* shape of this claim is not coincidental. It is only as the church 'per- forms' the epistles in the ongoing context of its sharing in the life of the Holy Trinity that such performances will contribute to the shaping of a holy people.

This is not to be understood as an excuse for a conservative compla- cency in defence of some traditional moral status quo. Nor is it a basis for a liberal (or even liberationist) moral relativism. Over against both these ten- dencies in Christian ethics, the model sketched here is one which fully acknowledges that the moral import of the epistles has to be re-evaluated with changing times and changing circumstances. At the same time, by its contextualisation of the 'performance' of the epistles in the church's sharing in the trinitarian life of God, it shows a clear recognition that the boundaries of such performance are not infinitely flexible.

A CASE STUDY: THE 'HOUSEHOLD RULES' AND CHRISTIAN SOCIAL ETHICS

We conclude with a case study. How might the 'household rules' (from the German form-critical term *Haustafeln*) of the New Testament epistles inform Christian ethics – for example, in the sphere of family life? This is an important question both because of the prominence of 'the family' in current political and ethical discourse[15] and because of the influence of the New Testament 'household rules' on Christian patterns of sociality over the last two millennia.

The household rules are a recurrent feature of the moral teaching of the epistles (e.g. Eph. 5:22–6:9; 1 Peter 2:18–3:7; also 1 Tim. 2:8–15, 6:1–2; Titus

2:1–10). They are found also in early post–New Testament texts.[16] A good
example is Col. 3:18 – 4:1 (RSV):

> Wives, be subject to your husbands, as is fitting in the Lord. Husbands,
> love your wives, and do not be harsh with them. Children, obey your
> parents in everything, for this pleases the Lord. Fathers, do not provoke
> your children, lest they become discouraged. Slaves, obey in everything
> those who are your earthly masters, not with eyeservice, as men-
> pleasers, but in singleness of heart, fearing the Lord . . . Masters, treat
> your slaves justly and fairly, knowing that you also have a Master in
> heaven.

Following a fairly regular pattern, with strong precedents in standard discussions from Greek antiquity on matters of 'household management' (*oiko-
nomia*),[17] the rules set out how relations within households are to be ordered
as between husbands and wives, parents and children, and masters and
slaves. Generally, the three sets of relations are addressed in that order, and
the subordinate in each pair (i.e. wife, child, slave respectively) is addressed
first. What is of evident concern is the importance of preserving orderly
relations and the proper social hierarchy in the households of Christians or
in households which have Christian members. That hierarchy consists in
the subordination of wives to husbands, children to parents and slaves to
masters. It is a hierarchy which is pervasively patriarchal, as feminist scholarship in particular has drawn to our attention.[18] It is also a hierarchy which
assumes a class structure in which the institution of slavery is morally
acceptable.

All this is a world away from contemporary western society (even if it
may be closer, in some respects, to traditional non-western cultures). We
may characterise the contrast as between inequality in social relations then
and egalitarianism now; the obligation then to know your place over against
the obligation today to exercise your rights; and the expectation in antiquity
to conform to patterns laid down in traditions held as venerable over against
the expectation today to experiment and choose from the range of options
currently 'on the market'. In the face of this undeniable distance between
contemporary social values and the world of the text, what is the Christian
ethicist to do with the New Testament household rules?

One important step is to remember that this kind of issue is not new. In
an earlier generation, for example, Rudolf Bultmann attempted to deal with
the questions of interpretation raised, not by the problem of 'political correctness', but by the problem of (for want of a better phrase) 'cosmological
correctness': how to enable 'modern man' (*sic*) to be confronted by the true

'scandal' of the gospel in a way that did not demand assent to the outmoded cosmology and mythology of the biblical writings. His solution was to deny that the truth of the gospel is bound indissolubly to an ancient world-view, and to provide a method of interpretation (which became known as 'demythologisation') that allowed the deeper meanings behind the biblical mythology to come to expression. These deeper meanings have to do with an understanding of human existence; and in the existentialist philosophy of his day, Bultmann found ready to hand the categories of interpretation that made possible the 'translation' of biblical myth into terms intelligible in modernity.[19]

The adequacy of Bultmann's approach need not detain us here;[20] but it does provide pointers to possible ways forward in dealing with other kinds of 'problem texts'. For Bultmann recognised that the way to deal with problem texts is not to excise them or censor them, but to interpret them *in a larger theological-hermeneutical framework*. Related to this, Bultmann showed that responsible interpretation involves ongoing acts of engagement between the reader and the text in openness to God's justifying grace in Christ. The true meaning of the text is never static. It resides in the transcendent, living Word of God to whom the words of the text bear frail witness.

Having recognised that the 'problem' of the household rules is endemic to New Testament interpretation *as a whole* and that a theological–ecclesial framework of understanding is essential, we need to ask, What is the fundamental subject matter of these rules? What is the basic question to which the *Haustafeln* are an answer? Could it be that the essential issue is not the laying down of a divinely ordained pattern of hierarchical family relations (which, on a literal reading, would include slaves!) under male 'headship', but rather something to do with *the relationship between church and culture*: specifically, with how as families (or households) to be the church, how the *already given* structures of personal and social existence are to be renewed in the light of membership of the Body of Christ?[21]

Seen in this way, the household rules continue to speak as Christian scripture in a number of ways. Above all, they show that the revelation of the grace of God in the death and resurrection of Christ and the coming of the eschatological Spirit forced the early church to re-examine fundamental questions of personal identity, social obligation and power and authority. Noteworthy in the epistles, for instance, is the way in which theological and christological affirmation is followed by reflection on how to live: christological indicative is followed by moral imperative.[22] In the light of Christ, things could never be the same again. Christian believers could not be complacent about even the most taken-for-granted aspects of their individual and social lives, including life in families.

The household rules are, at least in part, an outworking of this process of critical, theological re-examination. Now, the measure of relations between husbands and wives is *Christian existence 'in the Lord'* (Col. 3:18). Husbands – and this in a patriarchal society – are to love (not abuse) their wives, and the measure of that love is laid down as Christ's self-giving love for the church (Eph. 5:25–7). Wives, especially those married to unbelievers, are to 'be subject' to their husbands, not out of servility and weakness, but for the higher good of 'gaining' their unbelieving husbands for Christ (1 Peter 3:1–2). Children are to obey their parents 'in the Lord', and fathers are not to abuse their authority by 'provoking' their children: rather, they are to bring them up 'in the Lord' (Eph. 6:1–4). Similarly, relations between masters and slaves are framed in terms of their mutual belonging to a 'master in heaven' (Col. 4:1). In other words, what we are witnessing in these texts is the criticism and gradual transformation from within of Jewish and pagan household ties in the light of Christ.

If this is so, then the attempt to reject the household rules wholesale by those who consider them inegalitarian, oppressive and out of date may be as inappropriate a response as the attempt to impose the household rules wholesale by those who consider them to be the church's last hope in the face of contemporary moral indiscipline and social disintegration. Neither the 'liberal' nor the 'conservative' response will do. Both are too 'sectarian', too totalitarian in their desire, either to wipe the slate clean and start somewhere else or to wipe the slate clean and return to 'what the Bible says'.[23]

Understood in their historical context and evaluated theologically in terms of what the Spirit of Christ might be saying to the church about human sociality, the household rules help us to see instead that what is required is something more modest, realistic, local and concrete, but no less demanding. What is required is day-by-day participation in the life of families and other social and political structures in ways which witness with full integrity to our true, eschatological identity as members together in a *new* household, the 'household of God'. That we today are obliged to participate in ways which do not reproduce the domestic pattern of those early Christian household rules does *not* mean that they no longer have anything to say. What is required is *creative fidelity*, where fidelity involves recognisable continuity with our scriptural faith tradition, and creativity is an openness to the Spirit to inspire us to interpret and 'perform' that tradition in ways which are life-giving.

Notes

1 Cf. Wayne A. Meeks, *The Moral World of the First Christians* (London: SPCK, 1987), 19–96.

2 Cf. Rowan Williams' claim earlier: 'So perhaps the most important challenge to some of our conventional Western ways of talking about morality comes from the biblical principle that sees ethics as essentially part of our reflection on the nature of the Body of Christ' (*Anglican Theological Review*, 81/2, p. 300).

3 John Barton, *Ethics and the Old Testament* (London: SCM Press, 1998), 14–15.

4 For an expanded version of the following, see Stephen C. Barton, 'Christian Community in the Light of 1 Corinthians', *Studies in Christian Ethics*, 10/1 (1997), 1–15.

5 Cf. Dieter Georgi, *Remembering the Poor: The History of Paul's Collection for Jerusalem* (Nashville: Abingdon Press, 1992).

6 Cf. Stanley Hauerwas, *A Community of Character* (Notre Dame: University of Notre Dame Press, 1981).

7 Cf. Brian Rosner, *Paul, Scripture and Ethics* (Leiden: Brill, 1994).

8 For a major recent account, see Richard B. Hays, *The Moral Vision of the New Testament* (San Francisco: HarperCollins, 1996); also his J. J. Thiessen Lecture, *New Testament Ethics: The Story Retold* (Winnipeg: Canadian Mennonite Bible College Publications, 1998), ch.1.

9 Exemplary here are writers like Wayne A. Meeks, *The Origins of Christian Morality: The First Two Centuries* (New Haven: Yale University Press, 1993), and Dale B. Martin, *The Corinthian Body* (New Haven: Yale University Press, 1995).

10 Cf. Nicholas Lash, 'What Might Martyrdom Mean?' in his *Theology on the Way to Emmaus* (London: SCM, 1986), 75–92.

11 Cf. David W. Brown, *Tradition and Imagination* (Oxford: Oxford University Press, 1999).

12 Cf. Rowan Williams, 'Interiority and Epiphany: A Reading in New Testament Ethics', *Modern Theology*, 13/1 (1997), 29–51, esp. 29–36.

13 See further Stephen C. Barton, *Invitation to the Bible* (London: SPCK, 1997), 12–27.

14 Cf. Nicholas Lash, 'Performing the Scriptures', in his *Theology on the Way to Emmaus*, 37–46.

15 Cf. Don S. Browning et al., *From Culture Wars to Common Ground: Religion and the American Family Debate* (Louisville: Westminster John Knox Press, 1997).

16 See further J. D. G. Dunn, 'The Household Rules in the New Testament', in S. C. Barton, ed., *The Family in Theological Perspective* (Edinburgh: T & T. Clark, 1996), 43–63. The relevant texts are laid out at 44–6.

17 Cf. David L. Balch, *Let Wives Be Submissive: The Domestic Code in 1 Peter* (Society of Biblical Literature Monograph Series 26, Chico: Scholars Press, 1981).

18 Cf. Elisabeth Schüssler Fiorenza, *In Memory of Her: A Feminist Theological Reconstruction of Christian Origins* (London: SCM Press, 1983), ch. 7.

19 See Rudolf Bultmann, 'New Testament and Mythology', in Hans Werner Bartsch, ed., *Kerygma and Myth: A Theological Debate* (London: SPCK, 1972), 1–44, and the essays in response collected therein.

20 Cf. Anthony C. Thiselton, *The Two Horizons: New Testament Hermeneutics and Philosophical Description* (Grand Rapids: Eerdmans, 1980), chs.VIII–X.

21 Cf. Miroslav Wolf, 'Soft Difference: Theological Reflections on the Relation between Church and Culture in 1 Peter', *Ex Auditu* 10 (1994), 15–30.

22 Cf. Victor P. Furnish, *Theology and Ethics in Paul* (Nashville: Abingdon Press, 1968), esp. 224–227.

23 On Stephen Toulmin's analysis of the 'myth of the clean slate' as a characteristic of modernity, see M. Wolf, 'Soft Difference', 23.

Part two

Approaches to Christian ethics

6 Natural law and Christian ethics

STEPHEN J. POPE

ORIGINS

Themes akin to natural law emerged in Greek civilisation. The tragedian Sophocles (497–406 BCE), for example, gave some indication of it in his depiction of the conflict between Antigone's obedience to King Creon and her stronger obligation to a higher law. Plato (428–348 BCE) countered the relativism of the Sophists by arguing that goodness consists in living a life in accord with our rational nature and not in thoughtless social conformity.[1] Aristotle (383–322 BCE) followed suit in distinguishing the deeper 'natural justice' from what is legally just.[2] For Aristotle, the good for every organism is 'to attain fully its natural activity'.[3] Living 'according to nature' (*kata physin*)[4] for human beings means living virtuously.

The cosmopolitan Stoics distinguished the human nature that pertains to all human beings as such from laws instituted by particular societies. They held that the right way to live can be discovered by intelligently conforming to the order residing in human nature. Their characteristic maxim – that we ought to live 'according to nature' – was an injunction to live virtuously rather than at the whim of fluctuating emotions or social approval.

Stoic notions were assimilated and popularised by the Roman philosopher Cicero (106–43 BCE), who maintained that 'True law is right reason in agreement with Nature; it is of universal application, unchanging and everlasting; it summons to duty by its commands, and averts from wrongdoing by its prohibitions'.[5] According to Cicero, 'natural law' (*lex naturalis*) grounds ethical universalism, unchanging standards pertaining to all times, people and places – 'there will not be one law at Rome, and another at Athens'.[6] Awareness of the 'brotherhood of man'[7] grounded Stoic objections to slavery.

Christian writers discerned a harmony between Greco-Roman invocations of natural law and St Paul's observation that the Gentiles were instructed by 'the law written in their hearts' (Rom. 2:15). St Paul observed that even pagans have some knowledge of God: 'what can be known about

God is evident to them ... Ever since the creation of the world, his invisible attributes of eternal power and divinity have been able to be understood and perceived in what he has made' (1:19, 20). Yet when pagans failed to give thanks to God, they fell into idolatry and other vices, including unnatural sexual relations (1:26–7). Yet at times, Paul observed, pagans have done 'by nature' deeds required by the Law even without the benefit of positive biblical revelation. Thus all people will justly receive divine judgement: Jews according to their observance of the Law of Moses, pagans in terms of their observance of the 'law written on their hearts' (2:15).

St Paul was later taken to support Christian adoption of natural law by the Patristic authors in the early centuries of the church. St John Chrysostom (d. 407), for example, believed that every person has access to natural law in his or her natural reason: 'In creating man at the beginning, God placed within him a natural law.'[8] The 'law of nature' exists prior to civil statutes and is their judge. The Fathers also believed natural law was indicated in various scriptural texts, including denunciations of the violation of basic moral awareness by the 'nations' (Amos 1), appreciation of the ordering of creation (Ecclesiasticus 39:21), and appeal to God's original intention in creation (Matt. 19:3–8).

St Augustine (354–430) distinguished the 'temporal law' of particular communities from the 'eternal law' displayed in the providential governance of creation through the eternal and immutable ideas in the mind of God.[9] Eternal ideas are 'impressed' upon the human mind by the Creator, so that, for example, Cain knew that murdering his brother was wicked.[10] Natural law, as he explains in *On Free Choice* (395), teaches that the lower parts of the person ought to be ordered to the higher – the passions and the 'spirited' parts of the soul to reason and reason to God.[11] Natural law is 'the divine reason or will of God prescribing the conservation of the natural order and prohibiting any breach of it'.[12]

Before Augustine, the civil lawyers of the second and third centuries of the Roman empire were forced by practical demands to account for the informal legal customs – called the 'law of nations' (*ius gentium*) – that applied to all people, e.g. concerning fraud, the right to self-defence, promise-keeping etc. 'Natural right' (*ius naturale*) exists in the nature of things and governs civil law (*ius civile*). As recorded in the sixth century by the compilers of the emperor Justinian, the Roman lawyer Gaius, writing around 180, distinguished civil law from the 'law of nations', which he identified with natural right proper to humanity.[13] In the next generation, however, the jurist Ulpian (170–228) came to separate the 'law of nations' from natural right, and to define the latter as 'that which nature teaches all animals', e.g. the sexual union of male and female and the rearing of off-spring.[14]

In the seventh century, Ulpian's threefold distinction – natural law, the 'law of nations', and positive law – was incorporated into the encyclopedic *Etymologies* of St Isidore of Seville (560–636), from which it was transmitted into the mainstream of medieval legal thought. The influential *Decretum* (1140) of Gratian (d. 1160) coordinated Ulpian's threefold division with the human law and the divine law. Gratian took the natural law to be 'that which is contained in the Law and Gospel',[15] which added yet another level of ambiguity to an already complex terminological legacy.

MEDIEVAL SCHOLASTICISM

Theologians in the twelfth and thirteenth centuries subjected these inherited distinctions to careful philosophical analysis. Anselm of Laon (d. 1117) and his disciples understood the natural law to be inherent in human reason, supplemented by divine law and capsulised in the Golden Rule. The Franciscan Alexander of Hales (d. 1245) provided the first systematic scholastic treatise on law. He understood natural law as an innate 'habit' in the human soul. St Albert the Great (1206–80) identified natural law with the first principles of practical reason that exist naturally in the human mind – as proper to our rational nature and not, contra Ulpian, something we share with animals.

St Thomas Aquinas (1225–74) developed a well-ordered synthesis of previous Stoic, Ciceronian, Aristotelian, Patristic, juristic and canonical themes. Aquinas explained in the *Summa theologiae* that theology attempts, as much as reasonably possible, to uncover and enter into the intrinsic intelligibility of what Christians already believe on the basis of 'sacred doctrine.'[16] In moral matters, theologians refer to the natural law as a way of giving the reasons behind Christian moral teachings. We are first taught by the divine law that killing, stealing and lying are forbidden, and then come to know why they are forbidden through a deeper grasp of how these kinds of acts violate the good of rational creatures made in the 'image of God'.

Aquinas defined law as 'an ordinance of reason for the common good, promulgated by him who has care of the community'.[17] He thus placed ethics in the wider context of an overarching theological vision of the cosmos as a hierarchical order created by God. Employing the term 'law' analogously in different spheres, Aquinas distinguished the eternal law governing the universe, the positive divine law revealed first in the Old Law and then in the New Law, the natural law comprising the basic moral standards for human conduct, and positive human law, both civil law and the 'law of nations'. Positive human law, whether statutory or customary, must always be consistent with the higher requirements of the natural law.

Aquinas is best known as the theologian who critically assimilated the philosophy of Aristotle, including his rich theory of 'nature' that provided an important conceptual counterpart to 'supernature'. Aristotle defined nature as 'an intrinsic principle of motion and rest',[18] as a principle of a being's operation that could be clearly explained in terms of its intrinsic purposes or ends. Since we are 'rational animals', natural law is defined as the 'rational creature's participation in the eternal law'.[19] Every person naturally experiences desires for goods also needed by 'irrational creatures', including self-preservation, water, food, air and sex. We also have desires proper to our rational nature, including those to form political community, to develop friendships and to know the truth about God. We 'participate' in the eternal law by freely deciding to act in morally good ways, that is, in accord with the 'dictates of reason', the knowledge 'written on the heart', and the natural ends built into human nature.

Natural goods are proper objects of human action as long as they are pursued with reasonable moderation and in accord with their natural purposes. For Aquinas, some acts are always in violation of natural law. Lying is wrong because 'false signification' violates the natural purpose of human speech.[20] Baptism of infants against their parents' wishes usurps natural parental responsibility.[21] Suicide is wrong in part because it attacks natural self-love as well as love of the common good,[22] usury because it violates the purpose of money,[23] and masturbation because, like other 'sins against nature', it fails to comply with the reproductive purpose of our sexual organs.[24]

Every person, Aquinas believed, has access to the first principles of practical reason by means of an innate capacity that he called *synderesis*. We know that we ought to seek good and to avoid evil and that we ought to treat others as we wish to be treated. Just a little reflection on these primary precepts leads us to recognise more focused requirements to honour our parents, protect human life, respect the property of others, tell the truth and maintain fidelity within marriage. These injunctions are revealed in the Decalogue, Aquinas held, but in fact they are observed within any decent community and their force is recognised by reasonable people everywhere.

Human reason, then, has broad competence to grasp the goods proper to human nature and to identify the virtues by which they are attained; he even stated that there would be no need for divine law if we were ordered only to a natural rather than to a supernatural end.[25] However, reasoning from the widely known primary precepts of the natural law to their application in secondary and even more remote precepts can be complex and difficult.

Moreover, it is not always clear what we ought to do in concrete situations; that is, how to make amends for wrongdoing, whether deceiving another is justified morally, when it might be legitimate to use another's property etc. Good judgement is more elusive, less reliable and less certain than is desirable or necessary. To make up for the limitations of human reason, Aquinas held, God has explicitly revealed what we need to know. Reason is competent to grasp precepts that promote imperfect happiness in this life, but revelation alone instructs us about our true end, the beatific vision.

Aquinas certainly did not equate all of Christian morality with observing the natural law. Natural law constitutes the fundamental moral standards to which rational and free creatures conform when they act reasonably. But the essence of the Christian life lies in a spiritual journey towards God made possible only by the grace-inspired theological virtues of faith, hope and charity. Natural law thus plays a subordinate but important role within the Thomistic vision of the Christian moral life.

VOLUNTARISM AND PROTESTANTISM

The late Middle Ages witnessed the emergence of a growing theological emphasis on the sovereignty of the divine will. In Thomistic realism, the content of the natural law follows from the divine essence, reason and eternal wisdom.[26] In theological voluntarism, on the other hand, the natural law flows from the divine will. It ought to be obeyed, therefore, not because it is intrinsically intelligible or constitutive of human flourishing, but because it is decreed by the divine lawgiver. If natural law is a form of divine positive law, then we can only judge acts to be wrong by referring to their extrinsic prohibition rather than to their unsuitability to human nature.

Duns Scotus (1266–1308) emphasised the freedom of God's will and its priority to the divine intellect. While Aquinas defined law as an ordinance of reason (presupposing an act of the will), Scotus regarded law as preeminently an act of the will. Since the divine will is the first rule and the cause of good, a human act is made good or evil only because God wills it as such. He agreed with Aquinas that God creates a natural law that not even God can abrogate, but, maintaining the radical freedom of God, he significantly reduces its scope. The 'First Table' of the Ten Commandments belongs to the natural law; Scotus thought, for example, that it would be logically impossible for God to have commanded idolatry. But God's freedom is not limited when it comes to the 'Second Table', that concerned with our duties to one another. Scotus thus thought that, though he obviously did not do so, God was perfectly free to have commanded fornication, perjury or human sacrifice. These commandments, then, might be congruent with the natural law, but they cannot, properly speaking, be claimed to belong to it.

William of Ockham (c. 1290–1350) extended the voluntarist ethic much further, claiming that nothing is good or evil as such but only as determined by the divine will. Ockham continued to identify natural law with right reason, but regarded right reason as whatever God decrees to be so. God is not subject in the slightest degree to any superior will, law or logical necessity; therefore there is no immutable standard derived from the unchanging human good as such. This even applies to the 'First Table' of the Decalogue, so, departing from Scotus, Ockham held that God could have commanded that the natural law obligated us not only to hate our neighbour but even to hate God himself.[27]

Protestant theological ethics has often been characterised as a voluntaristic replacement by biblical ethics of natural law. Martin Luther's (1483–1546) emphasis on the omnipotence, inscrutibility and arbitrariness of God's will clearly reflects a voluntarist emphasis at odds with the theological underpinnings of Thomistic natural law. Yet Luther never denigrated natural intelligence in ordinary life, valued the use of 'regenerate reason' in service of the church, and acknowledged the presence of the natural law in the conscience of each person: 'For nature, like love, teaches that I should do as I would be done by'[28] (Matt. 7:12).

At the same time, Luther thought that the profoundly corrupting influence of sin undermined radically any chance for building ethics on the basis of natural law or any teleology explicated by the 'heathen' Aristotle. Luther's primary animus in this regard was directed toward the view that acting in accord with the natural law is salvific. While conceding that unbelievers can at times know and even obey the moral law, he regarded doing so as utterly irrelevant to the key question of justification. Even if identified by 'regenerate reason', the wisdom found in the natural law – or any law, for that matter – pales in significance before the 'foolishness' of the gospel.

Similar themes were sounded in John Calvin (1509–64).[29] While the reformers' natural law was dominated by biblical exegesis, the explicitly Thomistic strain of natural law continued later in the work of the Anglican theologian Richard Hooker (1554–1645), notably in *Of the Laws of Ecclesiastical Polity* (1593–7).

THE 'SECOND SCHOLASTICISM'

International law, the body of principles and binding agreements which regulate conduct taking place outside the legal boundaries of states, began with scholastic reflection on the moral status of native peoples and the responsibilities of Christian nations towards them. The greatest development of natural law in the sixteenth century began with the 'second scholasticism' of the Dominican theologians of the University of Salamanca.

Francisco de Vitoria, OP, (1492–1546) has been described as the founder of 'international law'. Vitoria held that the 'law of nations', though recognised by all societies, stands in need of explicit formulation into a specific legal code governing the conduct among different political communities. Its provisions are established by international agreement and positive law, but they take their deepest ethical justification from the principles of natural justice. Natural law precedes and governs positive law. Indeed, later Thomists like Francisco Suárez, SJ, (1548–1617) held that the natural law governed human nature before political community even existed and that its observance lies behind the establishment of legitimate commonwealths.

Many of Vitoria's disciples went on to become influential scholars. These include the Dominicans Melior Cano (1509–60), Fernando Vazquez (1509–66), and Domingo de Soto (1494–1560). Vitoria's intellectual influence was also registered, though in different ways, in the work of Jesuits Robert Bellarmine (1542–1611), Luis de Molina (1535–1600) and Suárez, perhaps the most influential Jesuit legal philosopher of his day.

Vitoria's influence was reflected in the work of Bartolomé de las Casas, OP, (1474–1566), whose *In Defence of the Indians* argued against forced conversions on the Thomistic basis that by its very nature faith must be a free act and cannot be forced by threats of violence. Empirically, las Casas argued that native cultures were quite sophisticated, that the natural intelligence of their people proved their human dignity, and that their morality, while at certain points deficient, showed many signs of natural virtue and an 'inherent justice'. Ethically, he agreed with Vitoria that the natives have political dominion over their own communities and therefore that they are owed immunity from illicit aggression. Las Casas had some success before the Spanish court in providing a natural-law argument for the rights of natives to be free from attack, enslavement, torture and economic exploitation.

'MODERN NATURAL-LAW' THEORY

The historical context for the emergence of modern natural-law theory includes the widespread desire for peace in the wake of the Wars of Religion in the sixteenth and seventeenth centuries. The length, ferocity and destruction of these wars, especially the Thirty Years' War (1618–48), created an intense desire for a theory of morality, law and political organisation that could transcend confessional boundaries and allow for peaceful coexistence in the international order. Secondly, the stunning growth of scientific knowledge in this period inspired philosophers and lawyers to attempt to put ethics on a rational foundation that is consistent with the mechanistic science of the day.

Dutch Protestant Hugo Grotius (1583–1645) is the founder of modern natural-law theory. Against sceptics and antinomians, Grotius argued that nature provides a discernible and objective law governing human conduct. He included within natural law the older *objective* sense of natural right as a just relation between parties, along with a newer sense of natural right as the *subjective* claim of individuals. The former is exemplified when we see that 'it is right' that a parent cares for his or her child and the latter when the employee claims her 'right' to a just wage. Aquinas had used natural law and natural right interchangeably in the objective sense, but Grotius exhibits the modern emphasis on natural right as subjective claim of individuals.

Society is made possible only, Grotius held, when people agree to recognise one another's natural rights, for example the right to own property. Grotius' system was in fact 'the first reconstruction of an actual legal system in terms of rights rather than laws'.[30] He also attempted to justify ethical norms in terms of rights, so that lying, for example, is wrong because it violates the right of the person who is told the lie.[31]

Grotius' major work, *On the Law of War and Peace* (1625), offered the first systematic attempt to regulate international conflict by means of just war criteria. States were related to one another the way individuals were in the state of nature. Since natural rights precede civil society, states too have rights that can be protected through the use of force. Natural law thus regulates human behaviour occurring outside as well as inside the boundaries of nation-states.

Grotius held that natural law gives rational norms that would have obligatory force even if, though impossible, there were no God – the 'impious hypothesis' usually described as the beginning of the secularisation of natural-law theory. Grotius himself was a sincere Christian who desired to construct a version of natural law that could be widely agreed upon in an intensely combative religious age. Though he had no intention to divorce God from natural law, this move established an agenda for the rest of modern natural-law theorists and led to the abandonment of speculation on the highest good or anything beyond a minimal version of Christian belief.

Thomas Hobbes (1588–1679) undercut the scholastic basis for natural law by more sharply repudiating teleology. In *Leviathan* (1651) Hobbes insisted that nature is best understood in terms of material and efficient causes, especially as exhibited in the science of Galileo, and without any reference to the 'obscure' formal and final causes of scholasticism. Hobbes, unlike Aquinas and Grotius, depicted human nature as profoundly pleasure-seeking and selfish rather than naturally social and oriented to friendship. Thus in his state of nature 'every man is enemy to every man',[32] and each lives under a constant threat of violent death. In this condition each person has complete liberty – an unlimited and amoral natural right – to do whatever is necessary for self-preservation.

Individuals seek security by replacing the state of nature with political community based on social contract. To this end, reason trades the insecure and unlimited liberty of natural right for the secure restrictions of natural law. Breaking with his predecessors, Hobbes argued that moral obligations are authorised not by natural right but rather by contracted 'natural laws', for example, to fulfil contracted agreements, which is the basis of justice. Though highly individualistic in anthropology, Hobbes' political theory granted nearly absolute power to the state and rendered positive law all but immune from evaluation by natural law.

In Germany, Lutheran Samuel von Pufendorf (1632–94), author of *Law of Nature and Nations* (1672), strove to construct a rational science of morals that could be superimposed on a Hobbesian amoral nature. Pufendorf believed that in the state of nature there are neither natural rights nor a natural law imposing moral obligations – both were creations of civil society, so there are, for example, no natural property rights prior to the social contract.

While not 'social animals', he thought, we nevertheless recognise that belonging to civil society provides a degree of order necessary for individual survival. Reason can deduce the norms necessary for social life in the abstract state of nature, for example those governing marriage and family, property, truth-telling etc., and these constitute the natural law. The natural law ought to be instantiated as much as possible in the array of particular civil laws enacted by lawmakers in political society; the former provides the basis for correcting, when necessary, the latter. This position eroded the distance between natural law and civil law, thus providing more authority to the latter than had obtained in earlier theories.

John Locke (1632–1704), especially in his *Second Treatise on Civil Government* (1690), argued that individuals are motivated by self-interest to trade the somewhat insecure state of nature for more orderly civil society in order to better protect their self-evident, inalienable and natural rights to life, liberty and 'estate' (private property). Extending Grotius' ideas and contradicting those of Pufendorf, Locke held that the natural rights of individuals *precede* the social contract and provide the ultimate moral standards for judging the performance of government. These rights present restraints on political regimes and were subsequently adopted by Thomas Jefferson (1743–1826) in the U.S. Declaration of Independence (1776).

Locke wanted to limit quarrels by establishing empirically justifiable laws not dependent on sectarian religious beliefs or metaphysical claims about the highest good or the ideal regime. For Locke, the question of the highest good was in principle rendered unanswerable by the diversity of subjective preferences. Having abandoned classical teleology, he saw not a common human good but only an aggregate of preferences pursued by self-interested individuals – a theory suited to the ethos of early capitalism. Locke's moral individualism, metaphysical nominalism and epistemological empiricism display his distance from pre-modern views of natural law.

Immanuel Kant (1724–1805) continued to employ selectively the language of natural law, but scholars generally consider his work an alternative to rather than a development of the main lines of preceding modern natural law. In *Foundations of the Metaphysics of Morals* he criticised previous moral philosophies for being fatally guilty of 'heteronomy', that is, of encouraging individuals to leave moral decisions to authorities rather than requiring them to function as autonomous moral agents. Though he understood nature in mechanistic Newtonian terms, he held that we need to act as if nature as a whole is purposive. He also maintained that the natural ends ought to be incorporated into the moral life, but that their normative significance derives not from their 'naturalness' but only from the fact that reason determines that their fulfilment is the necessary condition for the possibility of living ethically; we cannot function as moral agents if we do not exercise responsible caring for one's own physical and emotional well-being. Yet the ground of ethics for Kant, in contrast to Aquinas, is rational *rather than* natural.

Kant's separation of reason and nature was employed in the later academic division between the natural sciences (*Naturwissenschaften*), which study purposeless, mechanistic nature, and cultural studies (*Geisteswissenschaften*), which examine symbolism and systems of meaning. It also inspired, along with other influences, Max Weber's (1864–1920) division between 'value-free' social science and value-laden morality.[33]

By this time, nature has been stripped of all vestiges of normativity and natural law theory is moribund. Ethical theory was dominated by positivism and utilitarianism. The former view, expressed by John Austin (1790–1859), held that law is simply what is commanded by political authority. The latter was developed by Jeremy Bentham (1748–1832) and his followers on the basis of Hume's focus on utility. They abandoned 'the' human good of classical teleology and substituted for it various procedures designed to identify the aggregate of pleasure and pain that would best advance 'the greatest happiness of all those whose interest is in question'.[34] Bentham dismissed natural law as merely an expression of the subjective moral feelings of the speaker. So 'repugnant to nature' means 'I do not like to practise it: and consequently, do not practise it. It is therefore repugnant to what ought to be the nature of everybody else'.[35] Anything of value in natural-law theory ought to be expressed more scientifically in terms of utility.

THOMISTIC REVIVAL: PAPAL SOCIAL TEACHINGS

Pope Leo XIII's encyclical *Aeterni patris* (1879) inaugurated the renewal of Thomism, and Thomistic natural law, within Roman Catholicism, a movement which gained momentum around the time of the Second Vatican Council (1962–5). Papal social teachings respond primarily to pastoral rather than theoretical concerns; for this reason they never offer theoretical justification of natural law. The popes simply assume the philosophical validity of natural law and draw upon it to provide a philosophical framework within which they can speak about particularly troubling moral and social issues.

Pope Leo's own social encyclical, *Rerum novarum* (1891), applied natural-law ethics to the problems of workers in unfettered industrial capitalism. Leo taught that the rights to private property and to a just wage are guaranteed by the natural-law rather than simply granted by social convention or the will of employers. Subsequent popes invoked natural law to support the doctrine of subsidiarity, the prohibition of active euthanasia and sterilisation, duties of solidarity and international development, freedom of religion, the right to life of the unborn and the severely handicapped, and the prohibition of *in vitro* fertilisation.

NEO-THOMISM IN MID CENTURY

The major twentieth-century ethical thinker in the Thomistic tradition was the French philosopher Jacques Maritain (1882–1973). In his major work, *Man and the State* (1951), Maritain defined natural law as 'an order or a disposition that the human reason may discover and according to which the human will must act to accord itself with the necessary ends of the human being'.[36] We know natural law by 'connaturality' rather than by logical deduction or empirical observation. Adapting personalism, Maritain held that natural law regards persons as ends and not merely objects to be used by the state or the collectivity. Natural law thus supports an 'integral humanism' enjoining a balanced concern for human rights and the common good, a principle that has been profoundly influential in the Christian Democratic political parties of Europe and Latin America.

John Courtney Murray, SJ (1904–67) was the foremost twentieth-century American proponent of natural law. In *We Hold These Truths* (1960), Murray employed natural law to show Roman Catholics the legitimacy of participating in American democracy without compromising their faith. He held that natural law – and its explication in what he called the 'tradition of reason' – depends on three basic presuppositions: 'that man is intelligent; that reality is intelligible; and that reality, as grasped by intelligence, imposes on the will the obligation that is to be obeyed in its demands for action or abstention'.[37] Because natural law is grasped by reason, it stands independent of religious faith and thus can provide a broad basis for the moral consensus needed to unite the diverse citizens of a pluralistic society.

Murray's Thomistic identity was revealed in his acknowledgement that natural law presumes a 'metaphysic of nature, especially the idea that nature is a teleological concept . . . [and] that there is a God who is eternal Reason or Nous, at the summit of the order of being'.[38] His understanding of these assumptions as non-controversial presents a poignant indication of the difference between his intellectual context and ours. His creativity, however, was displayed in the employment of this framework in support of the American experiment in democracy, human rights, religious liberty, the separation of church and state, and the importance of moral consensus for public life. Murray continues to influence Roman Catholic social ethics.[39]

NATURAL LAW AND ARTIFICIAL BIRTH CONTROL

The most controversial debate in Roman Catholic moral theology in the century took place over the use of natural law to support the church's prohibition of artificial birth control. Pope Paul VI's encyclical *Humanae vitae* (1968) decreed that since procreation is the natural purpose of intercourse, all efforts to obstruct it are 'intrinsically evil'. Neither good motives nor consequences (e.g. humanitarian concern to limit escalating overpopulation) can justify any deliberate violation of the divinely given natural order of sexual activity.

Critics argued that this 'physicalist' interpretation of natural law fails to appreciate sufficiently the complexities of particular circumstances, the primacy of personal mutuality and intimacy in marriage, and the difference between valuing the gift of life and requiring its specific expression in openness to conception in each and every act of intercourse. As one theologian put it, 'it is one thing to say that both sexuality and marriage are intrinsically ordered towards procreation and that this must, therefore, be respected in a marriage; it is another to say that this provides a principle which must govern every marriage act'.[40]

John Paul II reiterates the moral prohibition, but rather than reiterating the 'physicalist' objection he employs the personalist and phenomenological argument that love as self-gift is always violated by artificial birth control.

THE REVISIONISTS

Revisionists (described pejoratively as 'proportionalists' by their detractors) seek to maintain the moral realism and eudaimonism of Thomistic natural law but without the conjoined physicalism, authoritarianism and legalism sometimes exhibited by natural-law moralists. Revisionists generally promote traditional positive moral norms and ideals but not in a way that yields universal and exceptionless non-formal prohibitions. So, for example, they would typically see good reasons in some cases for making an exception to the prohibition of artificial birth control or of artificial insemination (e.g., in some cases in which the husband is the donor of gametes). Similarly, some revisionists justify the threat of nuclear retaliation as a means of deterring nuclear aggression, a position which natural-law rigorists condemn on the grounds that it employs an intrinsically evil means (the threat of killing civilians) to promote a good end (national self-defence).

Revisionists conceive of human flourishing much more strongly in affective, imaginative, narrative and interpersonal terms than in dominantly natural terms.[41] Revisionists hold that, rather than conforming to natural ordering, we must be selective in our judgements about what aspects of nature contribute to the human good. The crucial issue for the moral assessment of human conduct turns not on its 'naturalness' but on its relation to human flourishing. Revisionists understand themselves to be engaged in the creative development of the natural-law tradition, particularly its emphasis on right reason, its appeal to the common good, its appreciation of knowledge by connaturality, its consideraton of moral norms as intelligible ways of identifying the human good, and its willingness to engage in moral dialogue across religious boundaries.

THE 'NEW CLASSICAL NATURAL-LAW THEORY'

This school of thought was inaugurated by philosopher Germain Grisez and then systematically elaborated upon by John Finnis, Joseph Boyle and others. It attempts to offer a constructive alternative to the dominance of scepticism, consequentialism and rationalism in ethics, yet it seeks to do so not simply by repeating neo-Thomistic commitments but rather by constructing a 'new classical natural law theory'.[42]

In his major work, *Natural Law and Natural Rights* (1980), Finnis begins with the claim that every person seeks happiness and that practical reason directs us to the basic human goods. It is self-evident, Finnis holds, that there are a variety of inviolable and basic goods – including life, knowledge, marriage, aesthetic experience, friendship, practical reasonableness and religion – the pursuit of which comprises the meaning of every reasonable human action. These goods are incommensurable, unable to be ranked in a priority system; they are never to be directly attacked and never to be seen as mere means to other ends. In practice, this means, for example, that we ought not betray religious faith to save face, nor destroy a friendship to get ahead, nor use artificial birth control to make our lifestyle more comfortable, nor engage in active euthanasia out of merciful motives etc. This position provides arguments for negative moral absolutes, for example never to support a policy of capital punishment, never to lie under any conditions etc.

This methodology avoids the 'naturalistic fallacy' – illicitly moving from 'facts' to 'values' – by holding that natural law is generated by practical reason's recognition of self-evident human goods rather than by any a priori descriptive claims about human nature. Practical reason does not need the assistance of metaphysics to understand the requirements of 'integral human fulfilment'. Interestingly, this position, although often employing scholastic language, is methodologically much closer to modern than to Thomistic methodology in its stress on law rather than virtue, on the individual rather than the common good, and on the independence of natural law from metaphysics and theology.

NATURAL LAW TODAY

Some of the major criticisms of natural law have been suggested earlier but can be recapitulated in light of contemporary debates. First, at the start of the twentieth century anti-naturalist philosophical criticism repudiated any attempt to derive moral 'values' from 'facts' about human nature.

G. E. Moore's *Principia Ethica* (1903) argued that naturalistic theories commit the 'naturalistic fallacy' by attempting to move invalidly from descriptive 'is' statements to normative 'ought' statements. Moore directed his criticism at the evolutionary social thought of Herbert Spencer (1820–1903), but others applied it to natural-law theory as well. Philosophers found precedent for this criticism in passing observation made by David Hume (1711–76) in *A Treatise of Human Nature* concerning the introduction of 'ought' statements within the course of argument that had been descriptive.[43] Over the course of the century, natural-law theorists have incorporated this stricture as a warning to avoid hasty, naive and simplistic derivations of 'values' from 'facts' rather than as requiring a complete abandonment of any descriptive bases for ethical reflection.[44]

Second, some Christian theologians attack natural law theorists for overestimating the powers of 'fallen' human reason and for calling into question the sufficiency of the Word of God. Early in the century this line of attack was expressed poignantly by Swiss theologian Karl Barth, especially in his attack of Emil Brunner's (1889–1966) theological ethics based on an 'orders of creation'.[45] Though categorised as a debate between Protestants and Roman Catholics, this debate runs within as well as between the Christian churches. More recently, 'narrative theologians' have criticised natural-law theory for minimalising or even ignoring Jesus, the Kingdom of God and the community of disciples embracing a distinctive way of life in favour of an accommodating universal ethic based on abstract and rationalistic metaphysics, anthropology and law.[46] Yet narrative need not in principle be opposed to natural law.[47]

Third, the anti-realist critics, informed by radical historicism, attack the 'essentialism' implied in Thomistic natural law. If there is no such thing as 'human nature' at all, then the notion of natural-law ethics is nonsense. They also charge modern natural law (or its philosophical descendants) with promoting a 'foundationalism' that ignores the radical limitations of its own suppressed historical particularity. If there is no properly rational practical reason, but only a raw human capacity for enculturation and socialisation, then it makes no sense to talk about a natural-law ethic. Anti-realists also point to its destructive consequences, particularly through the ways in which natural law has been invoked to give moral legitimation to dominant power structures and to repress prophetic demands for greater freedom.[48] Natural-law theorists have responded to anti-realism in a variety of ways, from denouncing it as nihilist to cautiously appreciating its insightfulness and taking up the challenge of presenting a more self-critical, historically conscious methodology.[49]

It needs to be said that in an age of moral pluralism we have become acutely conscious of the serious and widespread mistake of projecting the moral beliefs or social customs of a particular culture onto what is 'natural' to all human beings everywhere. Knowledge of history enables us to see as cultural what was once assumed to be 'natural' – the inferiority of women, the double standard for males and females in sexual morality, the disgracefuness of long hair on men (1 Cor. 11:14–15), the enslavement of captives of war etc. The same is true of practices that were once dismissed as 'unnatural'. Invocation of natural law has indeed been a tactic used by people in power to maintain their privileged position, and of course the same is true of appeals to scripture, tradition, philosophy and other sources of legitimation.

While much of its analysis in the universities is fairly abstract, one can observe the practical appeal of natural law. The horrors of the century – from the Holocaust to Rwanda – point to a level of moral perversity that is unimaginable. There is widespread recognition by all but the most indifferent and cynical that these evils amount to something more than a violation of mere social customs, aesthetic taste or sentiment. These horrors have led governments, religious institutions and humanitarian organisations to call for a level of philosophical backing for human rights that carries stronger moral authority than conventional treaties.

The practical force of natural law can thus be seen in legal documents from the 1946 Nuremburg trials of Nazi war criminals and in the formulation of the U.N. Declaration of Human Rights in 1948. Its soaring idealism is evidenced in Martin Luther King, Jr's 'A Letter from a Birmingham Jail', which denounced laws enforcing racial segregation with the Augustinian maxim that 'an unjust law is no law at all'.[50] It offers a basis for moral analysis of the content of human rights, the requirements of the international common good and the demands of ecological responsibility. It has recently been invoked to criticise slavery in the Sudan, to support the rights of prisoners in China, to attack the practice of genital mutilation in Africa, to provide backing for the justice due to immigrants in Europe, to counter the death penalty in the United States and to authorise the priority of human rights over the claims of national sovereignty in the former Yugoslavia.

The natural-law tradition has been strongly associated with Roman Catholicism. Yet the reformers acknowledged the natural law, and all of the major theorists of the modern version, from Grotius through Locke, came from Protestant nations. In the twentieth century its major defenders were often Roman Catholic, but its advocates have also come from the Greek Orthodox, Anglican and Protestant traditions (though sometimes employing the language of 'general revelation', 'created order' and the like). While the language of natural law has an undeniably Christian character, many of its themes find resonance with themes found in Confucius, Mencius and thinkers from different religious traditions.

Whatever their differences, natural lawyers believe that it offers a superior alternative to the relativism that discourages serious public moral discourse and to the subjectivism that undermines personal moral deliberation. More sophisticated proponents of natural-law ethics wish to employ it as a way of searching for a shared understanding of the human good, or at least of the major components that constitute the human good, both within their own religious communities and also in broader public contexts. They recognise that the common good can only be discerned through active participation in conversation by all the members of a community. For all their differences, natural-law ethicists share a belief that there is such a thing as the human good, commensurate with human nature, however complex its manifestations and various its possible modes of fulfilment.

Notes

1 See *Rep.* 428e–429a.
2 See *Nic. Eth.* 1134b 18–29.
3 *Eud. Eth.* 22.
4 *Pol.* 1.2.1253A.
5 *De Rep.* III,28,33–34.
6 *De Rep.* III,27.
7 *De Off.* III.3.
8 *On the Statutes* 12.3.
9 See *De lib. arb.*, i.6.
10 See *De Trin.*, xi.15.
11 See *De lib. arb.* i.8.
12 *Contra Faustum Manichaeum* xxii.27.
13 See *Digest* I.1.
14 *Digest* I.1.1–4.
15 *Decretum* 1.
16 ST I.
17 ST I–II 90.4.
18 *Phys.* II.1 193a28–29.
19 ST I–II 94.2.
20 II–II 110.3.
21 II–II 10.12.
22 II–II 64.5.
23 II–II 78.1.
24 II–II 154.11.
25 ST I–II 91.4.

26 This is emphasised by Heinrich A. Rommen, *The Natural Law: A Study in Legal and Social History and Philosophy*, trans. Thomas R. Hanley, OSB (St Louis: B. Herder, 1946), ch. 2.

27 *In Sent.* II, q.19P.

28 'Secular Authority', iii.4.

29 Calvin held that, though it does not provide saving knowledge, God's law is inscribed on our hearts (Inst. 1.3.1), that human nature is endowed with a natural sense of justice that is not completely obliterated by sin (2.2.13), and that the content of the natural law conforms to what is taught in scripture (4.20.14,15).

30 Richard Tuck, *Natural Rights Theories: Their Origin and Development* (New York: Cambridge University Press, 1979), p. 66.

31 Grotius, *De iure belli et pacis*, I.iii.

32 *Leviathan* I.13.

33 See Max Weber, 'Political as Vocation' and 'Science as Vocation' in H. Gerth and C. Wright Mills, ed., *Max Weber: Essays in Sociology* (New York: Oxford University Press, 1958), chs. 4–5.

34 Bentham, *An Introduction to the Principles of Morals and Legislation* (New York: Macmillan, 1948), p. 1.

35 *Ibid.*, pp. 18–19.

36 *Man and the State* (Chicago: University of Chicago Press, 1951), p. 86.

37 *We Hold These Truths: Catholic Reflections on the American Proposition* (New York: Sheed and Ward, 1960), p. 109.

38 *Ibid.*, pp. 327–328.

39 For recent attempts to develop Murray's work, see J. Leon Hooper, SJ, and Todd David Whitmore, ed., *John Courtney Murray and the Growth of Tradition* (Kansas City: Sheed and Ward, 1996). The continuing influence of Murray is seen in the work of Roman Catholic theologian David Hollenbach, *Justice, Peace, and Human Rights: American Catholic Social Ethics in a Pluralistic World* (New York: Crossroad, 1988), and Protestant theologian Robin W. Lovin, *Christian Faith and Public Choices: The Social Ethics of Barth, Brunner, and Bonhoeffer* (Philadelphia: Fortress, 1984), and Robin W. Lovin, ed., *Religion and American Public Life* (New York/Mahwah: Paulist, 1986).

40 Joseph Komanchak, '*Humanae Vitae* and Its Reception', *Theological Studies* 39 (1978):253.

41 See L. Cahill, *Sex, Gender, and Christian Ethics* (Cambridge: Cambridge University Press, 1995).

42 The seminal essay was Germain Grisez, 'The First Principle of Practical Reason: A Commentary on the *Summa theologiae*, 1–2, Question 94, Article 2', *Natural Law Forum* 10 (1965):168–201. This school is represented in many of the essays in Robert P. George, ed., *Natural Law Theory: Contemporary Essays* (Oxford: Clarendon Press, 1992).

43 *Treatise of Human Nature* iii.1.1.

44 See, for example, Mary Midgley, *Beast and Man: The Roots of Human Nature* (Ithaca, NY: Cornell University Press, 1978).

45 For the debate see Emil Brunner and Karl Barth, *Natural Theology*, trans. P. Fraenkel (London: Geoffry Bles, Centenary Press, 1946). A helpful discussion of Protestant views of natural law is found in Michael Cromartie, ed., *A Preserving*

Grace: Protestants, Catholics, and Natural Law (Washington, DC: Ethics and Public Policy Center; Grand Rapids, MI: Eerdmans, 1997).

46 See Stanley Hauerwas, *A Community of Character: Toward a Constructive Christian Social Ethic* (Notre Dame: University of Notre Dame Press, 1981).

47 See Pamela Hall, *Narrative and the Natural Law: An Interpretation of Thomistic Ethics* (Notre Dame: University of Notre Dame Press, 1999, reprint).

48 See Jeffrey Stout, *The Flight from Authority: Religion, Morality, and the Quest for Autonomy* (Notre Dame: University of Notre Dame Press, 1981), and also his essay in George, ed., *Natural Law Theory.*

49 See, for example, Lisa Sowle Cahill, 'Natural Law: A Feminist Reassessment', in Leroy S. Rouner, ed., *Is There a Human Nature?* (Notre Dame: University of Notre Dame Press, 1997), pp. 78–91, and also Susan Frank Parsons, *Feminism and Christian Ethics* (Cambridge: Cambridge University Press, 1996).

50 *A Testament of Hope: The Essential Writings of Martin Luther King, Jr.*, ed. James Melvin Washington (San Francisco, CA: Harper and Row, 1986), p. 293.

7 Virtue ethics

JEAN PORTER

A virtue is a trait of character or intellect which is in some way praiseworthy, admirable or desirable. When we refer to somebody's virtues, what we usually have in mind are relatively stable and effective dispositions to act in particular ways, as opposed to inclinations which are easily lost, or which do not consistently lead to corresponding kinds of action. And so, for example, someone who has the virtue of generosity will consistently respond in generous ways in a variety of situations, including those in which generosity is difficult or costly, in contrast to someone who is moved by pity to one uncharacteristically generous act, or someone whose generous impulses are frequently overcome by desires for self-indulgence. Today, the virtues are normally understood to be morally praiseworthy traits of character, but this has not always been the case; for example, many ancient and medieval writers considered intelligence and wit to be virtues.

Probably every society has identified certain human characteristics as being especially praiseworthy and worth cultivating, while also identifying others as vices, which are morally corrupt, contemptible or otherwise undesirable. These traditions of virtues, in turn, have frequently given rise to systematic reflection on what it means to be virtuous. Virtue ethics, understood as a process of systematic, critical reflection on the virtues and related topics, is particularly likely to emerge in conditions of social change, when received traditions of the virtues undergo development and criticism. These observations apply to Christian societies as much as to any others. From the outset, Christians have identified certain traits of character as virtues which are distinctively characteristic of their way of life, while condemning others as vices which undermine the life of the soul and the well-being of the community. At some points, these Christian virtue traditions have given rise to systematic theories of virtue in response to encounters with other traditions of virtue or to internal criticisms and developments.

What follows is an overview of the development of a Christian tradition of the virtues and of the theoretical reflections on virtue which have emerged out of that tradition. This overview will necessarily be brief and schematic, but hopefully it will serve as a guide to a more in-depth study of different aspects of this rich and varied tradition.

SOURCES

Two sources have been formative for Christian reflection on the virtues, namely the ideals and theories of virtue which emerged in Greek antiquity and were further elaborated in the Hellenistic Roman empire, and the ideals of virtue set forth or implied in scripture.[1]

In Athenian society, the heroic virtues which were appropriate to the warlike society of archaic Greece became increasingly problematic in the more settled, urban conditions of that society. These social changes, in turn, gave rise to systematic philosophical reflection on the virtues. The philosopher Socrates (469–399 BCE) is portrayed by his pupil Plato (c. 428–348 BCE) as someone who continually challenged the ideals of virtue cherished by his fellow-citizens, not in order to undermine the virtuous life, but to arrive at a more adequate conception of virtue.[2] It is difficult to say how far Socrates' views as expressed in Plato's dialogues should be taken as reflecting the position of Socrates himself, as opposed to reflecting Plato's own thought. However, a number of scholars consider it likely that the views expressed by 'Socrates' in the early dialogues do go back to the historical Socrates. On this basis, Socrates is thought to have held that virtue is a kind of wisdom or knowledge concerning what is truly good, possession of which is the only genuine human happiness. Furthermore, since all the virtues are forms of this wisdom, they are all essentially expressions of one quality, a view which came to be known as the unity of the virtues.

At any rate, Plato almost certainly took the starting points for his own theory of virtue from Socrates.[3] Like Socrates, he understood virtue to consist in knowledge or insight into what is truly good, but he goes beyond his teacher to assert that this insight can only be attained through an immediate perception of the Forms of Beauty, Goodness, Justice and the other Forms. Thanks to this perception, the human person is enabled to bring the different components of the soul into right relation with one another, with reason governing the passions. Furthermore, he or she will be inspired by these Forms to attempt to create their images in human society through sustaining right relations with others. In an ideal society, philosophers (including women as well as men) would rule in accordance with their vision of the Forms, and other members of society would function in the way best suited to the talents of each individual under the direction of the philosophers, with all working together harmoniously for the good of the whole. In this way, justice would be embodied in the society, just as the harmonious relation among the capacities of the soul embodies justice in the individual.

Plato's disciple Aristotle (384–322 BCE) is sceptical of the former's claim that the virtues are grounded in a vision of the Forms, an idea which Aristotle rejects for its lack (in his view) of conceptual clarity.[4] Instead, he argues that we should analyse the virtues in terms of our best understanding of the distinctively human form of goodness, which he identifies as action in accordance with reason, or more specifically, practical wisdom, or equivalently, virtuous action.[5] In contrast to Plato, Aristotle does not equate virtue with knowledge *tout court*, but considers it to include appropriate emotional responses as well as correct judgements.[6] He asserts that the virtues are connected, since all of them depend in some way on practical wisdom, but not that they are all forms of one quality.[7]

The most distinctive aspect of Aristotle's theory of the virtues is his doctrine of the mean, according to which the virtues are stable dispositions leading to reactions and behaviour in accordance with a mean as that is determined by practical wisdom.[8] Aristotle's mean is sometimes equated with moderation, but this is inaccurate; it is better understood in terms of the degree and kind of passions and actions appropriate to a particular situation. (In a given situation, the most appropriate response might consist in intense passion or drastic action; for example, extreme anger would be an appropriate response to the sight of someone torturing a child.) This line of analysis provides a way to distinguish true virtues from their similitudes, and thus to deal with the competing claims about virtue prevalent in Athenian society. For example, Aristotle offers an extended discussion of that pre-eminently heroic virtue, courage, in which he distinguishes true courage, grounded in reasoned judgements about the kinds of risks which a good person should undertake, from the skill of the professional soldier and the recklessness which (we might suspect) would have characterised warriors in archaic Greece.[9]

Among later classical philosophers, the most important for subsequent Christian reflection on the virtues is undoubtedly the Roman statesman and philosopher Cicero (106–43 BCE); indeed, his general influence on subsequent Christian ethics can scarcely be overstated.[10] Although Cicero's reputation as an original philosopher is not high today, he is credited with finding ways to express Hellenistic philosophy in forms accessible to the Latin-speaking, practical-minded Roman world of his time. In the process, he developed an account of virtue, predominantly although not exclusively

Stoic in origin, which was to be formative for medieval Christian reflection on the virtues. Specifically, he endorsed the Aristotelian/Stoic view that virtue should be understood as a disposition to act in accordance with right reason.[11] He also offered a fourfold division of the virtues into practical wisdom or prudence, justice, courage and temperance, which, under the rubric of primary or cardinal virtues, was to be highly influential in the medieval period.[12] At the same time, he offered a critique of the Aristotelian view according to which practical wisdom is the primary virtue, arguing that we should assign this honour to justice instead.[13] It is not hard to see that this reflects yet another shift in socially sanctioned ideals of virtue, away from the intellectual qualities prized by Athenian society and towards the ideals of justice and equitable administration cherished by the Romans.

It may seem surprising that so little has been said so far about the other primary source for Christian reflection on the virtues, namely scripture itself.[14] Yet at first glance, the scriptures do not appear to have much to say about the virtues. In the Hebrew scriptures, there is no term corresponding to 'virtue', and while much attention is given to moral questions, these are generally answered by appeals to God's Law and the wisdom which it confers. Nonetheless, the Hebrew scriptures do present distinctive ideals of character, especially in the wisdom literature, which offers the exemplary types of the wise person and the fool as representative of personal characteristics which should be cultivated or shunned. Furthermore, the prophetic literature reflects an emphasis on interior disposition, seen in contrast to outward observance, which resembles the focus on character that we find in most accounts of the virtues.

Similarly, while the virtues do not form a central theme in the New Testament writings, these do offer some accounts of the character traits which are especially appropriate to, or inconsistent with, the Christian life. Paul offers a number of lists of such character traits, for example at Gal. 5:22ff, which have provided starting points for Christian reflection on the virtues up to the present day. However, his formulation of faith, hope and love as the guiding ideals of the Christian life has been even more important for Christian virtue ethics than these summary lists (1 Cor. 13:13). Subsequently, faith, hope and love came to be identified as the paradigmatic theological virtues, seen in contrast to the cardinal virtues. In addition, later Christian thinkers have drawn on New Testament images of Jesus and of the early church to identify other distinctively Christian virtues, for example, the humility which Jesus displayed in his human condition and the meekness which he showed towards his persecutors during his Passion and crucifixion.

PATRISTIC AND EARLY MEDIEVAL ACCOUNTS OF VIRTUE

Among patristic authors, the bishop and theologian Augustine of Hippo (354–430) stands out for the extent and depth of his reflections on the virtues.[15] Like those of the classical authors we have been considering, Augustine's theoretical reflections on virtue were driven by, and in turn helped to guide, his engagement with the ideals of virtue which he inherited from his society. In Augustine's case, this meant the ideals of virtue which informed the society of the later Roman empire, including justice, courage and a high-minded regard for one's reputation among other men and women of virtue. In the *City of God*, Augustine remarks that because the virtues of the pagans are not grounded in knowledge of the true God, they should be understood as vices, expressions of pride rather than true virtues.[16] Taken in isolation this comment is misleading; Augustine hesitates to condemn the so-called virtues of the pagans as vicious without remainder, and he does acknowledge that they are praiseworthy in some respects. Nonetheless, he insists that the seeming virtues of the pagans cannot be true virtues, because they are not informed by knowledge and love of God, the only source of true goodness.

This re-evaluation of classical virtue correlates with Augustine's more theoretical analysis of true, that is to say Christian, virtue. Augustine follows both Plato and the Stoics in claiming that the virtues are all fundamentally expressions of one quality, but for him that quality is Christian love.[17] This love bestows the ability to place all human affections in their right order, loving God above all, and loving creatures as expressions of God's goodness, within the parameters set by God's decrees. As his thought developed, Augustine became increasingly conscious that love of God leads naturally to love of the neighbour, whom we are called upon to regard as a potential companion in the enjoyment of divine goodness and to cherish for God's sake.

In the long term, Augustine probably had a greater impact on subsequent Christian virtue ethics than any other patristic author. However, in the short term his account of the virtues was probably less influential than the practical, pastorally oriented discussions of the virtues and vices offered by the monastic writer John Cassian (c. 360 – c.435) and Pope Gregory the Great (c. 540–604).[18] Cassian wrote primarily for monks and ascetics, whereas Gregory was more concerned with offering guidelines for the pastoral care of lay Christians. But for both of them, the most urgent challenge of the Christian life is to identify and eliminate the vices which lead to sin. To aid the Christian in this task, the abbot or pastor needs some practical knowledge of the virtues, understood as qualities which correct the vices. That is what both Cassian and Gregory attempt to provide, in the form of analytic lists of the most serious vices and the virtues which serve to correct them. Seen from the perspective of the sophistication and psychological insight of Augustine's analysis, this approach might appear to be a step backwards. Yet it met a real need, and it was much imitated in later patristic and medieval times. For example, in the *Summa virtutum de remediis anime*, a late-thirteenth-century pastoral handbook on which Chaucer drew in his *Parson's Tale*, the virtues are arranged in accordance with the seven deadly vices which they counteract; hence, humility is presented as the remedy for pride, charity is said to be the remedy for envy, and so forth.

In the early-medieval period, moral reflection was practically oriented, and the virtues did not receive extended theoretical analysis. Nonetheless, pastors and preachers continued to discuss the virtues and vices, together with related topics such as the gifts of the Holy Spirit and the beatitudes. As a result, by the time of the emergence of scholasticism in the twelfth century there was a considerable tradition of reflection on the virtues which invited reflection and synthetic analysis.

MEDIEVAL DEVELOPMENTS

In the eleventh century, Western Europe began to experience far-reaching social and economic changes, which were consolidated through reforms and innovations in religious and intellectual life. These social and institutional changes led to systematic reformulations of existing moral traditions, including centrally the Christian tradition of the virtues.[19]

In the early scholastic period, we find two contrasting approaches to the virtues, as exemplified by the writings of Peter Abelard (1074 – c. 1142) and Peter Lombard (c. 1100–60).[20] Abelard understood virtue in Aristotelian terms as a stable disposition which enables persons to act morally.[21] In contrast, Peter Lombard proposed a strictly theological account of the virtues in his *Sentences*, a highly influential analytic compendium of key statements from patristic authorities. In this work, he defines virtue as a good quality of the mind which God brings about in us without our activity – a definition which takes its terms from Augustine's writings, although the formulation is Peter's own.[22] As he goes on to explain, God brings about virtue in the soul, while we bring about the acts of virtue through our exercise of free will in cooperation with God's grace. Hence, there can be no true virtue without grace, and by implication there is no place in Christian theology for a distinctively philosophical analysis of the virtues.

Subsequently, most scholastics attempted to combine philosophical and theological perspectives on the virtues. One very common approach, exemplified by William of Auxerre (c. 1150–1231) in his *Summa aurea*, was to distinguish between the theological virtues of faith, hope and charity, which are dependent on grace, and the political virtues, identified with the classical cardinal virtues, which are necessary for all social life. In William's view, the political virtues stem from the basic principles of the natural law. These in turn are known through a vision of God as supreme good which, in William's view, is present in every human soul.[23] William expressly attributes to Augustine the view that the fundamental principles of virtue are known through direct divine illumination; he is almost certainly wrong in his reading of Augustine, but it is nonetheless apparent that his theory reflects the strong influence of Augustinian and Platonic conceptions of virtue.[24] Because the principles of the political virtues are knowable to all persons, they are attainable without grace, and for this reason they cannot lead to salvation. Yet they do serve as a preparation for the theological virtues, and they provide a medium through which the theological virtues can be expressed in external acts.[25]

We find a second approach to synthesising philosophical and theological perspectives on the virtues in the writings of Thomas Aquinas (c. 1225–74), who offers the most influential scholastic theory of the virtues and their place in the Christian life. In his last theological treatise, the *Summa theologiae*, Aquinas identifies Peter Lombard's Augustinian definition of virtue as the best definition overall: 'Virtue is a good quality of the mind, by which we live righteously, of which no one can make bad use, which God brings about in us, without us.'[26] However, he goes on in this article to say that the last clause applies only to the infused virtues, which God bestows on us without action on our part. In this way, he introduces a distinction between infused virtues, which have union with God as their direct or indirect aim, and acquired virtues, which are directed towards the attainment of the human good as discerned by reason.[27] This takes the place of the distinction between political and theological virtues as an organising principle, although Aquinas does comment briefly on the latter division.[28]

The acquired virtues are identified with the cardinal virtues, which can be understood either as general qualities of moral goodness or as specific virtues with their own characteristic forms of expression.[29] However, the infused virtues include not only the theological virtues, but also infused cardinal virtues, which are specifically different from their acquired counterparts because they are directed towards a different end.[30] While on Aquinas' view no one can attain salvation without the infused virtues, he also holds that those virtues which are acquired by human effort are genuine virtues, albeit in a limited sense.[31]

Like Abelard, Aquinas follows Aristotle in the view that a virtue is a stable disposition which inclines the person to act in one way rather than another.[32] Earlier, he had explained that such dispositions are necessary for the rational creature to be capable of action at all; for example, the basic human capacity for speech will not enable a person actually to speak until he or she has learned a language.[33] As this example suggests, the virtues include intellectual capabilities, such as knowledge, which are morally neutral.[34] The virtues which shape the passions and the will, and the intellect insofar as it is oriented to action, are of course moral qualities.[35] Each distinct faculty of the soul has its corresponding virtue, identified with one of the four cardinal virtues. Prudence or practical wisdom, which is strictly speaking a virtue of the practical intellect, enables the agent to choose in accordance with her overall conception of goodness; justice orients the will towards the common good; fortitude shapes the irascible passions in such a way as to resist obstacles to attaining what is truly good; and temperance shapes the passions of desire in such a way that the agent desires what is truly in accordance with the overall good.[36] The theological virtues are likewise associated with specific faculties; faith is a virtue of the intellect, while hope and charity are virtues of the will.[37] Aquinas also follows Aristotle in holding that the virtues are connected; all of them presuppose prudence for their exercise, and in the case of the infused virtues they presuppose charity as well.[38]

So far, we have focused on academic discussions of the virtues. However, throughout the later medieval period the virtues were also a favourite theme for literary works, preaching and practical pastoral advice. These treatments of the virtues tended to employ the older schema of the virtues as correctives to the vices, yet in the writings of Chaucer and Dante this old schema took on unprecedented beauty and power.

CHRISTIAN VIRTUE ETHICS IN THE MODERN PERIOD

Interest in the virtues began to wane with the advent of the modern period in the fifteenth century. This 'turn from the virtues' reflected the theological critiques of Martin Luther (1483–1546) and other reformers, as well as the thoroughgoing rejection of virtue ethics by modern natural-law thinkers beginning with Grotius (1583–1645).[39] (In these latter critiques, we see the beginnings of a sharp dichotomy between virtue and law which was unknown to the ancients and the medieval scholastics, but which has shaped so much recent work on the virtues.) More fundamentally, the turn from virtue-oriented approaches to ethics reflected the growing complexity of modern moral discourse, which could not readily be accommodated within the traditional schemas of virtues and vices.[40]

Yet during this period, the virtues were not altogether neglected, either by moral philosophers or by theologians. The moral-sense theorists, who attempted to account for morality in terms of natural sentiments of approval or disapproval, suggested a new way of thinking about the virtues.[41] This approach was fully developed by the most significant of these theorists, David Hume (1711–76). According to Hume, morality is grounded in feelings of approval and disapproval towards motives for action (one's own or another's), such as courage, generosity or parental affection. He explicitly links these motives with virtues, which he takes to be dispositions to respond and act in particular ways. He goes on to argue that the passions and desires which give rise to the virtues do not depend directly on reason, which differs from the passions precisely in that it cannot move us to action. This represents a break with the dominant classical and medieval understanding of the virtues, according to which they are always at least informed by rational judgements even if they do not consist in knowledge or reasonableness alone. However, Hume does grant that one important class of virtues depends on reason indirectly, namely artificial virtues such as justice, which presuppose rational social conventions for their origin and exercise.

Hume's reputation as an anti-theological philosopher has perhaps led theologians to underestimate his importance for virtue ethics. Yet his account of the virtues continues to be influential among moral philosophers, and deserves consideration by anyone interested in the virtues.[42] The moral-sense approach to ethics also gave rise to one of the most interesting theological theories of virtue in the modern period, namely *The Nature of True Virtue*, written by the Puritan theologian Jonathan Edwards (1703–58).

Edwards follows Hume and the other moral-sense theorists in the view that moral judgements are founded in sentiment rather than reason.[43] This sentiment he describes as a sense of delight in the presence of virtue, described by him as a kind of beauty of disposition and action. So far, his account of virtue is reminiscent of Hume's, but the distinctiveness of his theory becomes apparent in what comes next. According to Edwards, the beauty of virtue can be understood on two levels, which correspond to two distinct stances of the will. On one level, it consists of harmony and proportion, expressed in human relationships by justice. On another level, virtue is understood as benevolence towards Being in general, which necessarily implies love of God as the supreme and infinite Being. Love of virtue in the first sense, that is, natural virtue, is not salvific. Yet this natural virtue is a genuine excellence, and it is subsumed and transformed rather than being destroyed by the love of Being as such. Virtue in this latter sense is true virtue, the expression of grace in the human heart, and as such it is an effect and sign, although not a cause, of election.

Still more important from the standpoint of theological virtue ethics is the work of Friedrich Schleiermacher (1768–1834), considered by many to be the originator of modern Protestant theology.[44] According to him, all genuine religion stems from an awareness of the infinite and eternal ground of finite realities, together with a sense of our absolute dependence on that divine reality. For the Christian, this sense of dependence on the divine is expressed in terms of the role of Jesus Christ as the mediator between us and God, although Schleiermacher does not claim that this is the only possible expression for an authentic religious sense.

Schleiermacher's most significant contribution to virtue ethics probably lies in this overall theology, which has inspired a theological ethics of piety or Christian disposition among both English-speaking and German theologians.[45] At the same time, his explicit theory of virtue is also worthy of note. In his view, ethical reasoning necessarily incorporates three ideas, namely the highest good, duty and virtue. Although these ideas are interconnected, each provides a distinctive perspective on moral reasoning. In particular, he interprets virtue as a capacity which enables the individual to understand and to act upon the concrete implications of the moral law. In this respect, his concept of virtue is very similar to the Aristotelian idea of practical wisdom, an idea which is not otherwise much represented until recently in modern moral reflection.

The classical antecedents of Schleiermacher's theory of virtue become even clearer when we turn to his analysis of specific forms of virtue. He analyses particular virtues in terms of a taxonomy of the basic structures of human action and experience. Action is always either internal or external, directed either towards the acquisition of symbolic knowledge within the agent, or towards bringing about something in the outside world. Human existence more generally considered is structured by reason and sensuality, which sometimes work together and sometimes conflict. Hence, the capacity for action will sometimes take the form of reason struggling with sensuality, while at other times it will be expressed through the operation of reason as informed by sensuality, in which case reason becomes a power of inspiration. This analysis leads to a fourfold division of the virtues: the capacity for symbolic knowledge generates wisdom when it is inspired, and it is expressed in reflectiveness or mental temperance when it reflects reason's control of sensuality; the power of external action gives rise to love when it is inspired, and to fortitude when the agent's rational control of sensuality is expressed in external actions. In this way, Schleiermacher reformulates the traditional cardinal virtues.

CONTEMPORARY THEOLOGICAL VIRTUE ETHICS

During the early part of the twentieth century, virtue was not a major theme among either Catholic or Protestant theologians. Among Catholics, the lack of interest in the virtues stemmed from an emphasis on the natural law understood as a set of rules which came to dominate Catholic moral theology after the Council of Trent. In contrast, virtue ethics was an important theme in the nineteenth century, thanks to the work of Schleiermacher, Albrecht Ritschl and others.[46] But the critiques of Karl Barth and other neo-orthodox theologians in the early twentieth century led many Protestants to reject the central themes of liberal evangelism, including its emphasis on virtue.

However, throughout the twentieth century, a number of theologians, both Catholic and Protestant, rediscovered traditions of virtues and virtue ethics as a resource for theological ethics. In fact, there were several efforts to retrieve the idea of virtue for Christian theology which were more or less distinct from one another.

The first of these came about as part of a wider effort to free Catholic moral theology from what was seen as an overly legalistic emphasis on the natural law. The best-known and most influential of the theologians involved in this effort was Bernard Häring.[47] For Häring, the Christian moral life leads naturally to a cultivation of the sense of God's presence. Hence, ordinary Christian moral duties are inseparable from the practice of some form of spirituality, and, correlatively, spiritual practices are not just for those who are seeking a higher perfection. By the same token, the moral life cannot be reduced to the observance of moral laws. Häring develops his vision of the Christian moral life by drawing on Aquinas' claim that the virtues, especially the theological virtues, are the principles through which grace becomes active. Similarly, the Jesuit moral theologian Gerard Gilleman attempted to retrieve Aquinas' account of charity as the root of the Christian moral and spiritual life.[48]

A second effort to retrieve virtue ethics has been predominantly philosophical rather than theological, but it has had a widespread influence among theologians. This movement originated in the pioneering work of Elizabeth Anscombe, Philippa Foot and Iris Murdoch, and it began to attract widespread attention through Alasdair MacIntyre's *After Virtue*.[49] In this book, he argued that moral discourse today consists of fragmented survivals from earlier moral traditions, and that that is why it is so acrimonious and unsatisfying. Coherence in moral discourse requires a more or less unified moral tradition, in which ideals of virtue will necessarily play a central role. Subsequently, a growing number of philosophers have turned their attention to the virtues and related topics, including the moral significance of the emotions and the importance of particular communities and traditions for moral judgement.

Since the early 1970s there has been a further revival of interest in virtue ethics among both Protestant and Catholic theologians. One strand of this most recent revival has developed in tandem with a growing interest in the recovery of Aquinas' moral thought among both Catholic and Protestant theologians.[50] Another strand takes its starting points from the work of the U.S. theologian Stanley Hauerwas, for whom the ideas of virtue and character, rather than moral rules, provide the most appropriate framework for reflection on the Christian moral life.[51] According to him, the Christian community is rooted in ideals of non-violence and communal solidarity quite different from those which prevail in the dominant culture, and Christian ethics should reflect these differences by focusing on the virtues which enable the individual to live in a truly Christian fashion. Hence, Hauerwas places considerable emphasis on retrieving a particular tradition of virtues. Among Protestant scholars on the Continent, there has been less interest in the virtues until recently. This situation is changing, however, as German theologians rediscover those aspects of Lutheran and Reformed theology which are more friendly to the idea of virtue, in particular its emphasis on the active dispositions through which God's grace works in individual lives and in the community.[52]

There is some tendency among theologians to assume that the only options for developing a Christian virtue ethics are those presented by the Aristotelian/Thomistic tradition and the communitarian approach of Hauerwas and his followers. Yet, as this summary indicates, Christian virtue ethics comprises many different approaches. Similarly, theologians today are turning to virtue ethics out of a variety of different concerns. For this reason, it would be a mistake to assume that there is one definitive form of virtue ethics, or even that all virtue ethicists would agree about the meaning and implications of the concept of virtue. For many of these ethicists, there is a critical difference between virtue ethics and an approach to morality based on rules. For them, the moral life should be understood in terms of dispositions of character and prudential judgement, rather than in obedience to clearly formulated moral laws. For others, virtue ethics is valuable because it provides a framework for reflection on the place of knowledge, will and the passions in the moral life. Those who take this approach recognise the importance of responsiveness and judgement in the moral life, but they do not necessarily draw a sharp dichotomy between virtue and rule-based approaches to morality. A growing number of theologians are following Hauerwas' lead by reflecting on the specific virtues which are particularly characteristic of the Christian life, and, similarly, some Protestant theologians are beginning to explore virtue ethics as a way of formulating some individual and communal aspects of the experience of God's grace. Although the most recent revival of virtue ethics has already produced much distinguished work, the Christian tradition of the virtues still offers many unexplored possibilities for theological ethics.

Notes

1 For an illuminating overview of reflection on virtue in the ancient world, see Julia Annas, *The Morality of Happiness*, Oxford: Oxford University Press, 1993, pp. 47–134; for a discussion which emphasises the social contexts for this reflection, see Alasdair MacIntyre, *After Virtue*, Notre Dame: University of Notre Dame Press, 1984 (second ed.), pp. 121–164.

2 In what follows, I draw on Terence Irwin, *Classical Thought*, Oxford: Oxford University Press, 1989, pp. 68–84. For examples of Socrates' method as applied to moral questions, see Plato's *Euthyphro* 4b–e, 5c–d, and *Laches* 191a and following; for his claim that the virtues are all a form of knowledge, and therefore all expressions of one quality, see for example *Laches* 198a–99c; for the equation of wisdom and happiness, see for example *Euthydemus* 280b, 281 d–e.

3 For my account of Plato's theory of virtue, I rely on Irwin, *Classical Thought*, pp. 85–117, and Gregory Vlastos, *Studies in Greek Philosophy II: Socrates, Plato, and Their Tradition*, Daniel W. Graham, editor, Princeton: Princeton University Press, 1995, pp. 69–146. Many examples could be offered for the claims summarised here; for an example of a passage which brings together many of the leading themes of Plato's thought, see the parable of the cave, *Republic* 514a–520e.

4 *Nicomachean Ethics* 1096a 10–1096b 15.

5 *NE* 1098a 10–15, 1144b 1–1145a 14; for more on Aristotle's account of reason and virtue, see Richard Sorabji, 'Aristotle on the Role of Intellect in Virtue' in *Essays on Aristotle's Ethics*, Amelie Oksenberg Rorty, editor, Berkeley and Los Angeles: University of California Press, 1980, pp. 201–200.

6 *NE* 1102a 5–1103a 10.

7 *NE* 1144b 15–30.

8 *NE* 1106b 35–1107 a 25; for further discussion, see J. O. Urmson, 'Aristotle's Doctrine of the Mean' in Rorty, ed., pp. 157–170.

9 *NE* 1116a 15–117a 29. However, he is not the first to apply an analysis of the virtues to the task of distinguishing true and false courage; see Plato's *Laches* 191a–193e.

10 In what follows, I draw extensively on Maria L. Colish, *The Stoic Tradition from Antiquity to the Early Middle Ages*, Vol. I: *Stoicism in Classical Latin Literature*, Leiden: Brill, 1990, pp. 61–79 and 85–89.

11 *De inventione* II, LII 159.

12 *Ibid.*

13 *De officiis* I, 157–158.

14 For a helpful discussion of the concept of virtue in scripture, particularly in the Hebrew Bible, see John Barton, 'Virtue in the Bible', *Studies in Christian Ethics*, 1999, 12.1, pp. 12–22.

15 For an especially illuminating account of Augustine's theory of virtue seen in relation to its classical antecedents, see John M. Rist, *Augustine: Ancient Thought Baptized*, Cambridge: Cambridge University Press, 1994, pp. 148–202.

16 *De Civitate Dei* 19.25.

17 *De moribus ecclesiae catholicae* I 15.25.

18 I rely here on Siegfried Wenzel, 'Introduction' in *Summa virtutum de remediis anime*, S. Wenzel, editor, Athens: University of Georgia Press, 1984, pp. 2–12.

19 The best account of the development of reflection on the virtues in the medieval period is provided by the essays collected in Odon Lottin, *Psychologie et morale aux XII et XIII siècles*, vol. III, part 2.1 and part 2.2, Louvain: Abbaye du Mont César, 1949; for a more recent and very illuminating discussion, focused primarily on the later medieval period, see Bonnie Kent, *Virtues of the Will: The Transformation of Ethics in the Late Thirteenth Century*, Washington, DC: Catholic University of America Press, 1995.

20 On Abelard and Peter Lombard, see Lottin, *Psychologie et morale*, 2.1, pp. 100–104; for a more detailed account of Abelard's theory of virtue, see John Marenbon, *The Philosophy of Peter Abelard*, Cambridge: Cambridge University Press, 1997, pp. 282–287.

21 *Dialogus inter philosophum, judaeum et christianum*, PL 178, 1651 C – 1652 A.

22 *Libri II Sent.* 27.1.

23 *Summa aurea* III 18 intro, 18.4.

24 *SA* III 18.4.

25 *SA* III 19 intro.

26 *Summa theologiae* I–II 55.4, quoting II *Sentences* 27.5.

27 *ST* I–II 63.3.

28 *ST* I–II 61.5.

29 *ST* I–II 61.1.

30 *ST* I–II 63.3, 4.

31 *ST* I–II 62.1, 2.

32 *ST* I–II 55.1.

33 *ST* I–II 49.4.

34 *ST* I–II 56.3; 57.1; 58.3.

35 *ST* I–II 58.1.

36 *ST* I–II 59.2; 60.3–5.

37 *ST* II–II 4.2; 18.1; 24.1.

38 *ST* I–II 65.1.

39 For Grotius' critique of virtue, see J. B. Schneewind, *The Invention of Autonomy: A History of Modern Moral Philosophy*, Cambridge: Cambridge University Press, 1998, pp. 75–78.

40 This point is argued in J. B. Schneewind, 'The Misfortunes of Virtue', *Ethics*, 1990, 101, pp. 42–63.

41 For an account of the recovery of virtue among the moral-sense theorists, see Schneewind, *Invention of Autonomy*, pp. 285–309; for an account of Hume's theory of virtue, see *ibid.*, 1998, pp. 354–377.

42 For a good example of a contemporary appropriation of Hume's theory of the virtues, see the essays collected in Annette C. Baier, *Moral Prejudices: Essays on Ethics*, Cambridge, MA: Harvard University Press, 1994.

43 In my account of Edwards' theory of virtue, I draw extensively on William K. Frankena's foreword in Jonathan Edwards, *The Nature of True Virtue*, Ann Arbor: University of Michigan Press, 1960 (originally published 1765), pp. v–xiii; the main lines of that theory are set forth by Edwards in the first chapter of that book, pp. 1–13.

44 For a very helpful overview of Schleiermacher's theology, see B. A. Gerrish, *A Prince of the Church: Schleiermacher and the Beginnings of Modern Theology*, Philadelphia: Fortress Press, 1984; in my account of his account of virtue, I depend on John Wallhausser, 'Schleiermacher's Critique of Ethical Reason: Toward a Systematic Ethics', *Journal of Religious Ethics*, 1989, 17.2, pp. 25–40, and Eilert Herms, 'Virtue: A Neglected Concept in Protestant Ethics', *Scottish Journal of Theology*, 1982, 35, pp. 481–495.

45 Most notably, James Gustafson, *Ethics from a Theocentric Perspective*, vol. I: *Theology and Ethics*, and vol. II: *Ethics and Theology*, Chicago: University of Chicago Press, 1981 and 1984, and Konrad Stock, *Grundlegung der protestantischen Tugendlehre*, Gutersloh: Chr. Kaiser/Gutersloher Verlagshaus, 1995.

46 On the turn from virtue ethics in twentieth-century Protestant thought, and prospects for its revival, see Herms, 'Virtue'.

47 Bernhard Häring, *Law of Christ: Moral Theology for Priests and Laity*, two volumes, translated by Edwin Kaiser, Westminster, MD: Newman Press, 1965; for a good summary of his basic position, see vol. 2, 3.

48 Gerard Gilleman, *The Primacy of Charity in Moral Theology*, translated by William F. Ryan and André Vachon, Westminster, MD: Newman Press, 1959.

49 Anscombe's highly influential essay 'Modern Moral Philosophy' was first published in 1958; it is reprinted as in G. E. M. Anscombe, *Ethics, Religion and Politics: Collected Philosophical Papers*, vol. III, Minneapolis: University of Minnesota Press, 1981, pp. 26–42. In addition, see the essays collected in Philippa Foot, *Virtues and Vices and Other Essays in Moral Philosophy*, Berkeley and Los Angeles: University of California Press, 1978; Iris Murdoch, *The Sovereignty of Good*, New York: Methuen, 1970; and MacIntyre, *After Virtue*.

50 See for example Giuseppe Abba, *Lex et Virtus: Studi sull'evoluzione della dotrina morale di san Tommaso d'Aquino*, Rome: Libreria Ateneo Salesiano, 1983; Diana Fritz Cates, *Choosing to Feel: Virtue, Friendship, and Compassion for Friends*, Notre Dame: University of Notre Dame Press, 1996; James Keenan, *Goodness and Rightness in Thomas Aquinas's 'Summa Theologiae'*, Washington, DC:

Georgetown University Press, 1992; Daniel Mark Nelson, *The Priority of Prudence: Virtue and Natural Law in Thomas Aquinas and Its Implications for Modern Ethics*, University Park: Pennsylvania State University Press, 1992; Jean Porter, *The Recovery of Virtue: The Relevance of Aquinas for Christian Ethics*, Louisville, KY: Westminster/John Knox Press, and London: SPCK, 1990; and Martin Rhonheimer, *Praktische Vernuft und Vernunftigkeit der Praxis*, Berlin: Akademie Verlag, 1994.

51 Hauerwas' writings are very extensive. Stanley Hauerwas, *The Peaceable Kingdom: A Primer in Christian Ethics,* Notre Dame, IN: University of Notre Dame Press, and London: SCM Press, 1981, provides a good statement of his overall views, and S. Hauerwas and C. Pinches, *Christians among the Virtues: Theological Conversations with Ancient and Modern Ethics*, Notre Dame, IN: University of Notre Dame Press, 1997, offers a more recent statement of his views, together with some indication of the directions in which others are developing his ideas.

52 See in particular Stock, *Grundlegung.*

8 Gender and Christian ethics

LISA SOWLE CAHILL

The term 'gender' refers to the personality characteristics, behaviours and social roles that are expected of or assigned to an individual, depending on whether that individual is a male or a female.

Gender is different from biological sex. Although some individuals have ambiguous sex characteristics, the human species is in general sexually dimorphic. Humans come in two sexes, male and female, that cooperate for reproduction. Thus the sexual differentiation of individuals into male and female is taken for granted in virtually all societies, and some biologically based behaviours and roles are almost as universally associated with sexual differentiation. These are the behaviours and roles required for reproduction through sexual intercourse, pregnancy, birthing, and lactation and the associated care of infants.

Because pregnancy, birth and infant care require a protected environment, and because these activities have historically tended to reduce the ability of pregnant and child-bearing females to fend off enemies and obtain food for themselves and their young, corresponding male roles of hunter and protector have also developed. But it is precisely here that gender enters the picture as a problematic category. Even if some gender differentiation in the reproductive sphere is the natural consequence of sexual dimorphism, how far need gender difference extend in prescribing different psychological and cognitive traits in women and men, or different social roles in other areas? To what degree are women by nature designed for childbearing and child care, and men for warfare and material productivity? Are women meant to fulfil duties only in the domestic sphere, while men control the economic and political domains? To what degree are these roles pliable, able to be shared by adults of both sexes? Over the centuries and in many cultures, ethics (normative theories of morality and society) has included either explicit or implicit answers to such questions.

'Ethics' refers to interpretations of and ideals or norms for moral beha-viour, at both the individual and the societal levels. Sometimes ethicists dis-tinguish between personal ethics and social ethics as two separate branches of inquiry. However, they really are closely interdependent. This is espe-cially true and evident in the case of gender. For example, what is considered proper female or male behaviour is important in defining the nature of the family (a social group). It also defines the way men and women participate in social institutions like education, the workplace, government, the mili-tary, religious institutions and so on. Conversely, assumptions about gender roles in a social institution like family, government or religion are very important in establishing options for one's self-understanding and personal behaviour. 'Gender and Christian ethics' indicates Christian views of the characteristics and roles of women and men as they relate to personal and social behaviour, as well as to the institutions of society (like family, work, politics and religion) where personal and social meet.

For most of Christian history, it has been taken for granted that biologi-cal sex entails specific gender roles that go beyond reproduction and child care to include significant differentiation in most domestic and social roles. Behind this assumption is the idea that women were created primarily for reproduction, and are in all other ways weaker than men. Men are assumed to be the natural leaders in public affairs, as well as the supervisors of women's fulfilment of domestic responsibilities. Feminists criticise this world-view and its 'patriarchal' social system. Feminism includes both men and women, especially since patriarchy narrows the range of opportunities and acceptable behaviours open to both. Some thinkers take up the topic of masculinity in its own right, exploring what masculine gender identity might look like in an era in which the old patriarchal stereotypes have broken down.[1]

Christians differ about whether there are innate gender characteristics that go beyond basic reproductive requirements, what they might be, and how they should be institutionalised socially and in the church. For example, many Christians still believe that women's most important respon-sibility is raising a family, while others defend the right of women to enter public and professional roles and receive equal pay for equal work. Many Christians believe men have a duty to exercise headship in the family and to support wife and children economically, while others advocate a more egali-tarian model of marriage and family, in which men and women share both economic and child-nurturing responsibilities.

Christians arguing diverse positions all appeal to the Bible, Christian tradition and contemporary experience and practice for support. Therefore, this chapter will devote much of its attention to what Bible and tradition have said. In the past, since the fact of gender differentiation was assumed, the key ethical question was to define the respective moral obligations of and just treatment towards the 'opposite' sexes. In recent decades, it has been increasingly suggested that gender differences as any culture knows them are not innate, but are largely the product of social conditioning. This opens up the possibility that just treatment within just social institutions may require changing some standard cultural practices and norms of gender behaviour. Therefore, an interesting question to explore in the tradition, especially the New Testament, is whether some standard expectations about gender were in fact challenged more than has been generally appreciated. Does the Bible or other authoritative teaching confirm or unsettle the idea that women and men have distinct and different natures that prescribe certain gender roles, around which family and society are structured? The present overview of gender and Christian ethics will begin with the Old and New Testaments and proceed with some major Christian theologians, before concluding with a discussion of the problem of gender in Christian ethics today.

THE BIBLE AND GENDER

In the Christian Old Testament (or Hebrew Bible) men's and women's roles are clearly differentiated, reflecting the cultural practices of ancient Israel, as of other ancient Near Eastern societies. Men have the primary responsibility to herd and tend flocks, to engage in agriculture, to fulfil religious duties (especially cultic duties associated with the Jerusalem temple and with the priesthood) and to govern. Most of the important figures in the narratives of the Old Testament are male, and the history of the community and its encounters with God is recounted primarily in terms of divinely chosen patriarchs (Abraham, Isaac and Joseph; Moses; King David). The most important duty of Israel's leadership and of the male head of every family was to hand down the religious traditions and practices that constituted Israel as the covenant people of God.

The continuation of Israel depended on the births of heirs, especially sons. Hence, the most important functions of women were to be wives and mothers. Sons were essential to safeguard the patrimony of the family or kin group, and to transmit the traditions of Israel. Marriage in Israel was occasionally polygamous until about the time of the monarchy (tenth century BCE), which allowed men to sire more children. But even in monogamous marriages, concubinage was permitted. The familiar story of Abraham and

Sara illustrates the picture (Gen. 16–17). Sara resorted to using her slave Hagar (who was not consulted) as a sort of 'surrogate mother'. As Sara says to her husband, 'You see that the Lord has prevented me from bearing children; go in to my slave-girl; it may be that I shall obtain children by her' (Gen. 16:2). Hagar does indeed bear a son (Ishmael), but the consequent friction between Sara and Hagar leads to the eventual expulsion of Hagar and her child (albeit under divine protection). After God establishes his covenant with Abraham, however, and promises to make him 'the ancestor of a multitude of nations' (Gen. 17:4), Sara miraculously bears a son (Isaac) in her old age (verse 17:19). Both Hagar and Sara are means to the propagation of Abraham's line of descendants, through which they acquire status in the biblical tradition.

Despite this generally patriarchal framework, some women in the Old Testament are important in their own right, including Deborah, a prophetess who leads forces into battle (Judg. 4–5); Judith, who saves the Jerusalem temple from the Assyrians by getting the general Holofernes drunk and chopping off his head (Jth 12); and Esther, who successfully intercedes for her people with her husband, the Persian king Xerxes, bringing their enemy, Haman, to the gallows (Esther 7).

Even more significantly, the story of the creation of man and woman (Gen. 1–3), so often interpreted to justify female subordination, can be seen in an egalitarian light. As many Christians learn this tale, God created Adam first, then took Eve from his rib, showing a subordinate state that God in fact confirms by pronouncing Eve to be Adam's 'helpmeet'. Worse is Eve's intellectual and moral weakness, for she is deluded by the serpent (Satan) and, desiring to be like God, eats of the forbidden fruit. So enter sin and death into the world through the misdeed of a woman.

The real story is not so simple. First of all, God begins the creation process with inanimate creatures, then living things: animals, then man – and finally woman (Gen. 2). Why not see this as a progression from lower to higher? Moreover, the Hebrew word sometimes translated 'helpmeet' does not have to connote inferiority (it can also mean 'saviour'). Indeed, the New Revised Standard Version of the Bible portrays God as saying that Eve has been made so that Adam can have 'a helper as his partner' (2:18). The story of the pair's disobedience and fall does not necessarily portray Eve as the more weak or guilty party. She is the one who debates with the serpent, while 'her husband, who was with her' the whole time (3:6), waits and does unquestioningly what she suggests. Certainly God sees them as equally deserving of punishment. The divine observation that, after the fall, the man will till the gound in toil and sweat, and the woman will suffer in childbearing and have a husband who will 'rule over' her, is an observation on the consequences of sin – not on the original creation as designed by God (3:16, 19).[2]

The New Testament presents a similarly mixed picture. Many feminist critics make the argument that equality and non-traditional roles for women sound a radically new note in the gospels and epistles, perhaps even louder than the occasional reaffirmation of traditional roles. First, kinship, marriage and the procreation of children are relativised in the New Testament by the imminent approach of God's reign. Early Christians thought Jesus would return soon, maybe even in their own lifetimes, and bring the end of the world as we know it. Disciples are called to replace old ways of life with a 'single-hearted devotion' to Christ that hardly has time for the cares of marriage and family (1 Cor. 7:35). Men no longer pass on the faith by procreating sons, nor are women fulfilled by maternity above all. Instead, each individual is called to conversion and personal faith, women as well as men. Unusually for a Jewish man of his time and place, Jesus approaches women directly, not through a male intermediary (John 4:7, 27). Women are among his personal friends (Luke 10:38–42; John 4:5). And, without necessarily implying disrespect for his mother, he tells followers that his mother has not been blessed by God simply for giving birth to him; the only way to achieve discipleship is to 'hear the word of God and do it' (Luke 8:19–21). An often neglected woman is Mary Magdalene, erroneously maligned in Christian memory as a prostitute (the Bible simply says that Jesus drove from her seven demons (Luke 8:2)). She is actually recorded by all four gospels as the first witness to the resurrection.

Both the gospels and the letters of St Paul show a tendency to downplay the importance of procreation, to see women and men as mutually responsible partners in marriage (Mark 10:11–12; 1 Cor. 7: 3–5), and to place women in somewhat non-traditional roles. Paul writes to or about women leaders in the churches he founded (Rom. 16:1–2, 3–5; 1 Cor. 1:11). However, other texts in the New Testament reaffirm traditional gender roles, especially the subordination of women to men in the family. The so-called household codes (Col. 3:18 – 4:1; Eph. 5:21 – 6:9; 1 Pet. 2:18 – 3:7; 1 Tim. 2:8–15; Titus 2:1–10; 3:1) reflect ancient Greek and first-century systems of household order and management (see above, pp. 68–71). They command wives to be submissive to their husbands, slaves to their masters and children to their fathers, and include instructions to men to love wives in return and not rule subordinates harshly. Like their pagan counterparts, the Christian codes may actually be reactions against signs of greater equality for women that were already appearing in the culture. Feminist New Testament scholar Elisabeth

Schüssler Fiorenza has theorised that the codes were attempts to make the emerging Christian 'discipleship of equals' seem more acceptable to the surrounding patriarchal culture, and not like a subversive cult.[3] In any event, the household codes provide supposed evidence for the divinely ordained subordination of women in marriage and the family under male 'headship'. However, these codes are far from the only image of gender present in the Bible, and they are arguably not the most prominent one. Though they occur in the Pauline epistles, they are contradicted by St Paul himself, who not only encouraged female leadership but recorded this baptismal formula: 'There is neither Jew nor Greek, there is neither slave nor free, there is neither male nor female; for you are all one in Christ Jesus' (Gal. 3:28).

CHURCH HISTORY AND GENDER

Although a complete discussion of views of gender in Christian history is impossible here, a few key and exemplary figures may be noted. Most Christian thought and practice has reverted to cultural norms about gender. Women have been more or less confined to domestic space, and men expected to take responsibility in the economic and political realms (and expected *not* to be overinvolved in domestic and family life). Men have been seen as more aggressive and rational, women as more nurturing and emotional. While the deficits of these stereotypes for women are obvious, their damaging, unfair and constraining results for men are sometimes overlooked.

In the first four centuries of Christianity, 'church Fathers' like Jerome, Chrysostom, Tertullian, Clement, Origen and Augustine specifically taught that women were weaker than men in intellectual capacity and judgement. They nonetheless regarded women as equally able to be saved, especially through their ordained maternal role, or by remaining virgins dedicated to God. In fact, the possibility of adopting a life of vowed virginity gave women an opportunity to escape the patriarchal household and achieve holiness on a par with celibate males.[4] Several of the Fathers, like Tertullian, Jerome and Chrysostom, had close female associates and companions who joined the search for spiritual perfection and were patrons supporting the men's work. These women achieved some freedom from typical gender standards through holiness, asceticism and sometimes independent control of their property. The wealthy young widow Olympias, resisting all pressures to remarry, used her resources to support Chrysostom and other notable churchmen, as well as to engage in charitable works and building programmes.[5]

Mention must also be made of martyrdom as a way of transcending gender difference in following Christ. Christians have died for their faith throughout the history of the church, but stories of early Christian martyrs are perhaps most numerous and most formative for Christian self-understanding. The example of women martyrs like Felicitas, Perpetua, Catherine of Alexandria, Cecilia and Margaret gave rise to the motif of the 'virile woman', who in her endurance, humility and faith becomes the equal of or surpasses men, and shows that virtue ('virility') is determined by character, not biology.[6]

One of the most influential of all Christian theologians, Augustine, had what many modern critics would see as an unfortunately pessimistic view of sex, which he almost unequivocally identified with lust. He even wished that God had arranged that women and men could procreate without having to engage in what we know as sex at all.[7] Nevertheless, Augustine was not a misogynist. The strict sexual norms he laid out applied equally to men and women, and he saw faithful, procreative marriage as a good for both. He shared the assumption of his time that men would be leaders in church and society, but gave spiritual credit to women like his mother, Monica, who had faithfully prayed for her son's conversion in his youth.[8]

For the long period of the Middle Ages, four touchstones can reveal how Christians viewed personal relationships and social institutions through the lens of gender, and what they saw to be normative for the expression of gender in human relations, both personal and social. These four are the greatest medieval theologian, Thomas Aquinas; canon law regarding marriage and divorce; the role of religiously vowed celibate women; and the presence of a few notable women mystics and theologians, who were able to carve out iconoclastic roles for themselves by redefining the significance of gender.

Thomas Aquinas thought that women are less rational and physically weaker than men, and were created to be subordinate to men, though not to be men's servants. The primary role of women is childbearing, for men are more competent in everything else.[9] Still, women are equally called to eternal union with God. On this earth, Aquinas is concerned about fair treatment of women in marriage and family, arguing that if men had free rein to have sex outside of marriage or abandon an older wife for a younger one, neither women nor their children would be properly protected.[10] Aquinas sees in marriage between a woman and man the most intense type of love that is possible outside of friendship with God.[11]

Up until about the fourth century, marriage was a secular and family affair. Christians followed the marriage laws and customs of the surrounding Roman culture, though Christians were expected to aim for holiness in marriage and family, as in all else. However, marriage and family were among the key institutions of society affected by gender, with very unequal results. For instance, the paterfamilias had ultimate control over marriages and divorces; young people, especially girls, were often married without their consent to politically or economically advantageous mates; and women had many fewer rights in the family than had men. Men often had control over their wives' property; adultery was punishable by death for a wife but not a husband; and in the event of a divorce (typically a male prerogative), children belonged to the husband. As a result of Germanic invasions into Europe in the fourth through the sixth century, which introduced barbarian folk customs, gender relations became even more unequal. For example, a man could claim a woman for marriage by raping her. Throughout the Middle Ages and especially in Gratian's codification of church law in 1140, the church took gradually greater control over marriage. Ecclesiastical legislation equalised gender relationships, controlled adult male bahaviour, and offered greater protection to less-powerful parties: women, children and young people. A valid marriage had to result from the free consent of both parties, marriage could not be dissolved once it had been consummated (even if the wife were infertile or a better prospect came along for the husband or one of the families), and sex outside marriage was forbidden for women and men alike (at least in theory).

The ideal of virginity that had characterised primitive Christianity also continued to offer a way of life outside marriage, which likewise served to modify gender differences somewhat. Communities of religiously consecrated women or men had existed since the patristic period. For both sexes, the convent or monastery offered an alternative to strongly gendered family and social norms. This opportunity was perhaps especially valuable to women, since it was women who were most constrained by their subordinate position in family life and their limitation primarily to that sphere. Although in the Middle Ages women did exercise some economic independence in occupations like brewing, the normal vocations of wife and mother came under male authority. Convents could serve as a refuge for women seeking another way of life, for unmarriageable daughters and for widows; noble women could use their resources to found convents, where they could educate their daughters and later themselves retire.[12]

Finally, recent decades have seen a theological and popular 'rediscovery' of some women of the Middle Ages who were theologians and mystics, advisers of lay people and church dignitaries, and spiritual visionaries who made religious use of sexual, bridal and maternal imagery and symbolism. Among them are Teresa of Avila, Catherine of Siena, Mechtild of

Magdeburg, Julian of Norwich and Hildegard of Bingen. Though such women sometimes felt they needed to justify their claim to religious authority, since they were simply women, they were still effective in presenting their unique experiences of God. Julian experienced sixteen visions or 'showings' of Christ's death and God's love, which she spent the rest of her life pondering and committing to writing. Proclaiming her mission to teach, she asks, 'Because I am a woman, should I therefore believe that I ought not to tell you about the goodness of God since I saw at the same time that it is His will that it be known?'[13]

The Protestant Reformation modified the Christian perspective on gender and ethics. Both Luther and Calvin still saw procreation as the primary purpose of sex, but they emphasised companionship and domestic partnership as purposes of marriage more than had the theologians of the patristic period and the Middle Ages. This opened up the possibility of greater reciprocity and mutuality in marriage, even though, theoretically, women were still the weaker vessels, requiring male oversight and functioning mainly in the home and family. Luther interpreted Genesis in accord with modern-day feminists insofar as he granted that women and men were created to be equal in every way, including public leadership and governance, with subordination resulting only from the fall. This did not lead Luther to challenge the legitimacy of the patriarchal institutions that *de facto* exist, though.[14] Calvin in particular, and later the Puritans, construed marriage as a covenant relationship blessed by God for the holy ordering of life, the mutual sanctification of the couple and the righteous upbringing of children.[15] (The Puritans, it must be noted, were quite strong on enforcing the household codes as a framework for these worthy aims.) On the other side, by eliminating clerical celibacy and closing the convents, the reformers also narrowed the options for a socially viable way of adult life outside the household, especially for women. More radical were the Quakers, who affirmed a spiritual equality for men and women, and supported the active ministry of women as preachers, missionaries and leaders of women's meetings.[16]

MODERN TIMES

Since the Protestant Reformation and the Enlightenment, both of which give new emphasis and importance to the individual, to freedom and responsibility, and to equality, the movement for gender equity has gained in both energy and effectiveness, especially in western (North Atlantic) cultures. The struggle for women's rights has brought drastic changes in social relationships and institutions based on gender, with major consequences for men and women. As women have gained the vote and improved access to education and employment, men have taken on new roles in the domestic sphere, developing capacities and talents once assigned to 'feminine' nature. Men and women strive to redefine masculinity and femininity under new economic, political and familial conditions. Christians are participating in these same cultural developments, and share in the same uncertainties, controversies and conflicts over gender that characterise contemporary western cultures as a whole.

Susan Parsons has developed a framework for understanding Christian feminist theologies that can serve as an entry point for comparing various models of gender that exist in Christian ethics.[17] Parsons compares *liberal*, *social constructionist*, and *naturalist* paradigms of feminist theology. Male–female difference in social roles can be understood similarly in light of these three philosophical foundations or perspectives. Liberal theorists (and much of popular culture) focus on equality and freedom as basic moral values, essential to preserve human dignity. The most important moral obligations of persons and of society are to respect individual autonomy, self-determination and human rights. Above all, the just society should protect these requirements of individual freedom. In the liberal view, gender roles are minimised; all persons are equal and have equal rights to education, work and pay. There is no intrinsic reason women and men should not share equally in domestic and public roles, with health-care and child-care support given so that the burdens of pregnancy and early child care on women will be minimised, or shared as far as possible with men. Christian ethicists supporting this general approach might make appeal to the equality of roles in the original creation; the saving grace and faith offered to every individual, male or female; the equal responsibility of all persons in Christ; or the covenantal model of relationship in much Reformation thought.

A second paradigm, the social constructionist, holds that all or most moral values are culturally created and manifest the deep influence of social and moral ideologies that serve those already in power. Gender and the family are often construed as such ideologies. In this paradigm, the moral aim is to be suspicious of and resist all reigning world-views or interpretations of 'the way things are'. What seems natural or divinely ordained may simply reflect the propaganda of the power elites. Gender, in such a view, is not natural, and has no legitimate right to define personal and social relationships. Women and men must seek new identities and patterns of relationship that take into account the voices of previously marginalised or oppressed groups (women, for example), and that aim for liberation from patriarchal, class-biased and heterosexist false norms about how the sexes should relate to one another, personally and in social institutions such as the family, education and labour. Christian ethicists sympathetic to such a critique might note that the Bible includes many subversive portraits of male and female behaviour, and that Jesus' treatment of women overturned the norms of his day. They would go back to an iconoclastic reading of traditional texts, trying to recover the destabilising subtext 'behind' standard interpretations.

A third paradigm is what Parsons calls 'naturalist' feminism, really an approach that tries to re-examine whether there are any innate human characteristics that exist within and despite an admittedly large component of socialisation and cultural shaping, and whether any universally human experiences or values can give rise to moral standards or ideals. From the standpoint of gender, the issues would be whether reproductive differences, which few deny, can yield any guidance for the ethics of relationships and institutions, and whether these differences and the resulting moral standards are fairly minimal or fairly extensive. On these questions, of course, there is room for significant disagreement. Some would argue that natural differences are so limited that virtually no differentiation of social roles is in order, save those absolutely necessary for reproduction. Others would say that male and female gender roles and characteristics are naturally 'complementary', based on sexual and reproductive complementarity, and resulting in at least some and perhaps major differences in suitable social functions for women and men.

The view that male and female nature is equal but complementary typifies official Roman Catholic thought, especially the writings of John Paul II, who sees motherhood as women's highest calling and says only men can be ordained priests. However, the pope maintains at the same time that both men and women have responsibilities in the family, that women should have access to all public functions and receive equal pay, and that discrimination or violence against women is wrong.[18] Christians following out a 'naturalist' line of inquiry might turn to the fact that human existence as two sexes is part of creation; and that modern scientific research is revealing at least some biologically based sex differences in humans as in other animals, such research being relevant to Christian ethics, given the doctrine of creation. The variations in conclusions to be drawn within this approach, however, could still be high, depending on the weight given to freedom and biology as interdependent human characteristics that are both aspects of morality.

A MORE GLOBAL, INTERCULTURAL PERSPECTIVE ON GENDER

Just as Christian theology and ethics in general have been generated primarily from a Eurocentric (and more recently North American) perspective, so have Christian interpretations of gender and the moral relations gender demands. Many authors, especially women authors, from Latin America, Asia and Africa object that even the new, revisionist Christian views of gendered relationships are culturally biased. For example, the battle for equal rights among First World women has focused on access to higher education and a male-dominated workplace, whereas many poor women in the Third World are more frequently victims of domestic violence and lack even basic education, health care and the means to feed their children. Moreover, in less individualistic and more community-oriented cultures, women may derive more satisfaction from familial roles and be less interested in a liberal, rights-based approach to social access. Women around the globe are increasingly speaking and writing in their own voice about gender issues, looking for ways to reconstruct their societies to be more just without necessarily replicating western solutions to gender inequity.[19]

Broader ethical questions that are especially affected by gender assumptions and practices (and that will be treated elsewhere in this volume) concern family and bioethics (for example, reproductive technologies). Yet almost every ethical question conceivable – from war and peace to ecology – is to some extent defined by whether we see reality in general and human behaviour in particular in binary, oppositional terms (aggression, power and rationality opposed to relationality, compassion and emotionality) or in reciprocal, dialogical and fluid terms (such qualities can coexist and interpenetrate). While differences in human experience and in moral value or responsibility are certainly real and important – for both cultures and individuals – such differences should not become divisive in Christian ethics, nor should they be the basis of exclusionary or oppressive social structures. The Christian doctrines of redemption and reconciliation counsel an inclusive and liberating vision of gender in Christian ethics.

Notes

1 See James Nelson, *Between Two Gardens: Reflections on Sexuality and Religious Experience* (New York: Pilgrim Press, 1983); and *Body Theology* (Louisville, KY: Westminster John Knox Press, 1992).
2 For the groundbreaking version of this interpretation, see Phyllis Trible, *God and the Rhetoric of Sexuality* (Philadelphia: Fortress Press, 1978).

3 Elisabeth Schüssler Fiorenza, *In Memory of Her: A Feminist Theological Reconstruction of Christian Origins* (New York: Crossroad, 1983).

4 Peter Brown, *Body and Society: Men, Women, and Sexual Renunciation in Early Christianity* (New York: Columbia University Press, 1988); Rosemary Radford Ruether, *Women and Redemption: A Theological History* (Minneapolis: Fortress Press, 1998).

5 Elizabeth A. Clark, *Jerome, Chrysostom, and Friends* (Lewiston, NY, Edwin Mellen Press, 1979).

6 Katherine Gill, 'Martyr', in Letty M. Russell and J. Shannon Clarkson (eds) *Dictionary of Feminist Theologies* (Louisville, KY: Westminster John Knox Press, 1996) 174.

7 Augustine, *City of God*, trans. Henry Bettenson, ed. David Knowles (New York: Penguin Books, 1972) XIV.19, 21, 23–24.

8 Peter Brown, *Augustine of Hippo: A Biography* (New York: Dorset Press, 1967).

9 Thomas Aquinas, *Summa Theologica*, Vol. I, Part 1, Q I.92 (New York: Benziger Brothers, n.d.) 466–69.

10 Thomas Aquinas, *Summa Contra Gentiles*, Book Three/2, chapters 121–26 (Notre Dame: University of Notre Dame Press, 1975) 141–56.

11 Thomas Aquinas, *Summa Theologica*, Vol. II, Part 11–11, Q.26.11 (New York: Benziger Brothers, n.d.) 1302–03.

12 Angela M. Lucas, *Women in the Middle Ages: Religion, Marriage, and Letters* (New York: St Martin's Press, 1983) 30–42.

13 Ruether, *Women and Redemption*, 106.

14 See Martin Luther, 'The Estate of Marriage', in *Luther's Works*, Vol. 45, ed. Jaroslav Pelikan (Philadelphia: Fortress Press, 1966) 13–49.

15 See John Calvin, *Commentaries on Genesis*, Volume One, 2: 18–25, 3: 16–18 (Grand Rapids, MI: Baker Book House) 128–37, 171–76.

16 Ruether, *Women and Redemption*, 137.

17 Susan F. Parsons, *Feminism and Christian Ethics* (Cambridge: Cambridge University Press, 1996).

18 John Paul II, *On the Family* (Washington, DC: United States Catholic Conference, 1981); and *On the Dignity and Vocation of Women* (Washington, DC: United States Catholic Conference, 1988).

19 See Ursula King, ed., *Feminist Theology from the Third World: A Reader* (London and Maryknoll, NY: SPCK and Orbis Books, 1994).

9 Liberation ethics

TIM GORRINGE

Whilst it would be an overstatement to say that there are as many liberation theologies as there are practitioners, it is certainly true that liberation theology is not all of a piece. This is not just to point to the varieties of liberation theology – black, Asian, African, Jewish, feminist, womanist and so forth (and since feminist ethics are treated elsewhere in this volume, I will not deal with the subject here) – but to the variety of standpoints even within Latin America, where the movement started. Juan Luis Segundo, for example, had an essentially evolutionary understanding of reality which he shared with his fellow-Jesuit Teilhard de Chardin. He can cite with approval the view that every vice was probably at some time a virtue, and that what we call 'human beings' are only slowly emerging from the tangle of primitive drives and instincts.[1] He frankly avows a situation ethic, an ethic in which the ends justify the means, but on the understanding that Christian ends are the most communitarian and generous-hearted imaginable.[2] Míguez Bonino, on the other hand, offers us a survey of twentieth-century social ethics, but allows himself to formulate a principle which is virtually identical with utilitarianism: 'The basic ethical criterion is the maximising of universal human possibilities and the minimizing of human costs.'[3] Any economist would recognise this as a version of Pareto optimality. Enrique Dussel, for his part, who represents an appropriation of the work of Levinas long before that thinker became fashionable in Europe, describes ethics as 'fundamental theology', that which constitutes both the rationality and the possibility of theology.[4] Like Levinas, his ethics are grounded in the face-to-face encounter. Meanwhile, if we were to concentrate on the appeal to liberation spirituality which is so marked a feature of the work of theologians like Gutiérrez or Pieris, we might derive a virtue ethic from them. Or, given the role of scripture in Gutiérrez' theology, we might take it as a form of a Barthian command ethic. There is, then, no one 'liberation ethic', and what we have to do is to look for commonalities amidst the vigorous discussion which constitutes the discipline. The first of these represents a strong line on the relation of theory and practice.

OVERCOMING THE DUALISM OF THEORY AND PRACTICE

Aristotle, theorising on behalf of the elite free group in the Athenian polis, and dependent on slaves for all of his basic needs, distinguishes between wisdom (*sophrosune*) and practical wisdom (*phronesis*), knowledge (*theoria*) and praxis, and traces them to different parts of the soul; the former is concerned with what is eternal, the latter with what is disputable. Although practical wisdom is indispensable to the realisation of the human end, it is not superior to contemplative knowledge. Such a conclusion would make politics of supreme importance, which would be to rank the temporary and negotiable above the eternally true (*Nicomachean Ethics*, bk 6). This ranking of theory and practice is reflected in the medieval distinction between the *vita contemplativa* and the *vita activa*. Although the crucially important Benedictine tradition sought to integrate the two, contemplation remained prior to praxis until the process of inversion began in the sixteenth century. It was completed by the emergence of utilitarianism in the eighteenth century, which is the ethic of the industrial revolution and the capitalist order, and which prioritises what produces results over all mere theorising. Facts are what count, as Gradgrind insists in Dickens' *Hard Times*, an attitude which has had fateful consequences in economic theory up to the present in the (in fact nonsensical) idea that economics can be pursued without values. At the same time as utilitarianism emerged, in remote Königsberg, in a state which had to wait another fifty years for the industrial revolution, Kant articulated the philosophy of the cultured bourgeois, separating the three critiques of 'pure' and 'practical' knowledge and taste. The new theology which followed this move made a stark separation between doctrine and ethics so that ethics form no part, for example, of Schleiermacher's *Christian Faith* (1819).

Liberation theology represents a challenge to the entire distinction, something which was already made plain at Medellín which insisted that it was necessary to 'end the separation between faith and life, because in Christ Jesus the only thing that counts is 'faith that works through love' (Medellín, Message 6). Similarly, the EATWOT (Ecumenical Association of Third World Theologians) declaration in 1976 rejected as irrelevant 'an academic type of theology that is divorced from action'. This insistence has profound methodological consequences. Critics have often alleged that liberation theology lacks an ethic. This may mean nothing more than that

Dussel's five-volume magnum opus on liberation ethics has not been translated, but it is also true that, as with Karl Barth, liberation theology integrates doctrine and ethics. Gustavo Gutiérrez offers us no treatise on ethics for the simple reason that *A Theology of Liberation* is itself a theological ethic, the theory of a *practice*. According to his well-known formulation, theology is a second step, reflection on the presence and action of the Christian in the world.[5] It is critical reflection on praxis, or alternatively on ethical action. If ethics is reflection on what reasons are offered for particular forms of action or behaviour, then liberation theology clearly does this in expounding its major loci. Exactly as for Barth, every doctrinal postulate has its ethical correlate. More clearly than in Barth, liberation theology has spelt out what those ethical correlates are.

It is in virtue of the unity of doctrine and ethics that liberation theology has often not elaborated an ethic. The foremost Latin American ethicist, however, Enrique Dussel, does so and follows Levinas in making a distinction between ethics and morality. For him, morality refers to the norms of the established order, the order of what John's gospel calls 'the world'. The established order constitutes a self-referential system with its own norms, and therefore with a good conscience. It is a 'totality', that situation which determines the limits of the thinkable – in our case the situation of global capital. The moral law can tell me if something is wrong according to the principles of the system, but not whether the totality is wrong. The system creates a 'peaceful remorseless conscience vis à-vis a practice that the system approves but that may originally have been . . . a practice of domination'.[6] Ethics, on the other hand, begins with the capacity to hear the voice of the other, which is the moment of conversion. Ethical conscience, as opposed to moral conscience, consists in knowing how to open up to the other.[7] To be moral, we might say, means to be law-abiding; to be ethical is to be open to the other as person, and therefore as sacred.

As the Medellín text makes clear, liberation theology offers us *an ethic of discipleship*. For this reason, when Gutiérrez does come to speak explicitly of ethics, he does so by speaking of discipleship, which is the following of a way, a learning by doing.[8] It is when we reflect on discipleship that the meaning of theology as a second step becomes clear. In the gospels the disciples' questions arise from action in which they are involved. They do not first take a degree in theology and then 'get involved', but the other way about. Though not derived as a principle from the gospels, which would be self-contradictory for liberation theology, the 'priority of praxis' is evangelically grounded.

THE PRIORITY OF PRAXIS

The 1976 EATWOT declaration mentioned above speaks for liberation theology as a whole in assuming 'a radical break in epistemology which makes commitment the first act of theology and engages in critical reflection on the praxis of reality of the Third World'. The priority of praxis is a shibboleth of liberation thought, though, like the overall understanding of ethics and theology, what is meant by praxis is rather differently defined. Gutiérrez echoes Marx in speaking of praxis as the process by which human beings transform themselves. 'By working, transforming the world, breaking out of servitude, building a just society, and assuming his destiny in history, man forges himself.'[9] Dussel offers a Levinasian definition of praxis as 'any human act directed to another human being', the manner of our being in the world before another person.[10] C. Boff offers a definition with which most liberation theologians could agree in speaking of praxis as 'the complex of practices orientated to the transformation of society, the making of history'.[11]

To speak of the priority of praxis may mean that it is the most urgent concern of theology, and that theology cannot properly be done without it, but characteristically liberationists have wished to grant epistemological priority to praxis, which, on any of these definitions, is problematical. Segundo, for example, formulates the hermeneutic circle thus: experience of oppression leads to a questioning of received ways of understanding reality and of reading scripture; a new reading of scripture leads to a new praxis which then goes on to a new understanding of reality, and so on.[12] What is concealed here is the reason for outrage, the moment in which the process gets started. Outrage is the proper moral response to an immoral situation, but it is not, like Kant's categorical imperative, innate in human nature. Social conditioning, the fatalism of centuries, can make it seem improper even to the victims, a process which psychology has deeply illuminated in its account of the internalisation of oppression. The famous story of Bartolomeo de las Casas illustrates the way in which illumination can come. It was whilst reflecting on the portion of scripture set for the mass (Ecclesiasticus 34) that he finally came to see that Spain's treatment of the indigenous population was impossible for Christians.[13] Of course, the dehumanising treatment he had himself been involved in was the necessary presupposition of his illumination, like Saul's persecution of Christians, but a spark was necessary to break the old presuppositions. As Gutiérrez has emphasised, *conversion* stands at the root of the process.[14] Segundo prefers to speak of commitment, which he insists cannot simply follow from knowledge of the gospel message and its demands, because interpretations of the gospel differ according to one's political commitment.[15] Well, of course they do, but exactly the same applies to experience. The question is, then, how one acquires commitment, or comes to the moment of conversion, and it seems that the answers to that question are infinitely varied, and may very well involve the 'priority' of the text, as in las Casas' case.

This fact is above all theorised by Paulo Freire as the necessary *dialectic* between action and reflection.[16] The problem, as many of the early liberation practitioners recounted it, was one of fatalism, a view of the world reinforced by an 'otherworldly' Christianity.[17] Experience did not teach poor peasants the need for freedom, it taught them despair. It was priests and educators who saw that this situation was incompatible with the biblical promise, who therefore challenged it and who, through adult education and the formation of base communities, sought to conscientise people to become aware of their oppression and actors in their own history. Freire found that acquiring literacy meant becoming aware of oneself as a creative subject. As people became able to 'name reality', so they exercised creative freedom and participated in social change.[18]

The reasons for insisting on the priority of praxis are bound up with the situation of oppression in which all liberation theologies have emerged, and also with the hostility to the kind of deductive theology many of the practitioners had learned. But when it comes to method, as Segundo himself notes, we cannot argue for ever about the chicken and the egg.[19] Recognition of the necessarily dialectical nature of all human experience makes this unnecessary.

THE NEED FOR SOCIAL ANALYSIS

In Latin America liberation theology emerged in the wake of the failure of the economic developmental model of the 1950s, the increasing immiseration of the bulk of the populace, and the imposition of the national security state. Developmental theory came (and still comes) in the guise of an angel of light. Its concern is the 'ascent of man', the great move from millennia of poverty to affluence. Its imperatives are industrialise, mechanise, rationalise agriculture.[20] Pursued with passion by good people, the problem is to understand why the poor then get poorer. Wrestling with this puzzle, priests had to lay aside their theology books and study sociology, economics and politics. Since they discovered that the causes of increasing poverty involved the operations of global capital, they had, to the scandal of the Vatican, to study Marx. Understanding of the actual mechanisms of the global economy led further to the appropriation both of a theory of ideology, as an attempt to understand how false beliefs about situations are both generated and internalised, and of dependency theory. The good intentions of economists, they realised, masked a global power struggle in which ruthless means were adopted to maintain the hegemony of the OECD nations, and increasingly of transnational corporations.

This experience taught them that all knowledge, including both economics and theology, is socially situated and serves particular interests. The sociology of knowledge had already arrived at these conclusions, but it was the struggle for new perception in the Latin American context which burned this into theological consciousness in an entirely new way and established social analysis as an indispensable aspect of all theological reflection. In the words of the liberation theologians, theology needs a social-analytic mediation.[21] In the choice between a functionalist and a dialectical sociology, they opted for the latter, understanding society as badly structured, full of conflict and in need of transformation. This means, as critics of liberation theology were not slow to point out, that an ethical decision is implicit in the adoption of this method. Conflict and violence are recognised as part of all human reality and even as a necessary part of the process of salvation.[22]

Methodologically the recognition of the need for social analysis involves the commitment, shared, for example, by Alasdair MacIntyre, to the historical materialism of the early sections of Marx and Engels' *The German Ideology*. To understand any ideas properly, and *a fortiori* ethical ones, we have to ask about the social situatedness of the author. Pace Max Weber, no form of knowledge is value-neutral. If we accept the position that you cannot do ethics without social analysis, a rather dense and multi-levelled ethical reflection is inescapable. For social analysis itself, the prerequisite for ethical reflection, is ethically driven, and to avoid an endless regress we revert once more to the notion of commitment. In the case of liberation theology the bottom line, the commitment of which Segundo speaks, is the *option for the poor*. The assumption of this option is not that the poor are morally better than the rich, but that they are in a different situation and therefore see things differently. In Dussel's terms, they stand outside the totality of capitalism. Revelation cannot occur within the totality, but only from without, in this case through the poor, through whom God speaks. 'The criterion of the discernment of the word of God is the standpoint of the poor.'[23] The Sri Lankan theologian Aloysius Pieris puts this slightly differently. According to him, what distinguishes Christianity from the traditional religions of Asia is precisely God's defence pact with the poor.[24] All liberation theology is built on the two principles of the irreconcilable antagonism between God and mammon and the irrevocable covenant between God and the poor. The poor are not passive victims of historical process, but have a messianic role. They are those through whom God shapes history.

THE BIBLE IN THE ETHICS OF LIBERATION

If praxis and social analysis are the first two methodological pillars of liberation ethics, the third is appeal to scripture. Liberation theology has never been solely a Roman Catholic enterprise, but on the other hand Vatican II is one of the preconditions of its happening, and in particular the 'return to the sources' it urged. This was especially important in Latin America, where the base community gathered round scripture and sought to understand its situation in the light of it. 'It is in the conflict between the word of God and actual reality that the Base Communities seek light and strength for their journey. And it is from the same conflict that the theology of liberation draws its prophetic power.'[25] In some cases a deeply scriptural theology emerged, especially, for example, in Gutiérrez, whose theology above all proceeds through exegesis. He defines theology as 'critical reflection on Christian praxis *in the light of the word*'.[26] Unconsciously echoing the preface to Barth's first edition of the commentary on Romans, he writes that to read the Bible is to begin a dialogue between the believers of the past and the believers of today. The Bible is the Word of God which reads us before we read it.[27] As indicated by his actual practice, Gutiérrez expects ethical illumination from scripture in much the way that Barth does.

Segundo, on the other hand, whose theological method derives from the Catholic version of liberalism, believes that what we have in scripture is a picture of the educational process between God and humanity. In reading scripture we do not learn this and that, but we learn how to learn. We keep reliving the experiences recorded in scripture, 'thereby giving them an absolute value', but we do not derive concrete norms for the present from them. He adopts this position on the grounds of the need to be aware of the ideologies implicit in scripture and of the difficulty in moving from the past to the present. Scripture, then, has a deutero-pedagogical function. No ethical directives are to be expected from it, but rather instruction in how to frame ethical directives.[28]

In Africa, the Accra conference of 1977 spoke of the Bible as 'the basic source of African theology'. Of course there are huge differences between the French-speaking Catholic liberation theology of Jean Marc Ela, on the one hand, and the theology which has been hammered out in contest with

Calvinist Afrikaanerdom on the other. In a vast continent there are a multiplicity of cultures. What is widely affirmed, however, is a resonance between indigenous traditions and the narrative cast of scripture and the origins of scripture in oral tradition.[29]

In Asia, in the context of a dialogue with traditions at least as ancient as, if not more ancient than, Christianity, and with highly sophisticated ethical systems, Aloysius Pieris can still speak of scripture as 'a source of revelation ... God's Word ... our authoritative past as well as our norm of orthodoxy for the present'.[30] What he finds in scripture, however, is the record of the religious experience of the poor, and it is this aspect of it which guides his ethical appeal. This in effect relegates much of the wisdom literature to what Luther would have called 'right strawy' status. The 'canon within the canon' which in practice guides any Christian decision-making is decisively narrowed.

In South Korea, decisively influenced by a nineteenth-century Protestant mission, scripture functioned as a means of community self-understanding during the long years of Japanese occupation, and since then Korean theology has made a fundamental identification between the *minjung*, the oppressed, and the New Testament *ochlos* (crowd).[31]

In sum, the way in which scripture is resourced by liberation theology is as varied as it has been by the church through the ages. In the first decade it is fair to say that exodus was a guiding theme, but this has more recently been overtaken by a much more nuanced and wide-ranging appeal, as evidenced by Gutiérrez' study of Job or the Bible studies of Carlos Mesters. In parts of Latin America the base communities at first played a pivotal role, whilst in Asia these could not function in anything like the same way, and 'base human communities' do not form a mass movement as the CEBs did for a while in Brazil. In every area, however, the placing of the task of scriptural exegesis in the hands of the people is a key feature.

LIBERATION ETHICS IN RELATION TO OTHER ETHICAL SYSTEMS

Beginning with praxis and defining the ethical norm and goal as liberation serves as a point of delimitation from other ethical systems. Gutiérrez' appeal to scripture, for example, cannot be regarded as a form of command ethic, because of the priority he gives to praxis. Segundo's version of situation ethic differs from Fletcher in that the 'situation' which determines our ethical response is properly historically specified. In contrast with classical utilitarianism, pleasure or happiness is not the goal in view, but justice, and it is not the greatest good of the greatest number which is aimed at (despite the careless remark of Bonino, cited above) but the specific good of the poor. 'The criterion . . . of ethical lawfulness, and moral unlawfulness, is . . . "Liberate the poor." '[32] Moreover, all liberation ethics are an ethic of community. 'Community relationships of justice, real ethical relationships . . . are the essence and foundation of ethics.'[33] Dussel can say this on the ground that domination is only overcome in community. This emphasis marks it off from consequentialism, for it has yet to be demonstrated that this ethic can ever sustain a political community other than that of liberal individualism, which is in fact that of capitalism.

Much of the comparative discussion within liberation theology has been in relation to Kant's ideal of autonomy, which is, in its own way, an ethic of freedom.[34] Kant prioritises individual freedom, and the need for persons to make their own ethical judgements in the light of practical reason and independently of the deliverances of tradition. Having himself had a close shave with the Prussian censor as a result of the first part of *Religion within the Bounds of Reason Alone*, he has in mind the courageous citizen resisting the tyranny of either the state, the majority or a reactionary or fanatical church.

Despite this liberative origin, Kant's ethics have been criticised as bourgeois, Promethean, closed to the transcendence of solidarity and therefore of grace.[35] In particular it has been argued that the autonomous individual cannot sustain a moral world.[36] Liberation theology argues, likewise, that Kantian ethics do not take account of the fact that we all live in communities with histories. If we take this fact seriously, we are bound to articulate a community, which is to say a political, ethic. As Vidal argues, some form of ethics of autonomy, as the undergirding of human rights, is a necessary part of any liberation ethic, a fact insufficiently acknowledged by liberation ethicists. This omission is due to the origin of liberation theology in the failure of development economics and the emergence of the national security state.[37] Small surprise that liberation ethics has been concerned first and foremost with questions of class, economics, the nature of the state and latterly the environment. Where, as in Dussel's case, sexual ethics have been addressed, this has not been through the conventional topoi of marriage, procreation, abortion and so forth, but through Levinas' phenomenology of the caress, and so through the affirmation of the body in sexual relations as a part of integral human liberation.[38]

Gutiérrez spoke of a threefold liberation: from political oppression, from sin, and the path towards 'a new man and a qualitatively different society' through the whole of human history.[39] This last represented a crucial eschatological and utopian perspective which has characterised much liberation ethics, so that they can properly be described as 'kingdom ethics'. Where in the view of Reinhold Niebuhr's 'Christian realism' utopian thought signifies a failure to face reality, for most liberation theology there cannot be an ethic without a utopian element which guides the present into the future. The belief that God 'unblocks' the future beyond its perceived limits constitutes a call that commits human beings to action.[40] The dissenting voice is that of Segundo, who believes that in the language of hope 'the historical thrust and content of decision making gets lost'.[41] But what he put in place of eschatology was, as noted above, a strongly evolutionary trajectory, in which he finds himself in uncomfortable proximity to Hayek.

Precisely because liberation theology has a kingdom ethic, most liberation theologians insist on the eschatological proviso to the point of tedium. Temporal progress and the growth of the kingdom have the same goal, but they are not identical. The eschatological promises are fulfilled throughout history but cannot be identified completely with any given social reality. Every implementation of political liberation is part of the growth of the kingdom, according to Gutiérrez, and helps to overcome the negation of love, but is never 'all of salvation'. The need for liberation from sin always remains.[42]

A distinctive mark of the political ethic of liberation has been its centring on the notion of idolatry, making a contrast between the idols of death and the God of life. Idols take the place of God, and in so doing destroy human lives. To place idolatry at the centre of ethical analysis acknowledges that sin is not manifest only, or indeed primarily, in individual lives, but in structures which determine and dehumanise us all. That idolatry is an ethical category is shown in a most impressive way in Franz Hinkelammert's critique of capitalist economy, *The Ideological Weapons of Death*. In the famous section on commodity fetishism in *Capital* Marx had argued that in capitalist society money became the medium of relationships, a process in which commodities are personified and persons commodified. Persons become subordinated to things, and in particular to money and capital. Hinkelammert takes up the theological meaning of fetishism and argues that capitalism involves idolatry. Capital demands an act of faith from capitalists, and submission from those they employ. It comes to decide on the life and death of human beings, and demands the abandonment of aspirations to freedom.

Another example of the liberation critique of idolatry is the opposition to apartheid. As Manas Buthelezi put it, 'Race is a gift of God. When it is elevated to the level of the ultimate, when it becomes a decisive factor in the manifestation and direction of public morality ... it becomes a god that competes with the Father of Jesus Christ.'[43]

Ethics relate to ethos. Whilst it is probably true that most societies are a jumble of what is life-nurturing and life-destroying, it is undeniable that some societies get locked into necrophilia. Rome after Nero, National Socialist Germany, Stalin's Soviet Union, apartheid South Africa are all clear illustrations. Liberation theology extends this critique to capital, both in relation to what happens to the poor and in relation to the environment. Idolatry as a tool of ethical analysis is self-evidently a theological preserve and offers a very powerful critique of the heart of a culture, what really makes it tick. This brings us to the connection of ethics and spirituality.

SPIRITUALITY AND THE ETHICS OF LIBERATION

The fact that ethics springs from ethos is the reason for liberation theology's concern with spirituality. All ethics presuppose a spirituality, but in philosophical ethics this fact is deeply hidden, not to say buried. Liberation theology brings it out into the light of day. The spirituality of liberation has been the special concern of Gutiérrez and of Pieris. According to the former, the spirituality of liberation involves conversion, as we have already seen, but also gratuitousness and joy.[44] It is gratuitousness which allows me to encounter the other fully, precisely because it teaches me that everything is gift, and there can be real love only when there is free giving. Although he does not spell it out in so many words, Gutiérrez demonstrates that grace is the foundation of any political ethic, a profoundly political and not just a privatised reality.

Pieris, writing in the context of widespread involuntary poverty, and also of three millennia of traditions of Asian voluntary poverty, describes spirituality as a combination of the struggle against mammon (the struggle to be poor) and the struggle to eliminate want (struggle for the poor). In strong contrast to many Latin Americans (for example Hinkelammert), who deprecate any form of poverty, he believes that voluntary poverty needs to be embraced as a protest and precaution against forced poverty. For Pieris, voluntary poverty is both a spiritual antidote to mammon and a political strategy in the battle against the principalities and powers of mammon.[45] In Asia, theologians have to be awakened to the liberative dimension of poverty and the poor conscientised into the liberative potentialities of their religiousness.

The overt roots of liberation ethics in spirituality constitute its greatest strength. It signifies that a Christian ethic is always pushed back to prayer, and therefore to reliance on grace, and to scripture in the hands of community. Grace, however, is known in the flesh. It is a historical material reality and generates values which serve, in Engels' phrase, the production and reproduction of real life, in conflict with the abstract values of the idols of death. It is known and experienced in following the way of the God of life from bondage into freedom.

Notes

1 J. L. Segundo, *Evolution and Guilt*, Gill & Macmillan, London 1980, p. 119.
2 J. L. Segundo, *The Liberation of Theology*, Orbis, Maryknoll 1976, pp. 172–3.
3 J. M. Bonino, *Towards a Christian Political Ethics*, SCM Press, London 1983, p. 107.
4 E. Dussel, *Ethics and Community*, Burns & Oates, London 1988, p. 220.
5 G. Gutiérrez, *A Theology of Liberation*, SCM Press, London 1974 (orig. 1971), pp. 11–12.
6 Dussel, *Ethics*, p. 34.
7 *Ibid.*, p. 39.
8 G. Gutiérrez, The God of Life, SCM Press, London 1991, p. 118.
9 Gutiérrez, *A Theology*, p. 159.
10 Dussel, *Ethics*, p. 8.
11 C. Boff, *Theology and Praxis*, Orbis, Maryknoll 1987, p. 6
12 Segundo, *Liberation*, p. 9.
13 G. Gutiérrez, *Las Casas*, Orbis, Maryknoll 1993.
14 Gutiérrez, *A Theology*, p. 205.
15 Segundo, *Liberation*, p. 84.
16 P. Freire, *Pedagogy of the Oppressed*, Penguin, Harmondsworth 1969.
17 H. Camara, *Revolution through Peace*, Harper & Row, New York 1971.
18 P. Freire, *Cultural Action for Freedom*, Harvard University Press, Cambridge 1970, p. 20.
19 Segundo, Liberation, p. 7.
20 R. Marris, *Ending World Poverty*, Thames & Hudson, London 1999.
21 Boff, *Theology and Praxis*, p. 11.
22 Segundo, *Liberation*, p. 161.
23 Dussel, *Ethics*, p. 229.
24 A. Pieris, *An Asian Theology of Liberation*, T. & T. Clark, Edinburgh 1988, p. 120.
25 A. Moser, 'The Representation of God in the Ethic of Liberation', in D. Mieth and J. Pohier (eds), The Ethics of Liberation and the Liberation of Ethics, Concilium 172, T. & T. Clark, Edinburgh 1984.
26 Gutiérrez, *A Theology*, p. 13.
27 Gutiérrez, *God of Life*, p. xvii.
28 Segundo, *Liberation*, p. 180.
29 J. Mbiti, 'The Bible in African Theology', in R. Gibellini (ed.), *Paths of African Theology*, SCM Press, London 1994.
30 Pieris, *Asian Theology*, p. 113.
31 Christian Conference of Asia, *Minjung Theology*, Zed, London 1983.
32 Dussel, *Ethics*, p. 73.
33 *Ibid,.* p. 80.
34 D. Mieth and J. Pohier (eds), *The Ethics of Liberation and the Liberation of Ethics*, Concilium 172, T. & T. Clark, Edinburgh 1984.

35 M. Vidal, 'Is Morality Based on Autonomy Compatible with the Ethics of Liberation?' in Mieth & Pohier, *Ethics.*
36 Alasdair MacIntyre, *After Virtue*, 2nd edn, University of Notre Dame Press, Notre Dame 1984.
37 J. M. Bonino, *Revolutionary Theology Comes of Age*, SPCK, London 1975.
38 E. Dussel, *Ethics and the Theology of Liberation*, Orbis, Maryknoll 1978.
39 Gutiérrez, *A Theology*, pp. 36–7.
40 Bonino, *Revolutionary Theology*, p. 93.
41 Segundo, *Liberation*, p. 149.
42 Gutiérrez, *A Theology*, p. 177.
43 P. Frostin, *Liberation Theology in Tanzania and South Africa*, Lund University Press, Lund 1988, p. 107.
44 Gutiérrez, *A Theology*, p. 205.
45 Pieris, *Asian Theology*, p. 37.

10 Christian ethics: a Jewish perspective

RONALD M. GREEN

I am a Jewish Christian ethicist. I realise that this professional self-description admits of multiple interpretations, so let me explain. Both my parents were Jewish and I was raised in a home steeped in Jewish values. At the same time, neither parent was particularly devout in terms of religious practice. Hence, the word 'Jewish' in my self-description should be understood in broad cultural rather than explicitly religious terms. At university I studied moral philosophy and Christian ethics, continuing both emphases in my graduate work. As a result, I probably know more about the ethics of Thomas Aquinas, Reinhold Niebuhr, and Henry Sidgwick than I do about Solomon ibn Gabirol and Moses Maimonides.

Nevertheless, my Jewish background remains a permanent influence in my life. Over the years, it has led me back to issues or questions in Jewish ethics and has resulted in numerous publications in which I have tried to interpret Jewish ethics to a non-Jewish audience or apply Jewish ethical thinking to emergent issues in applied ethics.[1] Although I certainly lack the intense formal training in Jewish thought and philosophy of some who are professionally identified as Jewish ethicists, I am perhaps better qualified than many of them to think about Christian ethics from a philosophically informed Jewish perspective.

In what follows I want to look at Christian ethics from a Jewish point of view. Specifically, I want to draw on my understanding of the Jewish tradition to compare and contrast these two traditions. My aim is to highlight some of ways in which these two daughter traditions of biblical faith have come to differ over key features of the moral life. Of course, there are many important similarities between these religious–ethical traditions. Both believe that moral righteousness is an essential expression of faith in God. Both stress adherence to the most basic moral norms found in the Hebrew Bible. Reflecting their common debt to the Exodus traditions, both exhibit a special concern for the marginal and oppressed.

Nevertheless, within these broad areas of agreement there are important differences in the Jewish and Christian ethical traditions. These differences often represent polar choices on some central issues of the moral life. They reflect a series of stands that were taken partly *because* the competing community opposed them. Among the most important of these polarities are (1) the polarity of ethics versus law; (2) of universality versus particularity; and (3) of a positive valuation of suffering versus an aversion to suffering. Although these sharp differences are historically understandable, the fact that each tradition has chosen over time to emphasise only one pole of a complex moral reality suggests that neither one of these choices is adequate by itself. This will lead me to my conclusion: that these two sibling traditions must learn from one another in order to form a more complete picture of the moral life.

LAW VERSUS ETHICS

I can roughly summarise this initial polarity as the tension between 'law and gospel', 'law and spirit', or 'law and love'. Unfortunately, as the very use of these terms suggests, the topic has been overlaid with centuries of mutual recrimination. From St Paul onward, Christian theologians have frequently felt the need to loosen Christianity from its antecedent anchorage and to prove its superiority to the 'old' tradition.[2] As a result, Judaism is often portrayed as concerned with obsolete rites and ceremonies, at its worst a 'religion of pots and pans'. In contrast to this, in the words of one Christian ethicist of an earlier generation, 'The principle of love . . . and the principle of moral inwardness' are the 'distinctive Christian contributions to ethics'.[3]

Of course, these depictions are caricatures. The rabbis, like the prophets before them, understood that ethics is the soul of religious observance. The Jerusalem Talmud tells us that 'the entire body of biblical precepts and rituals are not equal to one ethical principle'.[4] Over the years, the rabbis constantly shaped the received body of commandments so as to match the community's developing ethical sensibilities. One small example among many illustrates this point. Biblical law was interpreted as requiring that suicides be buried outside hallowed ground. What, then, is one to do with a young person who takes her own life? Can parents be asked to endure the further torment of exclusion of a deceased child? The rabbis solved this problem by defining a suicide in such a way that no adolescent could ever be so described. Retaining the commandment, they eliminated its barbarous implications. Again and again in halakhah – classical Jewish law – we find evidence of such humane and progressive reasoning tempering or subverting the letter of outdated ordinances.[5]

Nevertheless, despite its deep ethical intentionality, Judaism remains a religion of law. Ethical life had always to be pursued by means of legal reasoning and legal development. The Christian willingness to subordinate law to the moral requirement of neighbour-love is not shared by Jewish teachers.

In Judaism, this commitment to law stems from two factors. One is the religious aim of creating a ritually and ethically 'holy community' where every word, thought and deed is an act of obedience to God. This aspect of Jewish religious law involves commitment to outer as well as inner forms of ritual purity. Christianity, on its side, has chosen to reject the Jewish emphasis on outer expressions of purity. Of course, no less than Judaism, Christianity retains the religiously universal emphasis on pure and impure. This is reflected in the importance given the cleansing ritual of baptism, and the commensality rules and table rituals determining who can share in the Lord's supper. Nevertheless, from its inception, Christianity has chosen to focus on interior, 'intentional' or spiritual expressions of purity as opposed to outer physical forms.

The other factor contributing to the importance of law in Judaism is the effort by Jewish teachers to communicate and enforce ethical ideals by means of institutionalised communal practice. Indeed, this aspect of Judaism has led some scholars to question whether the category of ethics even exists in Judaism, since most normative requirements are instantiated as binding or socially enforced rules of behaviour.[6] Harold Schulweis captures the spirit of this impulse to law when he observes that in classical Judaism

> Such guiding principles of ethics as the conservation of health, life, and property . . . were concretized into legal precepts. The issue of philanthropy, for example, was not left solely to the whim and caprice of the individual. Laws of tithing and restrictions even as to the generosity of the charity given were articulated . . . The Levitical formula 'to love one's neighbor as oneself' was not allowed to waste away into pious declaration. The rights of adjoining neighbors were spelled out pragmatically in the Talmud. A property owner has a prior claim over any other person to purchase property adjoining his. If the owner, lacking neighborly feeling, ignores his neighbor's rights by selling the property to a third person, the latter may be compelled to turn over the bought property to the adjacent neighbor for the

purchasing price. Theological ethics [thus] embraced reality through the implementation of law in the daily activities between man and man.[7]

This legal pole of the law–gospel, law–ethics debate is of abiding importance. Even within Christianity, despite the primacy given to inner ethical transformation and acts of loving kindness, there have always been efforts – perceived as *expressions* of Christian love – to organise Christian life around shared and binding normative standards. Various Reformed and sectarian groups evidence this impulse, as does the Roman Catholic Church. The Catholic tradition of medical ethics is illustrative. Understanding that crucial matters of life and death that affect everyone in the community cannot be left to the untutored whims of individuals, Catholic ethicists have striven over the years to develop a formal body of norms meant to guide individuals and institutions.

Of course, in Catholicism, as in Judaism, the impulse to law also sometimes reveals a negative side. This impulse runs the risk of turning into a series of inflexible injunctions and prohibitions. Spontaneity and inwardness in ethical decision can shrivel into a deadening conformity to some book of statutes.[8] Judaism offers abundant illustrations of this problem. A leading example is contemporary Orthodoxy's treatment of the *agunah* or abandoned wife. Traditional Jewish law stipulates that a woman whose husband has disappeared cannot remarry for fear that she and her new spouse may inadvertently commit adultery. In the State of Israel, where Jewish marital laws also govern civil life, this has left thousands of Holocaust survivors and even some young Israeli war widows in an intolerable situation. The inability of Orthodox rabbis to solve this problem creatively reflects the dead hand of the patriarchal past and the presence of legalism at its worst. Here we thirst for the freedom of which St Paul speaks and the sense that love of neighbour takes precedence over law.

There will always be a tension between the requirements of law and the need for immediate ethical responsiveness. The failures on both sides of the polarity, the extremes of legalism and asocial individualism, witness to this tension. This is one reason why Jewish and Christian ethics must stay in dialogue in order to learn from the other's mistakes and achievements.

UNIVERSALITY VERSUS PARTICULARITY

The second major polarity I want to discuss is the polarity of universality versus particularity. I can describe this succinctly by stating that

Christianity has always tried to extend its reach universally to embrace people of all backgrounds both in terms of its membership and in the scope of its ethical concern. In contrast, Judaism has tended to focus on the experience of one continuing ethnic community. In this sense, Judaism is an ethnocracy. Historically, Christianity accomplished the transition from ethné to individual primarily through a shift of focus in the divine redemptive activity from the people Israel to the person Jesus Christ. From this moment onward, peoplehood interpreted in terms of ethnic and historic continuity lost its redemptive significance. The single suffering servant, whose redemptive significance is accessible to all who acknowledge the salvific and moral meaning of his life, took its place.

Of course, putting matters this way overlooks many complexities that blur these sharp distinctions. In terms of membership, Christianity does not eliminate Hebrew peoplehood, but replaces it with a new, non-ethnic peoplehood of faith. For Christians, the destiny of this community – the new Israel – is no less important than the older ethnic peoplehood it replaced. On its side, Judaism, too, usually conceived its peoplehood in less than strictly ethnic terms. In the course of its history Judaism was sometimes a zealously missionary faith. It still possible for anyone to join the Jewish 'people' by means of a ritual conversion culminating in baptism. The rabbinical mind also saw no contradiction in holding that Israel stands in special relation to God and maintaining that 'the pious and virtuous of all nations participate in eternal bliss'.[9]

In terms of ethical scope, Christianity has known its moments of harsh exclusiveness and dehumanisation of those beyond its boundaries. It has sometimes not been averse to using the instrument of holy war against unbelievers. On its side, Judaism has harboured within it the prophetic impulse towards universality. Thus, classical Jewish law ordains that such pious acts as giving charity to the poor or consoling the bereaved are to be extended to the non-Jew as well as to the Jew.

Nevertheless, in their deepest instincts, I believe, these daughter faiths of the biblical tradition differ on this matter. Jewish concern and energy has always been directed inward towards protecting the Jewish people and developing their ethical and religious purity, whereas Christianity has sought to reach out to all human beings with its message of faith and compassion. I can put this distinction concretely by saying that the parable of the Good Samaritan, with its vision of individual acts of compassion beyond the bounds of one's community, is quintessentially a Christian story. True, it finds precedent and support in many Jewish sources – not least of all in the legally commanded concern for the sojourner in one's midst (Exod. 22:21).

But it is not a story that stirs the mind and heart of Jews as it does Christians. For an analogy in Jewish experience, one might look to the Book of Ruth. Here, too, we see openness to the outsider. But the emotional turning point of the story comes when Ruth joins her fate to that of the Jewish people, saying to Naomi, 'Your people shall be my people' (1:16). From this point onward, Ruth is a 'daughter of Israel', tied to its fate and entitled to its protections.[10]

No one can speak more positively about Christianity's transcendence of ethnic particularity and its spirit of compassionate universality than a modern Jew like myself. Coursing through a series of channels, this spirit has shaped democratic values and respect for human rights in the modern world. These channels include the Roman Catholic tradition of natural law, Protestant emphases on individual conscience, and sectarian protests against religious and political oppression. As a consequence of these formative developments, respect for the individual and the sanctity of every human being are among Christianity's greatest contributions to human civilisation. Ironically, some of that contribution was made through the efforts of the Enlightenment, which arose only after various misguided Christian imperialisms and triumphalisms failed to impose their wills on civilisation as a whole.

The Enlightenment is under attack from many quarters today, not least of all from some Christian ethicists who would replace its focus on disembodied individualism with a renewed attention to the historic communities of faith in which we dwell. I have no wish to enter into this debate, other than to say that there is truth on both sides. But I can add that when modern Jews hear such criticisms of Enlightenment ideals, they quiver. They instinctively respect these ideals of individualism, commitment to democracy and respect for the person that a reliance on reasoned arguments in public discourse represents. Jews also know that in any social order based on community identity, they are likely to be defined as outsiders.

The ironies here are multiple: steeped in ethnic identity, American and European Jews nevertheless fear renewal of a social order based on such identities. Valuing a transcendence of communal identities, they are in the deepest debt to Christian communities that, over the years, have struggled to preserve and embody such transcendence. A further irony is that in Israel, where older Jewish ethnocentric attitudes now sometimes fuel forms of Jewish nationalism and militarism, many citizens long for the universalism and individualism of the West that they see as founded on ancient Christian values and crystallised in the modern period in the ideals of the Enlightenment.

A leader of the Israeli Peace Movement, Yaron Ezrahi, expresses this viewpoint in a recent critical study of Israeli culture and political life. He writes:

> In Christian societies the idea of individual salvation . . . encouraged modes of introspection, reflection, self-examination, and moral and spiritual self-narration which enriched and consolidated the Western conception of the interior, inward self; liberal and democratic thinkers like Locke, Rousseau, and John Stuart Mill could elaborate on the 'technologies of the self' as the basis of modern conceptions of individual freedoms, rights, and citizenship. Where such traditions of spiritual individualism are weak invariably liberal-democratic individualism is depicted negatively as a form of degenerative, narcissistic, or materialistic egotism. In modern Israel, expressions of individualism have been perceived as symptoms of the breakdown of high ideals and the disintegration of communal life.[11]

> Ultimately a resilient Israeli democratic culture would have to be nourished by emancipated Israeli individuals capable of creating, or living in, personal narrative spaces resistant to the imperial power of the epic narratives of religion, ideology, and history.[12]

As we witness the clash of communities and ethnicities in the Middle East, Ezrahi's remarks serve to remind us of the historic importance of the universalised and individualised pole of the religious life that Christianity introduced.

Despite this, however, there is also much to be said about the pole of community and ethnicity, even with its dangers. Put succinctly, Jewish ethnic experience has created over time a community of shared fate that models the conditions of the moral life. Connected by ties of family, descent and culture, Jews have repeatedly been instructed in the truth that no human being stands alone, that no one is self-created and that no individual is stronger than the communities of support that she or he helps to sustain. A related lesson is that everyone's conduct affects everyone else.

An old Jewish story, part of the rich tradition of Jewish humour, illustrates this point. Two men are alone in a small rowboat far from shore. One of them takes out an augur and starts drilling a hole beneath his seat.

> 'You imbecile,' cries the other, 'what do you think you're doing?'
> 'Leave me alone', says the one who is drilling. 'It's none of your business. This is *my* part of the boat'.

Long ago, Jews learned the lesson that, like it or not, we are all in the same boat. In formal terms, the teaching was that all members of the community 'are bondsmen for one another'.[13] One stimulus to this was the awareness that misconduct by some in our midst provided a ready excuse for anti-Semitism that imperilled us all. We also learned that no matter how successful, how rich or how accomplished we are as individuals, in the eyes of the world we are still first of all Jews. This means that there is no personal escape from collective peril or hardship. All these lessons were driven home during the Holocaust, when ancient hatreds joined with an insane racist ideology to render individual forms of escape impossible. Rich or poor, wise or foolish, Jews – as Jews – became victims of injustice and cruelty. These experiences have forged for Jews an intense, almost family-like loyalty to the community. Eugene Borowitz captures some of the religious and ethical implications of this loyalty when he writes:

> [A] Jewish relationship with God inextricably binds selfhood and ethnicity with its multiple ties of land, language, history, traditions, fate, and faith. By this folk rootedness, covenantal Jewish identity negates the illusion that one can be loyal to humanity as a whole but not to any single people, and it rescues the messianic hope from being so abstract as to be inhuman. Ethnic particularity commits the Jewish self to the spirituality of sanctifying history through gritty social and political struggles. Internally as well, each Jew becomes implicated in this people's never-ending struggle to hallow grim social circumstances or the temptations of affluence . . .[14]

I am a student of John Rawls. During my graduate-school days at Harvard I first encountered Rawls' *A Theory of Justice* in manuscript form. As I studied Rawls' theory, I remember being overwhelmed by his concept of an 'original position of equality'. This idea gave rational substance to my own deepest ethical convictions. Now I realise how much my Jewish background prepared me for this idea. Jewish experience has repeatedly mimicked the original position of equality, stripping individuals of the privileges, ranks, possessions and distinctions which, in the course of social life, so easily come to be seen as earned or self-created. Only the repeated fracturing of these naive, self-serving illusions can lead people to see the deeper truths that our accomplishments are in part socially created and that we depend on one another's respect and cooperation for continuing survival and flourishing. These insights underlie Judaism's historic passion for justice. If Jewish teaching has always been sensitive to the needs of the orphan, the widow, 'the poor man when he called for help' (Job 29:12–20), it is because, from the Exodus experience onward, Jews have collectively known oppression. Ethnic peoplehood, a shared identity and a shared fate thus created for Jews a living, historical approximation of the 'original position of equality'.

The contrast here with Christianity is very complex. By no means do I wish to suggest that Christian communities have not known what it means to live and die together as a morally committed people. Certainly the Christian church during its early experiences of persecution learned this lesson. The family feeling of those early communities resonates through Paul's letters and other New Testament writings. As Wayne Meeks reminds us, being members of the Body of Christ grounded the unity and mutual care of those early Christian congregations.[15] Later Christian sectarian groups, committed to a distinctive ethical–religious ideal, have also known what it means to be 'a different people'. It is no accident that some of the most enduring contributions to Christian social ethics have come from sectarian groups or other oppressed religious communities. A commitment to Christian ideals often brought with it marginalisation that sustained and reinforced those very ideals. The willingness of the Huguenot citizens of Chambon sur Lignon to harbour Jewish refugees, as documented by Philip Hallie in his book *Lest Innocent Blood Be Shed*,[16] shows how effectively persecution and marginality can reinforce values of compassion to the stranger or the oppressed. In our own day, the value of ethical – and ethnic – peoplehood is most dramatically evidenced in the experiences of the black churches. I agree profoundly with Daniel Maguire's observation that 'African Americans can stake an impressive claim to being the geniuses of Biblical religion in our time.'[17]

However, it has not always been so with the Christian churches and denominations. Too often, they merely blended into existing majoritarian cultures and accepted prevailing social values. The very openness and inclusivity of the faith – one of its most important ethical impulses – thus led to loss of identity and shared community. In Kierkegaard's memorable words, one became a Christian merely by being born and living in Christendom.[18] The consequence is that Christian ideals often have no corresponding social base to illuminate their meaning, their value – or their price.

Let me insist here that this social base is not something that can be artificially created. However well intentioned the efforts, even gathered communities of idealism can lack the fatedness and the binding quality of ethnic or racial peoplehood. Here I find myself in multiple disagreements with a colleague like Stanley Hauerwas who looks to a reinvigorated church as the centrepiece of Christian ethics and the moral life.[19] For one thing, as Jew, I must say that the record of the churches has not been good. Some Christian communities have been bearers of genuine Christian values, but others have been centres of compromise or discrimination.[20] More important, there are limits to what can be accomplished by even the best voluntary community of morally committed people. However sincere such people are in their commitments, these commitments are still voluntary. Not only can individual members of such rededicated communities often escape suffering by opting out in times of hardship, even when they stand by their fellows and their beliefs a shared fate always remains something that has been willingly undertaken. This means that – even amidst martyrdom – an element of choice, decision and control remains. But it is precisely the absence of choice, decision and control that is an abiding truth of the moral life. Like it or not, we lack the ability to master our destiny. We are not the sole determiners of the degree of our vulnerability, nor are we the sole creators of our strengths and accomplishments. Precisely because of this, we must stand together in communities of mutual support and justice. These are the lessons of ethnic peoplehood. They are not easily learned in other ways.

What does this mean for Christian ethics? I am not sure. I know that to the extent that Christians wish to live and embody their own intensely idealistic ethics, they must somehow learn to recreate the community of shared destiny that, at least in the past, has come so naturally to Jews. They must also heed the experience of those – Jews, some Christians, and members of other faith communities – who have lived the experience of ethnic or racial peoplehood. Although Christians must never renounce their own commitments to ethical and communal universality – this is the glory of their tradition – they must also respect and pay attention to particularised ethical experiences. On this count, too, Christian ethics and Jewish ethics must be in dialogue with one another.

VALUATION OF SUFFERING VERSUS AVERSION TO SUFFERING

A final contrast between Jewish and Christian ethics that I want to develop has to do with the polarity of a religious ethic that spiritually values suffering versus one that strives to avoid suffering. My thinking about this issue was stimulated by my two years of service during the mid 1990s at the U.S. National Institutes of Health. As a part of my duties there helping to establish an office of Genome Ethics at the National Human Genome Research Institute, I repeatedly participated in conversations, panels and seminars with ethicists who expressed reservations about the growing

powers of genetic medicine. Some of the most thoughtful of these were
Christian ethicists working at the forefront of biomedical ethics (see below,
pp. 266f). Frequently, these ethicists raised the question of whether the new
powers of genetics were somehow making us less willing to accept imperfection in our midst. In the course of this work, I also had occasion to deal
with a number of Jewish thinkers and rabbis. Some of these were connected
with the screening programme for Tay-Sachs disease conducted in the
Orthodox and hasidic communities. What struck me were the energy with
which this programme was implemented and its wide acceptance by individuals of all Jewish backgrounds. Here, in a community perhaps more profoundly affected than any other by the horrors of eugenics in our era, there
was virtually no mention of the negative implications of genetic selection. A
similar contrast became apparent in the U.S. debates over cloning following
the announcement of the birth of Dolly the sheep. It is noteworthy that
Christian scholars testifying before the U.S. National Bioethics Advisory
Commission were almost uniformly negative about the human application
of cloning technology. In contrast, Jewish scholars, some of Orthodox background, tended to welcome the idea that cloning might be used to overcome
various disease conditions and infertility.[21]

These and many similar experiences led me to ask what there is in the
Jewish and Christian traditions that accounts for these differences. It is not
simply the formal teachings of the two traditions about prenatal life. Where
abortion is concerned, Orthodox Jewish teaching as interpreted today is
fairly restrictive, permitting abortion only when needed to save the life of
the mother. Despite this, Orthodox Jews remain broadly favourable to pre-
conceptional genetic testing programmes, and non-Orthodox (Reform or
Conservative) Jews are very supportive of most forms of prenatal testing.

In searching for an explanation of the differences between Jewish and
Christian responses to these issues, I conclude, we must look, in part, to each
tradition's attitude towards suffering. Jews and Judaism are deeply averse to
suffering in any of its forms. True, some isolated classical texts intone the
spiritual value of suffering, but these statements usually arise in the context
of discussions of the problem of theodicy.[22] They are anguished efforts to
understand the presence of innocent suffering in a world where it really
should not exist. Almost every other teaching in the tradition is averse to
suffering, be it psychological or physical. There is almost no tradition of self-
imposed ascetical discipline in Judaism.[23] Leading Talmudic sages
denounced the glorification of suffering and preferred to forgo future
reward if it involved present agony.[24] Acts which unnecessarily inflict suffering on others, even those causing embarrassment or humiliation, are

condemned. And, despite the importance of halakhic obedience, there is a willingness to suspend virtually any requirement when obeying it jeopardises human life or health.

I can only speculate here on why this aversion to suffering is so pronounced in this tradition. Part of it is the extreme this-worldly focus that Judaism inherited from its Hebraic past and never relinquished. In addition, I suspect that centuries of persecution have produced enough suffering in the lives of Jews to satisfy all useful moral purposes. One did not ever have to invite suffering to appreciate its spiritual benefits.

In the area of reproductive medicine, this sensibility has combined with many other factors to justify efforts to reduce familial burdens or maternal hardship. Thus even among the Orthodox we find a broad acceptance of women's efforts to avoid conception whenever a pregnancy is likely to threaten a woman's life or health. Anticipating modern efforts at genetic control, we encounter explicit rabbinic injunctions to avoid marrying into a family known to carry an inherited disease.[25]

In the area of biomedicine, this aversion to suffering led Jews to early and swift acceptance of medical interventions. Despite biblical pronouncements declaring God to be the healer, Judaism never exhibited any significant religious opposition to medical care. Indeed, some great rabbis combined scholarly endeavours with medical careers.

Christianity, too, has always been committed to medical care. But the Christian impulse, I believe, comes partly from a different direction. Here it is the effort to imitate God in Christ, to be present with those who suffer, that has most stimulated Christian efforts in this area. In terms of medical ethics, these different points of departure shape the resulting sense of what is most valuable in medicine. In Judaism, what are most admired are the healing skills of the individual rabbi/physician. It is the physician's task to slow or halt the progression of disease and reduce suffering. The most salient early Christian medical efforts, in contrast, involved the development of specialised religious orders and hospitals dedicated to succouring the infirm.

This subtle and nuanced difference becomes apparent in the area of genetic medicine today. Despite their bitter history of exposure to genetic abuses, Jews as a group raise few questions about the directions of these new technologies. In contrast, questions among Christian theologians and ethicists abound. These questions are not confined to Catholic ethicists or others who oppose prenatal testing because of its association with abortion. Consider the following remarks by Ronald Cole-Turner and Brent Waters, whose recent work focuses on the moral implications of the Human Genome Project:

Increased use of prenatal genetic testing seems to fit within a larger popular tendency to avoid pain at all costs. We seek not only pain-free dentistry but a pain-free life. We do not know nor do we want to learn how to make painful experiences part of the narrative of our lives. We shrink from these in the fear that they will infect our lives. Is prenatal genetic testing just another way to shrink from the pain of others, in this case by preventing them from living with us? If that is all that prenatal testing is, then it should be resisted as incompatible with the meaning of Christian life in the community of the cross. The aim of the Christian life is not the avoidance of pain but the faithful following of One who enters into the pain of those who suffer.[26]

This sensibility contrasts dramatically with the Jewish one, for which the avoidance of suffering by morally and religiously permissible means is an expected feature of life.

Biomedicine is on the eve of an era when we will have in our power new ways of reducing suffering and transforming the biological bases of human life. Each of these innovations – genetic manipulations, new birth technologies, cloning and beyond – will stimulate intense moral debate. Schooled in the minimisation of human physical or mental distress, individuals of Jewish background will predictably favour the availability of biomedical and genetic interventions to prevent a variety of conditions such as mental retardation or later-onset genetic disorders. In contrast, many individuals of Christian background will feel uncomfortable with such broad uses of this technology and will question whether our society's resort to it indicates a growing intolerance of imperfection and disability. These debates, of course, will not be confined to Jews and Christians, nor will the lines in the debates always be drawn in such religiously sharp ways. But the differing sensibilities I am pointing to will play a role.

I want to avoid the question 'Who is right?' The Jewish side of these debates responds favourably to technologies that can help improve the material conditions of human life. It also resists the tendency to allow an ultimate religious acceptance of suffering to become a moral encouragement to tolerating or increasing it. Christianity, in contrast, warns against the moral dangers of excessive zeal in trying to try to banish all suffering from our lives. It also fosters reflection on the long-term impact of new biomedical and genetic technologies in terms of our willingness to accept – and love – all who come into our midst. Once again we see two daughter traditions engaging in a family dispute and embodying two different ways of responding to some of the most difficult ethical choices we face. The lesson here is not that one pole of this debate is right and the other wrong, but that each must heed the other. Children of a common biblical faith, Jews and Christians in each generation must ask how the truths of their tradition are best understood, interpreted and applied in new circumstances of life.

CONCLUSION

I have tried to suggest that in terms of some very basic and abiding issues in religious ethics, the Jewish and Christian ethical traditions differ from one another. These differences emphasise the need for dialogue. Each of these broad traditions represents thousands of years of sustained effort to build human moral community. In the course of this experience, each has made terrible mistakes, and each has realised lasting achievements of wisdom and virtue. These streams of tradition cannot be kept apart. The task of Jewish and Christian ethicists is to learn from one another.

With apologies to Elie Wiesel, I would like end by offering a creative retelling of a story found in his novel *The Town beyond the Wall*.[27] In Wiesel's novel, the story concerns the relationship between God and man. But as I reread it recently, it occurred to me that it also applies to the relationship between the Jews and Christians and between Jewish and Christian ethics:

> Legend tells us that a Jewish teacher spoke to a Christian teacher in this way:
> 'Let us change about. You be Jewish and I will be Christian.'
> The Christian teacher smiled gently and asked, 'Aren't you afraid?'
> 'No,' the other replied. 'And you?'
> 'Yes, I am,' he said.
> Nevertheless, the request was granted. So neither one was ever again what he seemed to be.
> Years passed, centuries.
> As the liberation of one was bound to the liberation of the other, they renewed the ancient dialogue whose echoes come to us in the night, charged with hatred, with remorse, and most of all, with infinite yearning.

Notes

An early version of this chapter was delivered as the 1999 Presidential Address of the Society of Christian Ethics and appeared in the 1999 edition of the *Annual of the Society of Christian Ethics*.

1   See, for example, the following articles or book chapters by me: 'Jewish Ethics and the Virtue of Humility', *Journal of Religious Ethics* 1/1 (1973), 53–63; 'The Korah Episode: A Rationalistic Reappraisal of Rabbinic Anti-Rationalism', *Annual of the Society of Christian Ethics* (1981), 97–117; 'Abraham, Isaac and the Jewish Tradition', *Journal of Religious Ethics* 10/1 (Spring 1982), 1–21; 'Jewish Ethics and Beneficence', in Earl E. Shelp, ed., *Beneficence and Health Care* (Dordrecht: D. Reidel, 1982), pp. 109–125; 'Contemporary Jewish Bioethics: A Critical Assessment', in Earl E. Shelp, ed., *Bioethics and Theology* (Dordrecht: D. Reidel, 1985), pp. 245–266; 'Genetic Medicine in the Perspective of Orthodox Halakhah', *Judaism* 34/3 (Issue No. 135; Summer 1985), 263–277; '*Centesimus Annus:* A Critical Jewish Perspective', *Journal of Business Ethics* 12 (1993), 945–954; 'Guiding Principles of Jewish Business Ethics', *Business Ethics Quarterly* 7/2 (1997), 21–31; with Ehud Benor, 'The Successful Sarariiman: A Jewish Response', in Regina W. Wolfe and Christine E. Gudorf, eds., *Ethics and World Religions: Cross-Cultural Case Studies* (Maryknoll, NY: Orbis 1999), pp. 294–297.
2   Harold M. Schulweis, 'Judaism: From Either/Or to Both/And', in Elliot N. Dorff and Louis E. Newman, eds., *Contemporary Jewish Ethics and Morality* (New York: Oxford University Press, 1995), pp. 25–37.
3   *Ibid.*, p. 31, quoting Albert C. Knudson, *The Principles of Christian Ethics* (New York, 1943), p. 28.
4   *Jerusalem Talmud*, Peah 16a. Quoted in Schulweis, 'Judaism', p. 32.
5   For numerous examples of this process, see Elliot N. Dorff and Arthur Rosett, *A Living Tree: The Roots and Growth of Jewish Law* (Albany: State University of New York Press, 1988).
6   For an overview of this problem and a review of literature on the topic, see Louis Newman, 'Ethics as Law, Law as Religion: Reflections on the Problem of Law and Ethics in Judaism', in Dorff and Newman, *Contemporary Jewish Ethics*, pp. 79–93. A related but distinct problem is whether halakhah permits the kind of formalisation and resolution into basic principles that is appropriate to ethical theory. For a discussion of this see Leon Roth, 'Moralization and Demoralization in Jewish Ethics', *Judaism* 11 (1962), 291–302.
7   Schulweis, 'Judaism', p. 34.
8   *Ibid.*
9   *Sifra* on Leviticus 19:18. Quoted in Schulweis, 'Judaism', p. 31.
10 Ruth also becomes a 'daughter' in a familial sense, as Laurie Zoloth-Dorfman has emphasised – 'An Ethics of Encounter: Public Choices and Private Acts', in Dorff and Newman, *Contemporary Jewish Ethics*, pp. 219–245.
11 *Rubber Bullets: Power and Conscience in Modern Israel* (New York: Farrar, Straus and Giroux, 1997), pp. 96–97.
12 *Ibid.*, p. 74.
13 Moritz Lazarus, *The Ethics of Judaism* (Philadelphia: Jewish Publication Society of America, 1901), part II, p. 248.
14 Borowitz, 'The Jewish Self', in Dorff and Newman, *Contemporary Jewish Ethics*, p. 110.
15 Wayne A. Meeks, *The Moral World of the First Christians* (Philadelphia: Westminster Press, 1986), p. 130.

16 New York: Harper and Row, 1979.

17 Daniel C. Maguire, *The Moral Core of Judaism and Christianity* (Minneapolis: Fortress Press, 1993), p. 52.

18 Howard V. Hong and Edna H. Hong, eds. and trans., *Søren Kierkegaard's Journals and Papers* (Bloomington: Indiana University Press, 1967), Vol. 1, entry 407. See also Kierkegaard, *The Sickness unto Death*, Howard V. Hong and Edna H. Hong, eds. and trans. (Princeton: Princeton University Press, 1980), p. 56.

19 See for example Stanley Hauerwas, *A Community of Character* (Notre Dame, IN: University of Notre Dame Press, 1981), and his *After Christendom?* (Nashville: Abingdon Press, 1991).

20 Although a journalistic rather than scholarly account, John Cornwell's recent examination of the leadership of Pope Pius XII, *Hitler's Pope* (New York: Viking, 1999), offers a shocking depiction of the papal record of moral indifference and neglect at one of history's most decisive moments.

21 A listing of these presenters as well as a commissioned paper by Courtney Campbell reporting these differences of opinion, 'Religious Perspectives on Human Cloning', can be found on the World Wide Web at http://bioethics.gov/ pubs/cloning1/append.pdf. For an additional assessment of these debates, see Courtney Campbell, 'In Whose Image: Religion and the Controversy of Human Cloning, *Second Opinion*, No. 1 (September 1999), 24–43.

22 For a fuller discussion of these Jewish sources, see my article, 'Theodicy', *Encyclopedia of Religion*, Vol. 14, pp. 430–441. See also Lazarus, *The Ethics of Judaism*, part II, §§237–252; and C. G. Montefiore and H. Loewe, *A Rabbinic Anthology* (New York: Schocken, 1974), ch. 28.

23 On this point, the rabbis did not hesitate to subvert the biblical text. Thus, they deemed the offering to be brought at the end of the Nazirite's vowed term to be expiatory sacrifice 'for the sins of his asceticism' – *Babylonian Talmud*, Tractate Ta'anith, 11a.

24 *Babylonian Talmud*, Tractate Nedarim, 10a.

25 Immanuel Jakobovits, *Jewish Medical Ethics*, revised edition (New York: Bloch, 1975), pp. 155f.

26 *Pastoral Genetics: Theology and Care at the Beginning of Life* (Cleveland: Pilgrim Press, 1996), p. 139.

27 New York: Bard Books/Avon, 1964, p. 190.

11 Other faiths and Christian ethics

GAVIN D'COSTA

The area 'other faiths and Christian ethics' raises many questions, only three of which I shall deal with in this chapter. The three areas overlap and the divisions are artificial, but they serve a pedagogical purpose. First, there is a phenomenological question: Do other faiths have similar *material* ethical goals to those of Christianity? The allied question is whether other faiths also share *formal* similarities, in terms of ethical reasoning and the understanding of ethics. The way in which these questions are answered on an empirical–historical basis may or may not affect theological considerations, and it may well be the case that theological assumptions generate a particular way of reading the signifcance of empirical findings. I believe the latter is true. This leads to the second area: Are Christian ethics *sui generis*? On the one hand, there are those who would argue that whatever the historical–empirical findings, Christian ethics are *sui generis* and phenomenological comparisons are of limited value, and especially so in coming to theological assessments of other religions. On the other hand, there are those who argue that Christian ethics have much in common with ethics from other religions and therefore the phenomenological findings are important theologically and feed into broader questions. For example, can Christianity make unique claims about 'holiness' and 'salvation', when other religions have the capacity to produce 'saints' that equal or better Christian saints? The third area has, in part, developed out of the second: Can the religions support a common understanding of universal human rights? This question feeds into broader philosophical discussion as to whether human rights is a child of modernity and actually inimical to religious conceptions of virtue and duty.

Before turning to these questions, let me make four brief methodological points. First, I write as a Christian theologian broadly sympathetic to the virtue-ethics tradition of Aquinas. Second, I think that generalisations about 'religions', both Christian and others, should be avoided. Historically, there is vast diversity within a religion, and contemporary religions are no different. Third, 'ethics' is difficult to define, and in many traditions there would be an overlap between what might be called cultic duty and liturgical ritual. I will not seek to essentialise 'ethics'. Fourth, while I hope the reader will see the vigour and complexity of the many debates touched on, I shall make no attempt to disguise my own standpoint. I do not believe that 'pure description' is an option.

COMPARATIVE PHENOMENOLOGICAL QUESTIONS

Edward Conze, the great scholar of Buddhism, said: 'I once read through a collection of the lives of Roman Catholic saints, and there was not one of whom a Buddhist could fully approve . . . They were bad Buddhists though good Christians'.[1] Conze's remark highlights two important points in any comparative exercise. First, from where is the comparer starting? What are his or her ethical and religious commitments? Second, in Conze's careful phrase that a Buddhist could not 'fully approve' of any of these Christian saints, the point he is making is that comparisons happen between wholes and not parts. Each detail of ethical belief cannot be rent apart from the overall doctrinal beliefs and communal practices that give them their proper context and meaning. Pre-modernity, it is difficult to find examples of ethics within religions that did not operate in this interrelated and wholistic fashion. Hence, Conze is making the simple point that even if a particular Buddhist were to applaud St Francis of Assisi's relationship with animals, such a Buddhist might not approve of Francis' 'attachment' to God, from whom Francis' attitude to animals derives. Likewise, while politically pacifist Christians may approve and find much in common with the Jain doctrine of *ahimsā* (non-violence), they may not share the understanding and application of *ahimsā* seen in some Digambara monks who strain all water and refuse to bathe because they might harm vermin living in the water, and likewise refuse to brush their teeth. This difference may in part be because Christians do not share the Jain view that all animals have souls.

To return to our questions: Do other faiths have similar material ethical goals, and similar formal ethical assumptions, to Christianity? I think the answer requires not only an empirical–historical investigation, but a further question: How is ethics being envisaged? If, for example, one can simply speak of material ethical *goals* apart from the intentions, practices, and communal and cultic contexts within which such goals operate, then a certain amount of material similarity is forthcoming in a reasonably straightforward sense. For example, one can say that, in the main, modern orthodox Hinduism and Roman Catholicism oppose abortion on ethical grounds –

even if the ethical reasons differ. This is a common ethical *goal*. Examples can be multiplied on all sorts of ethical questions, such as not charging interest on loans; not killing innocent people; killing people guilty of certain crimes; not allowing women access to certain sacred offices; and so on. The United Nations Population Summit in Cairo in 1998 saw a remarkable concordat between the Vatican and many Islamic countries regarding 'birth control'.

On the other hand, if one envisages ethics in a less deontological fashion, and in a more virtue-based manner, then there will be a greater tendency for any similarity that is found to be kept in tension with the dissimilarities within which they exist. Hence, while another religion may share a virtue-based approach (formal similarity), the alleged material similarities of goals might now have to be called into some question, because the question is: What sort of character is being cultivated towards what sorts of ends? This added complexity arises quite simply because at a phenomenological level the *telos* of each religion is specified so very differently: Christians have a trinitarian God, while Jews and Muslims do not; and Buddhists do not have a God at all, while some Hindus are monotheistic and others not. Hence, if ethics are related to the *telos* of each tradition, to say another religion had materially the same ethical goals of Thomist Christiantiy would be to say that all religions explicitly strive for the beatific vision with God as trinity. Phenomenologically, that is clearly not the case, so from this perspective the extent of material ethical similarities must be very carefully contextualised. The differences will not necessarily inhibit cooperation over ethical matters. This is clearly illustrated by the Vatican cooperation with Islam cited above. Hence, while virtue-based approaches may differ substantially from deontological approaches, the resulting social consequences within each approach are not entirely predictable.

There are numerous studies of comparative ethics, and very few support the notion that there is a detailed common ethics found in all the world religions. Those that do come to that conclusion will be further examined below and criticised (mainly for assuming and imposing a universal deontological schema of ethics upon the world religions). However, many studies show that there are some, and very varying amounts of, practical overlaps within some religions in terms of specific commonly held ethical goals.[2] How these overlaps are interpreted and employed forms a further question to which I will turn in the next section. In conclusion, I would suggest that in terms of material ethical *goals* there is potentially a limited, but theologically significant, overlap between other faiths and Christianity;

and in terms of formal ethical assumptions, while there may be large overlaps, such overlaps are logically unrelated to material goals, for in themselves they do not specify the *telos* of the particular traditions. Hence, two
consequentialists, deontologists or virtue-based ethicists from two different
traditions cannot be guaranteed to find similar material goals on the basis of
formal similarities.

THEOLOGICAL ISSUES

We have seen above that findings on the comparative level are already
theory-laden according to the construal of ethics held by the investigator. In
this section, I want to pursue in more detail the theological presuppositions
that might be held by Christian investigators. For that purpose, I have artificially created three positions out of the materials related to this debate.

First, there are those who argue that since Christian ethics is *sui generis*
because Christ is *sui generis*, any such comparisons have extremely limited
theological consequences. Pragmatic cooperation might be appropriate, but
that is the extent of the significance of such commonality. For instance, Karl
Barth nicely exemplifies this point. For Barth, as with the Reform tradition
in general, salvation is not due to any action taken by the human person but
by *sola fide*. Hence, the question of looking at comparative ethics for theological reasons becomes spurious. We cannot be saved by being 'good', for
however impressive the ethical achievements of a religion, they are always
sinful human achievements and no more. Furthermore, when Barth is
pushed regarding the similarities of *sola fide* between Christianity and
Amida Buddhism, he quite rightly points out that the 'object' of faith is
entirely different in each case, so that such a similarity is inconsequential.[3]
Hence, for a position like Barth's, only the question 'how should Christians
treat others?' is a legitimate question. While Barth's position rightly stresses
discontinuity, it is in danger of failing to reflect sufficiently on the continuity within such discontinuity. This latter position, in contrast to Barth, can
be found in various Roman Catholic approaches, and the Reform/Catholic
difference here is not inconsequential.

Second, there are those who would agree with Barth about the *sui
generis* nature of Christianity and Christian ethics while also arguing that
there is a bridge, a point of contact, between Christians and others in terms
of 'natural law'. This does not erase difference, but acknowledges similarity
within the differences. Barth, of course, opposed any notion of the natural
law as *analogia entis*; that is, the supposition that one could come to God
apart from the triune revelation. Hans urs von Balthasar has gone some way

to show that within the Roman Catholic tradition the *analogia entis* operates only within the *analogia fides*, so that Barth's legitimate concerns about undermining revelation are actually shared by Roman Catholics – whom Barth (wrongly) opposes.[4] At this point, it is important to recognise that the natural law itself has been very differently interpreted within modern Catholic ethics.[5] There are those who tend to view it as a universal, found everywhere, despite any cultural construction. Such writers would come under Barth's and Balthasar's strictures. There are others who realise that the 'natural' law is culturally constructed and mediated. Hence, insomuch as natural law is detected in the world, then it can be said that there God is present (see above, pp. 83f).

For example, Pope John Paul II constantly encourages Christians to work together with those from other faiths to promote 'gospel values' such as justice and peace. He argues that such a commonality of ethical goals, when it does occur, has theological implications: 'It is true that the inchoate reality of the Kingdom can also be found beyond the confines of the Church among peoples everywhere, to the extent that they live "Gospel values" and are open to the working of the Spirit who breathes when and where he will (cf. *Jn 3:8*).'[6] Hence, on the one hand, John Paul II is able to affirm the inchoate presence of the kingdom of God within the world religions on the basis of such ethical values as conform to 'gospel values'. On the other hand, he is quite clear that this is not to equate or assimilate other religions to Christianity, thereby retaining its *sui generis* quality. This latter is seen when in the very next sentence following the one quoted above, John Paul II continues: 'But it must immediately be added that this temporal dimension of the Kingdom remains incomplete unless it is related to the Kingdom of Christ present in the Church and straining towards eschatological fullness.' In this last statement, there is a correct refusal to make a strict identity equation between the church and the kingdom within the temporal order, given its 'straining' towards a future identity and fullness, and given its inchoate reality outside the church. John Paul II balances an appreciation of the theological significance of other faiths' ethical systems which are capable of nourishing and cultivating 'gospel values', while still holding to the *sui generis* nature of Christianity, and he refuses to reduce Christian discipleship to ethical injunctions and principles. As he expresses it in the paragraph before the one just quoted: 'The Kingdom of God is not a concept, a doctrine, or a programme subject to free interpretation, but is before all else a *person* with the face and name of Jesus of Nazareth, the image of the invisible God.'

This second position seems to have the advantage of taking the phenomenological evidence of other faiths' ethical systems with due seriousness, without, on the one hand, erasing all points of contact (as does Barth) or, on the other hand, erasing serious differences and the *sui generis* nature of Christ (as do the third group that we shall look at in a moment). Sometimes missing from John Paul II's writings is the acknowledgement that ethical insights and forms of reasoning from other faiths might actually teach Christians something. The notion of 'gospel values' is sometimes rather statically rendered, as if the church were itself always in possession of these rather than being in the process of constantly discovering the ways in which it falls short of, and learns about, such values. For example, Christianity's environmental track record is poor, and something can be learnt from the eastern ethical traditions here. However, given what I have noted about *ahimsā* above, the learning cannot be a facile borrowing, but will always involve transformation, and sometimes mutual transformation, and even conflictual challenge.

The third position within this debate has moved towards using ethics as a way of judging authentic Christianity, and also therefore authentic religions. John Hick (Presbyterian) and Paul Knitter (Roman Catholic) have both argued, in different ways, that the actions of love and service towards others are what characterise the action of God, or the Real (as Hick calls it). Hence, we are able to distinguish between better and worse forms of Christianity on ethical criteria. For example, the German Christians who followed Hitler can be clearly judged negatively on these criteria, and the Rāmakrishna hospitals in India can be judged positively. Hick argues that all religions can and should be judged on these criteria, and historically they all fare equally well (and equally badly). Knitter argues this with a more liberation theology orientation, noting that while this process is called the kingdom by some Christians (and Marxism by others?), some from other religions also prize a similar social transformation. The theological significance of finding commonality is here used to develop a Christian theology of religions which holds that all religions, more or less, are equal paths to the one true God. Hans Küng has developed a slightly more nuanced but similar position in his call for a 'global ethics' that can be shared by all religions.[7]

There are two problems with this type of approach. First, has it displaced Christian ethics (centred on Christ who is *sui generis*) with the ethics of modernity? Kant argued that ethical truth could be known by reason alone, and Kant accordingly was able to judge and evaluate religions in accordance with their conformity to the Kantian Golden Rule. Kant saw in Christianity the highest historical embodiment of the ethics he was able to discover through reason alone. He argued that Christianity was helpful for those who were not able to arrive at the truth by reason.[8]

Inevitably, the trajectory of this position led to the subordination of Christianity to ethical universals. The only significant difference between Kant and these writers is that Kant's exclusive place for Christianity as the highest embodiment of the Golden Rule is extended. Other religions can offer equal testimony about the ethical truths of reason.

The second question follows on from the first: Do such positions simply extol abstract deontological injunctions like 'Love your neighbour as yourself'? This is cited by Hick, Knitter and Küng as the Golden Rule found in the major religions. However, Hick defines love as turning away from 'self-centredness' to 'Reality-centredness' without taking seriously the manifold different ways in which 'self' and 'Reality' are defined, and the different forms of social organisation which they lead to in the history of religions. 'Love' has meant burning other people's bodies, strict discipline enforced by physical punishment, the persecution of homosexuals, and caring for lepers. It has meant a wide variety of things. Küng says that such manifold differences (what he calls thick morality) can nevertheless be distilled into basic truths held by all, and this is what is important: do not lie, do not kill, do not commit sexual impropriety. However, it is only through the way in which these statements have been understood and practised ('thick' description) that we come to know what they mean, so that Küng's attempt to strip them of 'thick' description actually strips them of meaning. For example, we are never told what truth-telling constitutes, to whom it is due, what constitutes truth, and in what circumstances is it all right not to be truthful. To put it crudely, a Nazi could value truth-telling as much as a modern Tibetan Buddhist or a medieval pope, but this does not help in affirming either a serious commonality or a common ethic.

In this section we have seen how theological assumptions shape the interaction with other faiths' ethical systems, as well as how they lead to further theological outcomes. The situation is complex, as is the debate. I have tried to suggest that other faiths' ethics should have serious repercussions upon Christian practice and ethical reflection, such that Christians may learn from, as well as be called to challenge, the ethics of other faiths. I have very strong reservations about the coherence of the positions which advance an ethical foundationalism such as Hick, Knitter and Küng's; while nevertheless being extremely sympathetic to their concerns for world peace and cooperation. I also have problems with those positions that appear immune to history and minimise points of contact that are to be found, even if, admittedly, such similarities are always within a greater difference.

HUMAN RIGHTS AND RELIGIOUS ETHICS

From a Christian point of view the question of the relation between human rights and Christian ethics looms large in the contemporary debate. It is now also a question exercising those from other religions, given the global economy and the international nature of modern societies. Let us take both questions together by putting the problem thus: Is the Universal Declaration of Human Rights adopted by the United Nations General Assembly in 1948 acceptable to Christians and those from other faiths? Historically the answer is clearly yes and no, and both with a variety of qualifications. For example, many Arab countries objected to what they saw as the fundamentally secular assumptions behind the formulations; China now argues that the U.N. Declaration is against the 'Asian' spirit; many from the third world note how they were excluded in its formulation; and western commentators like Alasdair MacIntyre call the Declaration typical in stipulating all sorts of things and giving no reasons whatsoever for such injunctions. On the other hand, support for the U.N. Declaration has found important allies among some religions. His Holiness the Dalai Lama has publicly supported the Declaration, as has His Holiness Pope John Paul II.

This draws us back into an issue that has constantly surfaced in this chapter. It is the question of the relationship of human rights to modernity, and it affects not only Christian ethics but also the conception of ethics in many contemporary religions. The question can be put in the following manner: Is 'human rights' a recent western secular creation quite inimical to Christianity, and possibly to other religions as well? I want to outline three types of answer given to this question.

The first is that human rights is a creation of modernity and that it is inimical to Christianity (and possibly other virtue-based forms of ethics). The argument has been most persuasively put by Alasdair MacIntyre.

It can be summarised as follows. Aristotelian virtue ethics characterised ethical thinking in the west until the rise of modernity. Aristotelian virtue ethics was based on three fundamental insights, all of which were abrogated in the Enlightenment. First, that ethics was primarily a social, communal building task oriented towards the common good; the *telos* within the *polis*. Second, it was based on a syllogistic way of justifying the rules of morality in view of 'human nature as it is' and also what 'human nature, communally, was meant to be'. Third, it was through *phronêsis*, exercising judgement in particular cases, that virtue was learnt – somewhat analogous to the way in which an apprentice learns from a master. MacIntyre is sometimes uncritical of the Aristotelian exaltation of the *polis*, and has taken some time to ground his preference for virtue ethics in an actual community of practice (Roman Catholicism), but that is immaterial to our concerns. MacIntyre argues, in contrast, that the Enlightenment constructed its view of ethics fundamentally based on the notion of the authority of reason, which eroded the authority of tradition (and therefore religion's social vision, and with it the importance of perfecting practice by imitation – the first and third of the premises above). Furthermore, at least in the shape of Hume, Kant and others, the abandonment of the common good and a *telos* increasingly meant the inability to justify the rules of morality being advanced (through the eradication of the syllogism). Eventually, all that could be agreed upon was that people ought to be free to agree or disagree, and this freedom was the most essential quality of liberal society. Hence, the birth of the modern nation-state and liberal democracy, both founded on protecting one's own freedom to act as one wishes, as being the highest good. However, MacIntyre argues that with no common *telos*, even this minimal consensus would eventually be called into question.

Nietzsche was inevitable, given the unresolvable lacuna within the Enlightenment project which replaced the *telos* of the common good with that of 'individual freedom'. Nietzsche saw that there could be no real foundations for ethics and consequently celebrated the 'will to power' which always threatened to break out of this Enlightenment trajectory. The warring of nation-states and the rise of capitalism are testimonies to this. Hence, MacIntyre's argument is that the only communal enclave that can be free of destructive power and chaos (modernity and its child, postmodern nihilism) is in Thomist virtue ethics. MacIntyre's somewhat Eurocentric view, which fails to take seriously the ethical approaches of other religions, has been criticised, and most tellingly by a Muslim.[9] Nevertheless, what is important in this analysis is MacIntyre's indictment of the Universal Declaration of Human Rights as typical of Enlightenment ethics. It states universal ethical injunctions that must be followed by all, without any justification except the assertion that these are required for the four universal aspirations: freedom from fear and from want, and freedom of speech and of belief. Its lack of justification therefore undermines its own usefulness and authority. Furthermore, insomuch as this type of ethical document is based on modernity's concept of ethics, it is inimical to virtue ethics , which does not operate with 'rights', but rather with 'duties' based on role; and role is defined by a vision of the common good.

An example will help. In an opera, each singer has duties based on her or his role, and each singer is chosen for ability to play that role. If each performs the role well, and all do it together, a good opera results. Hence, if the main soprano fails to sing her aria well, she has failed in her duty, given that she is a good and auditioned soprano. She has not infringed human rights. The other singers cannot complain that their rights have in any way been infringed, but they can complain that the successful performance of the opera has been hindered. If one now looks at opera as rights-based activity, the entire conception of the enterprise and its character changes. If each singer has a right to be in a well-performed opera, only then can it be said that the soprano has infringed the rights of the other performers. The tenor may now sue the soprano for this infringement, and their relations become entirely contractual.

MacIntyre's view is shared by some from other religions, who complain that their religion has not been based on 'rights', and that such a term entirely misconstrues the nature of ethics within that tradition. Two examples will suffice. The first is from the great Indian legal historian P. V. Kane. After his magisterial survey of the tradition of Hindu legal ethics, he critically comments on the Indian Constitution of 1950, which in one stroke erased India's historical traditions. Kane writes:

> The Constitution makes a complete break with our traditional ideas. *Dharmasutras* and *Smṛtis* begin with the dharmas ('duties') of the people (*varṇas* and *āśramas*). Prime Minister Pandit Nehru himself says in his Azad Memorial Lectures on 'India today and tomorrow' (1959), 'All of us now talk of and demand rights and privileges, but the teaching of the *dharma* was about duties and obligations. Rights follow duties discharged.' Unfortunately this thought finds no place in the Constitution . . . The Constitution engenders a feeling among common people that they have rights and no obligations whatever and that the masses have the right to impose their will and to give the force of law and justice to their own ideas and norms formed in their own cottages and tea shops. The Constitution of India has no chapter on the duties of the people to the country or to the people as a whole.[10]

Of course, given that *varṇas* and *āśramas* entail caste, there are many low-caste Hindus who especially celebrated the Constitution. The chief architect of the Constitution, the minister of law in Nehru's cabinet, was an outcaste, a Mahar, and six years after the Constitution he finally became a Buddhist, some twenty-one years after leaving Hinduism because of the caste system. It should also be said that Kane was a Brāhmin. Whatever, the point Kane makes is germane. The Indian Constitution is inimical to Hindu ethics, which is based primarily on duties, not rights.

My second example comes from Buddhism. Craig K. Ihara presents an argument not unlike that of MacIntyre and Kane in noting the contrast between Buddhist ethics and the notion of rights. To summarise his succinct and well-illustrated argument against those who want to introduce the notion of rights into Buddhism:

> In my view there is a much more significant change being proposed and which I fear [they] are overlooking. The change to a modern concept of rights is one from conceptualising duties and obligations as the role-responsibilities of persons in a cooperative scheme to seeing them as constraints on individuals in their interactions with other individuals all of whom are otherwise free to pursue their own objectives.[11]

Ihara also makes the very important point that there are many duties, legal and non-legal, that are not logically correlated with the rights of other persons, while on the other hand rights always do entail duties.

This first position, then, can be stated as advancing the argument that human rights are a product of modernity and that modernity and rights language are inimical to religious ethics, which are founded on duties and communal role-playing towards the common good. Hence, to adopt rights language uncritically, religions may unthinkingly reconceptualise themselves to the point of a secret conversion to modernity! Two objections raise themselves at this point. First, if there are rights generated with some duties, then is there a limited place for the discourse of rights in religious ethics? For example, a virtue-ethics Thomism might well be able to subscribe to the notion of the 'universal right to life of an unborn child', even if usually it did not use this type of rights language. It is an interesting fact that the Vatican asked the Harvard professor Mary Ann Glendon, who is deeply critical of rights language, to head its delegation to the Cairo summit, where the 'right to life' was a major theme advanced by the delegation.[12] Second, if a religion sees its apologetic task as speaking in idioms familiar to its hearers (in the way Mahāyāna Buddhism and Catholic Christianity do) so as to convert them, then rights language might have a strategic importance that justifies it, within limits. Both these objections lead us to a second position.

This position might well be characterised by Vatican II's *Declaration on Religious Freedom* (1965) and John Paul II's pontificate, whereby universal human rights have been championed and given a basis in revelation and the natural law – based on the dignity of the human person. Hence, paragraph 2 of the *Declaration on Religious Freedom* seems to reverse Catholic papal social teaching that had developed prior to Vatican II, which held the view that since error has no rights, for it is a duty to avoid error and choose the truth, then holding to false religions (all those apart from Roman Catholicism) which perpetuate error, means that such adherents have no right to preach and teach their religion, or to gain converts. Hence, Gregory XVI (1832), and Pius IX after him, condemned as 'insane' and erroneous the view 'that the liberty of conscience and of worship is the peculiar (or inalienable) right of every man, which should be proclaimed by law'.[13] In 1965, the *Declaration on Religious Freedom* announced:

> This Vatican Synod declares that the human person has a right to religious freedom. This freedom means that all men are to be immune from coercion on the part of the individuals or of social groups of any human power, in such wise that in matters religious no one is to be forced to act in a manner contrary to his own beliefs . . . The Synod further declares that the right to religious freedom has its foundation in the very dignity of the human person, as this dignity is known through the revealed Word of God and by reason itself. This right of the human person to religious freedom is to be recognized in the constitutional law whereby society is governed. Thus it is to become a civil right.[14]

Such an extraordinary 'development' shows that the Roman Catholic Church is going through an important and not yet resolved transition from Thomist virtue ethics to an *ad hoc* employment of rights language.

This eclectic approach is also to be found in Buddhism and other religions, including Islam, which is often seen as the most resistant.[15] Historically, this second position is in its infancy. In my opinion, the integration of rights language into Catholic social ethics is still in a transition period. It suffers from the pitfalls noted by the first group above, but it also attempts to steer forward in the light of the two criticisms made against the first group (and noted above).

The third group of thinkers is not dissimilar to the previous third group (Hick, Knitter and Küng), and includes those like Leonard Swidler who advance *A Catholic Bill of Rights* (1988), such that the principles of the U.N. Declaration become determinative for judging the church.[16] Given my own sympathy with the first group, it seems to me that this third group cannot properly account for its ethical orientation and more often than not seems to have reconceptualised Christianity in the image of the Enlightenment. Nevertheless, it is clear that many in this group are only different in degree from those in the second; hence, the matter is far more complicated.

CONCLUSION

There are many theological, phenomenological and philosophical questions that require further exploration within the areas I have covered. There are also many other questions that might have been raised. However, in the field of 'other faiths and Christian ethics' I believe these three are the most important.

Notes

1 Edward Conze, *Thirty Years of Buddhist Studies: Selected Essays* (Oxford: Cassirer, 1967), p. 47.
2 See, for example, ed. Marcus Braybrooke, *Stepping Stones to a Global Ethics* (London: SCM, 1992); ed. Dan Cohn-Sherbok, *World Religions and Human Liberation* (Maryknoll, NY: Orbis Books, 1992).
3 See Karl Barth, *Church Dogmatics*, vol. 1, pt 2 (Edinburgh: T. & T. Clark, 1970), pp. 280–361.
4 Hans urs von Balthasar, *The Theology of Karl Barth*, trans. J. Dury (San Francisco: Ignatius Press, 1992).
5 See, for example, J. M. Finnis, *Natural Law and Natural Rights*, ed. H. L. A. Hart, Clarendon Law Series (Oxford: Clarendon Press, 1980).
6 *Redemptoris missio* (London: Catholic Truth Society, 1991), para. 20.
7 See John Hick, *An Interpretation of Religion* (London: Macmillan, 1989); Paul F. Knitter, *Jesus and the Other Names* (Maryknoll, NY: Orbis, 1998); Hans Küng, *A Global Responsibility: In Search of a New World Ethic*, trans. John Bowden (London: SCM, 1991). See my detailed criticism of this type of position in *The Meeting of Religions and the Trinity* (Maryknoll, NY: Orbis, 2000), pt I, esp. ch. 1.
8 Immanuel Kant, *Religion within the Limits of Reason Alone* (New York: Harper, 1960).
9 See Muhammad Legenhausen, review of *Whose Justice? Which Rationality?*, *Al-Tawhid*, 14, 2, 1997, 158–76. See also Leroy S. Rouner, *Human Rights and the World's Religions* (Notre Dame, IN: University of Notre Dame Press, 1998).
10 P. V. Kane, *History of the Dharmaśāstras*, 2nd rev. ed. (Poona: Bhandarkar Oriental Research Institute, 1968), pp. 1664–65.
11 Craig K. Ihara, 'Why there are no human rights in Buddhism: a reply to Damien Keown', in eds. Damien V. Keown, Charles S. Prebish & Wayne R. Husted, *Buddhism and Human Rights* (London: Curzon, 1998), p. 49.
12 See Mary Ann Glendon, *Rights Talk: The Impoverishment of Political Discourse* (New York: Free Press, 1991).
13 Pius IX, citing Gregory, as quoted in Michael Davies, *The Second Vatican Council on Religious Liberty* (Minnesota: Neumann Press, 1992), p. 60.
14 Para. 2 from ed. Walter M. Abbott, *The Documents of Vatican II*, trans. and ed. Joseph Gallagher (New York: Guild Press, 1966).

15 See the collections eds. Hans Küng & Jürgen Moltmann, *The Ethics of World Religions and Human Rights*, Concilium, 1990, 2, (London: SCM, 1990); eds. Keown et al., *Buddhism and Human Rights*; and Robert Traer, *Faith in Human Rights* (Washington, DC: Georgetown University Press, 1991).

16 See eds. Leonard Swidler & Herbert O'Brien, *A Catholic Bill of Rights* (Kansas City, MO: Sheed & Ward, 1988).

Part three

Issues in Christian ethics

12 Christianity and war

R. JOHN ELFORD

Christianity teaches that the world is in a state of what it describes as 'fallen' disorder. There have been two classic attempts to understand why this is the case. The first, by Irenaeus, claimed that God intended it to be so that God's creatures could live lives of 'recapitulation' in which they constantly grew in grace. The second, by Augustine, claimed that human disobedience caused the disorder.[1] Neither of these attempted explanations is satisfactory. Disorder and evil have to be lived with for the mystery they are. According to one biblical view, the state of conflict is represented by the 'principalities and powers' which are part of the created order (Rom. 8:38), and they are variously described in the Bible and its translations. Although they were among the 'all things' redeemed by Christ's death (Col. 1:20), they will remain in existence until Christ's return in glory. (1 Cor. 15:24). Only then will the struggle cease. This is a biblical way of describing the world's disorder. Human beings are part of this. They are seen as fallen creatures. Though they were created in and still bear the image of God as an alien dignity, their propensity to sin manifests itself in all that they do. Nothing remains untainted. Human beings are, however, the agents of God's grace in the world, but at the same time they remain part of its essential problem.

All this requires Christians to live in ways which bring the powers of redemption which were wrought on the cross to bear on every area of practical politics, including and especially areas of human conflict and suffering. This is why they are enjoined to be active 'peacemakers' in the present and are not permitted to believe only that peace will occur in some Messianic future. For this reason, peacemaking is a central Christian spiritual obligation. This alone explains its prominence in the New Testament and the contrast that that bears to the Jewish Bible in this respect. In this way, Christian approaches to war and peace are derived from its basic tenets. Other religions are similar in this respect. In general, it may be observed that: Judaism and Hinduism share a resigned acceptance of the inevitability of

war; Buddhism places it in the wider context of its central concern to eliminate all kinds of suffering; and Islam derives from Judaism its own more
prominent belief in war as an instrument of the divine wrath. In a pluralist
world in which religions are enjoined to unite in their similarities rather
than divide on their differences, there is a need for them to address matters
of war and peace more collectively than they have, for the most part, done
hitherto.

War, as a basic state of human affairs, has always been horrendous, and it
has become increasingly so with the advent of modern methods of war-fighting: biological, chemical, conventional and nuclear. All of these modern technologies impact on the means and the morality of war-fighting. We will
consider this in what follows. The horrendous fact, however, is that human
beings killed more of their own kind in the twentieth century than they did
in all the previous centuries put together. Add to all this the extensive worldwide trade in small arms, which through their use in civil and other wars kill
more people than any other type of weapon, and it becomes clear that war is
a greater problem than it has ever been.

Any satisfactory definition of war has to be specific enough to distinguish it from other types of human conflict short of war, yet also broad
enough to include wars of aggression and defence. This is why such a definition remains elusive. The classic definition of Clausewitz, 'war is an act of
violence intended to compel our opponent to fulfil our will', remains useful,
but it does not help with distinguishing war, as such, from individual acts of
violence and riots.[2] Riots do not take place in anything like the wider political context which is characteristic of war itself. 'Acts of violence' are also difficult to define. Are, for example, trading sanctions acts of violence? Some
will be and some not, but what precisely makes the difference? Nor is it any
longer satisfactory simply to say that war is a function of states. Just rebel-
lions against states and war waged by international bodies such as the
United Nations fall outside this restriction and are both common features
modern warfare. For these reasons war remains difficult to define theoretically, though when it occurs it is always clearly the all too readily recognisable human tragedy that it is.

Christian responses to war cover the spectrum of responses to be found
elsewhere and for this reason often overlap with non-Christian ones.
According to the classical typology of Roland Bainton, they fall, broadly, into
three categories; pacifist, crusading and the just war.[3] I will discuss each in
turn, but it must be kept in mind that these 'types' are abstract notions which
seldom occur in conceptually separate and neat instances. The actual
tragedy of war is more complicated.

PACIFISM

Jesus has been widely understood as a pacifist, notwithstanding his overturning the tables of the money-changers (Mark 11:15) and his claim that he came to bring a sword (Matt. 10:34). Too much has perhaps been made of these contrary indications by those who seek to justify their non-pacifism by tracing it back to Jesus himself. He was, it must always be remembered, a radically strange, to the point of being generally subversive, eschatological prophet.[4] His mission was to prepare people for the imminently expected world-to-come by examining their innermost motivations and actions, rather than to enable them to live permanently in the world as it then was. His generally pacifist approach naturally exerted a great influence on the earliest Christians. All of this, however, was to change gradually in the first three centuries as Christianity became less and less politically marginalised in a process which became complete on the conversion of the emperor Constantine to Christianity in 312CE. It is now often observed that up to this time Christianity was less pacifist than was once thought and that Christian reluctance to undertake military service arose as much from an aversion to taking the oaths of allegiance to Rome as it did from a desire to avoid military activity as such.

Jesus' teaching on peace was interpreted in the New Testament as being central to his wider message, and it contrasts with the understanding of peace in the Jewish Bible. In the latter, peace was something which would only occur in the Messianic future; in the meantime strife generally and war itself were seen as so much a part of the natural order of things that they were even thought to be the instruments of God's will – a belief which, as we shall see, persisted in later Christian thinking. For Christians, the coming of the Messiah changed all of that. Jesus was the Prince of Peace who gave his disciples the gift of peace and told them that they were blessed when they made it (Matt. 5:9). Peace was, therefore, a present reality in the new Messianic age. (We have already seen how the New Testament coped with all the evidence to the contrary.) Some Christian churches think this to be so central to the essential Christian message that they have given it prominence over all else. Examples are the Mennonite and Quaker churches. However, there is an important difference between them. The former believe that for this reason they are required to separate themselves from the fallen world, and the latter believe the contrary. Therefore, the Quakers, though pacifist, are frequently to be found in the midst of all manner of peacemaking activities, including non-combatant military service and often at the forefront of theatres of war.

More generally, Christian pacifists can be grouped, like others, under three headings: pacifists of principle, of pragmatism and of selection. The first group base their stance on their interpretation of the ministry of Jesus, claiming that that alone justifies it and that no manner of other circumstantial considerations can call it into question. It is right for that reason and no other. Whatever suffering might be encountered in the exercise of pacifism, so understood, it has to be endured as a means to the desired peaceful end; and here again the example of the ministry of Jesus is a powerful one. If suffering unto death is the means to that end, so be it. According to this view, only non-violence can beget non-violence. This sort of Christian witness is often powerful in the extreme, and never more so than when it leads to willing self-sacrifice. It is why some object conscientiously to any participation in activities relating to war, whereas others, who share the general pacifist view, choose to make whatever peace they can wherever the opportunity arises. Non-violence, so understood, is professed as an intrinsic moral duty which will not allow consideration of any consequences which would be contra-indicative. Taking one human life to save however many others is, therefore, never contemplated, since it is not allowed in principle. This view is generally held not to be as coterminous with the ministry of Jesus as many of its proponents claim it to be, but many Christians persist in it. It appeals to idealists of all kinds, not least the young. Its principal difficulty is that, noble though it appears, it seems to fly in the face of common sense. Few would now believe that the morality of our actions can be so divorced from a consideration of the desirability, or otherwise, of the consequences to which they give rise.

Pragmatic pacifists claim that their position is justified by this very point. Violence, they hold, is counterproductive and non-violence productive. The Mahatma Gandhi is often cited as an example of this position. His non-violent struggles against British rule in India, on most accounts, led directly or at least indirectly to its cessation. However, the fact that the power Gandhi was opposing had a moral conscience did much to insure the success of his methods. Ruthless opponent dictators would not have been so readily persuaded.

Selective pacifism is a version of pragmatic pacifism. It simply selects what things to be and not to be pacifist about. Nuclear pacifism is a clear example of this. There are many who would not call themselves pacifist in either of the first two senses and who would be prepared to contemplate war-fighting with conventional weapons but would not be prepared to use nuclear weapons. The reasons usually given are that there can be no winners in a nuclear war and that the means used would therefore be out of any proportion to any end achieved. The central problem for all types of Christian and other pacifists is whether or not and under what circumstances responsible citizenship is compatible with pacifism in a largely non-pacifist world where the peace, and the freedom of conscience on which pacifism depends, is largely wrought by military constraint of one sort or another.

Some Christian pacifists respond to this by claiming that their way of life is a vocation which is appropriate only for the few, like celibacy, and that it witnesses to a higher order of things to the many. There are, broadly, three things to which pacifists, with others, importantly contribute. First, they often help to politicise peace issues and thereby keep them in the public arena. Second, they often contribute to ongoing scholarly debate about war and peace. Third, they constantly and importantly remind the non-pacifist world that war is the terrible thing that it is. All of these things are important in any free society, which is why in Britain, for example, in the Second World War, pacifists were either granted exemption from military service per se or allocated non-combatant roles within it. No community could be asked to do more in the face of such a threat to national security and freedom. This is the only properly acceptable alternative to draft-dodging and dishonest hypocrisy of one sort or another.

CRUSADES

The second major category within which Christianity has approached war has been the crusades. Whilst the term has been used to describe actions the church has taken against heretics and its enemies generally, it more usually refers to the military actions specifically undertaken to regain Jerusalem from Islamic occupation in the eleventh, twelfth and thirteenth centuries.[5] They were also waged against any races and kingdoms which were thought to get in the way of this objective, such as the Visigoths, Ostrogoths, Lombards, Suevi, Vandals, Franks, Saxons and Jutes. The origins of the crusades can be found in the Old Testament concept of a holy war – a war fought for and on behalf of God and which, for that reason alone, required no other justification or legitimation of any kind. Traces of this idea are common in warfare. They are often associated with circumstances in which the crusaders are outnumbered and in impossible circumstances. Indeed, the concept even encouraged crusaders to attempt the seemingly impossible so that their success could be unequivocally interpreted as proof of God's favour. The later claim that the English fleet benefited from a 'Protestant wind' in the face of apparent overwhelming defeat by the

Spanish Armada is one often quoted example of this. Although the medieval crusades did much to create the myths of chivalry in the vivid imagination, they were, in fact, more noted for their brutal inhumanity. Wars fought in supposedly God-given righteous causes have often been thought to license the punishment of the wicked without either question or further justification. In the modern world, wars which are believed to be ethnically justified echo the depravity of similar and frightening certainties.

The medieval crusades occurred in a world where there was general anarchy and the voices of pacifist protest barely heard, if they were at all. In this world, overall authority was a meaningless concept. Religious, ethnic and generally sectarian self-interests were left to their own unfettered devices, awaiting events to trigger them into action. Two such events caused this in the eleventh century: the schism of east and west in 1054 and the fall of Jerusalem to the Seljukian Turks in 1072. Both alienated the western mind generally from what it then believed to be the sources of all civilisation and knowledge of God. Added to this, these events threatened vital trade with the east at a time long before the western world was to discover and become reliant on riches of its own. Given this western mind-set, it is little wonder that there should be uprising of one kind or another. This was directly encouraged by the fact that Pope Urban II made an influential speech at the Council of Clermont in 1095, which was convened specifically for the purpose of planning the First Crusade. This declared the 'Truce of God' which made all indulgence other than participating in the crusade superfluous. Following this, various popes similarly encouraged crusading, and the Third Lateran Council again went so far as to grant a limited indulgence to crusaders against heretics in 1197. From the start of the First Crusade in 1096, there followed some eight recognisable crusades, up to the last in 1270, which was concluded by negotiation. Though some crusades achieved limited aims, the first was the most successful and achieved the temporary repossession of Jerusalem. From the Second Crusade on, it became clear that the logistical problems of supporting such large movements of troops and protecting their weaker flanks were insurmountable. In spite of this, the crusading ideal remained a resilient one throughout the period. In the fourteenth century, however, the Christian west turned its attention to converting the east rather than subjugating it by force as it had so manifestly failed to do.

Martin Luther, like other Protestant reformers, rejected the crusading ideal as such but, in effect, revived it by using a version of the theory of the just war to justify religious war per se. This stressed the ultimate authority of the state under God and the necessity of individual obedience to it. The religious wars of the late-medieval period, which Christianity did so much to define and support, laid the foundation for political absolutism as a precursor to the justification of state militarisation in the modern world. This, in turn, reached back deep into Christian tradition in search of its legitimacy, and it found this in the just war tradition. This has been in the making since pre-Christian times, and it remains influential in modern Christian thinking about war.

JUST WAR TRADITION

Christian interest in the just war arose in the fourth century when Christianity became the officially accepted religion of the Roman empire. The foundations there laid have been built on ever since, and that work continues in what is called the 'just war tradition'. Again, this is not the exclusive preserve of Christianity, but Christian tradition has been and remains foremost in its continued development. In what follows I will outline some of the main features of this development, discuss its relevance to modern warfighting and conclude with mention of some problems now confronting the theory.

The Christian just war tradition has sought, from the fourth century on, to find answers to two questions. First, under what circumstances, if any, is it ever justifiable for Christians to engage in war at all – the *jus ad bellum* (justice in going to war)? Second, if there are ever such, what means of war is it ever permissible to use – the *jus in bello* (justice within war)? All attempts to answer these two questions fall in the area of relative moralising, in the sense that they seek to bring Christian faith and practice to bear on practical politics in general and on dire human need in particular. We will now see that the just war tradition did not originate with Christianity and that it still remains applicable as we still seek answers to these two questions with awesome powers of destruction at our disposal. These powers do not invalidate the tradition, as some claim. In fact they enhance the need for it. If some acts of war, such as biological, chemical and some nuclear ones, are to be declared morally illicit, then it is necessary for us to be clear about the reasons why. The just war tradition remains the sustained and rational way of defining them. We will see why this is the case and also why it bears importantly on the modern conventions of war-fighting.

The classic theory of the just war originated in the emergence of statehood and the need for citizens to protect the state with the same rationality that enabled them to found it in the first place. The Greeks were the first people to do this in a way we can still recognise and benefit from. Their first insistence was on the need for immediate mediation if war looked immi-nent. This was based on a panhellenism which valued the Olympian ideals. Historically, they had some notable success with this, though it did not prevent them from engaging in horrendous conflicts. We will see how this desire to avoid conflict in the first place became the primary requirement in Christian just war thinking. Plato was the first Greek to codify the principles of just war engagement and fighting under the heading 'civil strife', but he did not use the term 'just war' as such. That is attributed to Aristotle. The overriding aim was the restoration of peace, and nothing was tolerated which would make this more difficult than it inevitably was. In turn, the Sophists grounded these developments in their thinking about natural law in an attempt to locate the conduct of war in notions of natural justice. All of these influences have featured in the development of Christian just war theory and are still clearly discernible. Whereas the Greek interest in the just war was thus prompted by a quest for peaceful coexistence, the Roman con-tribution to its development was premised on a need to control and regulate the expansion of empire. The need for there to be a formal declaration of war by a state before it could be engaged arose from this time, and it was fol-lowed by the Roman legal codification of the possibilities and constraints of war. These, already centuries-old, developments were taken up by Christian thinkers in the fourth century because the civic societies they then served faced similar needs. The tradition stays alive for the simple reason that these needs still prevail.

The first Christian writers on the just war tradition were Ambrose of Milan and St Augustine of Hippo. Both drew on Old Testament notions of war as an instrument of God's righteousness. Such war was, therefore, intrinsically justified. Augustine began by distinguishing individual acts of violence and killing, which could not be justified, from those waged by col-lective or lawful authority, which could be justified. He writes:

> A great deal depends on the causes for which men undertake wars, and
> on the authority they have for doing so; for the natural order which
> seeks the peace of mankind, ordains that the monarch should have the
> power of undertaking war if he thinks it advisable, and that the
> soldiers should perform their military duties on behalf of the peace
> and security of the community.[6]

In so doing, he brought Christian biblical thinking in line with both Greek and Roman thought on the subject. As the theory developed, the church came to embrace a theory of civil society of non-Christian classical origin while at the same maintaining the prominence of the New Testament. This achievement was central to Augustine's genius as he more widely made Christianity credible in a changing and culturally alien world. His *City of God*, famously distinguished between the 'earthly city' and the 'heavenly' one, the one corruptible and the other not so.[7] This was and remains the profound foundation on which Christians base their dealings with all that is corruptible and imperfect, including war. The church, on this view, had to come to terms with its existence in the 'earthly city', and it could only achieve this if it always remembered that it was not the church in the heavenly one.

The foundations of western ecclesiology are to be found in all this, and they are inseparable from the origins of the Christian just war tradition. Hereby, the church was to play a central role in the fashioning of civil society, one which its central orthodoxy has maintained ever since. Deviations from that can all be traced back to this central issue in one way or another. Augustine's main focus was upon *jus ad bellum*, and from this focus a number of criteria have been developed over the centuries: namely, the need for war to be made only in a just cause, out of a right intention and authority, having a reasonable hope of success and a peaceful outcome, and doing a minimum amount of harm. (See chapter 13 for a detailed discussion of these criteria.) It is debatable whether or not Augustine also foresaw the later emphasis on the need for the observation of non-combatant immunity, the clear emphasis on which was a later, medieval development.

As civil needs changed and it became axiomatic that the church, so understood, would change with them, so the theory developed. Two such needs became apparent in the Middle Ages: the need to control the harm caused by newer forms of weaponry such as crossbows, and the need to protect the immunity of the innocent who found themselves caught up in wars through no fault of their own: children (prominently), the otherwise infirm and workers in non-associated occupations such as agriculture. In all this there emerged the notion of the *jus in bello*, which drew attention to the fact that constraint in war-fighting was as important as constraint in going to war in the first place. Several attempts were made through decree by the church in the early Middle Ages to achieve these ends, but the first time they became systematised in canon law was in the *Decretum* of Gratian in 1148. This drew heavily on the writings of Augustine and, thereby, effected a continuity from the classical world which lay behind it through to medieval Christian thinking. This work authoritatively combined theological tradition with legal process to such effect that many commentators observe that it, rather than the work of Augustine in its own right, is the foundation of Christian just war thinking in the modern world. Once the tradition was brought, in this way, into the tradition of canon law, it continued to be developed by canon lawyers; notably, the Decretists and the Decretalists. They focused on two questions neither of which, as we have seen, was new: namely, who was justified in declaring war, and how could non-combatants be protected? Throughout this period the theory also received the attention of theologians, principally Peter of Paris and St Thomas Aquinas. The latter stressed, again, the need for allowing only right authorities to go to war, for defined causes, pursued only with right intentions. He writes: 'the right intention of those waging war is required, that is, they must intend to promote the good and to avoid evil'. [8] He also stressed the need for proportion in the actions taken, and introduced the notion of *double effect* into the tradition. None of these remarkable developments in the theory solved all the even then existing problems. Lack of clarity persisted about who was and who was not lawfully constituted to go to war, as well as it did about the precise causes for which war could be waged. Later developments in the theory persisted in attempts to answer these questions.

In the Renaissance and Reformation this clarification focused on these needs: war must be a last resort; the means used should be proportionate to the end achieved; success should be achievable in the sense that the outcome should be a perceptible contribution to a wider peace. Luther was instrumental in all this for two reasons. He sought to marginalise the Anabaptist sects on the one hand and support the military pretensions of the northern European princes on the other. To achieve this he stressed the biblical basis of war in both the Old Testament and the New. He also saw it as the lesser evil and wrote:

> [People] should also consider how great the plague is that war prevents. If people were good and wanted to keep peace, war would be the greatest plague on earth. But what are you going to do about the fact that people will not keep the peace but rob, steal, kill, outrage women and children, and take away property and honour? [9]

Changes in the nature and means of warfare in the modern world have continued to bring about developments in the just war tradition. It has also had, and continues to have, an influence on international law.[10] The definition of legitimate authority has been called into question in wars of liberation where groups in opposition have claimed moral virtue. The notion of last resort has been called into question by national leaders such as Saddam Hussein who, apparently at least, use it to bluff weapons inspectors and others who represent the international community in the quest for peace. The proliferation and diversification in the types of nuclear weapons have put the tradition to perhaps its greatest test in the modern world. Some have argued that these weapons invalidate the theory on the ground that they would make all war disproportionate to any end which could ever possibly be achieved. Others reply to this by pointing out that some nuclear weapons, such as tactical ones, are smaller and less harmful than some conventional weapons. Christian writing on the morality or otherwise of the use of nuclear weapons is coterminous with their invention and has become a genre in its own right. (See, again, chapter 13.)

Five problems relating to the tradition of the just war still feature prominently in its debate. First, what is actually meant by saying that any means used in war must be *proportionate* to the end achieved? Second, the notion of *double effect* – what does it mean, for example, to say that we are not responsible for foreseen consequences of our actions? Third, there are the complex related notions of *intention, threat* and *bluff*. Fourth, there is the morality or otherwise of deploying weapons such as nuclear ones as deterrents, in the knowledge that their use would be immoral. Fifth, what happens when opposing sides both claim the justice of their cause?[11]

All of the mainstream churches have maintained debates on the issue, and this continues. More generally, many Christians have supported the Geneva Protocols, such as the one banning biological weapons in 1925, and the work of the United Nations Organisation. They have also been active in support of the Hague and Nürnberg legal traditions and the International Red Cross Association. All these have embodied the older traditions of the just war and brought them to bear in modern circumstances.

The extent and complexity of the vast international trade in small arms increasingly exercises the Christian conscience, for the simple reason that their accessibility and ease of use enables them to kill more people than any other type of weapon. Attempts to regulate this trade (and intergovernmental arms transfer) and subject it to international register, such as that by the United Nations Organisation in the Arms Transfer Register of 1992, are supported by Christians generally.

Throughout its history, Christianity has been in the midst and often at the forefront of discussions about the morality, or otherwise, of warfare, and it continues to provide an important forum for this in a changing world. Two features of the history of this involvement, as here discussed, particularly enable it to do this. First, it has always been in dialogue with appropriate secular resources and thereby brought them to bear alongside its own insights. And second, it has usually been responsive to new circumstances and technologies. By these and other means, Christian teaching in general, and in this subject in particular, has not been ossified or isolated. This enables Christians to work alongside all people of goodwill, whatever their faith or tradition might be, in the international quest for world peace.

Along with all of this, Christians pray constantly for peace as a matter of central spiritual obligation, for the reasons already discussed. This has been made possible, indeed, by their maintaining a broader theology of creation and the place of evil within it. In turn, this facilitates a political and military realism even in the face of the most horrendous challenges presented by war to the endurance of the human spirit. Short of the Kingdom of God, this will continue as successive generations of Christians make their contributions to seeking a peaceful world order and confronting the challenges to it – in theory, prayer and practice.

Notes

1 See John Hick, *Evil and the God of Love*, Fontana/Collins, London, 1968.
2 C. von Clausewitz, *On War*, trs. J. J. Graham, Kegan Paul, London, 1911.
3 Roland H. Bainton, *Christian Attitudes toward War and Peace*, Abingdon, Nashville, 1960.
4 See John Dominic Crossan, *The Historical Jesus: The Life of a Mediterranean Jewish Peasant*, T. & T. Clark, Edinburgh, 1993.
5 See Steven Runciman, *A History of the Crusades*, 3 vols., Cambridge University Press, Cambridge, 1962, and Elizabeth Siberry, *Criticism of Crusading 1095–1274*, Clarendon Press, Oxford, 1985.
6 Augustine, *Reply to Faustus the Manichaean*, XXII, 75. Quoted in Robin Gill, *A Textbook of Christian Ethics*, T. & T. Clark, Edinburgh, revised 1995, p. 274.
7 Augustine, *The City of God*, XIV, 27.
8 Aquinas, *Summa Theologica*, vol. XXXV, VII, 5. Quoted in Gill, *Textbook*, p. 282.
9 Martin Luther, *Whether Soldiers Too Can Be Saved*. Quoted in Gill, *Textbook*, p. 293.
10 See Sydney D. Bailey, 'International Law and the Nurnberg Principles', in Richard J. Bauckham and R. John Elford, eds., *The Nuclear Weapons Debate*, SCM Press, London, 1989, pp. 188–196.
11 See Sydney D. Bailey, *War and Conscience in the Nuclear Age*, Macmillan, London, 1987, pp. 28–34.

13 The arms trade and Christian ethics

ROBIN GILL

John Elford's chapter has set the broad context of Christian approaches to war and of attempts over the centuries to establish just war criteria. In this chapter I will focus, instead, upon the arms trade (or, more accurately, international arms transfer) set in the specific context of the wars or conflicts in the 1990s, first in the Gulf, then in Iraq and finally in the Balkans.

Christian versions of just war theory are essentially attempts to limit the horrors of warfare rather than means of justifying particular wars. Although initially derived by Ambrose and Augustine from pre-Christian, Greek and Roman sources, as John Elford has shown, just war theory has long been shaped by Christian theologians and now represents one of the more abiding theological heirlooms in the modern world.[1] It is intentionally a limiting framework. Given that countries are, and always have been, tempted on occasion to go to war, just war theory introduces notes of moral caution into a situation. It offers broad criteria in order to encourage people to see some forms of warfare as considerably less justified than others. Down the centuries many Christians have voiced strong anxieties about warfare and have sought to constrain countries from going lightly into battle and then to limit the horrors of war once it starts.

The highly influential 1983 pastoral letter of the United States Catholic Bishops, *The Challenge of Peace*, illustrates this point well. Early in this letter they explain the concept of comparative justice, which they believe is essential for a proper understanding of just war theory, as follows:

> Questions concerning the *means* of waging war today, particularly in view of the destructive potential of weapons, have tended to override questions concerning the comparative justice of the positions of respective adversaries or enemies. In essence: which side is sufficiently 'right' in a dispute, and are the values at stake critical enough to override the presumption against war? The question in its most basic form is this: do the rights and values involved justify killing? For

whatever the means used, war, by definition, involves violence, destruction, suffering, and death. The category of comparative justice is designed to emphasise the presumption against war which stands at the beginning of just-war teaching. In a world of sovereign states recognising neither a common moral authority nor a central political authority, comparative justice stresses that no state should act on the basis that it has 'absolute justice' on its side. Every party to a conflict should acknowledge the limits of its 'just cause' and the consequent requirement to use only limited means in pursuit of its objectives. Far from legitimising a crusade mentality, comparative justice is designed to relativise absolute claims and to restrain the use of force even in a 'justified' conflict. Given techniques of propaganda and the ease with which nations and individuals either assume or delude themselves into believing that God or right is clearly on their side, the test of comparative justice may be extremely difficult to apply.[2]

The clear logic of this is that just war theory, especially in the modern world, is intended primarily to be a constraint upon war rather than a means of justifying particular wars.

Again as John Elford has shown, different principles are important in just war theory within a war (*jus in bello*) and before a war (*jus ad bellum*). In both cases just war theory seeks to limit damage, but does so rather differently in each case.

Actually within a war, the principles of discrimination and proportionality receive particular attention. It is claimed that the increasing sophistication of modern weapons has allowed rockets and bombs to be deployed in conflict with a much greater capacity for target discrimination than hitherto. If we are to believe all that we read and hear, modern weapons can discriminate between military and civilian targets. The bombing by the United Nations in the Gulf and by NATO in the Balkans of course raised many doubts about this claim: according to some estimates, a tenth of bombs and missiles dropped are likely not to explode, leaving a legacy of unexploded weapons, and at least a tenth miss their military targets altogether. Both outcomes inevitably result in civilian casualties. A concern of western countries to be seen to act in accordance with international agreements – either those of the United Nations or those of NATO – has also entailed a new carefulness in deploying proportionate military resources. And the effects of media reporting upon home and enemy populations have also encouraged a more fastidious approach to both discrimination and proportionality in military engagements.

A complex mixture of increasing public awareness, digitised weapons and post-cold war political alliances has put a new (and welcome) emphasis upon these two ethical principles, which have historically attempted to limit the evil effects that occur in the context of warfare (*jus in bello*).

However, a broader set of principles has been developed over the centuries to test the morality of going to war at all (*jus ad bellum*). Most modern forms of just war theory contain at least the following additional elements. For a war to be considered just, it must:

(1) have been undertaken by a lawful authority
(2) have been undertaken for the vindication of an undoubted right that has certainly been infringed
(3) be a last resort, all peaceful means of settlement having failed
(4) offer the possibility of the good to be achieved outweighing the evils that war would involve
(5) be waged with right intention
(6) be waged with a reasonable hope of victory for justice.

Disputes about the moral legitimacy of the Gulf, Iraq and Balkan wars have focused upon the first, third and sixth criteria. For many commentators, the Gulf war satisfied the first criterion most clearly, since it was authorised by the United Nations and was halted when the United Nations' mandate expired. In contrast, the Iraq bombing was, arguably, legitimated only by the United States and Britain. The Balkans bombing, legitimated by NATO rather than by the United Nations, appeared to be halfway between these positions. Whether NATO, designed as a defensive alliance against a presumed Soviet enemy, had the authority to intervene remains disputed. Likewise the third criterion appeared to many to fit the Gulf war most clearly. In the 1999 Balkan war, the Russian government clearly believed that NATO countries had not exhausted all peaceful negotiations, although critics were not convinced that it, in turn, had exhausted peaceful means before bombarding Grozny in Chechnya later in the same year. This was also a point of considerable dispute in the earlier Falklands war. Did the British government really exhaust all peaceful means before engaging in the war, and, in particular, did Mrs Thatcher go through all the peaceful options before ordering the *Belgrano* to be sunk?

Prophetically, the U.S. Catholic Bishops recognised just how contentious these two criteria were likely to become in the modern world:

> For resort to war to be justified, all peaceful alternatives must have been exhausted. There are formidable problems in this requirement. No international organisation currently in existence has exercised

sufficient internationally recognised authority to be able either to mediate effectively in most cases or to prevent conflict by the intervention of United Nations or other peacekeeping forces. Furthermore, there is a tendency for nations or peoples which perceive conflict between or among other nations as advantageous to themselves to attempt to prevent a peaceful settlement rather than advance it. We regret the apparent unwillingness of some to see in the United Nations organisation the potential for world order which exists and to encourage its development. Pope Paul VI called the United Nations the last hope for peace. The loss of this hope cannot be allowed to happen.[3]

In the aftermath of the Gulf war it was hoped that the United Nations really would be able to have a crucial role in constraining and policing warfare in the modern world. Unfortunately, the Iraq and Balkan wars considerably undermined this hope.

However, it is the sixth criterion and, in part, the fourth which have proved the most troublesome in all recent wars. The Gulf war may have stopped Iraq's conquest of Kuwait, but it clearly did not stop Iraqi aggression. Neither the bombing of Iraq nor the 1999 bombing in the Balkans could expect any complete 'victory for justice'. Even the surrender of the Serbs following the NATO bombing produced at best an ambiguous 'victory for justice'. Indeed, some would argue that the evils of modern warfare make the achievement of either the fourth or sixth criterion unlikely. On this understanding, the full array of modern weapons (which still includes nuclear weapons) has become just too dangerous to be used any more as a means of achieving even the vindication of an undoubted right that has certainly been infringed.

This final point raises perhaps the most difficult issue of all. Even if modern warfare can be fought with a remarkable degree of discrimination and proportionality, is it finally a moral way of 'policing' the world? Those who believe that it is often use the analogy of a police force. In a fallen world, nations as well as people do need to be restrained and deterred at times from doing evil. The international community does properly act on occasion as a sort of police force to protect the vulnerable – whether they are the people of Kuwait or of Kosovo.

But there are still problems. Supposing the Soviet Union had won the cold war, would British Christians be quite so keen to see them rather than Americans acting as the police force of the world? We cannot be so confident that military superiority in the future will remain firmly in the hands of friendly democracies. There have, after all, been many examples of tyrannical, undemocratic countries using their superior military power to 'police' weaker countries. Unless we find effective non-military means of resolving all national, international and global conflicts, our long-term future may be bleak. In other words, just war theory in the future may need to insist that peaceful means of settlement must not be allowed to fail.

What implications does all of this have for the international arms trade? Weapons of mass destruction should cause us considerable anxiety, and it is, I believe, right that we should seek to constrain their proliferation and, especially, their use. In his important 1992 report *Profit without Honour? Ethics and the Arms Trade* for the Council on Christian Approaches to Defence and Disarmament, Roger Williamson argues that there is a broad consensus emerging across different churches. Having reviewed a rich variety of church statements and reports produced during the last three decades, he concludes:

> The accumulated evidence of the church statements of the British churches, European churches, the Roman Catholic Church (both centrally and in its national episcopal conferences), as well as international ecumenical bodies presents an increasingly clear voice in favour of bringing the arms trade under stricter control based upon moral principles. There are persistent pleas for greater openness and an insistence that the arms industry should not be allowed to be so dominant that pressure to sell arms overrides ethical considerations.[4]

If this trade is indeed to be brought under 'stricter control based upon moral principles', then applying just war theory rigorously – in terms of the criteria for use in war and those for use in advance of war – is an obvious way to do this. If this could be achieved, then the hope would be that just war theory might be able to constrain both the proliferation and use of weapons of war.

The principles of discrimination and proportionality have important implications for the arms trade. Once again the U.S. Catholic Bishops recognised this clearly in their pastoral letter:

> In terms of the arms race, if the real end in view is legitimate defence against unjust aggression, and the means to this end are not evil in themselves, we must still examine the question of proportionality concerning attendant evils. Do the exorbitant costs, the general climate of insecurity generated, the possibility of accidental detonation of highly destructive weapons, the danger of error and miscalculation that could provoke retaliation and war – do such evils or others

attendant upon and indirectly deriving from the arms race make the arms race itself a disproportionate response to aggression? Pope John Paul II is very clear in his insistence that the exercise of the right and duty of a people to protect their existence and freedom is contingent on the use of proportionate means.[5]

In contrast, those who support indiscriminate trade typically do so on the basis of a number of supposedly value-neutral or consequential grounds. So they might argue that it is not the buying or selling, or even transferring, of arms which is morally objectionable, but their use. Arms are a form of technology and, like all forms of technology, they can be used properly or improperly. It is the people who own arms who are the moral (or immoral) agents, not the arms themselves.

A more sophisticated version of this argument would maintain that, if it is legitimate for any particular nation to possess certain types of weapons, for whatever reasons, then it cannot be wrong for any other nation to possess them as well for the same reasons. So if it is considered right that one nation should have a set of weapons with which to defend itself, then it must be right that other nations should be allowed to defend themselves similarly. Of course this might change if you suspect that some nations wish to have such weapons for aggressive rather than purely defensive purposes. However, it is not wrong in itself to possess weapons which can be used for defensive purposes. Possession as such is morally neutral.

Unfortunately, there is an obvious flaw in this argument. It could be used successfully to defend horizontal nuclear proliferation. (In this context horizontal nuclear proliferation involves the spread of nuclear weapons into more and more countries, whereas vertical nuclear proliferation involves the production of ever more powerful nuclear weapons.) Presumably those countries which possess nuclear weapons believe that they remain important for the maintenance of peace in the world. During the cold war carefully articulated policies of nuclear deterrence depended upon such notions as a balance of nuclear weapons between the superpowers and threatened mutual assured destruction. Even though there is now considerable scepticism about the viability of these policies, a vast number of nuclear weapons do still exist, and the number of countries possessing them is still increasing. Presumably nations wish to become nuclear powers precisely because they believe that they will be better able to defend themselves from other nuclear powers with such weapons. Yet this is the Achilles heel of any policy of nuclear deterrence. If possessing nuclear weapons deters others from using them, then everyone should possess them; and then no nation will use them.

But if everyone possesses them, then surely it becomes more not less likely that someone, somewhere, sometime may indeed use them.

The U.S. Bishops reached the same conclusion:

> We fear that our world and nation are headed in the wrong direction. More weapons with greater destructive potential are produced every day. More and more nations are seeking to become nuclear powers. In our quest for more and more security, we fear we are actually becoming less and less secure.[6]

Jonathan Schell's remarkable 1998 book *The Gift of Time: The Case for Abolishing Nuclear Weapons Now* takes this argument further. He interviewed a wide variety of retired politicians and military, together with a number of leading academics, many of whom were once supporters of nuclear deterrence, but who now recognise it to be a deeply flawed doctrine. The observations of Robert McNamara, one of the architects of the policies of the Kennedy and Johnson administrations in the Vietnam war, are particularly striking. Once thoroughly convinced of the policy of mutual assured destruction, he now argues:

> I think it's not only desirable but essential that we eliminate nuclear weapons. They have no military utility other than to deter one's opponents from using nuclear weapons. And if our opponent doesn't have nuclear weapons, we don't need them. I am quoting almost exactly from a National Academy of Sciences report.[7]

There is an obvious difficulty in maintaining such a position even after the end of the cold war, and McNamara recognises this immediately:

> Now that report, oddly enough having made such a clear-cut and, I think, correct statement, goes on to say that we can't – we shouldn't – go below fifteen hundred or two thousand warheads. The reason they say it's not possible to get rid of nuclear weapons altogether is that we must protect against rogue-state or terrorist breakout.[8]

His response to this argument shows just how far his own position has now changed:

> Two or three reasons. The first is that it's very, very risky. Even a low probability of catastrophe is a high risk, and I don't think we should continue to accept it. If you don't believe it's a risk, then read the reports of the Cuban Missile Crisis Retrospective Meetings and the recently published Kennedy tapes. I believe that was the best-managed

Cold War crisis of any, but we came within a hairbreadth of nuclear war without realising it. There were mistakes made by Krushchev and his associates, and by Kennedy and his associates, including me . . . It's no credit to us that we missed nuclear war . . . So I want to say that's a risk I don't believe the human race should accept . . . [In addition] using nuclear weapons against a nuclear-equipped opponent of any size at all is suicide, and . . . using them against a non-nuclear-equipped opponent is, I think, immoral.[9]

There are also a number of considerably less honourable arguments that are used in defence of an indiscriminate arms trade. The most popular of these is that this is indeed trade which creates employment in Britain and which will simply be undertaken elsewhere in the world if the British do not do it. This is sometimes dubbed the 'slavery argument', since it was deployed by supporters of the slave trade in the eighteenth century. Undoubtedly there is considerable employment generated in Britain by the international arms trade (as there was once by the slave trade). Yet it is not a difficult argument to counter on more principled grounds. Doubtless child prostitution is popular and generates income in some parts of the world, yet few in Britain would seek to introduce it here on these grounds. Just because something is done by others elsewhere and generates employment for them does not make it right that we should do it ourselves. Indeed, within the slavery debate the very opposite conclusions were eventually drawn. The British government decided not just to ban it within Britain but to seek to abolish it elsewhere in the world as well. In the end it was decided that there was no such thing as a just slave trade.

Thoroughgoing Christian pacifists are most likely to agree whole-heartedly with this slavery argument. Since they believe that warfare is never justified, they will probably conclude that any trade/transfer in the weapons of warfare is also, like the trade in slaves, itself never justified. The response of just war Christians is likely to be more complex. Some might argue against a purely commercial arms trade, but nonetheless support carefully negotiated defensive arms transfers between those democratic governments which scrupulously uphold human rights. Others might argue that there is a proper place for commerce here but that it must be carefully subordinated to strict ethical criteria. Nonetheless, all of these groups would agree that an indiscriminate arms trade or transfer is wrong, however much employment it generates.

If an indiscriminate arms trade is not to be defended as a just arms trade, what about the principle of proportionality? There does seem to be a *prima facie* case for arguing that there are weapons of such monstrous proportions, such as nuclear weapons, that they should not be included in any notion of a just arms trade. Yet, as John Elford points out, the trouble here is that so-called conventional, let alone chemical and biological, weapons are also becoming potentially almost as destructive. The vertical proliferation of nuclear weapons is increasingly matched by the vertical proliferation of other forms of weapons as well.

Perhaps a distinction might be made between those defensive weapons which can actually be used for purely defensive purposes and those which certainly should not be used for such purposes. It is not difficult to see that there is a difference in kind and not simply in degree between, say, a nuclear bomb and a police truncheon. Both are types of arms and could in theory be bought and sold. Yet a police truncheon is unlikely to kill people if used, and has a clear and limited purpose to restrain violent criminals, whereas a nuclear bomb certainly will kill people if detonated in a populated area and will continue to contaminate that area for many years to come. In the hands of a tyrant a police truncheon will be of little use for aggressive rather than defensive purposes. In contrast, there is a very real fear that a terrorist group or a fanatical tyrant may one day be able to purchase nuclear-grade material and use it to commit an act of atrocity against a civilian population. As a result of this fear most people would regard trade involving nuclear weapons as distinctly more questionable than trade involving truncheons.

To return to Jonathan Schell's *The Gift of Time*, he finally argues for a policy of total abolition of nuclear weapons, believing that they have no justifiable use in the world today. He believes that both vertical and horizontal nuclear disarmament are now required:

> If vertical disarmament involves lowering the number of weapons in nuclear arsenals, horizontal disarmament involves progressively standing down, dispersing, disassembling, or partially dismantling arsenals. Establishing ceilings on nuclear arsenals, abolishing certain classes of weapons, and drawing down the number of weapons are steps along the vertical path. 'De-alerting' nuclear weapons, 'de-mating' warheads from delivery vehicles, storing warheads at a distance from delivery vehicles, removing parts from warheads or delivery vehicles (or adding parts that spoil their performance), or adulterating weapons-grade fissile materials are steps along the horizontal path. Vertical disarmament makes a catastrophe, should it ever occur, smaller. Horizontal disarmament makes a catastrophe of any size less

likely to occur. The verticalist looks at the size of the arsenals. The horizontalist looks at their operation.[10]

Schell is aware that nuclear weapons cannot strictly be 'disinvented'. Nuclear knowledge, in both civil and military forms, remains an inescapable part of our world. Yet that does not mean that we have to continue to possess, let alone trade in, nuclear weapons. Even the threat of terrorist groups using nuclear weapons is not, he believes, an argument for governments themselves retaining a residuum of nuclear weapons. Any advantage such groups gained in an otherwise nuclear-free world would at most be very temporary, and the very elimination of government weapons would make it less likely than at present that these groups would gain access to them.

Of course my contrast between nuclear weapons and truncheons is too easy. It becomes very much more difficult to distinguish between defensive and potentially aggressive weapons amongst those weapons that lie between these two extremes. It must be for others with much more technical expertise than myself to give advice here. Yet it does seem to be a requirement of just war theory that some such distinction is made. In terms of the criteria appropriate before war is undertaken, the second criterion assumes that just war is always a defensive response and not an initiating act of aggression. In addition, the fifth criterion does insist upon knowing something about the intentions of the one contemplating war. An ethical approach to the arms trade would surely wish to insist upon the same.

The fourth and sixth criteria applied to the arms trade would also forbid selling or transferring weapons to a country in a situation where there was no serious possibility of good outweighing the evils of war or where there was no reasonable hope of victory for justice. If applied rigorously, these two criteria would offend both pragmatists who regard technology itself as value-free and libertarians who consider such judgements to be patronising. However, a principled approach to the arms trade should be concerned about both the buyers and the sellers. If technology is regarded at the outset as potential power and not simply as value-free – power which can be used for good and ill – there is a proper sense of responsibility placed upon those developing and selling or transferring it. And, in contrast to a purely libertarian perspective, there is a strong dimension of social responsibility present in just war theory. It is for this reason that it insists in the first, and oldest, criterion that private citizens should not be allowed to initiate wars. Only lawful authorities can properly declare war.

It is, though, once again the third criterion that raises the most serious moral questions. If we conclude that our priority is to find effective non-military means of resolving all national, international and global conflicts, then the legitimacy of much of the arms trade becomes increasingly questionable. Roger Williamson, arguing from within a Christian just war position, reaches the same conclusion, but immediately offers a warning:

> More work needs to be done in emphasising that the only legitimations for arms transfers from the non-pacifist perspective are the preservation of peace, the defence of human rights and the preservation of life and dignity. From a Christian perspective, the concern for the protection of human rights must surely take precedence over arms sales . . . This is quite clearly *not* a platform on which a contemporary British political party could get elected. There is not a consensus of that kind – even against arms sales to highly questionable governments. One task facing the churches is thus the creation of a moral climate in which there is a strong presumption *against* arms sales unless a legitimate need for their transfer can be proven.[11]

The last few years may have seen more public discussion of an ethical policy on arms trade (however flawed) than Williamson anticipated in 1992. Nevertheless his overall point remains. He believes that churches should become much more active in attempting to change the prevailing moral climate: challenging unethical investments; monitoring and lobbying politicians; networking effectively for peace; encouraging a longer-term acceptance of alternatives to warfare; and engaging in a distinctly more critical dialogue on the ethics of arms trade and transfer.

In the last five years a group of twenty-three American theologians and international relations theorists have been meeting to produce a more systematic approach to peacemaking in the modern world. They have now published their initial conclusions in the stimulating book *Just Peacemaking*.[12] They share a common conviction that both pacifist and just war Christians should make a sustained attempt to promote strategies of peacemaking. Together they identify the following 'ten practices for abolishing war' – practices which specifically include arms reduction:

- Support non-violent direct action
- Take independent initiatives to reduce threat
- Use cooperative conflict resolution
- Acknowledge responsibility for conflict and injustice and seek repentance and forgiveness

- Advance democracy, human rights, and religious liberty
- Foster just and sustainable economic development
- Work with emerging cooperative forces in the international system
- Strengthen the United Nations and international efforts for cooperation and human rights
- Reduce offensive weapons and weapons trade
- Encourage grassroots peacemaking groups.

If just war theory in the future really does insist that peaceful means of settlement must not be allowed to fail, then the very use of weapons becomes a clear signal of that failure. One response to arms proliferation is to insist upon the right of everyone to own arms. Libertarian Americans have long insisted upon their personal right to carry arms, and the result, many believe, has been one of the most heavily armed and dangerous civilian populations in the world. A quite different response is to work hard for radical decommissioning and peacemaking. From this perspective a world containing fewer weapons will be a safer world for all of us. Since I share this perspective, I regard much of the present arms trade and transfer as deeply questionable.

Notes

1 See further my *A Textbook of Christian Ethics*, T. & T. Clark, Edinburgh, 1995, section 3.
2 United States Catholic Bishops, *The Challenge of Peace: God's Promise and Our Response*, National Conference of Catholic Bishops, Washington, DC, and CTS/SPCK, 3 May 1983, paras. 92–4.
3 *Ibid.*, paras. 96–7.
4 Roger Williamson, *Profit without Honour? Ethics and the Arms Trade*, Council on Christian Approaches to Defence and Disarmament, St Bride Foundation Institute, Bride Lane, London EC4Y 8EQ, and Methodist Publishing House, 20 Ivatt Way, Peterborough, PE3 7PQ, pp. 106–7.
5 U.S. Catholic Bishops, para. 107.
6 *Ibid.*, para. 332.
7 Jonathan Schell, *The Gift of Time: The Case for Abolishing Nuclear Weapons Now*, Granta Publications, London, 1998, p. 46.
8 *Ibid.*
9 *Ibid.*, pp. 47–8.
10 *Ibid.*, pp. 69–70.
11 Williamson, *Profit without Honour*, p. 184.
12 Glen Stassen (ed.), *Just Peacemaking: Ten Practices for Abolishing War*, Pilgrim Press, Cleveland, OH, 1999.

14 Social justice and welfare

DUNCAN B. FORRESTER

VARIETIES OF CHRISTIAN THOUGHT ON JUSTICE

The cultures in which Christianity flourished prior to the missionary expansion of recent centuries were deeply influenced by Christian notions, and in their turn shaped and perhaps sometimes distorted the expression of the Christian faith. It should not then be surprising if we discover that distinctively Christian ideas about justice which Christians, both Protestant and Roman Catholic, would wish to support and affirm have been deeply implanted in many modern cultures. The boundary between the religious and the secular in such matters is not always clear-cut or easy to discern. Themes like the human equality that the American Declaration of Independence thought 'self-evident' were not accepted as at all obviously true in a very different cultural environment such as that of traditional India. Indeed, in the course of time ideas and values absorbed from religious sources can become the almost unquestioned assumptions of later generations, commonly believed to be axiomatic, or the conclusion of a purely rational argument.

The complicated interaction between Christian thought on social justice and its intellectual, social, ecclesial and political context continues today. It is at this point that the first, and most obvious, distinction between Protestant and Roman Catholic thought on social justice emerges. In general terms Roman Catholic thought draws on classical Aristotelian philosophy as mediated and moderated by St Thomas, whereas Protestants tend to be suspicious of secular reason and seek to ground their thought on justice on revelation contained in scripture. The distinction is not as clear-cut as this remark might suggest. Roman Catholics have always used scripture, of course, and have a high doctrine of scriptural authority. Indeed, it is not hard to see an increasing emphasis on scripture in recent papal encyclicals. Nor have Protestants a uniform conviction that when addressing 'temporal issues' such as social justice, scripture should have the primacy it must possess within the heartlands of theology. Luther, for example, denounces Aristotle as 'this damned, conceited, rascally heathen' when considering his influence on theology.[1] And elsewhere he writes, 'Virtually the whole Ethics of Aristotle is the worst enemy of Grace . . . No syllogistic form is valid when applied to divine terms . . . The whole Aristotle is to theology as darkness to light.'[2] But in relation to 'temporal affairs' – and Luther would include social justice under this heading – the same Aristotle becomes a reputable authority: 'The heathen can speak and teach about this very well, as they have done. And, to tell the truth, they are far more skillful in such matters than the Christians . . . Whoever wants to learn and become wise in secular government, let him read the heathen books and writings.'[3]

Most Protestant thinkers would not accept the sharpness of Luther's disjunction between the sacred and the secular realms, or his suggestion that the one is the sphere of divine truth and revelation while the other is to be governed by secular reason. Theology, most Protestants would say, has something to contribute in the secular realm, while reason has a role in theology. But it is fallen reason that is at issue here, and most Protestant thinkers agree with Calvin in being suspicious of 'the great darkness of philosophers who have looked for a building in a ruin, and fit arrangement in disorder'.[4] It is incorrect, he continues, to 'maintain that reason dwells in the mind like a lamp, throwing light on all its counsels and, like a queen governing the will – that it is so pervaded with divine light as to be able to consult for the best, and so endued with vigour as to be able perfectly to command'.[5]

Protestants, therefore, in their thinking about social justice have a continuing ambivalence about the role of reason, and in particular about natural-law forms of thinking. They are not agreed among themselves as to where the boundary between the realms of the spiritual and the temporal comes, or about the role of a scripture-based theology in temporal matters. Some, like Luther and many Anglicans, affirm the role of reason in temporal affairs. Others, like most Calvinists, draw a less sharp distinction between the sacred and the secular, and argue that revelation should hold sway in both spheres. And the majority of Protestants in their treatment of issues of social justice seek to root their thinking in scripture and, particularly among liberals and charismatics, on experience of the justice of God.

Protestant accounts of social justice are diverse and tend to be episodic rather than systematic. Lacking a central authority like the papacy, Protestant thought on justice emanates from many quarters and is rarely coordinated. It is not cumulative, like official Catholic social teaching over the last century and more. Positively, this may mean that it can respond more creatively to changing challenges in the various contexts without the need to demonstrate that it is an unchanging and universally valid teaching. But this virtue of flexibility is sometimes at the expense of consistency.

What almost all Protestant theology shares with the whole of the Christian tradition is a belief in the authority of scripture. For most Protestant social thought, this stress on scriptural authority is the strongest single emphasis and the *sola scriptura* principle tends to make Protestant thinkers suspicious of using any secular language – say that of John Rawls – as an adequate vehicle for communicating Christian insights. Theology or Christian thought must have something distinctive to offer to the discussion, or it might as well keep its mouth shut – such is a typically Protestant approach. Since scripture is at its heart gospel, a scriptural theology of justice may be understood as public confession of the faith.

SOCIAL JUSTICE IN THE BIBLE

Biblical teaching on justice comes primarily in the garb of narrative and of injunctions, denunciations and the announcement of coming judgement and the restoration or establishment of God's just ordering of things, the messianic age, or the Reign of God. It is not a philosophy of justice, something that can appropriately be put alongside Aristotle or John Rawls. It cannot be detached from the faith of the people of God, of which it is an integral part. Its primarily narrative form allows it to articulate the cry of the oppressed for justice, and confidence in a God whose faithfulness is the assurance that the divine justice will be established, that God's just ordering of things will be fully expressed in the new Jerusalem, in the city of God, in the Kingdom, in the coming age.

James L. Mays speaks of 'the priority of justice for the prophets', for they believed that 'the entire history of Israel under God is subordinated to one purpose – righteousness expressed in justice'. The prophets understood justice as a theological term, inseparable from 'their knowledge of Israel's God, who is himself just and requires justice of people'. Talk of justice, accordingly, has a confessional element, for justice is an element of God's being and action. Justice is also a moral value which can be expressed in social relationships at least as much as in the courts.[6] Justice is integral to the faith of Israel and of the church. As Father John Donahue puts it, 'The doing of justice is not the application of religious faith, but its substance; without it, God remains unknown.'[7]

The prophet Micah's famous response to the question 'What does the Lord require of you?' – that we should do justice, and love kindness, and walk humbly with our God – is a fitting reminder of the centrality of the call for justice in the Hebrew scriptures, where justice is regarded in a remarkably broad and specific way. Justice is here linked with *hesed*, the steadfast loving-kindness which characterises God's covenant love, and with the humble walking with this God of justice and of love. And justice is regarded as something to be done, something that is inherently relational or social.

In the New Testament in the Matthean form of the beatitudes, the little band of disciples hear that those who hunger and thirst after justice (*dikaiosune*) are blessed and will be satisfied.[8] Justice is something about which we should be passionate, for it is essential to a fulfilled life and social flourishing. In the Bible justice appears again and again as the vindication of the poor and the oppressed. They can turn with confidence for redress to God and to those who seek to follow in the way of God. For the prophets 'made the treatment of the poor and the weak the functional criterion of a just society'. Furthermore, 'the justice they advocated must be capable of exception, of responsiveness to the individual's needs, of an estimate of worth based on the simple existence of a person'.[9] Justice here is proactive, healing, reconciling, forgiving, setting matters right so that people can live together in peace.

Justice in the Bible is always set within an eschatological frame; it is something we hope for, something that is not fully actualised here and now, for the full realisation, vindication, restoration lie in the future. Any manifestations of justice here and now can only be provisional and relative when measured against the coming justice of God. Thus disciples and others are enjoined to 'seek first God's Reign and his justice'.[10]

Because it is the justice of God's Reign, we can give it its distinctive content by examining the parables and the practice of Jesus as a proleptic manifestation of the life of God's Reign. These parables characteristically depict the conviviality of God's Reign as something to which everyone is welcome, but at which there is a kind of preferential invitation to the poor, the marginalised and the excluded. This was also manifested in the practice of Jesus, particularly in his relationship to women and in his open-table fellowship with all sorts of people. In both, Jesus breaks through the traditional rules of purity in order to establish a new form of community, anticipating the fellowship of God's Reign founded on justice and love. He ate with Zacchaeus and with Levi, with Pharisees and with quislings, with prostitutes and with notorious sinners. And at this table people found forgiveness, acceptance and the ability to make a new start in life. Zacchaeus was moved at the table to make restitution of what he had misappropriated. The forlorn found acceptance. In Jesus' eating and drinking the message of God's Reign was enacted, the life and justice of God's Reign exemplified.

The strange and complex relationship between the meals of Jesus and his death suggests that it is not at all fanciful to see these meals as a significant part of the work of reconciliation which is the establishment of justice by the creation of a new community through the breaking down of the dividing walls of hostility and suspicion, the bringing near of those who were far off, and the welcoming of strangers into the new Israel which prefigures God's Reign.

We see God's justice embodied and expressed in action most clearly in the life and death of Jesus, in his action as well as his teaching, and in his suffering. Bishop Lesslie Newbigin puts it thus: 'At the centre of the Christian understanding of justice there stands the cross, not a symbol but a historic deed in which the justice of God was manifested in his covenant faithfulness right through to the point where the just died for the unjust.'[11] In Acts, Jesus is declared to be 'the just One'.[12] And Paul proclaims that Jesus has become our justice.[13] In him we see the summing up of the Christian understanding of social justice.

The justice of God's Reign has an objective reality; it is something that we seek; we do not construct it or make it. It is a gift, not a prize to be earned. But the gift carries with it a call. Those who seek God's righteousness are called to walk in the ways of justice, to anticipate in their practice the justice of the coming Kingdom. Justice is pervasively relational. It has to do with the proper structure of relationships between God and people and among people.

JUSTIFICATION AND JUSTICE

Justification, according to the thought of the Reformation, is 'the article by which the church will stand or fall'. Luther's own experience of justification was definitive for his whole theological and reforming project. It gave him a radically new understanding of God's justice and indeed of the nature of God which helped him to a fresh reading of the Bible, particularly Paul's epistles, and an altered assessment of the significance of human ethical striving. Before this experience, Luther says he 'did not love a just and angry God, but rather hated and murmured against him'. When he realised that 'the justice of God is that righteousness by which through sheer grace and sheer mercy God justifies us through faith ... [t]he whole of Scripture took on a new meaning, and whereas before 'the justice of God' had filled me with hate, now it became to me inexpressibly sweet in greater love.' For Luther now knew God to be gracious and God's justice to be loving and forgiving.[14]

God's justice is not blind, impersonal, mechanical, retributive. It is rather gentle, forgiving, reconciling and above all loving. God's justice is his grace and forgiveness. We cannot earn the divine justification; we put our trust in God's faithfulness and grace, in the knowledge that God cares for us and accepts us just as we are. God's justice is displayed most clearly in God's grace and love, in his acceptance as just of those who are still sinners, and his special care for the excluded, the forgotten, the poor and the marginalised. In the experience of justification we discover the true justice of God, which is justice itself. In justification we encounter the justice of God, who declares us to be just, and sets us free to act justly and lovingly to our neighbours: we serve God and our neighbours for their own sakes, not because we wish to win our own salvation.

Lutheran thinkers have tended to treat justification as a rather private transaction between the believer and God, and to draw a sharp distinction between justice and justification. A number of biblical scholars have recently argued that the Lutheran reading of the Pauline doctrine of justification is far too dominated by Luther's characteristically late-medieval concern for the salvation of his soul. In fact, they argue, Paul's teaching on justification and on justice is set entirely within the context of the dispute about whether Jews and Gentiles could be reconciled to one another within the one community of faith, with the breaking down of barriers and the establishment of a community in which ancient hostilities and suspicions are overcome. 'Justification by faith', writes Professor James Dunn, 'is a banner raised by Paul against any and all such presumption of privileged status before God by virtue of race, culture or nationality, against any and all attempts to preserve such spurious distinctions by practices that exclude and divide.'[15] Justification and justice are relational terms; it is social justice which is at issue here, not a private transaction between God and the believer, or the measuring of people and actions against some impersonal ethical yardstick. God's justice is experienced as pure grace, and this justice is expressed in inclusive community in which there is a special care for the weak, the poor, the stranger, the orphan and the widow.

The Lutheran tradition has been particularly apt to draw another sharp division between the righteousness of faith which we experience in justification and in the church, and the 'civic righteousness' which is appropriate in secular affairs. It is often suggested that the justice of God that we encounter in justification may be radically different from the 'worldly justice' which is operative in temporal affairs. During the German church struggle of the 1930s this issue was thrashed out between more conservative Lutherans, who taught that they had no mandate to challenge Hitler and the

Nazis because they operated in the secular realm, which was beyond theological scrutiny, and the leaders of the Confessing Church, particularly the
Calvinist Karl Barth. 'Is there an inward and vital connection', Barth
inquired, 'by means of which in any sense human justice . . . as well as divine
justification, becomes a concern of Christian faith and Christian responsibility, and therefore a matter which concerns the Christian Church?'[16]
Barth answers his own question with a resounding yes, and an increasing
number of Lutheran thinkers who have learned from the experience of the
past would now agree with him. The experience of the divine justification
displays a model of social justice which is also of relevance to the secular
sphere. And a prominent contemporary American Lutheran theologian,
Ronald Thiemann, adds a crucial afterword:

> Because we know that God will remain faithful to his promises, we are
> liberated from the devastating fear that the accomplishment of justice
> in the world depends solely upon our efforts. The primacy and priority
> of God's grace frees us from the self-defeating effort of seeking our
> salvation in the quest for justice. Since our salvation has been secured
> by Christ's death and resurrection, we are now free to seek justice for
> the neighbor in need . . . We seek justice freely, because we have been
> freely justified.[17]

JUSTICE, FORGIVENESS AND RECONCILIATION

Mercy, forgiveness and reconciliation are at the heart of the divine
justice which Christians believe they experience, and which provides a
model for human justice. This theme is contained famously in Portia's
speech in Shakespeare's *The Merchant of Venice*. Portia, a woman disguised
as a man, brings the generous, merciful, healing and Christian understanding of justice characteristic of Belmont into the mechanical and impersonal
justice of Venice. She argues that God's justice is enriched with mercy and
forgiveness and that only thus can true justice be established:

> earthly power does then show likest God's
> When mercy seasons justice,

she proclaims.[18]

Mercy and forgiveness, Portia claims, season, that is bring out the true
flavour of justice, reveal what justice is really about. It is not vindictive,
unrelenting or mechanical, nor is it the cheap grace which disguises the
gravity of offence and broken relationships. Justice is essentially the healing

of relationships, the overcoming of animosities. Its *telos*, its goal, is reconciliation and the restoration of community. Justice seasoned with mercy is in the last analysis gracious. And narrower, thinner accounts of justice as fairness, or impartiality, or giving to each one what is due are actually harmful in as far as they are lacking in generosity, mercy and forgiveness.[19]

THE CHURCH AS EXEMPLAR OF JUSTICE

The American Methodist Stanley Hauerwas in a key passage wrote:

> The task of the church [is] to pioneer those institutions and practices that the wider society has not learned as forms of justice. (At times it is also possible that the church can learn from society more just ways of forming life.) The church, therefore, must act as a paradigmatic community in the hope of providing some indication of what the world can be but is not ... *The church does not have, but rather is, a social ethic.* That is, she is a social ethic inasmuch as she functions as a criteriological institution – that is, an institution that has learned to embody the form of truth that is charity as revealed in the person and work of Christ.[20]

But how is the church a social ethic, how does it 'pioneer new institutions and practices', how does it function as 'a paradigmatic community' demonstrating and exemplifying the justice of God? The church, Hauerwas is saying, is called to be a kind of anticipation of God's Reign and its justice, a preliminary and partial demonstration of the justice of God. Likewise John Milbank argues that although Augustine is right in suggesting that the world cannot yet live by the justice of God, the church ought to be an asylum, a place of refuge from the injustices of the world and a space within which a serious effort is made to pursue just practices and exemplify the justice of God.[21]

Hauerwas and his disciples are quite clear that the first ethical task is to be the church: 'Put starkly, the first ethical task of the Church is to be the church, the servant community ... What makes the church the church is its faithful manifestation of the peaceable kingdom in the world.'[22] The talk here is of the calling of the church rather than its empirical reality, which is often sadly different. A church which is serious about its faith must seek to shape its life by that faith; before it addresses 'the world' about God's justice and calls for obedience, it must make serious efforts to frame its structures and its relationships so that they show something of the truth and worth of what it proclaims. A blatant and unacknowledged contradiction between the teaching and the life of the church is a scandal which makes the message implausible.

Hauerwas and his allies have been deeply influenced by the Mennonite tradition, and tend by 'church' to mean the small local congregation of disciples, nurturing an absolutist ethic and existing as a kind of counter-culture, in tension with the broader society, when they speak of the church. But similar principles are true when different and broader ecclesiologies are involved. Magisterial social teaching on justice, on subsidiarity, on any social issue loses credibility if the church concerned appears to make little effort to apply the teaching to its own life and structures. In this sense it is indeed necessary to be a social ethic if that ethic and the faith of which it is an expression are to be credible in broader circles.

In worship, what Hauerwas calls 'the essential rituals of our politics',[23] there is an enacted anticipation of God's Reign and its justice, a proclamation and a call. Here Christians believe they have an authentic anticipation of God's future and a real, if incomplete, experience of the justice of God, a guarantee of its coming and an encouragement to continue to seek God's Reign and his justice with courage and steadfastness.

The church, Lesslie Newbigin says, is called to be 'an agency of God's justice', and in so doing it confesses the faith:

> In its liturgy it continually relives the mystery of God's action in justifying the ungodly. In its corporate life and the mutual care and discipline of its members it embodies (even if very imperfectly) the justice of God which both unmasks the sin and restores relation with the sinner. In its action in the society of which it is part it will seek to be with Jesus among those who are pushed to the margins. But in all this it will point beyond itself and its own weakness and ambivalence, to the One in whom God's justice has been made manifest by the strange victory of the cross . . . it can continually nourish a combination of realism and hope which finds expression in concrete actions which can be taken by the local community and more widely, which reflect and embody the justice of God.[24]

CHRISTIAN JUSTICE IN CONTEMPORARY DEBATE

There appears to be an extraordinary amount of confusion today about justice, and about social justice in particular. Hayek dismisses the concept as a dangerous mirage, a 'humbug', a dishonest notion, intellectually disreputable, socially divisive and subversive of freedom.[25] John Rawls develops with immense sophistication the theme that justice is fairness. Richard Nozick disagrees fundamentally. Alasdair MacIntyre and the communitarians declare that the Enlightenment project has come to an end, and inquire whose justice we are speaking about, and to which community and tradition it relates.

Disputes which appear to be irresolvable about justice and goodness represent not only academic difficulties but major problems of practice, for practitioners 'on the ground', as it were, and for ordinary folk, particularly for the victims of injustice. In such a context politics and policy-making easily degenerate into, in MacIntyre's telling phrase, 'civil war carried on by other means',[26] an arena in which interest groups compete for control, using ideas as weapons rather than constraints, and as justifications for volatile policy changes which in fact are little influenced by overarching moral considerations. Or the ideological pendulum swings from one extreme to another without the reasons for the change being clear or generally acceptable.

Practitioners often feel that they are making do with fragments of moral insight, and fragments which are frequently in unacknowledged conflict with other fragments, or are not recognised in the way the system or institution is run. And practitioners sometimes recognise that the fragments which are most important for them as insights into reality, as in some sense true, and which are central to the sense of vocation which sustains them in their practice, are derived from a tradition which was and is nurtured in a community of shared faith to which they may or may not belong, and which is now a minority view in society. There is a widespread awareness that the foundations of the practice of justice have been shaken. And in such a situation it is the weak and the poor who are hurt the most. But their cry of protest is often drowned out by the theoretical argument.

Roman Catholic social teaching is articulated in such a way that it is not too difficult to see where it may fit into the contemporary debate about justice. But the debate itself is flawed, MacIntyre suggests, by the fact that there is no agreed criterion against which conflicting views might be measured. Protestant thought, as we have already seen, is far more diverse and episodic. And in as far as Protestantism suggests it can only speak with integrity if it speaks theologically, whereas Roman Catholic social thought uses for the most part a more theologically neutral language of natural law, the question arises whether Protestant thought on justice can be more than the inner discourse of religious communities. Can it contribute creatively to the confusing debate on justice which is taking place in the public arena today? I think it can.

For instance, in the field of social justice, Christian theological ethics would suggest that more than fairness is necessary at the heart of a decent society. If Rawls is right that justice is 'the first virtue of social institutions', it must surely be a justice which is informed by love, by the *agape* of the Christian story, a justice which is more than fairness, a justice which is sometimes generous and sometimes is capable of eliciting sacrifice for others. Generous justice sometimes means giving people other than what is due to them, their deserts. In the gospel parable of the labourers in the marketplace, each receives the same wage independently of how long they have worked, of their desert. Their equality as human beings is recognised. But those who have worked throughout the heat of the day complain that they have been unjustly, unfairly treated. And so, in a sense, they have. The parable expands the notion of justice beyond the rules which protected the worker by insisting that a worker should be paid fairly, to a broader, more generous justice which responds to the misfortune and need, rather than the work, of those who stood waiting to be hired all day. Such a generous understanding of justice must find its place in public policy if we are not to have welfare policies which despise and mistreat the non-achievers, the handicapped and the poor.

A contemporary example is a now-familiar one from South Africa, the Truth and Reconciliation Commission, presided over by Archbishop Desmond Tutu. Here issues of guilt and of retribution are not avoided, and requests for amnesty are not invitations to amnesia: the memories of the past must be faced and healed. The truth must be confronted and moral responsibility accepted, for reconciliation is the aim. In the Commission's work they are using, according to its research director 'a different kind of justice' which is restorative and sees forgiveness as an essential element in justice. They believe this broader frame and fuller understanding of justice is necessary for the healing of South African society. And there is little doubt that this healing, restorative, relational understanding of justice comes as a Christian theological insight which has significant affinities in African traditional culture and is thereby recognised as public truth.

We need to note the particular historical context in which the contemporary renewed interest in the question of social justice has arisen, in particular the end of 'real socialism', the apparent collapse of Marxism as a plausible theory which commands wide support, and the problems faced by the modern welfare state. The collapse of the socialist regimes of Eastern Europe and their supportive ideology serves to remind us that what started as experiments in social justice disintegrated into tyranny and oppression. And in a very much gentler way, the various welfare states which emerged after the Second World War were also experiments in the implementation of social justice. It would, in my opinion, be far too strong to suggest that the welfare state projects have failed, but there is no doubt that they have run into serious difficulties and have not produced the degree of justice and equality that their progenitors hoped and expected from them. So here we have two experiments in social justice, one of which has failed dramatically, the other of which is no more than a qualified success and which in the opinion of most people cannot continue in its present form.

These developments for some people lend credence to frontal attacks on the whole notion of social justice from such as F. A. Hayek, who speaks of social justice as a mirage, a 'humbug', a dishonest notion, intellectually disreputable, which becomes profoundly destructive when efforts are made to embody it in social structures. 'As long as the belief in 'social justice' governs political action, this process must progressively approach nearer and nearer to the totalitarian system.'[27] For Hayek, a concern with social justice is subversive of freedom, socially divisive, and, ironically, 'one of the greatest obstacles to the elimination of poverty'.[28]

In the scriptures God's justice is displayed particularly clearly in the covenant in which he binds himself to his people in love and in grace. The covenant is not a contract in which God's grace is conditional on the response of God's people; God is constantly faithful to his covenant. Within the covenant, God's people experience the gracious, generous justice of God as care, discipline, protection and call. In the covenant the Israelites are required to accept special responsibility for the widow, the orphan, the poor and the stranger. They are expected to reflect the divine justice and covenant love in their dealings with their neighbours.

The covenant concept has been illuminatingly transposed by the American Bill May into the modern public sphere to illumine the proper, just relation between physician and patient. While there is an inevitable contractarian element in professional relationships, May suggests that covenantal relationships have a gratuitous, growing edge to them, for 'the biblical notion of covenant obliges the more powerful to accept some responsibility for the more vulnerable and powerless of the two partners. It does not permit a free rein to self-interest, subject only to the capacity of the weaker partner to protect himself or herself through knowledge, shrewdness, and purchasing power.'[29] A just society founded on covenant principles recognises obligations of care towards those who cannot, for one reason or another, contribute directly to social production – people who would be declared redundant in a society founded simply on a contractarian basis.

So perhaps biblical insights into justice of the sort that Christianity characteristically offers may still have something useful to say in the public forum and in the support of those who are striving to act justly, and to love kindness, and to walk humbly, with or without knowing that such is the way of God.

Notes

1 Luther, 'To the Christian Nobility of the German Nation', in *Philadelphia Edition of the Works of Martin Luther,* 6 vols., Philadelphia: Holman, II, p. 146.

2 Luther, 'Disputation against Scholastic Theology', Clauses 41, 47, 50, *American Edition of Luther's Works*, ed. J. Pelikan and H. T. Lehman, St Louis: Concordia, 1957, vol. XXXI, pp. 4ff.

3 Luther, 'Commentary on Psalm 101', *American Edition*, vol. XXXIII, p. 198.

4 John Calvin, *Institutes of the Christian Religion*, 1.15.8

5 *Ibid.*, II.ii.2.

6 James L. Mays, 'Justice: Perspectives from the Prophetic Tradition', in David L. Petersen, ed., *Prophecy in Israel: Search for an Identity*, Philadelphia: Fortress, 1987, pp. 146–7.

7 John R. Donahue, 'Biblical Perspectives on Justice', in J. Haughey, ed., *The Faith That Does Justice*, New York: Paulist Press, 1977, p. 76.

8 Matthew 5:6.

9 Mays, 'Justice', p. 155.

10 Matthew 6:33.

11 L. Newbigin, 'Whose Justice?' *Ecumenical Review* 44 (1992), p. 310.

12 Acts 3:14; 7:52.

13 1 Cor. 1:30; cf. Rom:1.17.

14 Cited in Ronald Bainton, *Here I Stand: A Life of Martin Luther*, New York: Abingdon-Cokesbury Press, 1950, p. 65.

15 J. D. G. Dunn, 'The Justice of God: A Renewed Perspective on Justification by Faith', *Journal of Theological Studies* 43.1 (1992), p. 15.

16 Karl Barth, *Church and State* [Rechtfertigung und Recht], London: SCM Press, 1939, p. 1.

17 Ronald F. Thiemann, cited in V. Mortensen, ed., *Justification and Justice*, Geneva: Lutheran World Federation, 1992, p. 15.

18 William Shakespeare, *The Merchant of Venice*, Act IV, scene i, lines 196–7.

19 I have argued this case in my book *Christian Justice and Public Policy*, Cambridge: Cambridge University Press, 1997.

20 Stanley Hauerwas, *Truthfulness and Tragedy*, Notre Dame: Notre Dame University Press, 1977, pp. 142–3 (my italics).

21 John Milbank, *Theology and Social Theory: Beyond Secular Reason*, Oxford: Blackwell, 1990, p. 422.

22 Stanley Hauerwas, *The Peaceable Kingdom: A Primer in Christian Ethics.* London: SCM Press, 1984, p. 99.

23 *Ibid.*, p. 108.

24 Newbigin, 'Whose Justice?' p. 311.

25 See F. A. Hayek, *The Mirage of Social Justice, in Law, Legislation and Liberty*, vol. II, 2nd edn, London: Routledge, 1982.

26 Alasdair MacIntyre, *After Virtue*, 2nd edn, Notre Dame: University of Notre Dame Press, 1984, p. 236.

27 Hayek, *Mirage of Social Justice*, p. 68.

28 *Ibid.*, p. 139.

29 William F. May, *The Physician's Covenant: Images of the Healer in Medical Ethics*. Philadelphia: Westminster Press, 1983, p. 124.

15 Ecology and Christian ethics

MICHAEL S. NORTHCOTT

The existence of an ecological crisis is increasingly recognised as one of the defining features of life in the late-modern era. The precise parameters of the crisis are described in different ways, but most accounts include the following features:

(1) Modern humans are witnessing the first major extinction of species originated by human action and the first such mass extinction to occur in a time frame of decades rather than millennia. Scientists estimate the number of lost species as a consequence of human activity at around 10,000 per annum. Biodiversity is reduced by deforestation in both tropical and boreal regions, by the conversion of forests, savannah and wetlands into land for agricultural monocrops or domestic animal grazing, by industrialised deep-sea fishing, by the destruction of coral reefs, and by the increased use of pesticides and herbicides in modern agricultural systems.

(2) The earth is said to be undergoing radical changes in its climatic patterns caused by human activities, and in particular the burning of fossil fuels for space heating, transportation industry and electricity production. Growth in rice-paddy cultivation and beef-cattle ranching, major sources of methane, also contribute to the enhancement of the greenhouse effect. Evidence for global warming is said to include rising sea levels, rising global air temperatures, the melting of the Antarctic ice shelf, the increasing number and ferocity of tropical cyclones, disturbances in the pattern of tropical monsoon rains, and related changes in ocean currents which dramatically enhanced the effects of El Niño in 1998.

(3) 'Pollution' by industrial, post-consumer and chemical wastes and residues is increasingly widespread in the oceans, rivers, air and land of the planet. Local pollution in industrial cities has been a long-standing problem since the industrial revolution in Europe and North America.

The spread of industrial production methods across the earth has now introduced pollutants into all parts of the planet. The pervasiveness of chemical pollution, and its deleterious effects on many life forms, is demonstrated by dramatic declines in the global frog population, as frogs are particularly sensitive to air and water pollution. Tree health is also affected on many continents, as evidenced in declining leaf canopies and reduced annual growth rates. The depletion of the protective ozone layer consequent on the industrial production of CFCs and their accumulation in the upper atmosphere has already produced rising incidences of blindness and skin cancers in humans and mammals, as well as fish, in regions close to the Antarctic ozone 'hole' such as Chile and New Zealand.

(4) Soil erosion and desertification affect growing areas of the planet including the Mediterranean basin, Saharan and sub-Saharan Africa, Australia, parts of central China and the Americas. Soil is essential to vegetable and plant life, and derivatively to mammalian and bird life. Soil erosion is linked with deforestation, poor farming methods, including some forms of peasant agriculture but on a much larger scale industrial tillage, overgrazing from domesticated animals, and inappropriate use of marginal lands such as hillsides for crop production. Forty per cent of global arable land is affected by serious soil erosion.[1]

Most accounts of the causes of the ecological crisis link it with the rapid growth in the human population in the last four centuries, which passed six billion in the year 1999. Most also highlight central features of the industrial economy which dominates food and artefact production, housing and transportation systems in the northern hemisphere, and in growing parts of the southern hemisphere. In particular, technological enhancement of the human capacity to adapt the physical environment for human purposes has deepened and globalised the invasiveness of agricultural and artefact production into the prior order of the natural world. Globalised production systems are partly driven by the increasingly materially comfortable lifestyles of modern North Americans and Europeans. These lifestyles depend upon access to reserves of fossil fuels, timber and land for exotic crops and animal feed which represent an 'ecological footprint' more than double the land area occupied by the people who enjoy them. The ecological impact of the enhanced human population is not therefore so much a consequence of the sheer numbers of humans as it is of the technological, economic and political processes which enable the more affluent of modern humans, and the large corporations which putatively meet their 'wants', to access natural systems across the globe for their own lifestyle maintenance. This unequal access to natural resources, and their consequent scarce availability to many others, particularly in the southern hemisphere, in turn forces around one billion people to degrade their environments simply in order to survive.[2]

Behind these changes in modern lifestyles, technologies and global economic processes are ideological and cultural changes, changes in the orientation and character of modern human life, which many see as the roots of the ecological crisis. Thus Anthony Giddens describes the ecological crisis as one of the intrinsic consequences of the economic and cultural forms of late modernity, and in particular of capitalism's tendency to disembed human life from prior attachments to place, custom and tradition which in the past helped to conserve the environment.[3] The examination of the roots of these changes in western culture, and hence of the environmental crisis, has produced what James Nash calls an 'ecological complaint' against Christian theology and ethics which is widely perceived as legitimate.[4] Other religious traditions, and in particular Buddhism, or at least the forms of 'spiritual' practice and pantheist theology which pass for this tradition in modern western culture, are by contrast said to offer a more sympathetic conception of the human relation to nature.[5]

The complaint against Christianity was first articulated in a now frequently rehearsed argument by the historian Lynn White, who claimed that the Christian idea of a creator God who is 'outside' creation contributed to the desacralisation of material space in medieval theology and culture, and helped to legitimate an increasingly utilitarian approach to nature as resource bank in the early-modern period.[6] Unlike other advocates of this ecological complaint, however, White does not propose the abandonment of the Christian religion. He believes on the contrary that only religion has the motive power to change the direction of modern civilisation, and that in particular the spirituality of St Francis has much to offer in this regard.

In the judgement of a number of contemporary theologians and historians of science, White is correct in his view that changes in attitudes towards nature, and in particular the modern technological treatment of nature as malleable matter available for reconstitution in the service of human wants, does have roots in medieval theology and early-modern scientific cosmology. However, the problem is not, as White suggests, with the Christian tradition of a Creator God as such, and the supposed desacralisation of space that this is said to involve as contrasted with pantheism, but rather with the understanding of the *relation* between the Creator and the world. Hans Blumenberg[7] and Amos Funkenstein[8] suggest that the nominalist mutation of the Trinitarian doctrine of creation in the late Middle Ages, and its subsequent abandonment and replacement with a mechanistic cosmology, is the true ideological root of the modern western attitude to nature and the technocentric forms of modern culture which this attitude has fostered.[9] In particular, William of Ockham's overemphasis on *creatio ex nihilo* (creation from nothing), and on the arbitrary will of God as creator, sustained a loss of connection between the loving and redemptive purposes of God for the world, as revealed in the Incarnation of Jesus Christ, and the original divine ordering of the world. Colin Gunton suggests that this emergent theological split between creation and redemption encouraged a view of God and of bodies, cosmic and organic, as existing in a direct causal relation of absolute power and will, unmediated by the loving purposes of God for creation from the beginning, and which are reaffirmed in the Incarnation.[10] In the absence of Christological mediation the creation appears in the early-modern mind as sheer mechanism, as a realm of brute facts whose prior ordering reveals nothing of the beneficent intentions of the Creator, though it may still be said to have been *caused* by the arbitrary will of God (defined in deist rather than trinitarian terms) at the beginning of the cosmos. Such divine intentions as God may have for the good of life, and especially human life, within the material world are only available to the inner eye of spirit, or faith, as aided by revelation. They are unknowable to reason, and irrelevant to the scientific study and technological mobilisation of bodies and the cosmos. A consequent dualism between God, the good, and the physical appearance of the exterior cosmos emerges in the scientific writings of Galileo, Descartes, Newton and their successors wherein matter and bodies are increasingly understood as pure mechanism both in their workings and ultimately in their origins.[11] The human refashioning of nature is thus freed from the moral restraints which arise in the Trinitarian doctrine of creation which posits an ongoing, purposive and ultimately redemptive relation between God and the order of creation. In a mechanistic cosmology the prior order of matter and organisms bears no intrinsic moral or teleological significance.

To put the matter another way, Christians traditionally valued the existing and material ordering of creation because they perceived that in Jesus Christ the original creative principle through which God had caused the world to come into being – the *logos* or divine Word – had been made known as a human fleshly body, and in space and time. And further the Resurrection revealed to Christians that it was God's intention to redeem life in the body of the material creation, and not just to rescue the souls or spirits of Christians from out of the organic and substantial cosmos.[12] Hence in the early Christian accounts of the future destiny of the material world, such as the

Revelation of St John the Divine, and the second-century anti-Gnostic theology of Ireneus of Lyons, we find the idea of the recapitulation of creation, in which the earth is said to have been reconstituted by God in the Incarnation of Christ. On this view, at the appointed time the original peace and fertility of creation before the fall are to be fully restored.[13]

RESURRECTION AND CREATION ETHICS

A Christian environmental ethic requires as its source and guide the knowledge of God as the creator and redeemer of all life which is definitively revealed in the life, death and resurrection of Jesus Christ, the Incarnate Word. In the startling and unprecedented events of the incarnation, crucifixion and resurrection of Jesus Christ the early Christians find that the God who made the world, and who lamented and at times punished the waywardness of sinful humans who were its crown, had also and always intended to redeem it from its captivity to sin by the same means through which God had created it. The affirmation that the creative and redemptive purposes and actions of God were originally related is repeated at a number of points in the New Testament. In the Epistle to the Ephesians we find the following claim: 'he [God] has made known to us the mystery of his will, according to the good pleasure that he set forth in Christ, as a plan for the fullness of time, to gather up all things in him, things in heaven and things on earth' (Eph. 1:9–10). And in the prologue to St John's Gospel we read that Jesus Christ the Incarnate Word was also with God before creation began: 'the Word was God. He was in the beginning with God. All things came into being through him, and without him not one thing came into being. What has come into being in him was life, and the life was the light of all people' (John 1:2–3).

These passages in the New Testament testify to a theological position which evidently was developed quite early in Christian reflection on the meaning of the Incarnation, and this was that the means by which God had created the world was the same means by which God had chosen to redeem the world from sin and death, this being Jesus Christ the Incarnate Word, whom Ireneus later described as one of God's 'hands' in the act of creation (the other being the Spirit).[14] From the outset Christians were encouraged to view the creation of the world, and its redemption, in an integral way, and in the light of their emergent Trinitarian understanding of God as Father, Son and Spirit. The early Christian understanding of Christ as redeemer already carried with it a new understanding of the meaning and character of creation and of bodies, and also of the weight and depth of human sin and of evil, both human and angelic.

All that Christians believe about the creative and redemptive purposes of God in Christ for themselves and for the material creation springs from their understanding of the bodily resurrection of Christ on the third day. St Paul and the gospel writers in their different ways affirm their belief that the resurrection of Jesus from the dead was not just a vision or a 'spiritual' happening. Jesus is described as appearing to the disciples as a body who walks and talks, breaks bread, eats fish and sits down with the disciples. The claim is made repeatedly that there *was* a relationship between his physical and personal existence on earth and the resurrected body of Jesus which is seen by the disciples. The resurrected body of Jesus is not the *same* as the body of Jesus before his death, for we also read it can pass through walls and appear and disappear. But the idea of continuity between this body and the body of Jesus which was crucified is also affirmed: to the apostle who doubts this, Thomas, Jesus even shows the marks of crucifixion, his wounded limbs and pierced side.

It would be hard to overstate the ethical significance of the resurrection of Jesus for Christian ethics, and for a Christian ethic of the environment. If there had been no resurrection, there would be no church, and the disciples would have dispersed to their former callings. If there is no resurrection then the central ethical claim that Christians make, that God has rescued them from the condition of sin and evil which has characterised created life since Adam, collapses. Through the resurrection Christians discover that the law of sin and death has been overturned and that the possibility of moral restoration in *this* life, which Jesus announces in his preaching and demonstrates in his miracles, is brought near after his death through participation in the Spirit of the resurrected Christ. And the implications of this restoration of life are not limited to the *minds* or *souls* of believers. Against the antinomians and proto-Gnostics who threatened to subvert the ethic of resurrection in the gentile churches, St Paul asserts again and again that Christians must show forth the truth of their salvation in their life in the body which has become 'the temple of the Holy Spirit' (1 Cor. 6:19).

And he goes further. The implications of the salvation of Jesus Christ are not limited to the minds, bodies and spirits of *Christians*: 'He rescued us from the domain of darkness and brought us into the kingdom of his dear Son, through whom our release is secured and our sins are forgiven. He is the image of the invisible God; his is the primacy over all created things' (Col. 1:13–15). Once again, as in the prologue to the Gospel of John, the theological insight that he whom Christians worship in Jesus is the means by which God made the world finds explicit affirmation in this epistle. The cosmic Christ is not only Lord of the lives and bodies of Christians but Lord of the whole created order, and the implications of the resurrection extend beyond the lives of Christians to reveal God's intention to restore the right-eous peace, or *shalom*, of the whole of creation. As Oliver O'Donovan puts the matter in *Resurrection and Moral Order*,

> In proclaiming the resurrection of Christ, the apostles proclaimed also the resurrection of mankind in Christ; and in proclaiming the resurrection of mankind, they proclaimed the renewal of all creation with him. The resurrection of Christ in isolation from mankind would not be a gospel message. The resurrection of mankind apart from creation would be a gospel of a sort, but of a purely Gnostic and world-denying sort which is far from the gospel that the apostles actually preached. So the resurrection of Christ directs our attention back to the creation which it vindicates.[15]

O'Donovan goes on to propose that this reading of the creational signifi-cance of resurrection is central to a fully Christian and theological account, as opposed to a secular or liberal theological account, of the divinely given ethical project of human life. For the resurrection does not vindicate crea-tion as it has been marred by sin and alienation between God and humans, although, as John Milbank rightly contends, this is the realm in which the modern project 'ethics', including liberal Christian ethics, is constructed.[16] On the contrary, the resurrection vindicates the original relational ordering of creation *towards* the Triune God, who not only originates creation but orders it after, and towards participation in, God's own relationality, even though this ordering to God is obscured by human sin.

As O'Donovan suggests, this approach to ethics involves a decision about the status of the ordering of creation as we still partially encounter it, both in ourselves and in the rest of created order:

> only if the order which we think we see, or something like it, is really present in the world, can there be an 'evangelical' ethics. Only so, indeed, can there be a Christian, rather than a Gnostic, gospel at all. The dynamic of the Christian faith, calling us to respond appropriately to the deeds of God on our behalf, supposes that there is an appropriate conformity of human response to divine act.[17]

In this perspective the original ordering of creation towards God, and inter-nally towards itself, and towards the human as the most godlike aspect of creation, has deep moral and theological significance. The Christian moral project therefore requires affirmation of the original *telos* (purpose or end) and shape of created and material life, and of the marks of creation's original relatedness to God which we may still find in ourselves and in the rest of the natural order. Without this affirmation our human response to the event of resurrection, even though enabled by the indwelling Spirit of Christ, would find no echo or correspondence with our life as embodied and reasoning humans, and this again would leave us in the Gnostic position. It would leave us with a Christian ethical project which was dangerously detached from the location of the Christian life in the time and space and bodies of this material world. And *such* a project could legitimately be said to be problematic for a conception of the flourishing of the natural world in which humans dwell before death, and hence for a Christian environmental ethic. By contrast, a vision of Christian ethics which springs from the resurrection is both an evangelical *and* a natural ethic, because it involves an understanding of the moral ordering of creation, and of its restoration in Christ, which is an order which addresses all people and not just Christians.[18]

FROM PERSONALIST TO CHRISTIAN ETHICS

This approach to ethics contrasts dramatically with the modern secular view of human ethics as a project of creative construction which is undertaken in opposition to the prior order which humans encounter in the physical nature of things. Enlightenment philosophers, including Immanuel Kant and David Hume, accepted the judgement of modern science that the cosmos is fundamentally characterised by mechanical laws which are available for description and theorisation by modern science, and do not need the hypothesis God. As a consequence Kant, Hume and others sought to mark off ethics from cosmology, and in Hume's case from metaphysics, arguing for a complete epistemological break between moral perception or moral reasoning and scientific observation and theorisation concerning natural order. The outcome, as Peter Singer succinctly puts it, is that in modern post-Enlightenment philosophy 'ethics is no part of the structure of the universe'.[19] Modern humans may *construe* the natural order as a realm of deep meaningfulness and purposiveness, but it cannot be said to present itself in this way. Nature as autonomous, uncaused mechanism is the outcome of a series of random organo-chemical events, and subsequently of the blind but 'selfish' determination of genes, which by their very nature can have no moral significance. And this philosophical move has tremendous cultural significance: the modern economistic and technocentric construction of nature as resource bank for industrial, chemical and organic reordering for human purposes represents in the dominant social forms of modernity the idea that the order of nature has no prior moral significance before the imputation of beauty or value or utility to it by its human observers and owners.

The rejection of the idea that we live in a world imbued with goodness and order by the Triune creator God, whose order has objective moral significance because it is made, and is promised redemption, by God, is, on this account, a central feature of the alienation between nature and modernity: the modern relocation of the good in a natural capacity of the human mind and/or will, whether Kant's *practical reason* or Hume's *moral sentiments*, rather than in the mind of God and the order which we encounter objectively in God's world, is the principal source of the deep opposition between the modern forms of human flourishing and the flourishing of the ecosystems which modern humans transform for their interest and comfort.[20] In modern cosmology as in modern ethics the original order of nature has no moral significance: it is available to humans for reordering at will. The only moral implications of such reordering are the possible ways in which a reordered nature may cause harms to persons, or may offend their aesthetic sensibilities about the appearance of the natural world.

Detached from any conception of the objectivity of the good, and of the teleological ordering of life in the body and in creation towards the good, through its continuing relation to a beneficent God, the modern project of ethics adopts a personalist ethical frame. Since morality is located exclusively in individual human consciousness, the principle of non-harm to other conscious individuals becomes the putative mode of operation of ethics. This principle finds expression in deontological and consequentialist terms. The deontologist makes *a priori* judgements that certain actions are *always* against the good of persons, while the consequentialist believes that all actions are best judged by the sum of their effects on the pleasure (or pain) of actually existing persons. It was, and continues to be, in relation to such personalist concerns that appeals to environmental conservation are principally made and environmental regulations and laws are framed. Thus the important report of the United Nations Commission on Environment and Development *Our Common Future* frames its appeal for a more environmental form of economic growth, or 'sustainable development', in terms of the interests of presently existing humans and their progeny.[21]

Anthropocentric approaches to environmental conservation are criticised by advocates of a broader sensibility to the value of the non-human world as insufficiently radical to halt or reverse the ecological depredations of modern civilisation. In order to supersede the personalist outcome of the modern ethical project, advocates of a thoroughgoing environmental ethic propose that the moral values located in certain capacities of persons be extended to beings in, and/or features of, the non-human world. The first extension, and one which is anticipated in the writings of early utilitarian philosophers such as Jeremy Bentham, is to include all beings that are judged to be capable of experiencing pain in the sphere of the morally considerable.[22] This extension of the consequentialist calculus to include sentient animals now finds widespread advocacy in modern western societies. It is advocated both by consequentialists such as Peter Singer in *Animal Liberation* and, by deontologists such as Tom Regan who argue for the 'rights' of animals on analogy with the modern ethical recognition of the 'rights' of persons.[23] The arguments between these two approaches are robust, and, relying as they do on different moral logics, they tend to incommensurability. And this incommensurability is reflected in ongoing public debates in Britain and elsewhere about the morality of hunting foxes or other wild animals, the morality of modern intensive animal breeding and mechanised slaughter systems, or the morality of animal experimentation. Consequentialists are able to tolerate certain harms done to animals in the pursuit of evident moral goods for humans: thus Singer is not opposed to the limited and careful use of animals in certain medical procedures, while other consequentialists who recognise animals as conscious sentient beings to whom duties of care are owed by humans still admit the morality of the humane slaughter of animals for meat production or for medical parts such as heart valves. In this approach it is the welfare of the animal when alive which is crucial.[24] Deontologists on the other hand will admit of no exceptions to their judgement that animals possess the same moral rights as humans not to be experimented upon, or to be killed before their lives naturally end, because as 'subjects-of-life' they are capable of experiencing pain and possess memories and some sense of identity; and, since in a personalist perspective moral value resides precisely in the qualities which make life personal, ethical consistency may be said to require that they are the object of moral respect in all life forms.[25]

However, personalist or anthropocentric ethics do not admit of the moral considerability of non-sentient forms of life such as trees or coral except inasmuch as they are of value to humans, and hence two alternative positions, biocentrism and ecocentrism, are proposed to extend the realm of moral considerability still further. The first of these is Aldo Leopold's proposal, developed and embellished by J. Baird Callicott, that the diverse and mutually dependent communities of life which characterise ecosystems are collectively judged to be morally considerable.[26] Leopold's position is summed up in the following statement: 'A thing is right when it tends to preserve the integrity, stability, and beauty of the biotic community. It is wrong when it tends otherwise.'[27] Leopold's is a classically holist position. As Callicott argues, in the land ethic value is not ascribed to individuals but to the good of the whole, and the flourishing of the community in the balance of its parts.[28] Against this approach Holmes Rolston argues that it is possible to discern moral value in the purposive activities of the individual life forms – from biota to conscious mammals and persons – of which species-communities are constituted.[29] Moral interests may in other words be said to correlate to all life forms which demonstrate that they are teleologically directed. Rolston proposes that the moral interests of different life-forms, where they compete, must be judged on the basis of the richness and complexity of purposes which life forms express, those of humans and the higher mammals being on this view the most valuable and those of biota the least.

These forms of ecocentrism represent attempts to reform the anthropocentric orientation of modern personalist ethics, in an effort to delineate an *environmental* ethic. This project may also be seen as part of the 'turn to nature' which characterises the romantic as well as the humanist response to the Enlightenment proclamation of the sovereignty of reason, and of persons, and the associated evacuation of God, or any relational connection to God, from the mechanistic cosmos.[30] With the loss of God as moral source, the modern moral project is concerned with identifying another locus for ethics, either in personal capacities such as reason or sentiment, or, in the Romantic approach, in certain features of the natural world, beauty in particular.

The first environmental flowering of the turn to nature is represented by the efforts of the early Romantics, such as Wordsworth, Ruskin and Muir, to set aside certain wilderness areas from the depredations of modern industrial activities such as quarrying and logging. The national park and the wildlife reserve are the first fruits of the turn to nature of which the recognition of the 'rights' of animals, of species communities or even biota may be said to be the logical extension. However, the nature 'reserve' presents a way of seeing nature which already assumes an intrinsic alienation between human and non-human flourishing. It fosters the idea that environmental exclusion of humans from nature is the only way to resolve their inherent tendencies to abuse and degrade their environment.[31] The turn to nature then has an ironic outcome. To 'save' the values moderns wish to find in nature, independent of their own gaze, this approach requires the exclusion of humans from nature, rather the way a radical animal-rights position requires that humans not be involved with the keeping of animals in any way, except, for some animal-rights activists, as pets. The problem is that the turn to nature is unable to put aside the original, prior and ordering scientific narrative of the nature of life as inherently conflictual, and a consequent vision of the moral life as constructed in basic tension with the material and biological character of life in the cosmos.

REDEEMING CREATION: ECOJUSTICE AND STEWARDSHIP

In the Christian tradition, as we have seen, the physical character of the universe is not said to be opposed to the human good but quite the reverse. The human good is directly related to the good of the Creator, and is also seen as existing in direct relational connection with the goods of the rest of creation. This relational connection is both marred by, and also revealed in, the sinful rebellion of the creature against God which is described in the second and third chapters of Genesis and interpreted by St Paul and others as paradigmatic for the subsequent divine 'rescue' of creation effected in Jesus Christ. And just as this rescue has significance for the whole creation, so the original rebellion against God has effects not just for humans, or the human relation to God, but for the whole creation. Thus Adam and Eve are said to have been turned out of the fruitful and peaceable garden of Eden, and the land and its non-human inhabitants are also said to have become subject to the effects of human sin. This story of sin is, though, said to be redeemed in the covenant which Yahweh makes with the people of Israel under the terms of which they are given once again a land which is close to paradise, flowing with milk and honey, rich in natural goods and fertility. Robert Murray shows how this original covenant is not limited to humans but includes the land and all its inhabitants within its purview and is in effect a 'cosmic covenant'.[32] However, in the context of this covenant the narrative of sin once again reasserts itself. As the Israelites become settled in the land, they follow other gods, they abandon the just laws which were to govern the community of the people of God, the poor are downtrodden and the rich take all the wealth of the land for themselves. And again, as with the sin of Adam, the consequence is not limited to human society: the land itself suffers as a result of the abandonment of the faithful worship of Yahweh and the moral frame of righteousness and justice which Yahweh had established. Thus in the prophecies of Isaiah we find the claim that the exclusion of the poor from the land and the land's loss of fertility are connected:

Woe to those who add house to house
and join field to field
until everywhere belongs to them
and they are the sole inhabitants of the land.
Yahweh Sabaoth has sworn this in my hearing,
'Many houses shall be brought to ruin, great and fine,
but left untenanted;
ten acres of vineyard will yield only one barrel,
ten bushels of seed will yield only one bushel.' (Isa. 5:8–10)

The prophets read the eventual exile of the Israelites from the land and its ecological degradation as consequences of the failure of the Israelites to keep to the covenant which God had made with them, and on the keeping of which their tenure of the land, and its continuing fertility, were said to depend:

See how Yahweh lays the earth waste,
makes it a desert, buckles its surface,
scatters its inhabitants,
priest and people alike, master and slave,
mistress and maid, seller and buyer,
lender and borrower, creditor and debtor.
Ravaged, ravaged the earth,
despoiled, despoiled,
as Yahweh has said.
The earth is mourning, withering,
the heavens are pining away with the earth.
The earth is defiled under its inhabitants' feet,
for they have transgressed the law, violated the precept,
broken the everlasting covenant.
So a curse consumes the earth
and its inhabitants suffer their penalty,
that is why the inhabitants of the earth are burnt up,
and few men are left. (Isa. 24:1–6)

What we find in such passages (and Murray argues that they are by no means isolated passages)[33] is the recognition of a deep connection within created order between human injustice with regard to the distribution of the wealth of God's creation, especially environmental exclusion of the poor, and ecological degradation. The righteousness and justice which are intrinsic to the being of God are also writ large in the material and moral framework of the creation which God has made, and with which God remains in continuing relationship. We have in this tradition, then, a powerful insight into the ecological nature of divine, and so of created, justice.

The term 'ecojustice' has a significant provenance in the environmental movement. In the United States it is associated with the recognition that environmental concerns have a deep association with social inequality and racism. Advocates of ecojustice note that toxic-waste dumps, chemical works, nuclear power stations, polluting factories and landfill sites are almost exclusively located in the neighbourhoods of poor people and people of colour. Similarly in the United Kingdom it is very rare to find major sources of pollution in middle-class residential areas. It is also notable that it is the children of the poor who are most frequently the victims of urban motor accidents, for it is through their neighbourhoods that urban motorways and major roads tend to run.[34] The wealthy tend to live on private roads or else on suburban streets well away from major traffic routes. Their streets are also more likely to be 'calmed' with the use of speed bumps, chicanes, dead-ends and other speed- and traffic-reducing devices.

Developed countries are beginning to address some of these internal environmental equity problems by removing their dirtiest technologies and manufacturing facilities from poor neighbourhoods to poorer countries in the developing world, where labour is cheap and environmental regulation often non-existent. The inconsistent morality of this new form of colonialism is shrouded in arguments about the legitimacy of 'free' trade and the benefits to both rich and poor of 'deregulated' global markets. In practice however the vast majority of the human victims of environmental abuses now live in developing countries, and the foremost abuse is that of environmental exclusion, whose agents are often those global corporations who exercise considerable power in a global system where local or national custom and law exercise diminishing constraint upon economic activity. From the first Act of Enclosure in England in the seventeenth century, modern industrial 'civilisation' has dragged commoners and tribal peoples into its wake by forcibly excluding them from environments where they previously met their bodily and cultural requirements without recourse to industrial production and monetary exchange.[35]

Environmental exclusion and poverty, both global and local, are, ironically, connected to a growing concern for environmental quality in the context of national and global political and economic structures in which decision-making processes favour powerful over powerless people. And herein lies the *real* limitation of modern personalist approaches to environmental dilemmas. As I have argued, these ethical procedures are designed to preserve a moral 'space' in human experience from the world of mechanism, hard facts and rationally verifiable truths which characterises the gaze of modern science and deist or atheist cosmology. But the Enlightenment effort to preserve this moral space has proven unsuccessful. Gradually, as postmodern critics recognise, the preserved space of personhood, moral sentiment, custom and tradition has been overtaken by the powerful partnership of science-informed knowledge, economic corporations mobilising and marketing new technologies, and the bureaucratic and executive powers of modern nation-states and super-state bodies such as the International Monetary Fund, the World Bank and the World Trade Organisation. The Enlightenment proclamation of the sovereignty of reason in a mechanistic universe now threatens the very humanist moral project of personalism which this proclamation also birthed. As Milbank puts it,

> once it is conceded, as by Kant, that ethics is to be grounded in the fact of the will, and of human freedom, then quite quickly it is realized that freedom is not an ahistorical fact about an essential human subject, but is constantly distilled from the complex strategies of power within which subjects are interpellated as unequal, mutually dependent persons. The production of an equality of freedom therefore collapses into the promotion of the inequality of power.[36]

Will-to-power is latent within the liberal and Enlightenment attempt to preserve some form of morality – and in particular respect for persons – from the nominalist metaphysics of absolute divine power, a cosmology of mechanism and the sovereignty of reason, which, in the social and material form of the industrial remaking of nature, has had such dreadful ecological consequences.

However, most secular or non-theist advocates of environmental ethics fail to recognise or adequately respond to this deep problem in contemporary western metaphysics. They argue instead, as we have seen, for various kinds of extension of the delimited but essentially non-factual realm of moral value, while missing the larger framing of power and violence which marks all forms of human environmental exclusion, as well as the technological forms of modern humanity's efforts to wrest wealth and security from the recalcitrant mechanical life forms of the non-human world.

Until the Enlightenment, the Christian tradition sustained the belief that God and not humans is the principal locus of consciousness and of moral purposiveness in the cosmos. Similarly the creation is first and foremost God's possession, not humanity's. Humans dwell in it and experience their own life, and the biophysical cosmos in which they live out their lives, as a gift or a loan from God rather than as their absolute possession.[37] In Jesus' parable of the steward, and in the apostle Paul's affirmation that we are not owners of our own bodies, nor of the mysteries of faith, but that all belongs to God (1 Cor. 6:19), we find reaffirmation in the New Testament of the ancient Jewish belief that humans enjoy the creation as gift and not possession. The duty of respect for natural order arises, then, from the original recognition that the world is not ours but God's, and that in its design and order it displays not an independent order of being from human being, available for human remaking at will, but a shared realm of *created* being. And according to the psalmists, monks, nuns and hymn-writers who have given ritual form to Jewish and Christian prayer and worship over the centuries, this recognition finds its paradigmatic form in worship, through which creation shares in the gracious relational abundance of the being of God from which it is birthed, and in God's contemplative rest from the labour of creation on the Sabbath. Christian worship and prayer forms 'part of the praise that the whole creation, consciously or unconsciously, offers to its Creator'.[38]

However, stewardship *apart from* worship and the recognition of the Trinitarian and incarnational relation of creation to creator is not unproblematic. If we imagine we are in control of the earth, that our duty to respect it stands independent of our and its relation to God who is its owner, we already conceive of our relation to the earth in terms conducive to the metaphor of scientific control and technological management which so dominates environmental management procedures, and with such ecologically deleterious consequences. Apart from the worship of God as sovereign and Lord of creation we always stand in danger of turning our control of the earth, or the earth itself, into a substitute for God, and worshipping the creature rather than the creator. The first commandment both enjoins the worship of God and prohibits idolatry. It involves the recognition that when we do not worship God with our whole heart, soul and strength we are in danger already of worshipping that which is not God. Idolatry – of technology, of consumer goods, of human control and corporate power – is at the heart of the collective and individual sins which constitute the environmental crisis. Turning back to God, not to nature, is the only truthful spiritual response to this crisis.

Jesus revisited the command tradition of ethics in his moral teaching and proposed that its essence is discoverable in the category of love, love of God and love of neighbour. Love between God and the creature involves both in a mutual relation in which the different being and order of both is recognised and affirmed. Created being apart from God stands in need of completion through relationship with God. The promise of this completion is realised in the resurrection of Christ, and is anticipated and brought near in the power of the Spirit. The Christian tradition for many centuries affirmed that this bringing near, this reconciliation of created life to God, was something which happened to the whole creation. There can be no more solemn and morally weighty conception of the moral value of created order than this incarnational tradition. It means that when Jesus summed up the import of the remaining commandments in terms of the command-ment to 'love your neighbour as yourself', we cannot limit the implications of this love to other persons. We are enjoined to love creation, to love nature, because we share with nature in the restoration which is promised in the resurrection of Jesus Christ.[39]

Envisaging the human relation to nature in terms of love has profound implications for the modern social form; for the cost–benefit calculus which insures that billions of animals every year are imprisoned in cruel and value-less life to provide cheap protein for humans; the corporate and inter-governmental calculus which sets as a price for international debt repay-ment the systematic clear-cutting of ancient forests and the environmental exclusion of peasant farmers and tribal peoples from their ancestral lands; the market ideology which sets the putative good of 'private' transport above safe space for children and walkers and wild things to play and relate and make community. Christians may not expect that the ethics which arises from the worship of the God who is in Jesus will convert the world. Christians can, though, seek to make connections between worshipping communities sustained by the love of God, and shaped by their love for God, for persons and for nature, and the social and natural environment in which those communities are set precisely because the social and the natural are *created*, and not just secular, spaces. These connections are all part of the relational and ethical force of the command to love the neighbour. They find expression in what elsewhere I have characterised as parochial ecology.[40] In a world in which neighbourly relationships find expression in international trade as well as in local communities, the pursuit of parochial ecology will involve local Christian communities in a quest for just and hence alternative ethical approaches to global economic exchange *and* in efforts to promote the flourishing of the local human and ecological communities in which worshipping communities are situated.

Notes

1 For a fuller account of the environmental crisis see Michael S. Northcott, *The Environment and Christian Ethics* (Cambridge: Cambridge University Press, 1996), pp. 1–39.

2 See further Piers Blaikie, *The Political Economy of Soil Erosion in Developing Countries* (London: Longman, 1985).

3 Anthony Giddens, *The Consequences of Modernity* (Cambridge: Polity Press, 1991), esp. pp. 151ff.

4 James Nash, *Loving Nature: Ecological Integrity and Christian Responsibility* (Nashville, TN: Abingdon, 1992), p. 68.

5 See for example J. Baird Callicott, *Earth's Insights: A Multicultural Survey of Ecological Ethics from the Mediterranean Basin to the Australian Outback* (Berkeley and Los Angeles: University of California Press, 1994).

6 Lynn White, 'The historical roots of our ecologic crisis', *Science* 155 (1967) pp. 1203–7.

7 Hans Blumenberg, *The Legitimacy of the Modern Age*, transl. R. M. Wallace (Cambridge, MA: MIT Press, 1983), pp. 149ff.

8 Amos Funkenstein, *Theology and the Scientific Imagination: From the Middle Ages to the Seventeenth Century* (Princeton, NJ: Princeton University Press, 1986), pp. 142ff.

9 See further Northcott, *Environment and Christian Ethics*, pp. 57–61 and 217–21, and Colin Gunton, *The Triune Creator: A Historical and Systematic Study* (Edinburgh: Edinburgh University Press, 1998), esp. chs. 5 and 6.

10 Gunton, *The Triune Creator*, pp. 124–5.

11 See further Michael Buckley, *At the Origins of Modern Atheism* (New Haven, CT: Yale University Press, 1987), pp. 99–144.

12 Gunton, *The Triune Creator*, p. 125.

13 See further Paul Santmire, *The Travail of Nature: The Ambiguous Ecological Promise of Christian Theology* (Philadelphia: Fortress Press, 1985), p. 37.

14 Gunton, *The Triune Creator*, p. 54.

15 Oliver O'Donovan, *Resurrection and Moral Order: An Outline for Evangelical Ethics* (Leicester: Intervarsity Press, 1984), p. 31.

16 John Milbank, 'The poverty of Niebuhrianism', pp. 233–254 in Milbank, *The Word Made Strange: Theology, Language, Culture* (Oxford: Blackwell, 1997).

17 O'Donovan, *Resurrection and Moral Order*, p. 36.

18 *Ibid.*, pp. 16–17.

19 Peter Singer, *How Are We To Live: Ethics in an Age of Self-Interest* (London: Mandarin, 1994), p. 188.

20 For a fuller account of this thesis see Northcott, *Environment and Christian Ethics*, pp. 57–76 and 243–7.

21 *Our Common Future: World Commission on Environment and Development* (Oxford: Oxford University Press, 1987).

22 See further Stephen Clark, 'How to calculate the greater good', pp. 9–15 in Clark, *Animals and Their Moral Standing* (London: Routledge, 1997).

23 See further Peter Singer, *Animal Liberation*, second edition (London: Jonathan Cape, 1990), and Tom Regan, *The Case for Animal Rights* (London: Routledge, 1988).

24 For a clear account of this approach see for example Michael Appleby, *Why Should We Care about Animal Welfare?* (Oxford: Blackwell, 1998).

25 Regan, *The Case for Animal Rights*, pp. 243ff.

26 Aldo Leopold, *A Sand Country Almanac and Sketches Here and There* (New York: Oxford University Press, 1968).

27 *Ibid.*, p. 225.

28 J. Baird Callicott, *In Defence of the Land Ethic: Essays in Environmental Philosophy* (Albany: State University of New York Press, 1989), p. 25.

29 Holmes Rolston, *Environmental Ethics: Duties to and Values in the Natural Environment* (Philadelphia: Temple University Press, 1988).

30 The phrase 'turn to nature' originates in Charles Taylor's insightful survey of this philosophical terrain in his *Sources of the Self: The Making of the Modern Identity* (Cambridge: Cambridge University Press, 1989), pp. 368ff.

31 See further Edward Pearce, *Green Warriors: The People and the Politics behind the Environmental Revolution* (London: Bodley Head, 1991), ch. 4.

32 See further Robert Murray, *The Cosmic Covenant: Biblical Themes of Justice, Peace and the Integrity of Creation* (London: Sheed and Ward, 1992).

33 *Ibid.*

34 See further Michael Northcott, 'Children' in Peter Sedgwick (ed.), *God in the City* (London: Mowbray, 1995).

35 See further Michael Northcott, *Life after Debt: Christianity and Global Justice* (London: SPCK, 1999).

36 John Milbank, *Theology and Social Theory: Beyond Secular Reason* (Oxford: Blackwell, 1990), p. 279.

37 On the idea of creation as a loan from God to humans see further Karl Barth, *Church Dogmatics*, vol. III, *The Doctrine of Creation*, transl. A. T. Mackay, T. H. L. Parker, H. Knight, H. A. Kennedy and J. Marks (Edinburgh: T. and T. Clark, 1961), part 4, pp. 327ff.

38 European Province of the Society of Saint Francis, *Celebrating Common Prayer: A Version of the Daily Office* (London: Mowbray, 1992), p. 677.

39 See further Nash, *Loving Nature*.

40 See further Northcott, *Environment and Christian Ethics*, pp. 308ff.

16 Business, economics and Christian ethics

MAX L. STACKHOUSE

Many of the debates that have preoccupied the public generally and Christian ethics specifically with regard to business are in desperate need of modulation – especially by recalling and recasting the deeper theological resources, now widely forgotten, that have shaped contemporary economic life. Without understanding the roots of what we have, the dynamics of the present will not be accurately grasped and the capacity to direct the present towards a humane and just future will be limited. The problem is that theological and ethical assessments of economic life have largely accepted secular, materialist and political views of our past. That perception has distorted our moral vision.

In the long, slow process of 'modernisation', the nation-state gradually asserted its dominance over the household-based economy of feudal society. Both traditional households and governments were later threatened by the rise of an industrial economy, but only the nation-state was understood to have the wherewithal to control it. The socially and politically short twentieth century, which lasted basically from the outbreak of World War I in 1914 until the fall of the Wall in 1989, was thus a century dominated by issues of political economy, especially of tensions between the haves and the have-nots. The struggles between and within nations about economic matters had essentially to do with the role of government in guiding industrial development and controlling its consequences. Most modern conventional understandings of business and economic ethics are shaped by these issues.

The conservative and business-oriented parties of the western developed nations all wanted less governmental 'interference' with the market internally, but more protection for national industries vis-à-vis international competition, and less accent on socialist and communist programmes. The progressive and labour-oriented parties meanwhile wanted more governmental 'involvement' in wage and price control, health and safety regulations, welfare and insurance provisions, racial and (belatedly) sexual equality in access to economic opportunity, and guarantees of both job security and a living wage. The debates about how to mix and blend these two macro-economic approaches were the decisive issues from the boom years after World War I, through the depression of the 1930s, World War II, the Korean War, the Vietnam debacle and the Cold War years to the end of the era.

While these issues continue, especially in those countries that have emerged from colonialism and are struggling still to establish viable modern political and economic systems, they are today secondary. Business-oriented parties now defend one or another form of social security and oppose international 'protectionism', while most labour-oriented parties defend one or another qualified version of 'responsible' capitalism. The debates between democratic capitalists and social democrats about a little more of this and a little less of that remain, and they make a great difference for certain percentages of the population. They have, however, become political ritual and quite tired.[1]

More pressing issues have to do with the forces now forming a global economy. No government can now control these complex developments, although a host of new international institutions have been established to try to stabilise them. The World Bank, the International Monetary Fund, the World Trade Organisation, the International Labour Organisation and an alphabet of U.N.-related organisations pose new questions for ethics which only a few are attempting to address. The spread of democracy plus concern for human rights, ecology, the poor, and the encounter with the world religions have altered the agenda of ethical reflection, although there is as yet no theologically grounded common perspective on these matters.[2]

Indeed, a number of influential contemporary voices in Christian ethics, often deeply attracted to anti-modern interpretations of theology, see little prospect for creative engagement with such issues. They view contemporary economic life as essentially foreign to the faith, an exercise in uncontrolled greed that provides some with more than is needed and many with the prospect of impoverishment. They distrust attempts to engage theology with business ethics, with the contemporary professions and the social sciences, especially economics, because they can find no place for God in them.[3] Not infrequently, their view of society blindly accepts the analysis found in liberation thought, although they differ with it because many are pacifist and suspicious of attempts to form a social ethic on any other basis than biblical, narrative-driven or dogmatic convictions, agreeing with the postmodern claim that public possibilities of meaning have been fundamentally eroded by the triumph of a market economy – an insistence that leads many to identify with the historic Anabaptist tradition and others to label them as 'neo-sectarian'.[4]

Doubt as to whether the statist, liberationist or neo-sectarian options are adequate to our present needs and to the deeper understandings of the Christian ethical heritage has led a number of Christian thinkers to develop a 'public theological' approach to ethics and economic life. This recent term, earlier associated with the 'Christian Realism' of Protestant ethicist Reinhold Niebuhr, was developed further by the contemporary Roman Catholic theologian David Tracy. 'Public theology' points towards a wider and deeper strand of theological reflection rooted in the interaction of biblical insight, philosophical analysis, historical discernment and social formation. It sees the moral interpretation of the common life as a fundamental task of theology and seeks to link that interpretation with the cultivation of a normative vision to form, guide and reform society.

The roots of such views are found in the biblical prophets, in Jesus' preaching and teaching and in Paul's encounters at the Acropolis. Augustine's *City of God*, Thomas' writings on justice, the Reformers' teachings about 'orders of creation', 'vocation', 'covenant' and the relationship of Law and gospel carried this tradition to the twentieth century, where it was adopted and adapted by Abraham Kuyper's theology of the 'spheres', Ernst Troeltsch's quest for a 'Christian social philosophy', Walter Rauschenbusch's 'theology for the social gospel', Emil Brunner's treatment of the 'orders of creation', and in the Roman Catholic social-encyclical tradition from Leo XIII to John Paul II. These perspectives all presume that 'theology', while always related to personal faith, particular faith communities and concrete social conditions, is at its most profound levels neither psychologically defined, contextually determined nor an unwarranted dogmatic claim about the way things are and ought to be. They differ from liberation thought, with which they otherwise share a deep concern for social justice, but they resist Marxist analysis, which they view as unscientific and finally subversive of justice and faith.

Tracy argued that although many today turn to human experience to find a basis for common morality and meaning, experience turns out to be more pluralistic than doctrine. Thus, at least three modes of public discourse are needed to ascertain experiential meaning – ecclesial, political and academic, all interpreted by philosophical theology and theological ethics.[5] Subsequent thinkers, in the face of current global trends, have added to these the technical/scientific and economic publics by asking what forms of production, finance, exchange, and distribution and kinds of social organisation best allow us, worldwide, to create plenty, to relieve want and drudgery, and to enable the material wellbeing of humanity.[6] This interpretation of economic life is, thus, less dominated by modern political frameworks of meaning than those which have included attention to those chapters of theologically shaped histories laden with implications for business and economic development.[7]

DEEP CONTINUITIES

Production and consumption have been a part of human life from the beginning, as is recognised by the authors of Genesis 1–3 when they write of tilling the garden and eating the fruits thereof. It is also the case that various techniques, competition, exchange and property have been a part of societies for as long as we can trace them into the past, often historically connected to the conflictual dynamics of familial and political life – as is recognised in Genesis 4. Indeed, in every recorded history, traders, caravans or boats bearing items for exchange are known, even if some peoples seem to have been settled and isolated for long periods of time, and even if they developed an economic life of extraction, production and consumption without an established trader class or a complex set of business practices. Even then, people met at the margins of society to exchange goods, services and know-how. At crossroads and harbours, near sacred sites and military encampments, farmers, weavers, hunters, merchants, peddlers, craftsmen and entertainers of all kinds appear with their wares at stalls, shops and marts.[8] Business is not a modern invention; humans are, among other things, economic beings who will interact over many social boundaries.

All over the world, some persons and groups became skilled at organising materials, labour, finance and transport for commerce; exercising those skills developed into a full-time occupation. Their work became second nature, a habit of mind, a way of life. Farmers and fishermen, peasants and priests, courtiers and commanders come to depend on them, yet for thousands of years business was largely marginal to the dominant economy. Most people lived by one or another form of agriculture which often required refined techniques and much ingenuity, but survival, even wellbeing, seldom required extensive or sustained systems of exchange. People depended on nature, and economic life centred in 'natural' kinship groups – the household, the clan, the band, the tribe. The processes of production, distribution, ownership and consumption centred in kinship networks, and both labour and claims on its fruits were ordered by age and gender-specific roles.

This 'familial' structure of the economy in primal and feudal societies more often than not was re-enforced by the authority of the patriarch, chief, lord of the manor or king, and was legitimated by religious authorities who claimed to be able to interpret extraordinary natural events, especially those related to birth, marriage, production, reproduction and death. The term 'economy' (Greek *oikos* + *nomos*) had to do with 'household ordering', even if the domains of some leading houses became larger and larger, establishing a polity that governed the fate of many families surrounding, supplying and serving the palaces of rulers or priests.

It is not surprising that most household elders and political authorities, including those treated in the Bible, manifested a profound doubt about the practices and people involved in business. The merchant, the trader, the artisan was not settled into anyone's hearth or realm. They did not produce or share as kith and kin, govern or defend as soldiers. They did not live in accord with the natural fecundity of the earth or according to the established loyalties to regime. Rather they built cities, travelled the earth and engaged in a restless quest for gain by a highly impersonal calculation of profit.

Opposition to the cosmopolitan bourgeois, their profits and the market's logic often meant also an opposition to new technologies, precisely because they undermined the values behind the social order of traditional societies. Thus the call for control was frequent, and not seldom needed, as the biblical prophets also saw. Laws were everywhere passed, not only in the laws of Moses, regarding fair weights and measures; taxes are everywhere levied, not only by the kings of Israel, on commodities or traffic; and penalties were everywhere assessed, not only in the Deuteronomic reforms for adulterating products, using dangerous materials or cheating. Justice as fair treatment in dealings became recognised by every known tradition as a standard to be enforced, however often it was honoured in the breach.

A moral sense of 'just price', 'honest dealing' and 'fair wage' in contrast to 'theft', 'deception' and 'exploitation' also appeared, however, in the actual practices of business, as the authors of the wisdom literature of the Bible as well as the ancient philosophers knew. Without it, the business is unsustainable.[9] Trust can only be sustained when people are, more or less, trustworthy – a virtue that business requires but cannot generate alone. Family and religion form character, even if law is necessary to control the untrustworthy. Thus, people tend to trust those who are members of the same household or polity, as we can see in most ancient and feudal societies and in the biblical and early western traditions.[10] But complex forms of business life seldom develop in such settings, and both family and political life can be corrupted by economic interests. Not only are 'familism' and 'nationalism' irrational, business eventually flees them, and social life based only on them collapses.[11]

One of the greatest insights of those great founders of modern economists, from Adam Smith to contemporary 'neo-liberals' and from Karl Marx to present-day 'social market theorists', is that the basic ends of economic life are not the same as those of kinship or politics and that, indeed, viable families and stable governments depend on flourishing economies. To be sure, one side focused on the division of labour and the other on the division of the classes, and one called for a highly limited state to preserve private property and the other for a widely expanded state, gradually fading away once the inequalities of property are overcome; but both in principle hold that technical and social dynamics are economically prior to familial and governmental relationships, and that economic life never is, and never can be, confined to household or regime.

The modern discipline of economics contrasts not only with traditional views, which continue to be held by family patriarchs and political oligarchs everywhere, but also with attempts to make the whole world develop a single way. Old-fashioned 'liberal capitalism' fomented colonialism, and modern 'scientific socialism' generated a new imperialism – both of which led to forms of 'statism' against their primary intent. But the modern discipline of economics seldom recognises what business discovers: when it reaches beyond the boundaries of tribe and regime, it finds it needs trust there also. Philosophers have sought to explain commonalities that reached over the practices of many cultures, and lawyers have tried to articulate them in the face of competing claims across legal jurisdictions. The relation of *jus gentium* to *jus naturale* and *jus civile* in economic matters is an ancient issue and again a current question.[12] It is not only interests that reach across boundaries, ethics does so as well. At some levels, a 'natural law' or 'common grace' ethic is necessary for understanding modern business and economics.

Yet the changes brought by 'supra-natural' conceptions of social and ethical life have also become more important for both our current understanding of Christian ethics in relation to business and to our contemporary economic situation, in part because they have historically generated a wider and deeper trust. The religions of revelation have accented the universal moral authority of the Creator over the natural familistic and nationalistic loyalties of people and generated a worldwide concern for human rights.[13] Christianity is particularly notable in this regard, with direct implications for our issues also.

The classical heritage taught that while the traces of God's good intent remained in the deep structure of creation, the natural world should be viewed as imperfect, incomplete or, more radically, 'fallen' – open to deep disruption by corrupting forces and choices which can be repaired finally only by divine grace. It is thus a moral – at least a human and at most a godly – project to transform nature, to use it to serve the neighbour and to reshape it to make it accord with holy laws and redemptive purposes. The *jus divinum* thus also was, and is, central to economic life generally and business practice particularly.[14] The implications have been increasingly recognised in several bodies of scholarship in the last generation as the root of our global economy.

TECHNOLOGICAL NOVELTY

The social forces now shaping the economic world are intensely technological. Traditional societies feel bulldozed by them. Many cultural patterns tied to older techniques guided economic behaviours for centuries, but are now overwhelmed by cyber-technologies that take place, as Pope John Paul II once wrote, 'over the heads of the people'. Why did this technology arise in the west?

A clue to its roots is found in Robert K. Merton's much-debated essay 'Puritanism, Pietism, and Science'. Using a post-liberal, post-socialist mode of social analysis influenced by Max Weber, he argued that not only was economic activism deeply stamped by religion as Weber had claimed, but that science was also. Tracing the motivations stated by the leading lights of the Royal Society, who are often seen as the fathers of the Industrial Revolution, he cites Boyle's highly typical argument that the purpose of 'the study of Nature is to the greater glory of God and the Good of Man'.[15] Indeed, while nature is stamped by its Creator with an intended 'Order of Things' that made science possible, it was also sufficiently disordered in its manifestations that it needed a reordering that could conduce it to 'good in the light of the Doctrine of Salvation by Jesus Christ'. But, obviously, this attitude did not arise only with seventeenth-century Puritans and Pietists, and Merton draws his study to a close by referring to a medieval set of assumptions standing behind science's ascetic engagement in the world.[16]

More recently, Nancy Pearcey has also argued that modern science and technology rest on assumptions that were provided by Christian belief – especially the assumption that the world has a rational, intelligible order because it is created by a singular and rational God, and the assumption that we can discover that order because we are created in God's image. She goes on to argue that three additional principles are necessary to produce the technology that we now have:

(1) The universe, while orderly at a very deep level, is also contingent

and malleable, a principle that challenged the ontocratic assumption that nature is teleological and imbued with a fixed order and rational purposes. Instead, the expectation of a 'new heaven and a new earth' indicated that nature will collapse and is less to be contemplated than to be altered for godly and humane purposes.[17]

(2) Humans find their primary kinship with a transcendent God and with other humans created also in that image. This generates a stance that gives permission for humans to have an active role in engaging nature and denies that humans are so embedded in nature that they can only conform to it.[18]

(3) Beyond the fact that the world is malleable and that humans can intervene in it is the claim that we humans have a duty to do so; that we are, indeed, commissioned by God to have dominion. We must care for our bodies and the biophysical universe not for personal ambition but to promote the public good, themes that are deeply rooted in scripture and the theological tradition.[19]

In a new study, David Noble put is this way: 'the dynamic project of Western technology . . . is actually medieval in origin and spirit . . . [It] was rooted in an ideological innovation which invested the useful arts with a significance beyond mere utility. Technology had come to be identified with transcendence, implicated as never before in the Christian idea of redemption . . . The other-worldly roots of the religion of technology were distinctly Christian. For Christianity alone blurred the distinction and bridged the divide between the human and the divine.'[20] It is not that technology sprang directly from the teachings of Jesus, but that profound assumptions in scripture about the relationship of the divine and the human interacted with philosophy and science over time to bring about a 'striking acceleration and intensification of technological development'.[21]

At least from the ninth century on, Noble argues, technological developments were seen as both a possibility and a moral demand, one that could help humans reclaim the humanity disrupted in the fall. And from the thirteenth century on, they were seen as useful for moving humanity towards perfection. Humanity had a duty to seek these ends, a view taken up by Thomas More, Francis Bacon and a host of others in a lengthy history that led directly to the Royal Society, the Industrial Revolution and the acceptance, in the west generally, of technological change as a moral good – a claim reinforced by the capacity to produce material goods at previously unbelievable rates.[22]

This cluster of arguments, of course, represents a complex appreciation and simultaneous critique of most 'modern' views of science and technology and its links to economics, and they point us to the necessity of taking into account historical and theological developments and self-reflective assessments of how ideas work in social life over time. This view opens the door to an expanded public theology and points to a new ecumenicity demanded by our global era, the nature of theological ethics, and an understanding of the redemptive purposes of God for the world.[23]

THE ROOTS OF SOCIAL NOVELTY

The second main clue to understanding our contemporary situation is the business corporation. The birth and growth of this institution is also rooted in a deep history, with striking implications. Indeed, from an ethical point of view we should call what we now have a 'corporate, technological economy' rather than a 'market economy'. Nothing is new about having markets; what is new is that the channels within which the market works have not only much to do with the technological transformations of nature but also the fact that technologically equipped corporations are now primary actors in the market and are able to sustain it around the clock and around the world. The laws of the market, if they are to be morally influenced, will not only be shaped by familial and political institutions but also by technological and corporate organisation.

In the nineteenth century, corporations began their dramatic growth, but powerful forces in opposition were marshalled. For more than a century, many tried to mobilise political parties, class interests, national identity and traditional loyalties against them. This opposition continues in many places and inevitably holds that more extensive state control is necessary.[24] These social oppositions have, however, faltered, failed or proven worse than what they opposed. Efforts to recover or discover a moral theory of the corporation are under way.[25]

It has been amply documented but largely forgotten that the roots of the modern corporation are in the religious institutions of the west.[26] Christians organised communities of faith distinct from the household, which often had its own hearth deities, and distinct from the state, which had its own civic cult. People joined the church irrespective of birth or citizenship, or of the economic status that was determined by these. Members lived under a covenanted discipline that was to pervade all aspects of life, in a community dedicated to a transformed world, a *corpus Christi* that anticipated a New Jerusalem – just as the life of Jesus transcended both family and state and promised a Kingdom of Heaven. For the first time in human history, an enduring model of a third centre of organisation, what sociologists today call voluntary associations (no one is born into them) and political theorists call, even less elegantly, NGOs (non-governmental organisations), was formed. On this basis, the church spawned independent religious orders, hospitals and schools, all managing to secure a right to exist, own property, buy and sell goods and services, and develop capital. They became highly successful institutions in the 'free cities' and expanded steadily from then through the twentieth century.

That organisational formation was supported by several other developments that eventually converged with it. One is a theory of the morality of property. Medieval scholastics such as Thomas Aquinas and Duns Scotus addressed questions concerning private ownership, independent groups holding property, and contract law in a Christian context. Over time, the idea that property is personal yet best administered in an associative mode by 'covenantal' agreements came to be accepted in civil society, leading to modern morally laden concepts of 'trusteeship', 'limited liability' and 'responsible management'. When the Reformers applied the concept of 'vocation' to all believers and not only to clerics, the 'corpus' was soon secularised to become a profit-oriented corporation, and participation in it was seen to be an opportunity to work out the implications of one's relationship to God and neighbour. The church, in short, fostered an institution that had decidedly material interests; but these material interests were, in principle, constrained by incarnate moral principles and spiritual purposes. For the first time in human history, economics had a potentially ethical organisational home outside the household and the state.[27]

In the Industrial Revolution, these developments converged with technological developments to establish the central agent of economic capitalisation, production and distribution. In non-statist and post-traditional societies, such as America and later the defeated countries after World War II, the modern corporation became also the primary model of organisation for universities, libraries, hospitals, political groups, unions, professional guilds and voluntary associations for a wide variety of cultural and service activities. This reinforced democratic tendencies towards pluralistic civil societies dedicated to 'freedom' – which meant especially the right to associate and organise for religious, political, cultural, medical, social and economic purposes outside the control of household and regime. It also added to traditional views of 'commutative justice', a legacy of family life, and of 'distributive justice', an egalitarian legacy of modern political theory, the notion of 'productive justice' – due reward for those who facilitate economic growth and the creation of wealth for the commonwealth.[28] Kinship groups became 'family firms'; self-sustaining governmental agencies became

'public corporations'. Traditions and regions that did not support the formation of corporations fell further behind global standards of productivity,
wealth and income.

The business corporation continues to expand its operations to include
people from many families and nations, and to develop partners and subsid-
iaries around the world, transforming familial and political life wherever it
goes and establishing transnational centres of production, finance, distribution, consumption, publishing and technological development. Whether or
not all this has yet created the material basis for a global civilisation is an
open question; but it is likely that no viable social ethic for the future can be
developed that does not wrestle with the presuppositions and social implications of these historic influences. They now join humanity together in a
single economic destiny, with some tragically left behind thus far, as has
been recognised by the many Christian groups which have passed major
statements or resolutions on economic issues in the last two decades.[29] But
what is remarkable is that no one wants to be left out or wants others to be.
It has become universal.

CURRENT IMPLICATIONS

These developments have evoked a new burst of interest in business
ethics in universities and the new professional graduate schools that train
business managers. But the textbooks written for these courses seldom treat
theological issues, focusing instead on some combination of Kantian principles, utilitarian calculus and various versions of social Darwinism, although
it is doubtful that these resources can create an ethic deep enough and wide
enough to offer moral or spiritual guidance to either the new professional
managers or the vast institutional linkages that reach across cultures. While
the lessons of the deeper past remain relevant, and intellectual honesty
requires the acknowledgement of the contributions of theological ethics to
what we now have, we also face massive problems of inequality and new
encounters with the world's cultures. This has brought about several
attempts to link Christian ethics to a redefinition of mission.[30] Still unset-
tled in this area is the question of the importance for Christian ethics of the
new encounter of the world religions facilitated by the globalising forces.
Max Weber's massive treatment of comparative religious ethics in regard to
economic life at the beginning of this century has triggered an enormous
amount of discussion, but that remains an unfinished agenda. He did not
foresee the question of whether the resurgent world religions – especially
nationalist Hinduism in India, neo-Confucianism in East Asia, fundamen-

talist Islam in the mideast and Africa, and, above all, revitalised Catholicism and the unprecedented growth of evangelical Pentecostalism in Africa and Latin America – would aid or inhibit the drawing of these regions into patterns of development that he identified with the influence of Protestantism. The relation of Christian ethics to the ethics of the world religions on economic issues remains an open issue and at least one of the most critical questions for the future.[31]

Notes

1 Representative perspectives, which now serve as excellent summaries of those debates, can be found in Robert Benne, *The Ethic of Democratic Capitalism: A Moral Reassessment* (Philadelphia: Fortress Press, 1981); Prentiss L. Pemberton and Daniel R. Finn, *Toward a Christian Economic Ethic: Stewardship and Social Power* (Minneapolis: Winston Press, 1985); J. Philip Wogaman, *Economics and Ethics: A Christian Inquiry* (Philadelphia: Fortress Press, 1986); Ronald H. Preston, *Religion and the Ambiguities of Capitalism* (London: SCM Press, 1991); and Richard J. Neuhaus, *Doing Well and Doing Good: The Challenge to the Christian Capitalist* (New York: Doubleday, 1992). Some themes were early anticipated in Denys Munby, ed., *Economic Growth in World Perspective* (London: SCM Press, 1966).

2 Provocative attempts to establish new approaches to these issues can be found in Lawrence Harrison, *Underdevelopment Is a State of Mind* (Lanham, MD: U. Press of America, 1985); Herman E. Daly and John B. Cobb, Jr, *For the Common Good: Redirecting the Economy Toward Community, the Environment, and a Sustainable Future* (Boston: Beacon Press, 1989); Amy Sherman, *Preferential Option: A Christian Neo-Liberal Strategy for Latin America's Poor* (Grand Rapids, MI: Eerdmans, 1992); Hans Küng, *Global Responsibility: In Search of a New World Ethic* (New York: Crossroad, 1991) and *A Global Ethic for Global Politics and Economics* (New York: Oxford U. Press, 1998); Don A. Pittman et al., eds., *Ministry and Theology in Global Perspective* (Grand Rapids, MI: Eerdmans, 1996); and Maura A. Ryan et al., eds., *The Challenge of Global Stewardship: Roman Catholic Responses* (Notre Dame, IN: Notre Dame U. Press, 1997).

3 I count a number of friends and colleagues among key advocates of one or another version of this view, although I think it is very dubious. See, e.g., M. Douglas Meeks, *God the Economist: The Doctrine of God and Political Economy* (Minneapolis: Fortress Press, 1989); Mark Ellingsen, *The Cutting Edge: How Churches Speak on Social Issues* (Geneva: WCC Publications, 1993), especially chapters 2, 3 & 9; and Shin Chiba et al., eds., *Christian Ethics in Ecumenical Context* (Grand Rapids, MI: Eerdmans, 1995), especially part II.

4 Stanley Hauerwas in the United States, Alister McGrath in Great Britain, and now John Milbank, who has moved from Britain to America, are noted examples of this, often identifying themselves as, above all, 'post-liberal'. A critique of their views and of liberationist assumptions as they bear on economic life is offered in my *Christian Social Ethics in a Global Era* (Nashville: Abingdon Press, 1997). In

one sense, these two overlapping trends represent what Ernst Troeltsch identified a century ago as the 'withdrawing sect-type' and the 'aggressive sect-type',
in contrast to 'church-' or 'spiritual-types', in *The Social Teachings of the Christian
Churches*, tr. O. Wyon (New York: Harper & Row, 1930; German, 1911).

5 David Tracy, *Analogical Imagination: Christian Theology and the Culture of
Pluralism* (New York: Crossroad, 1981), especially chapters 1–3. See also Dennis
McCann and Charles R. Strain, *Polity and Praxis: A Program for Practical
Theology* (Chicago: Winston Press, 1985).

6 See, for example, Robert Benne, *The Paradoxical Vision: A Public Theology for the
Twenty-first Century* (Minneapolis: Fortress Press, 1995); José Casanova, *Public
Religions in the Modern World* (Chicago: U. of Chicago Press, 1994); Dieter T.
Hessel, ed., *The Church's Public Role* (Grand Rapids, MI: Eerdmans, 1993);
Michael J. Himes and K. R. Himes, *Fullness of Faith: The Public Significance of
Theology* (New York: Paulist Press, 1993); and my *Public Theology and Political
Economy* (Lanham, MD: U. Press of America, 1986, 1991).

7 Such shifts in understanding can be seen even among politically engaged
authors, as in Robert Reich, *The Work of Nations* (New York: Knopf, 1991); Paul
Kennedy, *Preparing for the Twenty-first Century* (New York: Random House,
1993); and other political leaders around the world who are facing the issues of
globalisation directly – e.g., Lindsay Tanner, *Open Australia* (Annandale, NSW:
Pluto Press, 1999).

8 See David Landes, *The Wealth and Poverty of Nations: Why Some Are So Rich and
Some So Poor* (New York: W. W. Norton, 1998), who treats these matters from the
standpoint of economic history, as a revision of Adam Smith; and Jared
Diamond, *Guns, Germs, and Steel: The Fates of Human Societies* (New York: W. W.
Norton, 1997), who takes them up in terms of evolutionary anthropology.

9 See Francis Fukuyama's recent study of ten cultures on this matter, *Trust: The
Social Virtues and the Creation of Prosperity* (New York: Free Press, 1995). It is
especially useful to compare this work with Edward C. Banfield's classic *The
Moral Basis of a Backward Society* (New York: Free Press, 1958).

10 Compare linkages elsewhere between the *Arthashastra* and the *Kamasutra* in
Hinduism, the ties of familial clan and empire in Confucianism, and the overlap
of lineage and leadership in Islam and many tribal religions. All shape economic
status and behaviour. Some speak of pervasive bribery in contexts shaped by
these traditions, but it is likely, given 'insider/outsider' definitions, that those
whom one cannot trust must be bought.

11 See Wilhelm Roepke, *The Social Crisis of Our Time* (New Brunswick, NJ:
Transaction, 1992; in German, 1944), *The Moral Foundations of Civil Society*
(New Brunswick, NJ: Transaction, 1996; in German, 1944), and *International
Order and Economic Integration* (London: Wm. Hodge, 1950; in German, 1945).
The current difficulties of Russia, of sub-Saharan Africa and of Central America
show similar patterns.

12 This can be rather clearly seen in, for instance, influences such as Cicero's *Laws*,
a key example of Stoic philosophy that shaped key aspects of secular jurispru-
dence as well as Roman Catholic and Calvinistic thought. See, e.g., Brian Tierney,
The Idea of Natural Rights (Atlanta: Scholars Press, 1997); Guenther Hass, *The
Concept of Equity in Calvin's Ethics* (Waterloo: Wilfred Laurier U. Press, 1997);

Knud Haakonssen, *Natural Law and Moral Philosophy* (New York: Cambridge U. Press, 1996); and Michael Cromartie, ed., *A Preserving Grace: Protestants, Catholics and Natural Law* (Grand Rapids, MI: Eerdmans, 1997).

13 The literature in this area is vast, but much of the best of the research is summarised in John Witte, Jr, and Jon van der Vyver, *Religious Human Rights in Global Perspective*, 2 vols. (The Hague: Nijhoff, 1996).

14 See, for example, Elspeth Whitney, *Paradise Restored: The Mechanical Arts from Antiquity through the Thirteenth Century* (Philadelphia: American Philosophical Society, 1990). Cf. Lester K. Little, *Religious Poverty and the Profit Economy in Medieval Europe* (Ithaca, NY: Cornell U. Press, 1978).

15 In R. K. Merton, *Social Theory and Social Structure* (New York: Free Press, 1957), p. 575. See also his *Science, Technology and Society in Seventeenth-Century England* (New York: Harper, 1970). Merton's theory was, for a time, subject to critique at the hands of neo-Marxist critics of social history. However, a second wave of historical scholarship has reinvestigated the data and the disputes and suggests that in fact Merton was, on the whole, quite accurate in his findings. See P. Sztompke, ed., *On Social Structure and Science* (Chicago: U. of Chicago Press, 1996).

16 Merton, *Social Theory*, pp. 580, 583.

17 See Pearcey, *The Soul of Science*, with Charles Thaxton (Wheaton: Crossway, 1994). See also her 'Technology, History, and Worldview', in John Kilner et al., eds., *Genetic Ethics: Do the Ends Justify the Genes?* (Grand Rapids: Eerdmans, 1997), especially pp. 41f.

18 Pearcey, 'Technology', p. 43. Here, and elsewhere, she draws on Christopher Kaiser, *Creation and the History of Science* (Grand Rapids: Eerdmans, 1991).

19 *Ibid.*, pp. 43–4.

20 D. F. Noble, *The Religion of Technology: The Divinity of Man and the Spirit of Invention* (New York: Knopf, 1998), p. 9. Noble depends heavily on Lynn White, Jr, 'Cultural Climates and Technological Advance in the Middle Ages', *Viator*, 2 (1971), and Elspeth Whitney, *Paradise Restored*.

21 Noble cites here Lynn White, Jr's *Medieval Technology and Social Change* (New York: Oxford University Press, 1962), and Ernst Benz' *Evolution and Christian Hope* (Garden City, NY: Doubleday, 1975).

22 Older, but substantially compatible, accounts of these developments can be found in R. J. Hooykaas, *Religion and the Rise of Modern Science* (Oxford: Clarendon, 1974); and Eugene Klaaren, *The Religious Origins of Modern Science* (Grand Rapids: Eerdmans, 1977).

23 Many scholars are contributing to this alternative view. See *On Moral Business: Classical and Contemporary Resources for Ethics and Economic Life*, ed. M. L. Stackhouse, Dennis P. McCann, Shirley Roels et al. (Grand Rapids, MI: Eerdmans, 1995); and *Religion, Globalization, and the Spheres of Life: Theological Ethics in a Pluralistic World*, 4 vols. ed. M. L. Stackhouse, Peter Paris and Diane Obenchain (Harrisburg, PA: Trinity Press International, forthcoming).

24 See François Furet, *The Passing of an Illusion*, tr. D. Furet (Chicago: U. of Chicago Press, 1999; in French, 1995). Current critics of the corporation include Richard J. Barent et al., *Global Dreams: Imperial Corporations and the New World Order* (New York: Simon & Schuster, 1994), and David C. Korten, *When Corporations*

Rule the World (West Hartford, CT: Kumarian Press, 1995). Christian voices who share this critique and would question Furet can be found in Michael Zweig, *Religion and Economic Justice* (Philadelphia: Temple U. Press, 1991).

25 Michael Novak is one of the chief advocates of an almost uncritical view of the corporations. See, e.g., his *The Corporation: A Theological Inquiry*, ed. with John W. Cooper (Washington, DC: The American Enterprise Institute, 1981). Peter Berger, however, is probably correct that this particular view is unlikely to capture the moral imagination of a very wide group. See his *The Capitalist Revolution* (New York: Basic, 1985).

26 The classic source remains Otto von Gierke's massive and still unsurpassed *Genossenschaftsrecht*, 4 vols. (1861–1913), only parts of which are yet translated. His work is both appreciatively cited and corrected in view of more recent research by Harold Berman, *Law and Revolution* (Cambridge, MA: Harvard U. Press, 1983).

27 See my 'The Moral Roots of the Corporation', *Theology and Public Policy*, 5, no. 1 (Summer 1993), pp. 29–39.

28 David Krueger et al., *The Business Corporation and Productive Justice* (Nashville: Abingdon Press, 1996).

29 For examples, see the representative Roman Catholic, Lutheran, Anglican, Liberal Protestant and Evangelical statements gathered in *On Moral Business*, pp. 427–84, 916–61.

30 Some key themes were anticipated by theologians and church leaders. See, e.g., Arendt van Leeuwen, *Christianity in World History* (New York: Scribner, 1964); and Denys Munby, ed., *World Development: A Challenge to the Churches* (Washington, DC: Corpus Publications, 1969). More recent representative developments can be found in Max L. Stackhouse, Lamin Sanneh, Donald W. Shriver, et al., *Apologia: Contextualization, Globalization, and Mission in Theological Education* (Grand Rapids, MI: Eerdmans, 1988), Robert Schreiter, *The New Catholicity* (New York: Orbis, 1997), and Tim Dearborne and Scott Paeth, *The Church in a Global Era* (Grand Rapids, MI: Eerdmans 2000).

31 See Peter Berger, ed., *The Desecularization of the World* (Grand Rapids, MI: Eerdmans 1999). Cf. Peter Beyer, *Religion and Globalization* (London: Sage, 1994); Wade C. Roof, ed., *World Order and Religion* (Albany: State U. of New York Press, 1991); George Weigel, ed., *A New Worldly Order* (Washington, DC: Ethics and Public Policy Center, 1991); and Robert Nevelle, *The Human Condition and Ultimate Realities*, 3 vols., forthcoming). A crucial global issue is that some people are able to increase their wealth to unprecedented levels as more and more countries reduce taxation and state capitalisation. This has created a greater gap between the wealthiest and poorest parts of the world's population. It may have expanded the middle classes in many lands, but it has left those unable or unwilling to adopt these changes further behind. In addition, the ecological damage, if everyone adopted these changes without constraint, would be severe (see chapter 15 above).

17 World family trends

DON BROWNING

In what follows, I will summarise elements of the emerging world debate over the family. I will set forth some of the facts and reasons that suggest this debate is not simply a product of conservative political rhetoric, although at times it is that. I contend that there is an emerging world family crisis, that it is worse in poor countries than in wealthy ones, that it is very debilitating even for rich societies, and that it is an independent variable undermining human wellbeing that is not reducible to poverty, war or natural catastrophe – all of which take their own tolls on families. I also believe that this crisis must be addressed at several levels – first at the religio-cultural level, then at the legal and economic levels, and finally at the level of education and individual development, in that order. This chapter will address primarily the first, the religio-cultural level. Addressing this level of human action is the central task of a practical or transformative Christian theological ethics.

Family changes engulfing advanced western societies over the last four decades – divorce, out-of-wedlock births, father absence etc. – were first interpreted by social scientists as benign. The sociologist Talcott Parsons said in the 1950s that families were changing but still fulfilling their functions.[1] The feminist sociologist Jessie Bernard said in her influential *The Future of Marriage* (1972) that these changes were not dangerous, that they were not harming children, that marriage was not particularly good for women anyway, and that divorce, cohabitation and non-marital births would contribute to the increased freedom of women.[2] Some social scientists held that family changes were harmful only when they ended in poverty. A wider welfare net and a healthy economy, they argued, could prevent these negative consequences.

EVIDENCE OF FAMILY DECLINE

Since the late 1980s, there has been a worldwide change in the attitudes within the social sciences towards these family changes. Sociologists, psychologists and economists today are much more willing to acknowledge that they have been damaging to large numbers of people. The family changes have contributed to the declining wellbeing of children, the 'feminisation of poverty' (the shift of poverty from the elderly to single mothers and their children), and the 'feminisation of kinship' (the trend towards women alone sustaining families without the help of fathers and husbands). Although most social scientists now concur that these changes have been costly to individuals and society, they disagree over whether they can be reversed or must simply be accepted with the hope of mitigating their negative consequences.

Family structure, seen in the 1960s and 70s as a neutral factor in family wellbeing, was viewed by the early 1990s as highly relevant to the flourishing of children and their mothers. In the United States, Barbara Dafoe Whitehead wrote a 1993 article in the prestigious *Atlantic Monthly* summarising new research showing the average negative effects on children of divorce and non-marital births.[3] Around the same time, the social scientist Charles Murray created a sensation when he reported in the *Wall Street Journal* that out-of-wedlock births had reached 22 per cent in the white community in the U.S. – the same figure reached by the black community in 1960 before the rate exploded to the present 60 to 70 percent.[4] He predicted that a similar leap forward was about to occur in the white community, thereby creating a new white underclass as a result of the negative economic consequences of non-marital births. He also travelled to England, studied family issues in that country, and predicted that much the same thing would happen there.[5]

The most definitive research was reported by Sara McLanahan and Gary Sandefur in their *Growing Up with a Single Parent* (1994). Using sophisticated statistical tools to analyse the data of four national longitudinal surveys in the USA, these authors concluded that children raised outside of biological two-parent families were twice as likely to do poorly in school, twice as likely to be single parents themselves, and one-and-a-half times more likely to have difficulties becoming permanently attached to the labour market.[6] This was true when the data was controlled for the race, education, age and place of residence of parents. Income reduced these disadvantages, but only by one-half. Stepfamilies had no advantage over single parents; both were less successful than intact biologically related families.[7] This is so even though average income of stepfamilies is higher than for intact families, thereby challenging the idea that income rather than family structure is the chief predictor of child wellbeing. The English author Patricia Morgan in *Farewell to the Family? Public Policy and Family*

Breakdown in Britain and the USA (1995) makes similar claims for Britain; income helps, but within salary levels that are relatively comparable, children living with both parents do better on a variety of indices.[8] Such reports have influenced family-supportive policies in several countries – especially the USA, Britain and Australia.[9]

WORLD DECLINE IN FATHER INVOLVEMENT

Social science research suggests that the central result of these trends is the growing worldwide decline of involvement by fathers in families and the lives of their children. At the same time, new understandings of the importance of fathers has also arisen. Some interpreters believe that father absence in the USA and other countries is indeed the single most alarming feature of world family changes.[10] In earlier writings, I have called this trend 'the male problematic'.[11] Over 30 per cent of children in the USA under age eighteen do not live with their fathers, and nearly 50 per cent under that age will spend at least three years without their father's presence in the home. Furthermore, divorced fathers, on average, do poorly in financing and visiting their children. The fathers of children born out of wedlock are even worse. As Cherlin and Furstenberg say in their *Divided Families* (1991),[12] American men see marriage and parenting as a package deal; when the marriage breaks up, parenting deteriorates as well.

Trends towards father absence are not limited to the United States. Aaron Sachs reports that in a recent study of low-income couples in Chile, 42 per cent of the fathers were providing no child support to their firstborn child after its sixth birthday.[13] According to a recent study in Barbados of 333 fathers with eight-year-old children, only 22 per cent were still living with their child. Furthermore, the children of the fathers who did live with their children were performing significantly better in school.[14] The Population Council's *Families in Focus* (1995) reports that the number of female-headed households has risen significantly in almost every country in the world since the mid 1970s. Marital dissolution runs from 40 to 60 per cent for women by the time they are forty in poor countries such as the Dominican Republic, Ghana, Indonesia and Senegal. Divorce rates were 55 per 100 in the United States in 1990, although they recently have modified slightly. Rates have doubled since 1970 in Canada, France, Greece, the Netherlands and the former West Germany.[15] If current rates continue, 41 per cent of new marriages will end in divorce in England and Wales.[16] In the early 1990s, out-of-wedlock births were 1 per cent in Japan, 33.3 per cent in northern Europe, 70 per cent in Botswana and 27 to 28 per cent in Kenya.[17]

Divorce and non-marital births contribute to father absence and the number of lone-parent families, generally headed by the mother. Although the decline of fathers' financial and social support has been costly for both children and mothers in wealthy countries, consequences have been devastating in poor and underdeveloped countries. Poverty both contributes to and is further aggravated by fatherlessness.

Yet as John Snarey, David Blankenhorn, David Popenoe, and McLanahan and Sandefur show, fathers contribute not only financially but also cognitively and emotionally to the wellbeing of their children.[18] Furthermore, their contribution is not easily replaced. Although biological relatedness does not guarantee good parenting by either mother or father, it seems to be a pre-moral condition (a pre-moral good) that encourages parental investment and therefore correlates positively with moral qualities such as commitment, presence, steadfastness and positive regard – qualities which are directly related to child flourishing. As a pre-moral good, it is not to be absolutised but held as an important relative good to be encouraged. As we will see, the Christian tradition has tended to regard intact parenthood in this light.

The case for the two-parent biologically related family can be exaggerated. Not all biological fathers and mothers are competent parents. Not all two-parent families are just and life-enhancing. For instance, some men are tyrannical and abusive to wives and children. The facts indicate, however, that alternatives are on average worse, especially if they are systematically generalised. Single mothers are more likely to abuse their children physically than intact families, and children are many times more likely to be physically and sexually abused in stepfamilies and cohabiting arrangements than in intact families.[19] I argue that there should be, as a matter of ecclesial and public policy, a *presumption towards encouraging the formation and maintenance of intact families. This rule has exceptions, but they do not undercut its importance as a cultural and religious guide.*

THE LIBERAL THEOLOGICAL RESPONSE

Three theological–ethical responses to these trends can be identified – a liberal Protestant, a Catholic, and a conservative Protestant. Liberal religious communities, at least in the USA, tended to agree with the social science analysis of the 1970s and 80s that believed family changes were not harmful. Theological liberals around the world were also sensitive to civil rights issues and analogised a relation between equality for minorities and equality for various family forms. Single-parent families, stepfamilies, non-married cohabiting families and gay and lesbian families were seen as equally good for both children and adults if only the onus of prejudice could be removed.

The close approximation of liberal theological views of marriage and family to the growing contractualism of legal theories of marriage should not be ignored. With the advent in the USA of 'no fault' divorce in the 1960s and 70s, marriage agreements increasingly were seen as analogous to business contracts.[20] Unilateral divorce – divorce based on the will of one partner even if the other resisted – made marriage contracts among the weakest in societies that adopted the no-fault policy. Although liberal churches never officially accepted the secular contractual view of marriage, their thinking on this subject had analogies to contractual theory. Rather than contract as such, the liberal view sometimes talked of marital-type 'relationships.' Church documents from liberal denominations in Canada, the USA and Britain often spoke of 'committed relationships.' The religious meaning of these relationships was found in their affective quality, reputed justice, and alleged non-exploitative character. Although seldom spoken of as 'contracts,' these ideal relations nonetheless possessed features of contracts because of the voluntary way they were thought to be established and dissolved. Gradually the classic religious models of marriage – marriage considered as both legal contract *and* covenant (Protestant) or legal contract *and* sacrament (Roman Catholic) – began to yield to the ideal of a marital-type relationship that was privately created and only incidentally legally witnessed and religiously sanctioned.

The concept of 'justice love' between consenting adults – a concept found in the Presbyterian (USA) report called *Keeping Body and Soul Together* (1991) – is an example of this style of theological–ethical thinking. In this ethic, wherever loving and just interpersonal transactions occurred, valid marital-type relationships also existed. This view became widespread in liberal circles, both religious and secular. This view blurred distinctions between non-sexual friendships, sexual friendships, cohabiting couples, legally contracted marital couples and couples both legally contracted and covenantally or sacramentally sanctioned. All could be in 'committed relationships.' A new democracy of loving and just intimate relationships began replacing older understandings of covenant, sacrament and contract applied to the sphere of marriage and family.

This view of marriage and family was not troubled by the family trends of the 1970s and 80s. The task of theology, church and society was rather to create a new situation of acceptance, justice, normalisation, and social and governmental supports for these emerging family arrangements. Although the liberal theological response should be applauded for its openness, charity and sense of justice, it was slow in recognising the depth of family disruption and new evidence that mere social acceptance and state supports were inadequate remedies.

THE ROMAN CATHOLIC RESPONSE

A second response came from Roman Catholicism. This view was grounded on the shadows of medieval natural-law thinking and the principle of subsidiarity. In spite of the personalism of some contemporary Catholic theologians (even Pope John Paul II) that played down the natural law,[21] Catholic family theory values even today many of its historical family commitments. These include the natural bonding of a man and a woman for the purposes of procreation and education of children, sexual exchange as a defence against lust and infidelity, mutual assistance between spouses, and supernatural grace sufficient to empower couples to live this ethic.[22]

The principle of subsidiarity – a view of the family–state relation inspired by Aristotle but explicitly stated by Popes Leo XIII and Pius XI – has its own natural-law backing. This concept held that the family, because of biological tendencies of parents to give preferential care to their own children, has a *prima facie* competence and right to care for its offspring. This tendency of families, it was thought, is based on the intentions of God in creation and stamped into the structure of nature. Government should not intrude into the God-given natural inclinations of families to care for their own. Nonetheless, the state has a crucial role in protecting families from the dislocations of market economies and assuring the social conditions needed for a just family wage.[23]

The Roman Catholic response to family changes in most countries has been conservative on family ethics and relatively progressive on social policy. It has resisted trends towards divorce, out-of-wedlock births, cohabitation, the deinstitutionalisation of marriage, and abortion. The principle of subsidiarity, however, led Catholic social theory to support state-financed welfare for needy families and children, whatever the cause of their vulnerability. Although Catholics believed government should not unnecessarily intrude on families, they believed that the state should protect the family's resources, be this through the guarantee of fair wages, the right through labour unions to bargain with companies, or the right to an adequate education for children.[24]

CONSERVATIVE RELIGIOUS RESPONSES

Conservative religious and political forces did not share the early social-scientific optimism about family change that liberal theology accepted. Religious conservatives resisted these changes. Such conservative organisations in the USA as Focus on the Family, the Moral Majority or the Christian Coalition, and analogous conservative Christian organisations in other countries, affirmed the traditional family roles of wage-earning father and domestic mother. Furthermore, they resisted government intrusion into family life through welfare, progressive values in public schools and sex education in schools. Some Christian conservatives justified this thinking by fundamentalist uses of scriptures that appear to sanction male headship (Eph. 5:23; Col. 3:18; and 1 Pet. 3:1), forbid divorce (Matt. 19:6–9) or command women to silence in the church (1 Cor. 14:34–6). These groups believe that the nineteenth-century family with its working husband and stay-at-home wife was derived directly from the biblical plan for families. They seemed unaware that this image of family reflected an economic organisation of domestic life that had its roots in the Industrial Revolution rather than in the New Testament (see above, pp. 68f).

Although conservatives of this type were sceptical of government intrusion in family life, they seemed less troubled by the intrusions of the market. There were, however, exceptions to this rule. The conservative mind was often sceptical of market influences which promoted the subversive values of popular culture; hence its interest in developing an alternative popular religious music and the use of new musical genres in worship.

Other Christian conservatives grounded their thinking on more sophisticated theological models. Those working out of Reformed theological traditions were likely to invoke the idea of 'orders' or 'spheres' of creation to justify both a religious sanction for intact married families as well as a theory of the limited role of government in family life. Genesis 2:24 ('Therefore a man leaves his father and his mother and cleaves to his wife, and they become one flesh') was used to argue that God's intention for covenanted and permanent marriage was an 'order of creation'. Variations of this pattern of thinking can be found in the theologies of Martin Luther, John Calvin, Karl Barth, Helmut Thielicke, Emil Brunner and the Dutch educator–statesman Abraham Kuyper. Brunner and Kuyper developed an idea that the spheres of family, government and market are differentiated orders of creation all under the will of God.[25] Kuyper, whose influence is growing on the American scene, taught that each order or sphere should be governed by the sovereign rule of God. This view theoretically does not end in theocracy, since no specific manifestation of government is concretely sanctioned, just the general idea that Christians operating in the various spheres of life, including government, must be attentive to their covenant responsibilities before God.

Kuyper's form of thinking is being developed by such contemporary thinkers as Mary Stewart van Leeuwen, Max Stackhouse and legal theorist John Witte. They all affirm the centrality of the intact mother–father partnership but do not condone male headship or the public–private split of the nineteenth-century family, as do some evangelicals and fundamentalists.[26] Although cautious about the role of government in family life, this view sees a role for the state in protecting families from destructive market intrusions and providing appropriate supports as long as it does not undermine the prerogatives of families and their covenants with their religious communities.

A CRITICAL THEOLOGICAL THEORY OF FAMILY FORMATION

All of the theologies of the family discussed above lack a critical theory of family formation, although it is implicit in some forms of Catholic thinking. By critical theory, I mean one that is not solely dependent on the confessional beginning point of a particular religious tradition. For instance, arguments based on orders of creation may be theologically classic in that they come from the first two chapters of Genesis and are further shaped by subsequent interpretations from Jesus to Calvin.[27] But this form of argumentation does not convert easily into discourse that can stand up in the give and take of public discourse. Increasingly, such theological language is not even convincing to faithful Christians. They are basically affirmations or, as Paul Ricoeur says, 'attestations' based on faith and experience informed by faith.[28]

If hermeneutic theories of language and experience are correct – and I believe that they are – all thought begins in confession or, as Hans-Georg Gadamer says, the 'effective histories' that unconsciously shape us.[29] By this Gadamer meant that the communities that socialise us, be they religious or secular, shape our thought patterns long before we start reflecting more critically on what we have received. Since this is true, religious affirmations based on faith should be able to enter into public debate. Even allegedly secular views are shaped by pre-critical traditions of various kinds.

So religious voices functioning out of the orders of creation, or the New Testament pastoral epistles, or liberal Christian interpretations of the love

commandment, all have a right to speak in public. But they also have obligations to give reasons that have broader public intelligibility than their
simple affirmations in faith. A critical theory of family formation would
help give additional meaning to the unique contributions of a Christian
view of families, especially since the theory I will advance is actually
assumed by some past Christian theologies. It is also confirmed by certain
contemporary secular disciplines.

I first turn to the theory of family formation advanced by contemporary
evolutionary psychology. I will then show its similarities to a theory
assumed by the formative views on marriage and family in the medieval
Roman Catholic theologian Thomas Aquinas. Although I am liberal
Protestant and not Roman Catholic, I believe that outlines of his theological
ethics of family constitutes a rich resource for a public theology of families
today.

Evolutionary psychology is a new discipline that applies the theories
of evolution to the study of human mental functioning. It is related to socio-
biology, evolutionary ecology and behavioural biology, but is less determin-
istic than these disciplines and more concerned with higher-level cognitive
and emotional development. Evolutionary psychologists are also interested
in how families are formed at the human level. They point to the asymmet-
rical reproductive strategies between males and females in mammalian
species; this means that most mammalian males tend to procreate as widely
as possible with a variety of females but do not become involved in the care
of their offspring.[30] Humans are one of the very few mammals in which
males have become a relatively stable part of the nurturing of their children.
This raises the question, What were the conditions which led *Homo sapiens*
males long ago to become attached to mates and involved in the care and
socialisation of their children?

Answering this question *has relevance for contemporary theological–
ethical responses to the family crisis.* Insight into these conditions offers a
theory of pre-moral conditions and goods that facilitate family formation
and stability. Knowledge about these things is a way of reconstructing
Catholic natural-law theory on the family. In turn, this reconstructed
Catholic naturalism can offer what Paul Ricoeur calls a 'diagnostic' to the
naturalistic depth of the classical Protestant orders of creation. By diagnostic, I mean an indication that the orders of creation actually refer to certain
realities and regularities of human existence even though the idea of
'orders' means precisely that God shapes these regularities towards more
ideal patterns. Finally, the theories of evolutionary psychology and current
data about the effects of family disruption on children constitute a critique

of the naive justice–love perspectives of liberal Protestantism. Justice and love, without attention to details about finite conditions and goods, may not be enough to address the contemporary crisis of families.

One must begin with the work of W. D. Hamilton (1964). He provided a theory of inclusive fitness and kin altruism that had important implications for the theory of family formation. Hamilton's theory of inclusive fitness states that individuals are not concerned only with the survival of their own specific genes; they are also concerned with the survival of those who carry their genes – offspring and siblings first and then cousins, aunts and uncles, etc. This implies a theory of kin altruism that also explains why creatures are willing under some circumstances to sacrifice their own wellbeing or fitness for the wellbeing or fitness of their children, siblings or other extended-family members.

The theories of inclusive fitness and kin altruism show there are very specific reasons why natural parents, on average, care more for their children than do other people. These theories also suggest why thousands of years ago the emergence of the following conditions helped integrate human males into families. Four conditions appear to have made this possible: (1) 'paternal recognition', or a father's certainty that a particular child was his and therefore worth caring for, (2) the long period of human infant dependency, which required mothers to look for assistance from male consorts, (3) ongoing sexual exchange between mates and (4) reciprocal altruism (mutual helpfulness) between father and mother.[31] When Robert Trivers in 1972 introduced the idea that paternal certainty and recognition led *Homo sapiens* males to invest in the care of their offspring as a way of extending their own lives, it was thought that it alone could account for male bonding with mate and child. It is now believed that the other three conditions are needed as well.[32]

These conditions together constitute a naturalistic theory of the institution of matrimony – a theory similar, as we will soon see, to the naturalistic components of Thomas Aquinas' theology of marriage and the family. These four conditions are important pre-moral goods that can be integrated into a more fully ethical theory of marriage and family.

THOMISM, NATURAL LAW AND EVOLUTIONARY BIOLOGY

Christian family theory in the work of Thomas Aquinas, without the benefit of modern evolutionary theory, recognised the naturalistic conditions for family formation summarised above.[33] But Thomas added the theological belief that the 'natural' offspring of parents are also gifts of God and made in God's image.[34] In Thomistic theory, which deserves critical reappropriation, the natural and supernatural reinforce each other. Children, as Aristotle had said before, were seen by Aquinas as the semblance or partial image of their parents;[35] this, Aquinas thought, was part of the reason parents care for their children. Aquinas added, however, that children are also made in the image of God; therefore, we should love in our children the divine good that is in them just as we should love God who is the source of that good. In addition, since God's goodness spills over into all children, Christian adults should cherish all children whether they are directly their own or not. The power of the Thomistic formulation is this: although it emphasises the obligation to show a general benevolence towards all children, it affirms and protects the inclinations in parents to exert special energy on behalf of their own offspring.

I will list briefly evidence showing that Aquinas had his own version of the natural elements of family formation now being discussed by evolutionary psychologists. He was aware that long-term human infant dependency beckons the male to assist his consort in child care. He believed that since the human infant 'needs the parents' care for a long time, there is a very great tie between male and female' at the human level, in contrast to other species.[36] Second, he recognised the role of paternal recognition in binding males to both offspring and mate and discussed how this is disrupted in a system of sexual promiscuity. He wrote, 'Man naturally desires to be assured of his offspring: and this assurance would be altogether nullified in the case of promiscuous copulation.'[37]

Third, he believed that one of the purposes of matrimony 'is the mutual services that married persons render one another in household matters'.[38] And fourth, he understood in a distinctively medieval way the role of sexual exchange in integrating marital partners. Like Paul and Augustine before him, he advised the payment of the 'marital debt', acknowledging that although it was a venial sin, it was excused by the marriage blessing.[39]

Hence, the natural grounds for matrimony were well recognised by Aquinas, even though the biology that supported them was crude and at points inaccurate. But Aquinas did not remain at the naturalistic level in his theory of matrimony. His vision of matrimony entailed distinctively ethical and theological levels as well. The ethical level is found in his refutation of polyandry and polygyny.

His criticism of polyandry was largely still at the pre-moral level; one woman with several husbands would lower male investment in offspring, since it would work against paternal certainty and recognition. This would be costly to the flourishing of children. His critique of polygyny was more directly ethical. He admitted that polygyny can exist with relatively high degrees of paternal certainty and investment in offspring. He also observed, however, that wherever men 'have several wives, the friendship of a wife for her husband would not be freely bestowed, but servile as it were. And this argument is confirmed by experience; since where men have several wives, the wives are treated as servants.'[40] In the name of equity and friendship, polygyny should be rejected.

A theological argument, however, is the capstone that completes Aquinas' naturalistic and ethical arguments for marriage as a formal institution. He is all too aware of the fragility and vulnerability of human natural inclinations and moral capacities. For him, human commitment to marital permanence must be reinforced with the grace of God which flows from Christ's love for the church. Although this grace is interpreted by Aquinas as supernatural, we know today that to be accurate he should have translated the Latin *sacramentum* (Eph. 5:32) to mean *mystery* (the meaning of the original Greek word *mysterion*).[41] When this is done, the emphasis of the passage becomes more the narrative analogy between Christ's sacrificial love for the church and a husband's love for his wife (Eph. 5:21–33). The husband is to model his commitment to wife and children after Christ's sacrificial love for the church. The male's recapitulation of Christ's sacrificial love does not cancel or replace Aquinas' naturalistic or ethical arguments for matrimony. Instead, it stabilises and deepens these natural inclinations and gives them a more permanent ethical form. Nature's inclinations plus ethical reason push humans towards matrimony; participation in Christ's love transforms these natural and ethical tendencies into permanent marital commitment.

NEO-THOMISM AND A CRITIQUE OF THE LIBERAL AND REFORMED PERSPECTIVES

Although I write as a liberal Protestant theological ethicist and practical theologian, there are clearly problems with both the liberal and conservative Protestant perspectives. Catholic moral theology, with its naturalistic foundations, has its difficulties as well, even though it has important contributions to make. Catholic naturalism must be cleansed of those aspects of Aristotelian biology that depicted women as deficient in rationality. It also must be washed of those features of the Thomistic theology which render women as less completely made in the image of God than men (see above, pp. 79f).[42]

These corrections can be made on biblical grounds, as my colleagues and I demonstrated in *From Culture Wars to Common Ground: Religion and the American Family Debate* (1997).[43] When early Christianity is interpreted against the background of the surrounding Greco-Roman honour–shame codes and their strong emphasis on male dominance, it becomes clear that the New Testament theme of male self-sacrifice was in tension with the subordination of women so rampant in the ancient pagan world.[44] Once Aquinas is reconstructed at these points, his views have several advantages. They have the virtue of depicting the sacrificial love of the cross as working to restore friendships of equal regard and mutuality rather than being an end in itself. In the Thomistic view, as various contemporary neo-Thomists have argued, love as mutuality or equal regard (Catholic views of *caritas*) rather than love as self-sacrifice (Protestant views of *agape*) has the more central place. Even Aquinas believed that a relation between husband and wife should be one of friendship, although not a fully equal one.[45] With the amendment I have just proposed, the Thomistic view of marital love actually protects women from a life of perpetual self-sacrifice to husband and children in the name of a Christian theology of the cross.[46]

Furthermore, Catholic naturalism exposes the shallowness of Protestant liberalism on marriage and family. The implicit relational contractualism of this perspective has no way of determining why one family form actualises, on average, more pre-moral good than another. It has difficulty absorbing recent turns in the social sciences showing the unfavourable consequences of family disruption. In addition, since Protestant liberalism disregards both Catholic naturalism on family formation and the classical Protestant orders or spheres-of-creation argument, it has no way of discerning the central regularities of life that a just and loving 'committed relation' should nurture and organise.

Finally, a reconstructed Catholic naturalism can supplement classic Protestant perspectives on the orders of creation. The classic Protestant perspective, with few exceptions, understands these orders as given in scripture and tradition. They are generally presented as 'ordinances' (as they were in Luther) or 'commands' (as they are in Barth) of God and accepted by faith.[47] In a day when hermeneutic perspectives on knowledge have established the importance of tradition for all knowing, neither the eyes of faith nor the counsels of philosophy can object to beginning with the witness of a community of faith. On this score, the traditions of orders or spheres of creation are on *solid ground*, as far as they go. Furthermore, the witness of faith can justifiably be binding on the inner life of churches and religious movements. But when these traditions bring their faith assumptions into the public square and make claims about the common good (the good for

Christians and non-Christians alike), then the attestations of faith should be advanced only as strong hypotheses that can gain the force of public positions only if they are supplemented by clusters of additional reasons. It is precisely these additional reasons that evolutionary psychology and Catholic naturalism can bring to the hypothetical status of Protestant appeals to the orders of creation.

Beginning with the witness of scripture and tradition does not mean that naturalistic perspectives have nothing to contribute to the plausibility of faith. Especially is that true when these testimonies pertain to marriage and family. I want to conclude by reviewing two examples of Reformed theologians who contain a naturalistic moment within their broader use of orders-of-creation thinking – principally the work of Emil Brunner and the feminist evangelical Mary Stewart van Leeuwen.

Brunner in his *Divine Imperative* (1947) has an interesting way of combining naturalistic observations and a theology of 'orders'. He believes that a reasoned analysis of human action reveals the natural motivations that create the spheres of work, family and government. Within the sphere or order of the family, Brunner makes naturalistic observations similar to those found in Aquinas and in evolutionary psychology. Brunner contends that the natural energies creating human families have to do with sexual attraction, parental recognition by father and mother that offspring are part of their very substance, and the bonding and interdependencies that this creates between husband and wife and between parent and child. But he contends that revelation in creation reveals the ideal ordering, purpose and direction that should guide these natural inclinations – hence the importance of the Genesis scriptures dealing with procreation and the 'one-flesh' union of husband and wife.[48] Van Leeuwen uses another branch of psychology to give an element of naturalism to her use of the order-of-creations argument. Rather than biology, she uses psychoanalytic object-relations theory. The internationalisation of the images of both a father and mother give the child, so her argument goes, a necessary fund of psychological structures upon which a variety of adult values in love and work must build.[49]

The naturalism recommended here is not a scientistic one that wipes tradition away and builds an ethic on the basis of the accumulation of discrete natural facts. The naturalism advocated here uses insights gained from the relatively distantiated epistemology of the social and evolutionary sciences to add a dimension of realism to the attestations of faith. In the parlance of contemporary hermeneutical debates, this is a 'critical hermeneutics' of the kind advocated by Ricoeur or a 'hermeneutical realism' as promoted by my colleague William Schweiker.[50] The voice of tradition is heard first; science is used to uncover some of the regularities of life that tradition organises and idealises.

Liberal Protestantism has been, for the most part, blind to the world-wide trends towards father absence. Conservative Protestantism has resisted family change but has seldom framed the issue in this way. It also has, for the most part, been unconvincing in public debate. Some of Catholicism's conservative stands on population issues actually have in mind what I call 'the male problematic'. The Vatican's resistance to liberal solutions to the population explosion that depend on abortion and birth control is based on the fear that this strategy will lead to the worldwide collapse of marriage, the further drift of males away from families, and the consequent impoverishment of more women and children.

I will not debate the merits of this fear. My point, rather, is this: neither its older, scholastic natural-law arguments nor its more recent personalism has placed the Catholic Church in a favourable position to make its arguments clear in public debate. I believe that the reconstruction of Catholic naturalism along the lines advanced above has much to offer for a more robust participation of the churches, both Protestant and Catholic, in the growing international debate over family issues.

Notes

1 Talcott Parsons and Robert Bales, *Family, Socialization, and Interaction* (Glencoe, IL: Free Press, 1955).

2 Jessie Bernard, *The Future of Marriage* (New York: World, 1972).

3 Barbara Dafoe Whitehead, 'Dan Quayle Was Right', *Atlantic Monthly*, April 1993, pp. 47–84.

4 Charles Murray, 'The Coming White Underclass', *Wall Street Journal*, 29 October, 1993, p. 16A.

5 Charles Murray, 'The Next British Revolution', *Public Interest*, Winter 1995, pp. 3–29.

6 Sara McLanahan and Gary Sandefur, *Growing Up with a Single Parent* (Cambridge, MA: Harvard University Press, 1994), pp. 1–12.

7 *Ibid.*, pp. 70–1.

8 Patricia Morgan, *Farewell to the Family?* (London: IEA Health and Welfare Unit, 1995), pp. 130–3.

9 *Beyond Rhetoric: A New American Agenda for Children and Families* (Washington, DC: United States Government Printing Office, 1991); *Families First: Report of the National Commission on America's Urban Families* (Washington, DC: United States Government Printing Office, 1993); *Supporting Families* (London: Home Office, 1998); *To Have and To Hold: Strategies to Strengthen Marriage and Relationships* (Canberra: House of Representatives Standing Committee on Legal and Constitutional Affairs, 1998).

10 For a summary of this point of view, see David Blankenhorn, *Fatherless America* (New York: Basic, 1995).

11 Don Browning, 'Biology, Ethics, and Narrative in Christian Family Theory', in *Promises to Keep*, ed. David Popenoe, Jean Bethke Elshtain and David Blankenhorn (New York: Rowman and Littlefield, 1996), pp. 119–56.

12 Frank Furstenberg and Andrew Cherlin, *Divided Families* (Cambridge, MA: Harvard University Press, 1991).

13 Aaron Sachs, 'Men, Sex, and Parenthood', *World Watch* 7:2 (March–April 1994), p. 13.

14 *Ibid.*, p. 14.

15 J. Bruce, C. B. Lloyd and A. Leonard, *Families in Focus: New Perspectives on Mothers, Fathers, and Children* (New York: Population Council, 1995), pp. 14–20.

16 Sharon Breen, *Divorce Today* (London: One Plus One, 1998).

17 Bruce et al., *Families in Focus*, p. 73.

18 John Snarey, *How Fathers Care for the Next Generation: A Four Decade Study* (Cambridge: Harvard University Press, 1993); David Popenoe, 'The Evolution of Marriage and the Problem of Stepfamilies: A Biosocial Perspective', in *Stepfamilies: Who Benefits? Who Does Not?* ed. Alan Booth and Judy Dunn (Hillsdale, NJ.: Erlbaum, 1994), pp. 3–27; McLanahan and Sandefur, *Growing Up*, pp. 37, 56, 72.

19 One of the definitive analyses of the risk of abuse in non-biologically-related family structures can be found in Martin Daly and Margo Wilson, *Homicide* (New York: de Gruyter, 1988), pp. 86–90.

20 John Witte, 'From Sacrament to Contract: The Legal Transformations of the Western Family', *Criterion* 34:3 (1995), pp. 3–11. See also his entire book on this subject, *From Sacrament to Contract: Marriage, Religion, and Law in the Western Legal Tradition* (Louisville, KY: Westminster/John Knox Press, 1997).

21 For evidence of the personalism of Pope John Paul II that still conforms to the classic Catholic natural-law position on the family, see his early book: Karol Wojtyla, *Love and Responsibility* (New York: Farrar, Straus and Giroux, 1994).

22 Augustine, 'The Good of Marriage', in *The Fathers of the Church*, ed. Roy J. Deferrari (New York: Fathers of the Church, 1995); Thomas Aquinas, *Summa Theologica* (New York: Benziger Brothers, 1948), III, Q. 41. (Henceforth referred to as *ST*).

23 For key documents on the Catholic concept of subsidiarity, see the following: Pope Leo XIII, *Rerum Novarum*; Pope Pius XI, *Quadragesimo Anno*; and Pope John Paul II, *Centesimus Annus*, all in *Proclaiming Justice and Peace: Papal Documents from 'Rerum Novarum' Through 'Centesimus Annus'*, ed. Michael Walsh and Brian Davies (Mystic, CT: Twenty-third Publications).

24 Pope John Paul II reiterated both sides of Catholic teaching on the family – conservative personal family ethics and liberal social philosophy on the active but limited role of government – when he visited the USA during the autumn of 1995. See Gustav Niebuhr, 'Homily at Aqueduct Race Track', *New York Times*, 7 October, 1995, p. 12.

25 Karl Barth, *Church Dogmatics*, III, 4 (Edinburgh: T. & T. Clark, 1961), pp. 116–29; Emil Brunner, *The Divine Imperative* (Philadelphia, PA: Westminster Press, 1957), pp. 330–9; Abraham Kuyper, *The Problem of Poverty*, ed. James Skillen (Grand Rapids, MI: Baker Book House, 1991), pp. 29–30.

26 Max Stackhouse, *Covenant and Commitment: Faith, Family, and the Economic Life* (Louisville, KY: Westminster/John Knox Press, 1997); Mary Stewart van Leeuwen, *Gender and Grace: Love, Work, and Parenting in a Changing World* (Downers Grove, IL: Intervarsity Press, 1990); Witte, *From Sacrament to Contract*.

27 Witte, *From Sacrament to Contract*, especially chapters 2 and 3.

28 Paul Ricoeur, *Oneself as Another* (Chicago: University of Chicago Press, 1991), pp. 21–3.

29 Hans Georg Gadamer, *Truth and Method* (New York: Crossroad, 1982), pp. 267f.

30 Summaries of evolutionary theory on family formation, kin altruism and inclusive fitness can be found in the following: Pierre van der Berghe, *Human Family Systems: An Evolutionary View* (New York: Elsevier, 1979); Martin Daly and Margo Wilson, *Sex, Evolution, and Behavior* (Belmont, CA: Wadsworth, 1983); Don Symons, *The Evolution of Human Sexuality* (New York: Oxford University Press, 1979).

31 W. D. Hamilton, 'The Genetical Evolution of Social Behavior, ii', *Journal of Theoretical Biology* 7 (1964), pp. 17–52.

32 Barry Hewlett (ed.), *Father–Child Relations: Cultural and Biosocial Context* (New York: de Gruyter, 1992), pp. xi–xix.

33 For Aquinas' analogues to the four conditions listed in the text, see *ST*, iii, Q. 41–6; and *Summa contra gentiles*, iii, ii (London: Burns, Oates and Washbourne, 1928), pp. 112–23 (to be referred to as *SCG*). See Don Browning, 'Biology, Ethics, and Narrative in Christian Family Theory', in David Popenoe et al. (eds), *Promises to Keep*, pp. 119–55. See also Stephen Pope, *The Evolution of Altruism and the Ordering of Love* (Washington, DC: Georgetown University Press, 1994). Pope's work on the relation of evolutionary biology and Thomistic theories of love and the family has been groundbreaking.

34 *ST*, ii, ii, Q 26.

35 Aristotle, *Politics*, in *Basic Writings of Aristotle* (New York: Random House, 1941), ii, iii.

36 *ST* iii, Q. 41, 1.

37 *SCG*, iii, ii, p. 118.

38 *ST*, iii, Q. 41, i.

39 *Ibid.*, Q. 41, iv.

40 *SCG*, iii, ii, p. 118.

41 *ST*, iii, Q. 42, A 2.

42 *ST*, i, i, Q. 92.

43 Don Browning, Bonnie Miller-McLemore, Pamela Couture, Bernie Lyon and Robert Franklin, *From Culture Wars to Common Ground* (Louisville, KY: Westminster/John Knox, 1997). See especially the introduction and chapters 5 and 10 for a biblical development of the idea of an equal-regard family and marriage and the associated concept of 'critical familism'.

44 For a development of the relevance of research on the honour–shame codes surrounding, but also being subverted in, early Christianity, see chapter 5 of *From Culture Wars to Common Ground*.

45 *SCG*, iii, p. 118.

46 Louis Janssens, 'Norms and Priorities of a Love Ethics', *Louvain Studies* 6 (1977),

pp. 207–38; Barbara Hilkert Andolsen, 'Agape in Feminist Ethics', *Journal of Religious Ethics* 9:1 (Spring 1981), pp. 68–83; Christian Gudorf, 'Parenting, Mutual Love, and Sacrifice', *Woman's Consciousness, Woman's Conscience* ed. Barbara Andolsen et al. (New York: Winston, 1985), pp. 175–91.

47 Luther uses the language of 'ordinance' in 'The Estate of Marriage', *Luther's Works*, vol. 45 (Philadelphia, PA: Muhlenberg Press, 1962), pp. 13–48. Barth uses the metaphor 'command' and Brunner the metaphor of 'order'.

48 See *The Divine Imperative* (Philadelphia, PA: Westminster, 1947), pp. 330–8.

49 Mary Stewart van Leeuwen, 'Re-Inventing the Ties That Bind: Feminism and the Family at the Close of the Twentieth Century', in Anne Carr and Mary Stewart van Leeuwen (eds.), *Religion, Feminism, and the Family* (Louisville, KY: Westminster/John Knox, 1996), pp. 33–54.

50 Paul Ricoeur, *Hermeneutics and the Human Sciences* (Cambridge: Cambridge University Press, 1981), p. 60; William Schweiker, *Responsibility and Christian Ethics* (Cambridge: Cambridge University Press, 1995), pp. 4, 113–17.

18 Christian ethics, medicine, and genetics

JAMES F. CHILDRESS

From its beginnings, Christianity has encouraged and provided health care, an activity featured in Jesus' healing and in his parable of the Good Samaritan. Over the centuries Christian traditions have also provided guidance for physicians, other health care providers, familial caregivers and patients. While often distinctive, this guidance sometimes overlapped with or incorporated, with modifications, guidance in professional oaths and codes. 'Medical ethics', which was largely physician ethics until nursing emerged in the nineteenth century, was subsumed in the 1960s and 70s under 'bioethics' or 'biomedical ethics', a broader conception for new developments and a variety of felt problems in biomedicine. For instance, medical technologies could prolong life far beyond previous possibilities, transplant organs from one living or dead person to another, detect certain fetal defects in utero and offer new reproductive opportunities. Bioethics or biomedical ethics involves an interdisciplinary and interprofessional approach to ethical issues in the life sciences, medicine and health care.[1]

Christian reflections on these developments build, to varying degrees, on scripture and tradition, along with appeals to experience and reason, sometimes expressed in the language of natural law. How various Christian churches rely on and rank these different bases of authority has important implications for their views in bioethics – for example, whether they are distinctive or overlap with secular perspectives. Even though Christians share important theological perspectives – for instance, the conviction that God created human beings in his own image and that God is the giver of life – and substantive moral norms – for example, the decalogue, neighbour–love (*agape*) and justice – Roman Catholic, Eastern Orthodox, Protestant and Anglican (or Episcopal in the USA) traditions often disagree about what these perspectives imply, how to interpret and apply those norms, how to specify them for particular areas, such as medicine and genetics, and how to adjudicate any conflicts that emerge. Furthermore, many bioethical views are at different stages of development in different Christian traditions.

Obviously, it is impossible to do justice to all these Christian traditions of bioethical reflection. And the range of issues in bioethics is too great to permit an exhaustive treatment. As a result, this chapter will concentrate on bioethical issues that raise distinctive Christian concerns or provoke significant debates among Christians. Thus, it will largely neglect such topics as privacy and confidentiality, professional–patient relations, research involving human subjects, and public health, among others, not because they are unimportant but because Christian views on these topics generally overlap with secular views.

REPRODUCTIVE CHOICES: AVOIDING PREGNANCY, TERMINATING PREGNANCY AND USING NEW REPRODUCTIVE TECHNOLOGIES

Contraception

Not until the Lambeth Conference of the Anglican Church in 1930 did any Christian church officially move beyond its traditional opposition to birth control. Since that time virtually every Christian denomination, except the Roman Catholic Church, has accepted various forms of contraception. The official Roman Catholic position remains opposed to artificial means of contraception as a violation of the natural law, which requires that each and every sexual act be open to the possibility of procreation – one of the important ends of marriage and of sexual intercourse within marriage. By contrast, traditional Protestant opposition – and some lingering reservations, especially among evangelicals – focuses mainly on attitudes of distrust in God's providence and of selfishness in avoiding children.

In the 1960s, in the wake of the Second Vatican Council, many thought that the Roman Catholic Church might alter its traditional prohibition of the use of artificial means of contraception. The values that had supported the prohibition could, in a new context, support its modification – indeed, according to John Noonan,[2] the various arguments for the prohibition of contraception were not as weighty as the ones that supported the prohibition of usury, which the church had overturned.

Critics took various approaches, stressing that different ends of marriage can come into conflict (e.g. procreation and education of offspring may conflict); that a moral assessment of sexual intercourse within marriage should concentrate on persons and their relationships rather than on the functions of sexual organs; and that responsible parenthood could keep the marriage as a whole open to procreation while using contraceptive means to determine the number and spacing of children. Nevertheless, in

1968 Pope Paul VI's encyclical *Humanae Vitae* reaffirmed the traditional prohibition while recognising the rhythms of nature in determining the number and spacing of children. The Catholic Church also prohibits sterilisation, which may be defined as the temporary or permanent removal of the capacity to procreate, unless it is the indirect effect of a legitimate medical procedure.

Practice does not always conform to official teachings. In some countries, Roman Catholics are no less likely than participants in other religious communities to use contraceptives. However, the Roman Catholic hierarchy continues to hold that contraception is not only intrinsically wrong but also that the contraceptive ethos contributes to the 'culture of death',[3] which legitimates both active euthanasia and abortion, in contrast to those who argue that the easy availability of safe and effective contraception can reduce the number of abortions.

Abortion

Abortion is one of the most sharply divisive issues in Christian ethics – as well as in the society at large – and different moral assessments hinge largely, though not entirely, on different interpretations of the moral status of the fetus. At least three views of the moral status of the fetus appear in contemporary discourse – the fetus is mere tissue, is potential human life or is full human life. At one end of the spectrum, few Christians regard the fetus as mere tissue, while, at the other end of the spectrum, the official Roman Catholic position holds that the fetus is a full human being, with a right to life, from the moment of conception. With this interpretation of fetal status, and the moral principle that it is always wrong directly to kill an innocent human being, the Roman Catholic Church condemns all direct acts of abortion.

One challenge to this position disputes the factual premise about fetal status, contending that the very early embryo, before around fourteen days, is not yet fully individuated, because twinning and recombination may occur until then, and the primitive streak that becomes the spinal cord only emerges at that time. However, this challenge has been rejected in official Roman Catholic teaching.

A second possible challenge emerges when a pregnancy puts a woman at serious risk of death. In such cases, some critics of the official view wonder whether the fetus could be considered an aggressor and thus justifiably killed, but that interpretive option has also been rejected. In a few cases, however, actions that seek to save a pregnant woman's life but that also result in fetal death can be morally justified, under the rule of double effect.

According to this rule, an action must be good or at least indifferent; the agent must intend the good effect but not the bad effect, even though he or she may foresee that bad effect; the bad effect cannot be a means to the good effect; and the good effect must outweigh the bad effect or there must be a proportionate reason for allowing the bad effect to occur.

If a pregnant woman has cancer of the uterus or a pregnancy in the fallopian tube, she may choose and the physician may undertake procedures to save her life even though they will result in her fetus' death. In terms of the rule of double effect, removing the cancerous uterus is a legitimate medical treatment for cancer of the uterus; the pregnant woman and her physician do not intend the fetus' death, even though they foresee it; the fetus' death is not a means to saving the pregnant woman's life; and there is a proportionate reason (saving the woman's life) to undertake the procedure. This line of reasoning has limited application – it does not extend beyond these types of cases to others where continuing the pregnancy would also threaten the woman's health, for example, where continuing the pregnancy would put too much strain on her weakened heart, but where the death of the fetus would be considered to be directly intended and caused.

By contrast, many Protestant, Anglican and Eastern Orthodox theologians view the fetus as potential human life, which makes significant claims upon the pregnant woman and others. From this perspective, abortion is considered generally, *prima facie* or presumptively wrong – it stands in need of moral justification, but it can sometimes be morally justified, even though it may be considered tragic, mournful and the like. The burden of moral justification varies greatly for proponents of this broad middle position, depending on the weight of fetal claims. In general, this middle position accepts abortion to save the pregnant woman's life and to protect her health from serious risks. However, some Eastern Orthodox thinkers view abortion as virtually always wrong, except in the rare circumstances of a threat to the pregnant woman's life, when it might be judged to be prudentially right.[4]

Many Protestant and Anglican thinkers[5] would also accept abortion in cases of pregnancy resulting from rape or incest. And a number would accept abortion in cases where reliable evidence indicates that the child-to-be has a genetic condition that is incompatible with life or that will lead to intense pain and suffering for him or her. Prenatal testing for genetic or other anomalies is not uncontroversial, especially if the prospective parents intend to have an abortion if certain conditions are detected. For example, some Eastern Orthodox thinkers contend that this information should be used only to enable the parents to prepare for the birth of their child and to meet that child's special needs. Finally, Christian churches and theologians often recommend conscientious and prayerful reflection in the context of the Christian community when abortion and its alternatives are being considered.

Two other approaches to moral reasoning about abortion suggest that the moral status of the fetus is not decisive. On the one hand, Stanley Hauerwas, a Methodist theologian, argues that the Christian virtue of openness to new life and to strangers stands in opposition to abortion.[6] Hence he contends that it is not necessary or fruitful for Christians to enter the debate about when human life begins. Critics respond that exactly what this virtue requires depends, at least in part, on the moral status of the fetus.

On the other hand, some feminist theologians, in several traditions, including Roman Catholicism, argue that even if the fetus is considered a human being, or person, from the moment of conception, abortion is not necessarily wrong in all cases. From this perspective, opposition to abortion and to women's rights to make their own decisions proceeds from a distorted interpretation of the relationship between the pregnant woman and the fetus. Too often that interpretation construes pregnancy as a relationship between independent parties, with the pregnant woman (and the physician) having a duty not to kill the fetus. If, however, the relationship is interpreted differently, the moral question may become: 'When, why, and to what extent does a pregnant woman have an obligation to provide bodily life support to the fetus?' The pregnant woman's obligation, when it exists, is one of beneficence, the obligation of beneficence may hinge on her prior decisions about sexual intercourse, and it may be limited by the pregnancy's risks to her.

Connections obviously exist between a religious tradition's judgements about the morality of acts of abortion and its judgements about appropriate laws – for example, whether to permit, regulate or prohibit abortions – and other public policies – for example, whether to provide societal funds to cover abortion procedures. Nevertheless, those connections are not direct entailments. Whether or not a tradition holds that abortion should be illegal will depend on several factors, including not only the basis, scope and weight of its opposition to abortion but also its convictions about the appropriate role of religious beliefs in formulating public laws and policies, especially in liberal, pluralistic democracies. A 'common ground' may be available for some laws and public policies, based, for example, on moral judgements that earlier abortions are preferable to later ones, and that abortion should not replace contraception in family planning. It is also possible to affirm women's political–legal rights to make abortion decisions without at the same time supposing that every abortion decision is morally right.

New reproductive technologies

The biblical story of God's creation connects human dominion with the responsibility of procreation, of multiplying and filling the earth. Thus, it is not surprising that modern reproductive technologies – artificial insemination and in vitro fertilisation, with all their spin-offs – provoke vigorous debates about when human beings are most distinctively human and most distinctively reflect God's image.

At opposite ends of the spectrum are the pro-technologists – such as Joseph Fletcher – who view artificial reproduction as more human than natural reproduction, precisely because of the use of human reason to control nature through technology, and the anti-technologists – such as the Roman Catholic tradition – who view reproductive technology as intrinsically inhuman. In between – and more common – are positions that view some reproductive technologies as potentially but not necessarily dehumanising and their use as sometimes morally justified. These intermediate positions tend to recommend caution rather than uncritical endorsement or prohibition.

Roman Catholicism tends to stress natural limits set, for instance, by the God-created ends of sexual organs, sexual activities and marriage. Thus, according to the Vatican's *Instruction on Respect for Human Life in Its Origin and on the Dignity of Human Procreation*,[7] couples using contraception wrongly pursue the unitive purpose of marital sexual intercourse while thwarting its procreative purpose, and those using artificial reproduction wrongly pursue its procreative purpose apart from its unitive purpose. From this standpoint, the only acceptable forms of artificial reproduction assist but do not dominate nature. However, because most reproductive technologies dominate nature – and may involve other proscribed acts such as masturbation – Catholics should in general bear the suffering brought on by infertility in the light of Christ's suffering.

By contrast, Protestants, Anglicans and Eastern Orthodox Christians tend to assign less value or weight to natural limits on the use of reproductive technologies. As Max Weber stressed, Protestants in particular allow extensive interventions into and control over nature. In general, these traditions hold that many uses of reproductive technologies can be loving acts of a married couple. Nevertheless, disputes about the use of particular reproductive technologies often hinge on whether the offspring can still be viewed as 'gifts' rather than as 'products'.

In addition, considerable debate exists, even in the Christian traditions that accept some reproductive technologies, about whether it is appropriate to use 'donated' sperm and ova (in some contexts, such as the USA, 'donation' is often a euphemism for sales and purchases). Problems of third-party involvement and of confidentiality and secrecy require special attention. Despite a variety of views about donated gametes, Christian traditions tend to oppose commercial surrogacy, often on the grounds that it is analogous to prostitution or to baby-selling. Although altruistic surrogacy is more acceptable than commercial surrogacy, it is still morally problematic, again because of the introduction of a third person into the marital relationship.

Many churches and theological ethicists also express considerable concern about appropriate respect for embryos left over and cryo-preserved following in vitro fertilisation. Determining appropriate respect for such embryos depends in part on whether they are viewed as mere tissue, potential human beings or full human beings – the range of positions already noted in the abortion debate. For instance, many Eastern Orthodox thinkers view discarding fertilised ova as equivalent to abortion.

At the end of the twentieth century, scientific developments in human embryonic stem cell research sharply posed the question about whether couples who have decided not to implant their cryo-preserved embryos could donate them for research rather than to another couple for reproductive purposes. Through this research, which destroys the embryo – and through research using tissue from deliberately aborted fetuses – scientists hope to be able to learn how to use stem cells to develop tissues for transplantation. Those who view the early embryo as full human life tend to oppose this research, while those who view the early embryo as potential human life take a variety of positions – some accept research on the early embryo as long as certain conditions are met.

Views of and attitudes towards the early embryo also play some role in Christian responses to the prospect of asexual reproduction, that is, cloning human beings, a prospect that moved out of the realm of science fiction with the announcement of the birth of Dolly, the ewe that scientists in Scotland produced through cloning techniques using fully differentiated adult cells. A large number of early embryos, or blastocysts, were lost in the process that produced the first cloned ewe. In addition, many critics of the prospect of cloning human beings expressed concerns about possible physical harms to children who might be created this way, along with concerns about psychosocial harms, threats to the family and the like. For Roman Catholicism, cloning represents the extreme end of the spectrum of reproductive technologies, and the arguments that oppose the other reproductive technologies also extend to cloning. By contrast, many other Christian approaches set a strong presumption against creating children through cloning without ruling it out in all possible circumstances (see above, pp. 147f).

POSTPONING DEATH, ALLOWING IT TO OCCUR OR
DIRECTLY BRINGING IT ABOUT

Withholding and withdrawing life-sustaining treatments to let patients die

Several metaphors and analogies mark Christian discourse about God's creation of human life and about its implications for life-and-death decisions. They involve, as Margaret Pabst Battin notes, property relationships (for example, life is God's 'image', 'temple' or 'handiwork', or is a 'loan' or 'trust' from God) and personal and/or role relationships (for example, human beings are God's 'children', 'sentinels', 'servants' or 'trustees').[8] Viewing life as a 'gift' invokes both types of metaphors and analogies. Hence, the obligation to protect human life, including one's own, grows out of God's gracious gift of life. According to *Evangelium Vitae* (The Gospel of Life), Pope John Paul II's 1995 encyclical, 'Man's life comes from God; it is his gift, his image and imprint, a sharing in his breath of life. God therefore is the sole Lord of this life: Man cannot do with it as he wills . . . the sacredness of life has its foundation in God and in his creative activity: "For God made man in his own image".'

Christian discourse often probes these metaphors and analogies. Are there limits on what a recipient may do with a gift? If the gift is faulty – for example, there are serious genetic defects – may it be returned or destroyed? Is the gift, which may cause considerable suffering on the recipient's part, then viewed as a way for God to test or educate the recipient? Centrally important in such debates are the evaluation of human suffering – whether it is valued, merely tolerated or always opposed – and the implications of the 'quality of life' for Christians' responses to God's 'gift of life'.

Over time the Roman Catholic moral tradition formulated several distinctions that allow patients to refuse, and family members and health care professionals to withhold or withdraw, life-prolonging treatment under some circumstances. It specifies the commandment against killing in the decalogue to prohibit directly killing an innocent human being. The distinction between direct killing and indirect killing is crucial in separating unacceptable acts of suicide, assisted suicide and active euthanasia, on the one hand, from acceptable acts of forgoing life-prolonging treatment and of using medications that may hasten death, on the other hand. Even though it is wrong directly to kill a suffering patient even at his or her request, it may be permissible, under the rule of double effect, to relieve that patient's suffering through medications that will probably, but indirectly, hasten his or her death.

Roman Catholic moral theology further distinguishes ordinary from extraordinary treatments or, in more contemporary language, proportionate from disproportionate treatments. If patients forgo ordinary or proportionate treatments, their actions constitute suicide, or if families and clinicians withhold or withdraw such treatments, their actions constitute homicide. However, if patients forgo, or families and clinicians withhold or withdraw, extraordinary or disproportionate treatments, which are sometimes called 'heroic' or 'aggressive', their actions do not constitute suicide or homicide. And their actions may be morally justifiable. In general, treatments that offer no reasonable chance of benefit or that create burdens for the patient and others that outweigh these benefits may be considered extraordinary or disproportionate and thus may be forgone, withheld or withdrawn without incurring a moral judgement of suicide or euthanasia.

Although the language sometimes differs, similar views exist in Eastern Orthodox, Protestant and Anglican traditions on withholding or withdrawing medical treatments in some circumstances in order to allow patients to die, as well as on providing medications to relieve pain and suffering even though they could hasten the patient's death. A rough consensus exists that treatments with no reasonable chance of benefit or with burdens to the patient and others that outweigh their benefits are morally optional. Nevertheless, disputes continue in various Christian traditions about whether medically administered nutrition and hydration should be considered medical treatments that are subject to a similar benefit–burden calculus and about whether terminal sedation falls under the rule of double effect.

According to some Christian ethicists, the criteria for distinguishing ordinary and extraordinary – or obligatory and optional – treatments involve judgements about quality of life; according to other ethicists who worry that quality-of-life judgements would subvert the absolute value of (innocent) life, these distinctions concern treatments, not persons. Another effort to reduce the risks of quality-of-life judgements restricts decisions to withhold or withdraw treatments to patients who are irreversibly and imminently dying. Using modern technologies to extend the dying process would, for some Christians, deny our mortality and our finitude, make an idol of life itself and amount to (inappropriately) 'playing God' – just as much as directly taking human life. Letting nature take its course, letting God's will be done, is usually viewed as appropriate for the irreversibly and imminently dying patient. More disagreement exists about whether it is justifiable to let a patient in a permanent vegetative state die through withdrawing antibiotics and medically administered nutrition and hydration.

Active euthanasia and assisted suicide

The term euthanasia, with its roots in the Greek *eu* (good) and *thanatos* (death), broadly refers to a 'good death'. However, in contemporary debates, it has come to denote how the death is brought about as well as the goal that is sought. Thus, 'active euthanasia' is often equivalent to 'mercy killing'. The distinction between active euthanasia and assisted suicide hinges on who performs the final act – the individual whose death is brought about or someone else, such as a physician or a family member. In assisted suicide, others may provide considerable assistance to the person choosing to end his or her life, but that person performs the final act. In active euthanasia, however, someone other than the person who dies performs the final act. In voluntary active euthanasia, the person who dies chooses to be killed by someone else.

If assisted suicide and voluntary active euthanasia cannot be justified within a particular religious tradition, that tradition will almost certainly oppose non-voluntary active euthanasia (without that person's will) and involuntary active euthanasia (against that person's will). In contrast to 'active euthanasia', the term passive euthanasia usually refers to letting or allowing patients to die. Even though, as previously noted, most Christian traditions and thinkers hold that it is acceptable, under some circumstances, to let patients die, they tend to eschew the language of passive euthanasia in order to prevent misunderstanding and confusion.

Christianity's traditional judgement that assisted suicide and voluntary active euthanasia are wrong stems from its judgement that suicide itself is wrong. If suicide itself is not justifiable, then assisted suicide and voluntary active euthanasia are not justifiable. Christianity has held that suicide contravenes important biblical and natural laws set by God, who created human beings in his own image and who gives them life (Gen. 1:26ff.), and reflects a lack of gratitude towards, trust in and faithfulness towards God as creator, preserver and redeemer. Some Christian theologians challenge this view. For instance, James M. Gustafson contends that '[s]uicide is always a tragic moral choice; it is sometimes a misguided choice. But it can be . . . a conscientious choice . . . Life is a gift, and is to be received with gratitude, but if life becomes an unbearable burden there is reason for enmity toward God.'[9] From this perspective, assistance in suicide and even active euthanasia could arguably be an act of neighbour love.

However, much of the debate among Christians and others focuses less on whether particular acts of assisted suicide and voluntary active euthanasia are right or wrong and more on whether it is appropriate to maintain traditional professional norms and legal rules that prohibit these acts. A rough correlation exists between moral judgements about such acts and moral judgements about laws regarding them, but the latter judgements are more complex.

Suicide is generally no longer subject to criminal sanctions in the USA, the UK and many other countries, but persons attempting to commit suicide may be involuntarily hospitalised for their own protection. Nevertheless, both assisted suicide and active euthanasia remain illegal – or at least not clearly legal – in virtually all jurisdictions. One notable exception is the experiment in legalised physician-assisted suicide that was inaugurated in Oregon in 1998; the Netherlands provides another partial exception in that, even though assisted suicide and active euthanasia remain technically illegal, physicians who perform those acts will not be prosecuted if they follow certain guidelines. Debate continues about what these two experiments demonstrate. The one in Oregon is too recent to permit definitive conclusions, while different sides in the normative debate read the evidence from the Netherlands in quite different ways. Proponents of the traditional prohibition contend that breaches of the guidelines, including the requirement of the patient's voluntary choice, have become common, while opponents of legal prohibition argue that the guidelines have worked quite well in practice.

Not all arguments by Christians for or against legal prohibition are themselves religious arguments or even rest on premises about the morality of particular acts. Proponents of legal prohibition frequently appeal to the probable negative consequences of permissive laws, including the difficulty of drawing and maintaining defensible lines; the dangers of abuse, especially because modern societies often devalue the elderly and inadequately protect vulnerable persons; the risks of a 'slippery slope'; and the danger of creating or extending what *Evangelium Vitae* calls a 'culture of death'. Additionally, in the USA, which has failed to provide universal access to basic health care, proponents of the traditional legal prohibition contend that it would be major mistake to establish a legal right to assisted suicide before establishing a legal right to health care. Other practical ethical concerns focus on the risks of diverting attention away from efforts to develop and provide more effective palliative care, because assisted suicide would be a quick and easy way to deal with pain and suffering.

By contrast, opponents of legal prohibition generally believe that these dangers are exaggerated and/or that strong regulation could effectively reduce their threat. In addition, they stress the values of respecting personal autonomy and of compassionately relieving pain and suffering. Furthermore, they often point to the inconsistencies and incoherence in traditional moral and legal rules, particularly in their distinctions between killing and letting die or between omission and commission. Finally, as Robin Gill stresses, any discussion of Christian views is too limited if it attends only to official church statements – or even major theological statements – and neglects the perspectives of lay Christians, many (perhaps even a majority) of whom support legalisation of assisted suicide and voluntary active euthanasia in some cases.[10]

Determination of death

The obligation to sustain an individual's life ceases at his or her death, but determining death is by no means uncontroversial. Human death involves the irreversible loss of the qualities associated with human life. Thus, where the line is drawn between life and death depends in part on which conception of essential human characteristics is defensible. Traditionally, the irreversible cessation of spontaneous respiration and heartbeat marked death, but the cardiopulmonary standard became somewhat problematic with the arrival of new technologies that could sustain respiration and heartbeat.

Then, in the late 1960s, the conception of whole-brain death emerged, partly in response to the need to obtain viable organs for transplantation. According to this conception, death involves the irreversible cessation of the activity of the whole brain, including the brain stem, as measured by neurological tests, even if technologies can temporarily maintain a person's respiration and heartbeat. Most Christian traditions and thinkers now accept the whole-brain standard for determining death, along with the cardiopulmonary standard, but controversy continues in actual practice. When the whole-brain-death standard was under consideration, Protestant ethicist Paul Ramsey worried about society's acceptance of a standard of death for utilitarian reasons, such as increasing the supply of organs.[11] Such an approach, he contended, involves a conceptual and normative conflict of interest. For Ramsey sufficient reasons existed in the care of patients to support a whole-brain-death conception. More radically, some ethicists propose a conception of higher-brain-death – the irreversible cessation of the capacity for consciousness and social interaction – particularly in view of the conceptual and practical instability of the whole-brain-death standard. The higher-brain-death conception has not been adopted, in part because it would count as dead persons who are in a permanent vegetative state, who can breathe on their own often for many years, as well as anencephalic newborns, who have only enough brain stem to allow them to breathe on their own for a brief period. This standard would, in principle, permit the burial of or the removal of organs from an individual who is still breathing on his or her own without mechanical assistance, but who lacks higher-brain functions and thus the capacity for consciousness and social interaction.

ORGAN AND TISSUE TRANSPLANTATION

Questions remain about how to treat the dead body, the cadaver, particularly in view of the possibility of using its organs and tissue in transplantation. Perhaps no area of contemporary medicine so widely evokes religious, and often specifically Christian, imagery as organ and tissue transplantation, which involves removing biological materials from a dead body – or in some cases a living body – to provide life or enhance the quality of life for another person. The language of 'gift of life' and the norm of neighbour love often surround this practice.

William May offers a typology of basic religious attitudes towards the human body and their implications for transplanting body parts.[12] The first type is idealistic, monistic and optimistic. It recognises the reality of the spiritual realm, but denies the reality of the body, sickness and death. A modern version is Christian Science. The second type, represented by the ancient Manicheans, is dualistic and pessimistic. The third type, represented by ancient and modern Gnostics, is also dualistic, but it views the body as incidental rather than unreal (Christian Science) or evil (Manicheanism). The fourth type, which is dominant in mainstream Christianity, as well as in Judaism, holds that the body is essential, real and good. This fourth type recognises natural aversions to tampering with the living body or the corpse, but also develops symbols and rituals for disciplining those aversions.

Christian convictions about respect for the human cadaver permit the donation of organs and tissue for transplantation as well as for research. The doctrine of the bodily resurrection, understood as an affirmation of God's power, poses no barriers to donation, and the norm of neighbour love can provide a positive warrant for donation. In general, these Christian convictions support a policy of obtaining transplantable organs through a system of donation, whether expressed or presumed, rather than through state conscription or expropriation or through a market. Even if buying or selling organs is not considered intrinsically wrong, such a practice raises profound concerns about abuse, exploitation and, more broadly, commodification of human bodies.

Such concerns obviously also apply to the living donor of organs. In addition, given the convictions about the human body that support traditional opposition to suicide, Christian churches had to struggle with the new technological possibility of transferring some bodily organs and tissues from one living individual to another. They easily accepted and supported blood donation because of its benefits for others, its minimal risk and blood's replenishability. Generally, Anglican, Protestant, Eastern Orthodox and Roman Catholic churches and their theologians also came to accept living organ donation, particularly kidney donation, as a praiseworthy expression of neighbour love, as long as the risks are reasonable and the decision is voluntary. Roman Catholic moral theology had to update its traditional principle of totality, which, in affirming bodily integrity, held that a diseased part of the body could be removed for the benefit of the whole body, the totality. This principle appeared to rule out the removal of an organ to benefit someone else, but theologians reinterpreted 'totality' to refer to the whole person, as a moral and spiritual person, not merely a physical body. Hence, donating an organ to help others was consistent with an expanded conception of totality. Some theologians, such as Paul Ramsey, worried that the revised principle of totality or the norm of neighbour love could lead to neglect of bodily integrity in the context of benefiting others through organ donation. At the beginning of the twenty-first century, concerns increased about the risks to and possible undue pressures on living donors, particularly of portions of lungs and livers.

JUSTICE AND ACCESS TO HEALTH CARE

Perhaps more than any other type of medical treatment, organ transplantation raises difficult questions about allocating scarce medical resources – for example, which patient on the waiting list for a transplant should receive a donated organ? – and allocating scarce societal funds, because some transplants, such as liver transplants, are so costly. Most Christian theologians affirm a universal right to health care, based on such norms as neighbour love, solidarity, community and justice. Virtually all developed societies – the USA is a notorious exception–recognise this right, but, in implementing it, they all have to make hard decisions about the level and kind of health care that will be provided for particular conditions. Societal allocation decisions reflect a variety of values, including equity and utilitarian judgements about maximising human welfare within a limited budget. No society provides universal access to all health care that could benefit all patients in need. Because no society can avoid all rationing, the main ethical questions concern its mechanisms (e.g. whether by queuing or by ability to pay) and its extent. If formal justice requires treating similar cases similarly, societies must still determine relevant similarities and dissimilarities for purposes of allocating resources for and within health care. The relevant similarities and dissimilarities are expressed in material criteria of justice, such as need, probability of success, merit and the like. Theories of justice, whether in Christian or secular contexts, vary largely according to the material criteria they emphasise in particular spheres, such as health care. Vigorous controversies have centred on the moral relevance of age and of lifestyle in allocating health care.

APPLIED HUMAN GENETICS

Some ethical issues in applied human genetics emerge in the context of abortion – for instance, in prenatal testing, screening and counselling about genetic problems. In addition, genetic interventions, particularly in the form of human genetic engineering, evoke some Christian concerns.

Two sets of distinctions are important. The first is between gene therapy, which attempts to cure, correct or reduce the effects of a disease, and genetic enhancement, which seeks to enhance certain human qualities. The second distinction is between somatic cell interventions, which affect only the individual involved, and germ-line interventions, which affect off-spring.

To this point, most Christian thinkers accept, at least in principle, somatic cell gene therapy, on the grounds that it is merely an extension of non-genetic therapies. However, the first experiments in human gene therapy over the last decade of the twentieth century had few successes and many failures, including some deaths from the therapy itself. In addition to stressing the need for careful scientific and ethical evaluation of particular gene therapy experiments, some worry that crossing the line or threshold from non-genetic to genetic therapy itself invites more problematic genetic interventions. Some critics of human genetic engineering worry especially about efforts to enhance human qualities, such as intelligence, particularly when these efforts are combined with germ-line interventions. Even when individuals and couples make these choices, rather than the state, eugenics can be problematic because of an unwillingness to accept the so-called natural lottery, or what some Christians might call providence, and to view all human beings as equally worthy whatever their abilities.

Nevertheless, it is not always easy to draw a clear moral line between acceptable non-genetic interventions, such as education and medication, which are used to improve human qualities, and genetic interventions. Even though concerns about 'playing God' appear in several areas of bioethics, they often surface in debates about human genetic engineering. Those concerns mainly focus on transgressions or violations of certain limits and on inappropriate human hubris and arrogance. Critics charge that scientists or physicians 'play God' by usurping God's power over life and death and over the natural or genetic lottery. In general the charge of 'playing God' focuses on two features of divine activity that should not be imitated: God's unlimited power to decide and his unlimited power to act. Thus, critics of 'playing God' usually demand scientific and medical accountability along with respect for certain substantive limits, such as not creating new forms of life. Objections to this metaphor often challenge the rationale for asserting a particular limit or for holding that a particular course of action is wrong. In addition, the divine creation of human beings in God's image provides a positive warrant for 'playing God', at least in some senses. Hence, Paul Ramsey calls on those who allocate health care to play God in a fitting way: we should emulate God's indiscriminate care by distributing scarce life-saving medical technologies randomly or by a lottery rather than on the basis of social worth.

Notes

1 See Warren T. Reich, ed., *Encylopedia of Bioethics*, 2nd ed., 5 vols., New York: Simon & Schuster Macmillan, 1995.
2 John T. Noonan, Jr, *Contraception: A History of Its Treatment by the Catholic Theologians and Canonists*, enlarged ed., Cambridge, MA: Belknap Press of Harvard University Press, 1986.
3 See John Paul II, *Evangelium Vitae*, 1995.4
4 Stanley Harakas, *Health and Medicine in the Eastern Orthodox Tradition: Faith, Liturgy, and Wholeness*, New York: Crossroad, 1990.
5 David H. Smith, *Health and Medicine in the Anglican Tradition: Conscience, Community, and Compromise*, New York: Crossroad, 1986.
6 Stanley Hauerwas, *A Community of Character: Toward a Constructive Christian Social Ethic*, Notre Dame, IN: University of Notre Dame Press, 1981.
7 Sacred Congregation for the Doctrine of the Faith, *Instruction on Respect for Human Life in Its Origin and on the Dignity of Human Procreation*,1988.
8 Margaret Pabst Battin, *Ethical Issues in Suicide*, 2nd ed., Englewood Cliffs, NJ: Prentice Hall, 1995.
9 James M. Gustafson, *Ethics from a Theocentric Perspective*, vol. II, Chicago: University of Chicago Press, 1984.
10 Robin Gill, ed., *Euthanasia and the Churches*, London: Cassell, 1998.
11 Paul Ramsey, *The Patient as Person*, New Haven, CT: Yale University Press, 1970.
12 William F. May, 'Religious Justifications for Donating Body Parts', *Hastings Center Report* 15 (February 1985), pp. 38–42.

Select bibliography

See the notes for each chapter for additional bibliographical information.

Baelz, Peter, *Ethics and Belief*, Sheldon, London, 1977.

Bailey, D. S., *Homosexuality and the Western Christian Tradition*, Longman, London, 1955.

 The Man/Woman Relation in Christian Thought, SCM Press, London, 1959.

Bainton, Roland H., *Sex, Love and Marriage: A Christian Survey*, Fontana, London, 1958.

 Christian Attitudes toward War and Peace: A Historical Survey and Critical Re-Evaluation, Abingdon, New York, 1960, and Hodder & Stoughton, London, 1961.

Banner, Michael, *Christian Ethics and Contemporary Moral Problems*, Cambridge University Press, Cambridge, 1999.

Barth, Karl, *Ethics*, T. & T. Clark, Edinburgh, 1981.

Beach, Waldo, & Niebuhr, H. Richard, *Christian Ethics: Sources of the Living Tradition*, 2nd edn, Ronald Press, New York, 1973.

Bennett, John C., *Christian Ethics and Social Policy*, Scribner, New York, 1946.

 The Radical Imperative, Westminster, Philadelphia, 1975.

Bennett, John C. (ed.), *Storm over Ethics*, Bethany Press, Philadelphia, 1967.

Bock, Paul, *In Search of a Responsible World Society: The Social Teachings of he World Council of Churches*, Westminster, Philadelphia, 1974.

Bonhoeffer, Dietrich, *Ethics*, Macmillan, New York, 1955; rev. edn, SCM Press, London, 1978.

 Sanctorum Communio, Collins, London, 1963.

 No Rusty Swords, Harper & Row, New York, and Collins, London, 1965.

 The Cost of Discipleship, SCM Press, London, 1978.

Bonino, José Míguez, *Towards a Christian Political Ethics*, Fortress, Philadelphia, 1983.

Brown, David, *Choices: Ethics and the Christian*, Blackwell, Oxford, 1983.

Brunner, Emil, *Justice and the Social Order*, Harper, New York, and Lutterworth, London, 1945.

Cahill, Lisa S., *Sex, Gender and Christian Ethics*, Cambridge University Press, Cambridge, 1995.

Childress, James F., & Macquarrie, John (eds.), *A New Dictionary of Christian Ethics*, Westminster, Philadelphia, 1986 and SCM Press, London, 1987.

Chilton, Bruce, & McDonald, J. I. H., *Jesus and the Ethics of the Kingdom*, SPCK, London, 1987.

Chopp, Rebecca, *The Praxis of Suffering: An Interpretation of Liberation and Political Theologies*, Orbis, Maryknoll, NY, 1986.

The Power to Speak: Feminism, Language, God, Crossroad, New York, 1989.

Liberation Theology and Pastoral Theology, Journal of Pastoral Care Publications, Decatur, GA, 1990.

Clark, Stephen, R. L., *The Nature of the Beast: Are Animals Moral?* Clarendon, Oxford, 1982.

Civil Peace and Sacred Order, Clarendon, Oxford, 1989.

A Parliament of Souls, Clarendon, Oxford, 1990.

How to Think about the Earth, Mowbray, London, 1993.

Biology and Christian Ethics, Cambridge University Press, Cambridge, 2000.

Coleman, Peter, *Gay Christians: A Moral Dilemma*, SCM Press, London, 1989.

Cook, David, *The Moral Maze*, SPCK, London, 1983.

Countryman, L. William, *Dirt, Greed and Sex: Sexual Ethics in the New Testament and Their Implications for Today*, Fortress, Philadelphia, 1988, and SCM Press, London, 1989.

Cronin, Kieran, *Rights and Christian Ethics*, Cambridge University Press, Cambridge, 1992.

Cupitt, Don, *Crisis of Moral Authority: The Dethronement of Christianity*, Westminster, Philadelphia, and Lutterworth, London, 1972.

The New Christian Ethics, SCM Press, London, 1988.

Curran, Charles E., *Catholic Moral Theology in Dialogue*, Fides, Notre Dame, IN, 1972.

Ongoing Revision: Studies in Moral Theology, Fides, Notre Dame, IN, 1975.

Issues in Sexual and Medical Ethics, University of Notre Dame Press, Notre Dame, IN, 1978.

Curran, Charles E. (ed.), *Absolutes in Moral Theology?* Greenwood Press, Westport, CT, 1975.

Curran, Charles E., & McCormick, R. (eds.), *Readings in Moral Theology*, Paulist Press, New York, 1980.

Curry, Dean C. (ed.), *Evangelicals and the Bishops' Pastoral Letter*, Eerdmans, Grand Rapids, MI, 1984.

Dominion, Jack, *Passionate and Compassionate Love: A Vision for Christian Marriage*, Darton, Longman & Todd, London, 1991.

Dunstan, G. R., *The Artifice of Ethics*, SCM Press, London, 1974.

Dunstan, G. R. (ed.), *Duty and Discernment*, SCM Press, London, 1975.

Dussel, E., *Ethics and the Theology of Liberation*, Orbis, Maryknoll, NY, 1978.

Dwyer, Judith A. (ed.), *The Catholic Bishops and Nuclear War: A Critique and Analysis of the Pastoral 'The Challenge of Peace'*, Georgetown University Press, Washington, DC, 1984.

Fairweather, Ian C. M., & McDonald, J. I. H., *The Quest for Christian Ethics*, Handsel Press, Edinburgh, 1984.

Fergusson, David, *Community, Liberalism and Christian Ethics*, Cambridge University Press, Cambridge, 1999.

Fletcher, Joseph, *Situation Ethics*, Westminster, Philadelphia, and SCM Press, London, 1966.

Moral Responsibility: Situation Ethics at Work, Westminster, Philadelphia, and SCM Press, London, 1967.

Humanhood: Essays in Biomedical Ethics, Prometheus Books, Buffalo, NY, 1979.

Forell, George Wolfgang, *History of Christian Ethics*, Augsburg, Minneapolis, 1979.

Forell, George Wolfgang (ed.), *Christian Social Teachings: A Reader in Christian Social Ethics from the Bible to the Present*, Augsburg, Minneapolis, 1971.

Forrester, Duncan B., *Christianity and the Future of Welfare*, Epworth, London, 1985.

Beliefs, Values and Policies: Conviction Politics in a Secular Age, Clarendon,, Oxford, 1989.

Christian Justice and Public Policy, Cambridge University Press, Cambridge, 1997.

Gardner, E. Clinton, *Justice and Christian Ethics*, Cambridge University Press, Cambridge, 1995.

Gascoigne, Robert, *The Public Forum and Christian Ethics*, Cambridge University Press, Cambridge, 2000.

Gill, Robin, *The Cross against the Bomb*, Epworth, London, 1984.

A Textbook of Christian Ethics, T. & T. Clark, Edinburgh, 1985; rev. edn, 1995.

Christian Ethics in Secular Worlds, T. & T. Clark, Edinburgh, 1991.

Moral Leadership in a Postmodern Age, T. & T. Clark, Edinburgh, 1997.

Churchgoing and Christian Ethics, Cambridge University Press, Cambridge, 1999.

González, Justo, *Faith and Wealth: A History of Early Christian Ideas on the Origin, Significance, and use of Money*, Harper & Row, San Francisco, 1990.

Grant, Colin, *Altruism and Christian Ethics*, Cambridge University Press, Cambridge, 2000.

Green, Ronald M., *Religious Reason: The Rational and Moral Basis of Religious Belief*, Oxford University Press, New York, 1978.

Religion and Moral Reason, Oxford University Press, New York, 1988.

Gustafson, James M., *Christ and the Moral Life*, Harper & Row, New York, 1968.

The Church as Moral Decision-Maker, Pilgrim, Philadelphia, 1970.

Can Ethics Be Christian? University of Chicago Press, Chicago, 1975.

Protestant and Roman Catholic Ethics, University of Chicago Press, Chicago, and SCM Press, London, 1978.

Theology and Ethics, Oxford University Press, New York and Oxford, 1981.

Hallett, Garth, *Christian Moral Reasoning*, Notre Dame University Press, Notre Dame, 1983.

Priorities and Christian Ethics, Cambridge University Press, Cambridge, 1998.

Häring, Bernard, *The Law of Christ*, 3 vols. Newman Press, Westminster, MD, 1961–6.

Medical Ethics, Fides, Notre Dame, IN, and St Paul, Slough, Berks, 1972.

Free and Faithful in Christ, 3 vols, Seabury, New York, and St Paul, Slough, Berks., 1978.

Harned, David Baily, *Grace and Common Life*, University of Virginia Press, Charlottesville, 1971.

Faith and Virtue, Pilgrim, Philadelphia, 1973.

Harris, P. (ed.), *On Human Life: An Examination of 'Humanae Vitae'*, Burns & Oates, London, 1968.

Hauerwas, Stanley, *Vision and Virtue: Essays in Christian Ethical Reflection*, Fides, Notre Dame Press, IN, 1974.

Character and the Christian Life: A Study in Theological Ethics, Trinity University Press, San Antonio, TX, 1975.

A Community of Character, University of Notre Dame Press, Notre Dame, IN, 1981.

The Peaceable Kingdom: A Primer in Christian Ethics, University of Notre Dame, Notre Dame, IN, 1983, and SCM Press, London, 1984.

Against the Nations, Winston Press, Minneapolis, 1985.

Suffering Presence, University of Notre Dame Press, Notre Dame, IN, 1986, and T. & T. Clark, Edinburgh, 1988.

Christian Existence Today, Labyrinth Press, Durham, NC, 1988.

Naming the Silences, Eerdmans, Grand Rapids, MI, 1990.

After Christendom, Abingdon, Nashville, 1991.

Dispatches from the Front, Duke University Press, Durham, NC, 1995.

Hauerwas, Stanley, & Willimon, W. H., *Resident Aliens*, Abingdon, Nashville, 1989.

Where Resident Aliens Live, Abingdon, Nashville, 1996.

Hays, R. B., *The Moral Vision of the New Testament*, HarperCollins, San Francisco, and T. & T. Clark, Edinburgh, 1996.

Hebblethwaite, Brian, *The Adequacy of Christian Ethics*, Marshall, Morgan & Scott, London, 1981.

Helm, Paul (ed.), *Divine Commands and Morality*, Oxford University Press, Oxford, 1981.

Hengel, Martin, *Property and Riches in the Early Church*, SCM Press, London, 1974.

Victory over Violence, SPCK, London, 1975.

Hicks, Douglas, *Inequality and Christian Ethics*, Cambridge University Press, Cambridge, 2000.

Higginson, Richard, *Dilemmas: A Christian Approach to Moral Decision-Making*, Hodder & Stoughton, London, 1988.

Hollenbach, David, *Claims in Conflict: Retrieving and Renewing the Catholic Human Rights Tradition*, Paulist Press, New York, 1979.

Holmes, Arthur F., *War and Christian Ethics*, Baker, New York, 1975.

Ethics: Aproaching Moral Decisions, Baker Book House, Downers Grove, IL, 1984.

Houlden, J. L., *Ethics and the New Testament*, Mowbray, Oxford, 1973.

Hughes, Gerard J., *Authority in Morals*, Sheed & Ward, London, 1983.

Jones, Richard, *Groundwork of Christian Ethics*, Epworth Press, London, 1985.

Keane, Philip, *Christian Ethics and Imagination*, Paulist Press, New York, 1984.

Keeling, Michael, *The Foundations of Christian Ethics*, T. & T. Clark, Edinburgh, 1990.

Kirk, Kenneth E., *Some Principles of Moral Theology*, Longman, Green, London, 1920.

Conscience and Its Problems: An Introduction to Casuistry, Longman, Green, London, 1927.

The Vision of God: The Doctrine of the Summum Bonum, Longman, Green, London, 1931.

Knox, John, *The Ethic of Jesus in the Teaching of the Church: Its Authority and Its Relevance*, Abingdon, New York, 1961, and Epworth, London, 1962.

Küng, Hans, *A Global Ethic for Global Politics and Economics*, SCM Press, London, 1997.

Langford, Michael, *The Good and the True: An Introduction to Christian Ehics*, SCM Press, London, 1985.

Lehmann, Paul, *Ethics in a Christian Context*, Harper & Row, New York, and SCM Press, London, 1963.
The Transfiguration of Politics, Harper & Row, New York, 1975.
Linzey, Andrew, *Christianity and the Rights of Animals*, SPCK, London, 1987.
Compassion for Animals, SPCK, London, 1988.
Little, David & Twiss, Sumner B., *Comparative Religious Ethics: A New Method*, Harper & Row, New York, 1978.
Long, Edward LeRoy, Jr, *Conscience and Compromise: An Approach to Protestant Casuistry*, Westminster, Philadelphia, 1954.
A Survey of Christian Ethics, Oxford University Press, New York and Oxford, 1967.
A Survey of Recent Christian Ethics, Oxford University Press, New York and Oxford, 1982.
Lovin, Robin, W., *Reinhold Niebuhr and Christian Realism*, Cambridge University Press, Cambridge, 1995.
McClendon, James, W., Jr, *Ethics: Systematic Theology*, Abingdon, Nashville, 1986.
McDonagh, Enda, *Invitation and Response: Essays in Christian Moral Theology*, Gill & Macmillan, Dublin, 1972.
Gift and Call, Gill & Macmillan, Dublin, 1975.
Doing the Truth, Gill & Macmillan, Dublin, 1979.
McDonald, J. I. H., *Biblical Interpretation and Christian Ethics*, Cambridge University Press, Cambridge, 1993.
Christian Values: Theory and Practice in Christian Ethics Today, T. & T. Clark, Edinburgh, 1995.
McFague, Sallie, *Models of God: Theology for an Ecological Nuclear Age*, Fortress Press, Philadelphia, and SCM Press, London, 1987.
The Body of God: An Ecological Theology, Fortress, Minneapolis, 1993.
MacGregor, G. H. C., *The New Testament Basis of Pacifism*, James Clarke, London, 1936.
Mackey, James P., *Power and Christian Ethics*, Cambridge University Press, Cambridge, 1994.
McLaren, Robert Bruce, *Christian Ethics: Foundations and Practice*, Prentice Hall, Englewood Cliffs, NJ, 1994.
MacNamara, Vincent, *Faith and Ethics: Recent Roman Catholicism*, Gill & Macmillan, Dublin, 1985.
Macquarrie, John, *Three Issues in Ethics*, Harper & Row, New York, and SCM Press, London, 1970.
Macquarrie, John (ed.), *A Dictionary of Christian Ethics*, SCM Press, London, 1967. (See under Childress for rev. edn).
Mahoney, John, *Seeking the Spirit*, Sheed & Ward, London and New York, 1981.
Bioethics and Belief, Sheed & Ward, London, 1984.
The Making of Moral Theology: A Study of the Roman Catholic Tradition, Clarendon, Oxford, 1987.
Manson, T. W., *Ethics and the Gospel*, ed. R. H. Preston, SCM Press, London, 1960.
Markham, Ian S., *Plurality and Christian Ethics*, Cambridge University Press, Cambridge, 1994.
Marrin, Albert (ed.), *War and the Christian Conscience: From Augustine to Martin Luther King, Jr*, Henry Regnery, Chicago, 1971.

Mealand, David L., *Poverty and Expectation in the Gospels*, SPCK, London, 1980.

Meeks, Wayne A., *The Moral World of the First Christians*, Westminster, Philadelphia, 1986.

The Origins of Christian Morality, Yale University Press, New Haven, CT, 1993.

Mitchell, Basil, *Law, Morality and Religion*, Oxford University Press, London, 1967.

Morality: Religious and Secular, Oxford University Press, Oxford, 1980.

Murnion, Philip J. (ed.), *Catholics and Nuclear War: A Commentary on 'The Challenge of Peace'*, Crossroad, New York, 1983.

Nelson, James B., *Embodiment: An Approach to Sexuality and Christian Theology*, Augsburg, Minneapolis, 1978.

Neuhaus, Richard J., *Christian Faith: A Public Policy*, Augsburg, Minneapolis, 1977.

Doing Well and Doing Good: The Challenge of Christian Capitalism, Doubleday, New York, 1992.

Newlands, George, *Making Christian Decisions*, Mowbray, Oxford, 1985.

Niebuhr, H. Richard, *Christ and Culture*, Harper, New York, 1951.

The Responsible Self, Harper & Row, New York, 1963.

Niebuhr, Reinhold, *Moral Man and Immoral Society*, Scribner, New York, 1932, 1960; SCM Press, London, 1963.

An Interpretation of Christian Ethics, Harper, New York, 1935, and SCM Press, London, 1936.

The Nature and Destiny of Man, 2 vols, Nisbet, London, 1943; Scribner, New York, 1949.

The Children of Light and the Children of Darkness, Scribner, New York, 1944.

Faith and History, Scribner, New York, 1949.

Christian Realism and Political Problems, Scribner, New York, 1953; Faber & Faber, London, 1964.

Noonan, John T., Jr, *The Scholastic Analysis of Usury*, Harvard University Press, Cambridge, 1957.

Contraception: A History of Its Treatment by Catholic Theologians and Canonists, Harvard University Press, Cambridge, 1965.

Noonan, John T., Jr (ed., *The Morality of Abortion: Legal and Historical Perspectives*, Harvard University Press, Cambridge, 1970.

Northcott, Michael S., *The Environment and Christian Ethics*, Cambridge University Press, Cambridge, 1995.

Nygren, Anders, *Agape and Eros*, SPCK, London, 1953.

O'Donovan, Oliver, *Resurrection and Moral Order*, Intervarsity Press, Leicester, and Eerdmans, Grand Rapids, MI, 1986.

Peace and Certainty, Clarendon, Oxford, 1989.

The Desire of Nations, Cambridge University Press, Cambridge, 1996.

Ogletree, Thomas, *Hospitality to the Stranger: Dimensions of Moral Understanding*, Fortress, Philadelphia, 1985.

The Use of the Bible in Christian Ethics, Blackwell, Oxford, 1985.

Oppenheimer, Helen, *The Character of Christian Morality*, Faith Press, London, 1965.

The Hope of Happiness, SCM Press, London, 1983.

Marriage, SPCK, London, 1990.

Osborn, Eric, *Ethical Patterns in Early Christian Thought*, Cambridge University Press, Cambridge, 1976.

Outka, Gene H., *Agape: An Ethical Analysis*, Yale University Press, New Haven, CT, 1973.

Outka, Gene H., & Ramsey, Paul, *Norm and Context in Christian Ethics*, Scribner, New York, 1968, and SCM Press, London, 1969.

Outka, Gene H., & Reeder, John D., Jr, *Religion and Morality*, Doubleday, New York, 1973.

Pannenberg, Wolfhart, *Ethics*, Search Press, London, and Westminster, Philadelphia, 1981.

Parsons, Susan Frank, *Feminism and Christian Ethics*, Cambridge University Press, Cambridge, 1996.

Pierce, C. A., *Conscience in the New Testament*, SCM Press, London, 1955.

Porter, Jean, *The Recovery of Virtue: The Relevance of Aquinas for Christian Ethics*, SPCK, London, 1994.

Moral Action and Christian Ethics, Cambridge University Press, Cambridge, 1995.

Preston, Ronald H., *Religion and the Persistence of Capitalism*, SCM Press, London, 1979.

Explorations in Theology, vol. 9, SCM Press, London, 1981.

Church and Society in the Late Twentieth Century: The Economic and Political Task, SCM Press, London, 1983.

The Future of Christian Ethics, SCM Press, London, 1987.

Preston, Ronald H. (ed.), *Technology and Social Justice*, SCM Press, London, 1971.

Industrial Conflicts and Their Place in Modern Society, SCM Press, London, 1974.

Perspectives on Strikes, SCM Press, London, 1975.

Ramsey, I. T. (ed.), *Christian Ethics and Contemporary Philosophy*, SCM Press, London, 1966.

Ramsey, Paul, *Basic Christian Ethics*, Scribner, New York, 1951; University of Chicago Press, Chicago, 1980.

War and the Christian Conscience: How Shall Modern War Be Conducted Justly? Duke University Press, Durham, NC, 1961.

Nine Modern Moralists, Prentice-Hall, Englewood Cliffs, NJ, 1962.

The Limits of Nuclear War: Thinking about the Do-able and the Undo-able, Council on Religion and International Affairs, New York, 1963.

Deeds and Rules in Christian Ethics, Oliver & Boyd, Edinburgh, 1965; rev. edn, Scribner, New York, 1967.

Who Speaks for the Church? Abingdon, New York, 1967.

The Just War: Force and Political Responsibility, Scribner, New York, 1968.

Fabricated Man: The Ethics of Genetic Control, Yale University Press, New Haven, CT, 1970.

The Patient as Person, Yale University Press, New Haven, CT, 1970.

The Ethics of Fetal Research, Yale University Press, New Haven, CT, 1975.

Ethics at the Edges of Life, Yale University Press, New Haven, CT, 1978.

Rauschenbusch, Walter, *Christianity and the Social Crisis*, Macmillan, New York, 1907.

Christianizing the Social Order, Macmillan, New York, 1916.

A Theology for the Social Gospel, Macmillan, New York, 1918.

Robinson, N. H. G., *The Groundwork of Christian Ethics*, Collins, London, 1971.

Rowland, Christopher, & Corner, Mark, *Liberating Exegesis: The Challenge of Liberation Theology to Biblical Studies*, SPCK, London, 1990.

Rudman, Stanley, *Concepts of Persons and Christian Ethics*, Cambridge University Press, Cambridge, 1997.

Sanders, Jack T., *Ethics in the New Testament*, SCM Press, London, 1975.

Schillebeeckx, Edward, *Marriage: Human Reality and Saving Mystery*, 2 vols, Sheed & Ward, London, 1965.

Schrage, Wolfgang, *The Ethics of the New Testament*, T. & T. Clark, Edinburgh, 1988.

Schüller, Bruno, *Wholly Human: Essays in the Theory and Language of Morality*, Gill & Macmillan, Dublin, 1986.

Sedgwick, Peter H., *The Market Economy and Christian Ethics*, Cambridge University Press, Cambridge, 1999.

Spong, John Shelby, *Living in Sin? A Bishop Rethinks Human Sexuality*, Harper & Row, San Francisco, 1990.

Stott, John, *Issues Facing Christians Today: New Perspectives on Social and Moral Dilemmas*, Collins/Marshall Pickering, London, 1990.

Tanner, Kathryn, *The Politics of God: Christian Theologies and Social Justice*, Fortress, Minneapolis, 1992.

Temple, William, *Nature, God and Man*, Macmillan, London, 1934.

  Citizen and Churchman, Eyre & Spottiswoode, London, 1941.

  Christianity and Social Order, Penguin, London, 1942; Shepheard-Walwyn and SPCK, London, 1976 (with introduction by Ronald Preston).

Thielicke, Helmut, *The Ethics of Sex*, James Clarke, London, 1964; Baker, Grand Rapids, MI, 1975.

  Theological Ethics, 3 vols. Eerdmans, Grand Rapids, 1979.

Thomas, G. F., *Christian Ethics and Moral Philosophy*, Scribner, New York, 1955.

Tillich, Paul, *Love, Power and Justice*, Oxford University Press, New York, 1954.

  Morality and Beyond, Harper & Row, New York, 1963; Fontana, London, 1969.

Trowell, Hugh, *The Unfinished Debate on Euthanasia*, SCM Press, London, 1973.

U.S. Bishops, *The Challenge of Peace: God's Promise and Our Response: Pastoral Letter on War and Peace in the Nuclear Age*, U.S. Catholic Conference, Washington, DC, and CTS/SPCK, London, 1983.

  Economic Justice for All: Pastoral Letter on Catholic Social Teaching and the U.S. Economy, U.S. Catholic Conference, Washington, DC, 1986.

  Building Peace: A Pastoral Reflection on the Response to 'The Challenge of Peace', U.S. Catholic Conference, Washington, DC, 1988.

Walsh, Michael, & Davies, Brian (eds), *Proclaiming Justice and Peace: Documents from John XXIII to John Paul II*, Twenty-third Publications, Mystic, CT, 1984.

Ward, Keith, *Ethics and Christianity*, Allen & Unwin, London, 1970.

  The Divine Image: The Foundations of Christian Morality, SPCK, London, 1976.

Welty, E., *A Handbook of Christian Social Ethics*, 2 vols, Nelson, Edinburgh, 1960–3.

White, R. E. O., *The Changing Continuity of Christian Ethics*, 2 vols, Paternoster Press, Exeter, 1981.

Winter, Gibson, *Elements for a Social Ethic*, Macmillan, New York, 1966.

Wogaman, J. Philip, *Economics and Ethics*, SCM Press, London, 1986.

  Christian Perspectives on Politics, SCM Press, London, 1988.

  Christian Moral Judgment, Westminster/John Knox Press, Louisville, 1989.

  Christian Ethics: A Historical Introduction, Westminster/John Knox Press, Louisville, 1993, and SPCK, London, 1994.

Woods, G. F., *A Defence of Theological Ethics*, Cambridge University Press, Cambridge, 1966.

Yoder, John Howard, *The Politics of Jesus*, Eerdmans, Grand Rapids, 1972.

  The Priestly Kingdom: Social Ethics as Gospel, University of Notre Dame Press, Notre Dame, 1984.

Index